the food of
asia

the food of asia

a journey for food lovers through
China, India, Japan & Thailand

MURDOCH BOOKS

CONTENTS

the food of
ASIA

CHINA

AN ENORMOUS COUNTRY, WITH A LARGE POPULATION TO FEED AND A DIVERSE GEOGRAPHY AND CLIMATE, CHINA HAS ONE OF THE GREAT CUISINES OF THE WORLD.

A staple, or fan, such as rice, wheat, maize or millet is the basis of every Chinese meal. Rice, always white and polished, is usually steamed. Wheat is made into breads and noodles, especially in the north, while millet is more common in poorer areas, eaten as porridge.

The secondary dishes of meat, seafood, vegetables, pickles and condiments that accompany the fan are called cai, and regional specialties often reflect the local climate and soil quality.

In the capital, Beijing, Peking duck is cooked in specialist restaurants all over the city, but the everyday fare of this northern region is more humble, and includes warming dumplings and Mongolian hotpots. The harsh climate and predominantly poor farming favour hardy crops such as wheat, millet, turnip and cabbage. Flavours are strong, with salty bean pastes and soy sauces, vinegar, spring onions (scallions) and garlic all being important ingredients. Winter vegetables are preserved or pickled, while piquant condiments are eaten with bowls of steaming noodles or rice when little else is available.

In contrast, China's second city, Shanghai, is situated on the fertile plains of the Yangtze Delta in the east. Nicknamed 'the land of fish and rice', the area produces an array of vegetables – bok choy (pak choi), bamboo, beans and more – as well as some of China's finest seafood, meat and poultry. Much of the cuisine is slow-braised, (rather than steamed or stir-fried), and soy sauce, rice wine, black vinegar, garlic and ginger are used for this purpose in many recipes, sometimes balanced by a pinch of sugar.

In the west, Sichuan has a deserved reputation for its hot cuisine and varied cooking styles, summed up in the phrase 'one hundred dishes and one hundred flavours'. Sichuan pepper dominates many dishes. Unrelated to Western black and white pepper, it is hot and pungent, producing a numbing sensation in the mouth. Chilli peppers and ginger add even more layers of heat.

The flavours of the South are more delicate – especially those of Guangdong (Canton), home to China's finest dining and most accomplished chefs. The Cantonese will eat an extraordinary range of foodstuffs, from shark's fin to snakes, but pork is the real favourite, often bought from the take-away counters of roast meat restaurants, which may also sell roast duck. Other dishes tend to be stir-fried, steamed or boiled, and served with spicy or fragrant condiments such as soy, chilli, oyster, hoi sin, black bean and XO sauces. The subtropical climate sustains rice, vegetables and fruit, while an extensive coastline and inland waterways provide fish and shellfish. The emphasis is on the premium quality and freshness of the produce – in many restaurants, seafood is ordered while it is still swimming in a fish tank.

Although freshness is highly prized, the Chinese use a large amount of preserved and dried foods (particularly seafood), too. Dried ingredients are also a common feature of traditional Chinese medicine, which utilises dried berries, fruits, roots and bark from hundreds of plants.

Dietary advice may be dispensed alongside the herbal medicine prescription, for in China, food is integrally tied with health. Ingredients are selected for their ability to keep the body in a state of harmony, as well as for their taste. Every food has a nature (hot, warm, cold, cool or neutral) and a flavour (sweet, sour, bitter, salty or pungent), and recipes strive to achieve balance between these tastes. These qualities are often matched to an individual's imbalances, so, for example, pungent foods such as lemon and tomato may be favoured during periods of diarrhoea, because they are believed to help dry up excess bodily fluids.

At the other extreme, banquets involve eating for pleasure, not for sustenance. Banquet food is often symbolic and is as extravagant and plentiful as budgets allow, with multiple courses such as abalone, shark's fin and whole fish. Rice or noodles are served only at the end, and may be left untouched as a reflection of the host's generosity during the earlier courses. The customs and menu of banquets may be quite different to those seen at everyday meals, but they do share one common feature: for the Chinese, the best meal is always one that is shared with family and friends.

INDIA

LARGE IN BOTH SIZE AND POPULATION, MODERN INDIA IS A VIBRANT MELTING POT OF GEOGRAPHIC, HISTORICAL AND RELIGIOUS INFLUENCES – WHICH ARE REFLECTED IN THE DIVERSITY OF ITS CUISINE.

Although most Indian food is characterised by the liberal use of spices, specific combinations and flavours vary from region to region.

The northern areas favour garam masala or 'hot mixes', personal and regional blends of warm aromatic spices such as cloves, cardamom, black pepper, and cinnamon, that are used to temper dishes at the end of cooking.

Food from the south tends to be lighter, with fresher, more pungent flavours thanks to the use of chillies, mustard seeds and curry leaves, as well as souring agents such as lime juice and tamarind.

The central regions favour seed spices such as cumin and coriander, which grow in Gujarat, as do turmeric and chillies. In Bengal, a blend of fenugreek, mustard, fennel, cumin and nigella seeds, called panch phoron, dominates.

All of these are used to flavour a wide variety of meats, seafood, pulses and vegetables. However, meat is consumed in much smaller quantities than in many other cuisines. Over eighty per cent of the population is Hindu, and consequently many people are vegetarian. Amongst those Hindus who eat meat, the majority abstain from beef. Islam is India's second largest religion, and its followers avoid pork, and eat other meat only if the animals have been slaughtered according to Muslim law. Smaller religious communities and some sects within the mainstream faiths also adhere to dietary taboos.

For those people who do eat meat, regional favourites often have their basis in local history. Lamb and game are popular in the north, reflecting Moghul influences as well as those of other communities such as the Parsis and Sikhs, while southern dishes such as vindaloo may contain local ingredients, but utilise European cooking techniques.

Availability also dictates regional cuisine. Fish and seafood are popular ingredients in southern and central regions with proximity to inland and coastal waterways, and appear in many Bengali, Assamese and Orissan dishes. On the other hand, Rajasthani cuisine contains many dishes cooked in buttermilk, milk or butter, a cooking style that

evolved because water was scarce and its use as a cooking medium had to be avoided.

In any case, these dishes are never the main feature of a meal, but are viewed as accompaniments to rice and bread.

The most highly prized rice is basmati from Dehradun, where it grows on terraces in the Himalayan foothills. Chewy red patni rice grows in the centre and west of India, particularly on the coast, and is regarded as a good source of energy. In the south, rice is cooked with saffron and spices and transformed into biryani, or made into khichhari, a traditional breakfast similar to kedgeree, but eaten with poppadoms, chutney and minced (ground) meat.

Breads are more of a staple in the north, where the climate is not as well suited to growing rice. There is a huge range of breads to choose from, including Middle Eastern-style kulcha and sheermal, which are popular in Kashmir and Jammu. In the Punjab and Haryana, naan are cooked in tandoors, and parathas, puris, chapatis and roti are widely eaten.

Across India, poppadoms, appams, idlis and dosa are eaten with chutneys and stew-like dishes, or in the case of the dosa, holding a spicy potato filling.

The entire meal may be served on a thali, a large, flat plate made from metal or a banana leaf on which the food is placed in small mounds or bowls. Although more prevalent in Gujarat and the southern areas, they are a common element of Indian cuisine, used by all strata of society.

To follow, dairy-based sweets such as rossogollas, gulab jamun and sandesh are popular, especially around Kolkata (Calcutta), where there are numerous sweet shops. The northern use of saffron, gold and silver leaf is a hang over from the opulence and excesses of the Moghuls.

A collection of spices and aromatics wrapped in a betel leaf is often served at the conclusion of the meal to freshen the breath and act as a digestive. Called a paan, it is chewed before being either swallowed or spat out, depending on its contents, which may include pieces of betel nut, and either lime paste, red katha paste, chewing tobacco or mitha masala (spices).

JAPAN

JAPANESE COOKING COMBINES DELICATE, SUBTLE TASTES AND TEXTURES, ALWAYS PREPARED WITH A LIGHT HAND AND SUBLIMELY PRESENTED TO APPEAL TO THE EYE AS WELL AS THE TASTEBUDS.

The Japanese are accustomed to small portions, each with its own particular flavour or melange of flavours, and presented in its own serving dish. This calls for a large and eclectic assortment of small plates and bowls, in different shapes, colours, patterns and materials, even the most basic of which may be elegantly styled.

The bento box is an art form in itself. Filled with small nutritious morsels in a variety of flavours, colours and textures, these lunch boxes can be bought in supermarkets and convenience stores, but traditionally, women diligently prepared them each morning for their husbands and children, and today many continue to perform this task before going to work themselves.

Similar care is taken in preparing home-style meals, which typically include a soup, a meat or fish dish, a vegetable side, pickles, and a bowl of rice. One-pot meals are also popular at home, including nabemono, a meat or fish and vegetable hotpot, prepared at the table over a portable gas ring.

Cultivated for more than 2000 years, rice is the foundation of the Japanese diet, and most people eat it once or twice a day. For many, a meal is not fulfilling without a bowl of rice on the table. The aromatic, glutinous, medium-grained Japonica is overwhelmingly the preferred variety.

Noodles are also extremely popular, especially the buckwheat noodles called soba, and wheat noodles including the thick udon, and the thinner ramen and somen varieties. Noodles are often served in a hot soy sauce- or miso-based broth, with toppings that can include tempura, deep-fried tofu, dried sardines, or raw egg yolk. Cold noodle recipes include zaru soba, buckwheat noodles served on a bamboo mat or basket-tray with a dipping sauce into which spring onions (scallions) and wasabi are stirred to taste, and somen served in a bowl of iced water garnished with a few slices of cucumber and tomato, and perhaps a prawn (shrimp).

Noodles are frequently eaten outside the home, purchased from wheeled carts called yatai mise that are set up in the early evening on corners all over the business districts, or from more established noodle shops. The best of these make their own noodles, the master skilfully mixing, kneading, rolling and cutting in the front window, tempting customers to duck under the noren curtain for a real treat. Fine noodles deserve a fine broth and house recipes are closely guarded secrets.

Yakitori are another popular snack. These skewers of succulent grilled chicken and vegetables are sometimes purchased from makeshift open-air food stalls, but can also be found in the most elegant restaurants, perhaps transformed into more sophisticated offerings, such as duck breast basted with balsamic vinegar or shiitake mushrooms stuffed with ground (minced) ginger chicken.

Fundamentally, though, the island nation of Japan loves its seafood. Nearly 3000 tonnes of seafood are bought and sold at Tokyo's central fish market every day, and among the 400 varieties of fish and sea creatures for sale, some of the most highly prized, like sea urchin, sea cucumber intestines, and mullet roe, seem alien – or even abhorrent – to Westerners.

Much of the seafood will be served raw, as sushi or sashimi, and nothing beats the theatre of a sushi chef wielding his knife, with every precise cut and gesture the product of his 10-year apprenticeship. For a more relaxed experience, kaiten-zushi is sushi on a conveyor-belt, perfect for busy people, who pop in for a few bites and some tea, stacking up their empty plates so the bill can be reckoned from the plate count.

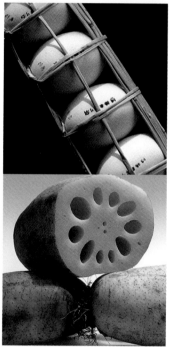

The Japanese also make extensive use of seaweed. Nori is used to wrap sushi and to garnish many dishes, while wakame is added to salads or floated in soups. Kombu (kelp) is an essential ingredient in dashi, the stock that is used in so many ways in Japanese cooking.

Soya beans too, are used in numerous ways. Aside from being soaked and boiled for many different dishes, soya beans are fermented to make soy sauce, miso, and sticky, aromatic natto. Cooked with water, the beans produce soy milk, which is heated with a coagulant to form tofu. Served fresh, edamame are green soya beans that have been boiled and shelled, and are a popular accompaniment to beer or sake.

Freshness is paramount to the Japanese, and every shopping street has a vegetable shop, with crates of fresh produce stacked out to the edge of the pavement. Shops and supermarkets sell both cultivated vegetables and a variety of wild plants called sansai – mountain vegetables such as fern fiddleheads and butterbur buds.

Even Japanese pickles seem fresher than western ones, since they are typically preserved for only a brief period of time and intended for relatively quick consumption. Called tsukemono, pickles are regarded as essential to the meal, and are made from almost every vegetable, particularly daikon radish and greens, cucumber, eggplant (aubergine) and ginger.

Seasonality has a strong influence on the ingredients chosen, especially as certain foods are used in the thousands of festivals that occur throughout the year, many of which have their basis in Japan's Shinto traditions.

The year begins with the biggest and most elaborate festival of all, O-Shogatsu, in which toshikoshi soba (literally 'year-crossing buckwheat noodles') symbolise long life and a smooth transition from one year to the next. Osechi ryori are dozens of different small delicacies artfully arranged in exquisite lacquered boxes, most of which have word, shape or colour associations with happiness, health, prosperity, peace, long life, fertility and abundance, so with each bite these hopes are internalised.

Another symbolism-filled ritual is sado, the famous Zen Buddhist tea ceremony, which involves vigorously whipping a finely powdered green tea called matcha into a thick, frothy beverage using a beautiful bamboo whisk. The bowl the tea is prepared and served in a way that may seem simple and humble at first glance, but often has considerable artistic value.

Green tea is also a beloved feature of everyday life, and is prepared at home or work at least several times a day, as well as being widely available in cans and bottles.

Of course, the Japanese are renowned for their love of a stronger drink, too. Sake is considered the perfect brew to accompany Japanese food, regardless of whether it is enjoyed as part of a traditional celebration or in an intimate, smoke-filled bar, called an izakaya.

THAILAND

THE FLAVOURS OF THAI COOKING ARE A HAPPY MARRIAGE BETWEEN AN ABUNDANCE OF LOCALLY AVAILABLE PRODUCE AND THE CULTURAL INFLUENCE OF THE COUNTRY'S NEIGHBOURS.

The food we think of as 'classic Thai' comes from the central region around Bangkok, the modern home of royal Thai cuisine. In 1960, King Bhumibol opened the court cookbooks to the general populace, and since then, decadent recipes from the palace kitchens – such as roast duck curry – have become popular in Thai restaurants around the world, as have other recipes from this region.

Curries from central Thailand include red, green and phanaeng (panang). Soups, salads and stir-fries are popular, with seasonings that combine hot, sour, salty and sweet flavours. The use of palm sugar (jaggery) makes many recipes sweeter than their southern counterparts, and chilli sauce, made at Si Racha on the Gulf of Thailand appears as a condiment on virtually every table.

The area is watered by many rivers, and constitutes the rice-bowl of Thailand. A network of canals further irrigates the region, providing both a means of transport and a host of freshwater fish, prawns (shrimp) and crabs. Chicken, pork and beef also feature in the cuisine.

This central region is exceptionally fertile and rice paddies cover most of the area. Cultivated vegetables include the popular Thai eggplants (aubergines), cha-om (a bitter green vegetable that resembles a fern), snake (yard long) beans, bamboo shoots, and European imports such as tomatoes. Vegetables grown in or alongside waterways include phak bung (water spinach) and lotus shoots. Fruit, sugar cane, maize, peanuts and taro are also farmed in this area.

The provinces to the south have always been culturally different from the rest of the country. Like areas of neighbouring Malaysia, they were once part of the ancient Indonesian Sriwijaya empire, and Malay-Indonesian culture has a strong influence.

The region is home to large numbers of Muslims, who contribute recipes such as massaman and roti to Thai cuisine. Muslim dishes tend to use ghee and oil rather than the coconut milk or cream that enrich the Thai (Buddhist) curries and soups of the south, amongst the most popular of which are the yellow curries that are coloured and flavoured with turmeric.

While the Thai recipes are hot with pepper and chilli, Muslim recipes employ a larger range of fragrant spices including cardamom, cumin and cloves. A smaller community of Chinese also lives in the south, so Chinese-style noodle dishes are popular here, too, as are barbecued meats, various deep-fried snacks, steamed buns, and dumplings.

However, seafood and fish are the predominate feature of southern cuisine and are acceptable to all, both culturally and in regard to religion. With the advantage of two long coastlines, fresh fish and seafood are eaten in abundance. It is grilled over charcoal, used in stir-fries or curries, and preserved by drying. Racks of dried squid and cotton-fish line many coastal roads. Locally made shrimp paste and fish sauce are used in quantity.

Northern and North-Eastern Thailand are more influenced by Myanmar (Burma), Laos and Cambodia, which border the country to the west and east.

The Burmese influence is seen in Northern Thai curries, which lack the coconut milk of their southern counterparts, giving them a thinner consistency and a more fiery flavour.

The most famous of these is Chiang Mai pork curry, (kaeng hangleh muu), and indeed, pork is very popular in the north, eaten both in its natural state and made into sausages.

Naem maw, fermented sausages made with pork rind and sticky rice, are common, as are sai ua, bright red sausages made with pork and chillies. German-style frankfurters appear in salads and are just one of the influences that the American soldiers stationed in the area during the Vietnam War had on the local cuisine. Deep-fried pork rind is served alongside cooked and raw vegetables as accompaniments to chilli dips called naam phrik.

Characteristic of the North-East is kai yang or kai ping. This grilled chicken is found all over the area, often sold by roadside vendors. The chicken skin is rubbed with garlic, fish sauce, coriander (cilantro) root or lemon grass and black pepper, and the chicken is then flattened and pinned on a bamboo skewer before being barbecued over coals and served with a chilli dipping sauce. Another favourite is laap, a minced chicken meat salad made with lime juice, fish sauce, lemon grass, chillies or chilli powder and roasted rice. Duck, fish and buffalo are also used to make laap, and neu naam tok, grilled strips of beef, are used for similar salads.

Som tam, a green papaya salad with chillies, peanuts, cherry tomatoes and dried prawns (shrimp), is a popular snack, sometimes transformed into a Laotian-style dish with the addition of pickled crabs. Individual portions are pounded together by hand and eaten with sticky rice.

Although North-Eastern Thailand was one of the first areas in Asia to grow rice, rainfall is patchy here, and the crop is less reliable than it is in other parts of the country. Nevertheless, rice is the staple food, and the pungent flavours and small quantities of the dishes that are served with it are an indication of the relative poverty of the region. Unfermented fish sauce and chillies are the main seasonings. Commonly used pickled and preserved foods are another symptom of an unreliable food supply – their piquancy adds more flavour to a diet of rice than the same quantity of these foods would in their original fresh state.

In fact, rice is the central component of nearly every Thai meal throughout the country. Regardless of the other dishes – curries, seafood, stir-fries, soups, salads or vegetables – that it is served with, everything else on the table is an accompaniment to the rice, rather than the other way around. On the whole, Thai meals are made for sharing, so portions are served on platters and meant for at least two people. It is good manners for your plate to contain mostly rice, topped up with only a couple of spoonfuls at a time of the other dishes, as this ensures that all your dining companions will have a chance to taste each of the many delicacies on offer.

When eating in Thailand, there are further subtle areas of etiquette to be observed. Platters of food are left on the table and not passed around, as stretching is not considered rude and someone on the other side of the table will always be happy to spoon things onto your plate.

SNACKS

FROM INDIA

SAMOSAS

THESE CRISP, DEEP-FRIED PASTRIES ARE THE MOST POPULAR SAVOURY SNACK IN INDIA, AND ARE USUALLY SERVED WITH CHUTNEY. THIS RECIPE HAS A DELICIOUS SPICY VEGETABLE FILLING BUT IF YOU PREFER A MEAT SAMOSA, YOU CAN USE THE SINGHARA FILLING ON PAGE 34.

PASTRY

450 g (1 lb) maida or plain
    (all-purpose) flour
1 teaspoon salt
4 tablespoons oil or ghee

FILLING

400 g (14 oz) potatoes, cut into
    quarters
90 g (3 oz/½ cup) peas
1½ teaspoons cumin seeds
½ teaspoon coriander seeds
2 tablespoons oil
½ onion, finely chopped
¼ teaspoon ground turmeric
½ teaspoon garam masala
    (see recipe on page 464)
2 green chillies, chopped
2.5 cm (1 inch) piece of ginger,
    chopped
1½ tablespoons lemon juice
2 tablespoons chopped coriander
    (cilantro) leaves

oil for deep-frying

MAKES 30

TO MAKE the pastry, sift the maida and salt into a bowl. Rub in the oil or ghee until mixture resembles breadcrumbs. Add 185 ml (6 fl oz/¾ cup) warm water, a little at a time, to make a pliable dough. Turn out onto a floured surface and then knead for 5 minutes, or until smooth. Cover and set aside for 15 minutes. Don't refrigerate or the oil will harden.

TO MAKE the filling, cook the potato in simmering water for 10 minutes, or until tender. Drain and cut into small cubes. Cook the peas in simmering water for 2 minutes. Drain and refresh in cold water. Place a small frying pan over low heat, dry-roast the cumin seeds until aromatic, then remove. Dry-roast the coriander seeds. Grind ½ teaspoon of the cumin and all the coriander to a fine powder in a spice grinder or pestle and mortar. Heat the oil in a heavy-based saucepan over low heat and fry the onion until light brown. Stir in all the cumin, the coriander, turmeric and garam masala. Add the potato, chilli, ginger and stir for 1 minute. Mix in the lemon juice and coriander leaves and salt, to taste, then leave to cool.

ON a floured surface, roll out a third of the pastry to a 28 cm (11¼ inch) circle, about 3 mm (⅛ inch) thick. Cut 10 circles with an 8 cm (3¼ inch) cutter and spoon ½ tablespoon of filling onto the centre of each. Moisten the edges with water, then fold the pastry over and seal with a fork into a semicircle. Repeat to use all the filling and pastry. Cover until ready to fry.

FILL a karhai or heavy-based saucepan one-third full with oil and heat to 180°C (350°F), or until a cube of bread browns in 15 seconds. Fry a few samosas at a time until lightly browned. Turn them over and brown on the other side. Drain on a wire rack for 5 minutes, then drain on paper towels.

SERVE warm or cold.

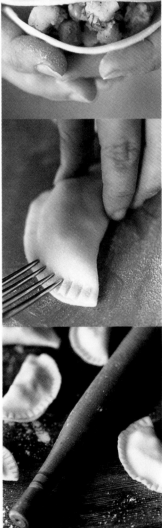

Don't over-stuff the samosas or they will burst during cooking. Seal them and use a fork to firmly press the edges together.

Spring rolls should look elegant rather than chunky, so use a small amount of filling in each and roll them neatly. Don't roll them too tightly or they are likely to burst open as they cook.

FROM CHINA

SPRING ROLLS

THE FAT, SOLID SPRING ROLLS FOUND IN MANY WESTERN RESTAURANTS ARE QUITE DIFFERENT FROM THE SLENDER AND REFINED SPRING ROLLS THAT ARE TRADITIONALLY MADE TO CELEBRATE CHINESE NEW YEAR. HERE'S AN EASY RENDITION OF THE CLASSIC.

FILLING
5 tablespoons light soy sauce
2 teaspoons roasted sesame oil
3½ tablespoons Shaoxing
    rice wine
1½ teaspoons cornflour (cornstarch)
450 g (1 lb) centre-cut pork loin,
    trimmed and cut into very
    thin strips
6 dried Chinese mushrooms
½ teaspoon freshly ground
    black pepper
4 tablespoons oil
1 tablespoon finely chopped ginger
3 garlic cloves, finely chopped
130 g (5 oz) Chinese cabbage,
    finely shredded
150 g (5 oz/1 cup) finely shredded
    carrot
30 g (1 oz/1 bunch) Chinese garlic
    chives, cut into 2 cm (¾ inch)
    lengths
180 g (6 oz/2 cups) bean sprouts

1 egg yolk
2 tablespoons plain (all-purpose)
    flour
20 square spring roll wrappers
oil for deep-frying

CONDIMENTS
plum sauce, to serve

MAKES 20

TO MAKE the filling, combine 2 tablespoons of the soy sauce and half the sesame oil with 1½ tablespoons of the rice wine and 1 teaspoon of the cornflour. Add the pork and toss to coat. Marinate in the fridge for 20 minutes. Meanwhile, soak the dried mushrooms in boiling water for 30 minutes, then drain and squeeze out any excess water. Remove and discard the stems and shred the caps. Combine the remaining soy sauce, sesame oil and cornflour with the black pepper.

HEAT a wok over high heat, add half the oil and heat until very hot. Add the pork mixture and stir-fry for 2 minutes, or until cooked. Remove and drain. Wipe out the wok.

REHEAT the wok over high heat, add the remaining oil and heat until very hot. Stir-fry the mushrooms, ginger and garlic for 15 seconds. Add the cabbage and carrot and toss lightly. Pour in the remaining rice wine, then stir-fry for 1 minute. Add the garlic chives and bean sprouts and stir-fry for 1 minute, or until the sprouts are limp. Add the pork mixture and soy sauce mixture and cook until thickened. Transfer to a colander and drain for 5 minutes, tossing occasionally to remove the excess liquid.

COMBINE the egg yolk, flour and 3 tablespoons water. Place 2 tablespoons of filling on the corner of a wrapper, leaving the corner itself free. Spread some of the yolk mixture on the opposite corner. Fold over one corner and start rolling, but not too tightly. Fold in the other corners, roll up and press to secure. Repeat with the remaining wrappers.

FILL a wok one-quarter full with oil. Heat the oil to 190°C (375°F), or until a piece of bread fries golden brown in 10 seconds when dropped in the oil. Cook the spring rolls in two batches, turning constantly, for 5 minutes, or until golden. Remove and drain on paper towels.

SERVE with plum sauce.

FROM THAILAND

SWEET CORN CAKES

400 g (14 oz/2 cups) corn kernels
1 egg
3 tablespoons rice flour
1 tablespoon yellow curry paste
2 tablespoons chopped Asian
   shallots
1 tablespoon fish sauce
1½ large handfuls roughly chopped
   coriander (cilantro)
1 large red chilli, chopped
peanut oil, for shallow-frying

CONDIMENTS
cucumber relish, to serve
   (see recipe on page 479)

MAKES 8

COMBINE the corn kernels, egg, rice flour, curry paste, shallots, fish sauce, coriander and chilli in a bowl. Shape the mixture into small patties, adding more rice flour, if necessary, to combine into a soft mixture.

HEAT the oil and fry the corn cakes for 3–4 minutes, turning once, until golden brown.

SERVE hot with cucumber relish.

SESAME PRAWNS ON TOASTS

280 g (10 oz) raw prawns (shrimp),
   peeled and deveined
2 teaspoons light soy sauce
1 egg
4–5 large garlic cloves,
   roughly chopped
7–8 coriander (cilantro) roots,
   roughly chopped
¼ teaspoon ground white pepper
½ teaspoon salt
7 slices day-old white bread,
   crusts removed, each slice
   cut into two triangles
3 tablespoons sesame seeds
peanut oil, for deep-frying

CONDIMENTS
cucumber relish, to serve
   (see recipe on page 479)

MAKES 14

USING a food processor or blender, whiz the prawns into a smooth paste. Transfer to a bowl, add the light soy sauce and egg and mix well. Leave for about 30 minutes to firm.

USING a pestle and mortar, pound the garlic, coriander roots, white pepper and salt into a smooth paste. Add to the prawns. (Using a pestle and mortar gives the best texture but you can also whizz the garlic, coriander roots, pepper, light soy sauce and egg with the prawns.) Heat the grill (broiler) to medium. Spread the bread on a baking tray and put under the grill for 3–4 minutes or until the bread is dry and slightly crisp. Spread the prawn paste thickly on one side of each piece. Sprinkle with sesame seeds and press on firmly. Refrigerate for 30 minutes.

HEAT the oil in a wok or deep frying pan over a medium heat. Drop in a small cube of bread. If it sizzles immediately, the oil is ready. Deep-fry a few toasts at a time, paste-side down, for 3 minutes or until golden. Turn with a slotted spoon. Drain paste-side up on paper towels.

SERVE with cucumber relish.

SESAME PRAWNS ON TOASTS

Abura-age is deep-fried sheets of tofu that should be rinsed with boiling water to remove excess oil before use in simmered dishes, such as soups or stews. The sheets can also be sliced and used in stir-fries.

FROM JAPAN

INARI SUSHI

THESE DELECTABLE LITTLE BUNDLES OF VINEGARED RICE IN POCKETS OF DEEP-FRIED TOFU CAN SERVE AS A STARTER, SNACK OR EVEN LUNCH BOX FARE. FRESH GREEN CHIVE TIES ADD A DECORATIVE TOUCH AND PINK PICKLED GINGER PROVIDES COLOUR AND FLAVOUR CONTRASTS.

20 pieces inari abura-age (prepared deep-fried tofu sheets)
1 quantity sushi rice
   (see recipe on page 460)
20 chives, optional

CONDIMENTS
shoyu (Japanese soy sauce),
   to serve
wasabi paste, to serve, optional
pickled ginger, to serve, optional

MAKES 20

PUT the prepared abura-age in a colander and drain off any excess liquid. Carefully insert a finger into the slit side of each sheet and gently prise the pocket open, trying not to split them.

FILL each pocket with 2 tablespoons of the prepared sushi rice, then fold over the open ends to enclose the rice as much as possible. You can dress these up by tying a chive around the middle and securing with a knot at the top – this also helps hold the open ends together to prevent the rice from falling out. Put the sushi rice pockets, seam side down, on a platter.

SERVE with a small bowl of shoyu for dipping into and, if desired, a little wasabi paste on the side to mix into the sauce and some pickled ginger as a palate refresher.

FROM THAILAND

FRIED FISH CAKES WITH GREEN BEANS

FISH CAKES ARE JUST ONE OF MANY DELICIOUS SNACKS SOLD AS STREET FOOD IN THAILAND. BATCHES ARE FRIED ON REQUEST AND SERVED IN A PLASTIC BAG, ALONG WITH A BAMBOO SKEWER FOR EATING THEM AND A SMALL BAG OF SAUCE FOR ADDITIONAL FLAVOUR.

450 g (1 lb) firm white fish fillets
1 tablespoon red curry paste
   (see recipe on page 472)
   or bought paste
1 tablespoon fish sauce
1 egg
60 g (2 oz) snake (yard long)
   beans, finely sliced
5 makrut (kaffir lime) leaves,
   finely shredded
peanut oil, for deep-frying

CONDIMENTS
sweet chilli sauce, to serve
   (see recipe on page 476)
cucumber relish, to serve
   (see recipe on page 479)

MAKES 30

REMOVE any skin and bone from the fish and roughly chop the flesh. In a food processor or a blender, mince the fish fillets until smooth. Add the curry paste, fish sauce and egg, then blend briefly until smooth. Spoon into a bowl and mix in the beans and makrut leaves. Use wet hands to shape the fish paste into thin, flat cakes, about 5 cm (2 inches) across, using about a tablespoon of mixture for each.

HEAT 5 cm (2 inches) oil in a wok or deep frying pan over a medium heat. When the oil seems hot, drop a small piece of fish cake into it. If it sizzles immediately, the oil is ready.

LOWER five or six of the fish cakes into the oil and deep-fry them until they are golden brown on both sides and very puffy. Remove with a slotted spoon and drain on paper towels. Keep the cooked fish cakes warm while deep-frying the rest.

SERVE hot with sweet chilli sauce and cucumber relish.

FOR a variation, make up another batch of the fish mixture but leave out the curry paste. Cook as above and serve both types together.

Using wet hands makes the fish mixture less likely to stick to your hands and also easier to handle.

Starting with the end nearest to you, roll up the sushi in the mat. Cut each roll into six slices, rinsing the knife after each slice.

CALIFORNIA ROLLS

ROLLED SUSHI IS EASY TO MAKE, SO EVEN THE NOVICE CAN SUCCEED ON THE FIRST TRY. CALIFORNIA ROLLS, BURSTING WITH A VARIETY OF LAVISH FILLINGS, WERE INSPIRED BY AMERICAN FREE-PLAY WITH SUSHI CLASSICS, AND THEY HAVE RECENTLY ALSO BECOME STYLISH IN JAPAN.

OMELETTE
1 large egg
1 teaspoon sake
pinch sugar
1 teaspoon oil

2 toasted nori sheets, 20 x 18 cm (8 x 7 inches)

FILLING
½ quantity sushi rice (see recipe on page 460)
2 crabsticks, 40 g (1½ oz) each, cut into strips
25 g (1 oz/¼ cup) pickled daikon, cut into julienne strips
5 cm (2 inch) carrot, cut into matchsticks
5 cm (2 inch) cucumber, cut into matchsticks

CONDIMENTS
shoyu (Japanese soy sauce), to serve
wasabi paste, to serve
pickled ginger, to serve

MAKES 12

TO MAKE an omelette, gently combine the egg, sake, a pinch of sugar and a pinch of salt. Heat the oil in a small frying pan. Pour in the egg mixture and cook until firm around the edges but still slightly soft in the middle. Roll up the omelette, then tip it out of the pan. Cool, then slice into strips.

PUT a nori sheet on a sushi mat, shiny side down. Add half of the prepared sushi rice, leaving a 4 cm (1½ inch) gap at the edge furthest away from you. Lay half of the fillings on the rice in the following order: omelette strips, crabstick, daikon, carrot and cucumber. Holding the filling in place with your fingertips and starting with the end nearest to you, roll the sushi away from you, tightly rolling the mat and the nori. When the roll is finished, press the mat down to form a neat, firm roll. Unroll the mat and put the roll, seam side down, on a cutting board. Repeat this process with the remaining ingredients to make a second roll.

USING a sharp knife, trim the ends and cut each roll into six slices. After cutting each slice, rinse the knife under cold running water to prevent sticking.

SERVE with shoyu, wasabi and pickled ginger.

FROM INDIA

CHUCUMBER

1 red onion, finely chopped
2 small cucumbers, about 200 g
   (7 oz), finely chopped
100 g (3½ oz) ripe tomatoes,
   finely chopped
3 tablespoons finely chopped
   coriander (cilantro)
1 red chilli, finely chopped
1 green chilli, finely chopped
1½ tablespoons lemon juice
1 teaspoon oil
125 g (4½ oz/¾ cup) unroasted
   peanuts, roughly chopped
1 teaspoon salt
½ teaspoon ground black pepper
1½ teaspoons chaat masala
   (see recipe on page 464)

SERVES 4

STIR together in a bowl the onion, cucumber, tomato, coriander, chillies and lemon juice.

HEAT the oil in a heavy-based frying pan over a high heat, add the peanuts and salt and fry for 1 minute. Sprinkle with the pepper and chaat masala and stir. Fry for 2 minutes. Remove from the heat and add to the onion mixture. Season with more salt, to taste, just before serving. The seasoning is added at the end to prevent the ingredients releasing too much juice before serving.

SERVE in small bowls. Chucumber can be eaten with a spoon or scooped up in pieces of roti or poppadoms.

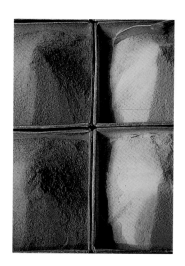

Chilli powder and turmeric marry well with small fish to make both spicy snacks and curries.

SPICY WHITEBAIT

350 g (12 oz) whitebait
½ teaspoon chilli powder
¼ teaspoon cayenne pepper
½ teaspoon ground turmeric
oil for deep-frying

SERVES 4

RINSE the whitebait and dry them thoroughly on paper towels.

MIX the chilli powder, cayenne pepper and turmeric together and toss the whitebait in the seasoning until well coated.

FILL a karhai or heavy-based saucepan one-third full with oil and heat to 190°C (375°F), or until a cube of bread browns in 10 seconds. Fry the fish in batches until crisp, drain on paper towels and sprinkle with salt.

SERVE hot and crisp.

SPICY WHITEBAIT

CHUCUMBER

Luk Yu Tea House,
Hong Kong.

FROM CHINA

CHAR SIU BAU

MANTOU, OR STEAMED BUNS, ARE A FILLING STAPLE EATEN ALL OVER CHINA, BUT ESPECIALLY IN THE

NORTH. HOWEVER, THESE FILLED, SLIGHTLY SWEET BUNS MADE WITH BARBECUE PORK (CHAR SIU)

ARE A CANTONESE SPECIALITY, ENJOYED IN EVERY DIM SUM RESTAURANT.

Gather in the tops of the buns as neatly as you can to make round balls. Bear in mind that they will open slightly as they cook to show their filling.

1 teaspoon oil
250 g (9 oz) barbecue pork
  (char siu), diced
3 teaspoons Shaoxing rice wine
1 teaspoon roasted sesame oil
2 tablespoons oyster sauce
2 teaspoons light soy sauce
3 teaspoons sugar
1 quantity basic yeast dough
  (see recipe on page 451)

CONDIMENTS
chilli sauce, to serve

MAKES 12 LARGE OR
24 SMALL

HEAT the oil in a wok. Add the pork, rice wine, sesame oil, oyster sauce, soy sauce and sugar and cook for 1 minute. Leave to cool.

DIVIDE the dough into 12 or 24 portions, depending on how large you want your buns to be, and cover with a tea towel (dish towel). Working with one portion at a time, press the dough into circles with the edges thinner than the centre. Place 1 teaspoon of filling on the dough for a small bun or 3 teaspoons for a large bun. Draw the sides in to enclose the filling. Pinch the top together and put each bun on a square of greaseproof paper. When you get more proficient at making these, you may be able to get more filling into the buns, which will make them less doughy. Ensure that you seal them properly. The buns can also be turned over, then cooked the other way up so they look like round balls.

PLACE the buns well apart in three steamers. Cover and steam over simmering water in a wok, reversing the steamers halfway through, for 15 minutes, or until the buns are well risen and a skewer inserted into the centre comes out hot.

SERVE with some chilli sauce.

FROM JAPAN

HAND-MOULDED SUSHI

TUNA, SALMON AND PRAWNS (SHRIMP) ARE AMONG THE MOST POPULAR OF ALL THE VARIETIES OF TOPPINGS FOR SUSHI. IN CONTRAST TO ROLLED STYLES, HERE THE WASABI IS PLACED BETWEEN THE RICE AND TOPPING, AND THE SHAPING OF THE RICE MOUNDS IS DONE BY HAND.

10 cooked prawns (shrimp)
1 tablespoon Japanese rice vinegar
½ quantity sushi rice
  (see recipe on page 460)
10 slices sashimi-grade tuna or
  salmon
wasabi paste, for spreading

CONDIMENTS
shoyu (Japanese soy sauce),
  to serve
wasabi paste, to serve, optional
pickled ginger, to serve, optional

MAKES 20

PEEL the prawns, leaving the tails intact if desired, then use a small knife to slit the prawns along their bellies, ensuring you don't cut through to the other side. Turn the prawn over and carefully remove the intestinal tract.

FILL a bowl with warm water and mix in the rice vinegar. Dampen your hands with the vinegared water to prevent the sushi rice sticking to your hands. Form a slightly heaped tablespoon of rice into a rounded rectangle about 5 x 2 cm (2 x ¾ inch), wetting your hands as needed. Put on a tray lined with plastic wrap, then cover with a damp tea towel (dish towel). Repeat with the remaining rice – you should make about 20 mounds.

PUT a slice of tuna or salmon sashimi in the palm of your left hand, then use a finger on your right hand to smear a little wasabi over the top. Put a piece of the moulded rice along the fish, gently cup your left palm to make a slight curve, then using the middle and index fingers of your right hand, press the rice firmly onto the fish, keeping the shape as neat and compact as possible. Turn the fish over so it is facing upwards, then neaten up the shape, keeping your left hand flat. Place, rice side down, on a plate and cover with plastic wrap while you repeat with the rest of the fish. Repeat the same process with the prawns, which should have the belly side against the rice.

SERVE with a small bowl of shoyu for dipping into and, if desired, a little extra wasabi on the side to mix into the sauce and some pickled ginger as a palate refresher. Eat with your fingers and dip the fish side, not the rice side, into the dipping sauce.

The shaping of the rice mounds is done by hand.

FROM INDIA

SINGHARAS

SINGHARAS, THE BENGALI VERSION OF SAMOSAS, ARE LITTLE PARCELS SERVED AT EVERY INDIAN WEDDING OR FESTIVAL AS WELL AS BEING A POPULAR TIFFIN DISH. SAMOSAS ARE SEMI-CIRCULAR IN SHAPE, WHILE SINGHARAS ARE TRIANGULAR. THE VEGETABLE FILLING FROM PAGE 17 CAN BE USED.

PASTRY
250 g (9 oz/2 cups) maida or plain
  (all-purpose) flour
2 tablespoons ghee

MEAT FILLING
4 ripe tomatoes
2 tablespoons ghee or oil
2 cinnamon sticks
6 cloves
1 cardamom pod
3 green chillies, chopped
1 large onion, finely chopped
3–4 curry leaves
4 garlic cloves, crushed
1 teaspoon ground turmeric
5 cm (2 inch) piece of ginger, grated
500 g (1 lb 2 oz) minced (ground)
  lamb
150 g (5½ oz/1 cup) peas
1 teaspoon garam masala
  (see recipe on page 464)

oil for deep-frying

MAKES 24

TO MAKE the pastry, sift the maida and a pinch of salt into a bowl. Rub in the ghee until the mixture resembles breadcrumbs. Add 125 ml (4 fl oz/½ cup) warm water, a little at a time, to make a pliable dough. Turn onto a floured surface and knead for 5 minutes or until the dough is smooth. Cover and set aside for about 30 minutes. Do not refrigerate or the ghee will harden.

TO MAKE the meat filling, score a cross in the top of each tomato. Plunge into boiling water for 20 seconds, drain and peel away from the cross, then roughly chop, discarding the cores and seeds and reserving any juices. Heat the ghee or oil in a karhai or large saucepan over low heat and fry the cinnamon, cloves, cardamom and chilli. Add the onion, curry leaves, garlic, turmeric and ginger and fry for 5 minutes, or until the onion is brown. Add the lamb and fry until brown. Then add the tomato and cover with a tight lid. Cook gently, stirring occasionally until the lamb is tender. Add the peas, cover and cook for 5 minutes. If there is any liquid left, turn up the heat and let it evaporate. Remove the whole spices. Season with salt, to taste, and sprinkle with garam masala.

DIVIDE the dough into 12 portions, roll out each to a 12 cm (5 inch) circle, then cut each circle in half. Take one piece and form a hollow cone by folding the dough in half and sealing the two edges of the cut side together. It is easiest to wet one edge and make a small overlap. Fill three-quarters full with filling. Don't overfill. Seal the top edges, then pinch to give a fluted finish. Repeat with the remaining dough and filling.

FILL a karhai or heavy-based saucepan one-third full with oil and heat to 180°C (350°F), or until a cube of bread browns in 15 seconds). Deep-fry the singharas in batches until well browned. Drain on a wire rack and keep them warm in a low oven.

Form a cone shape with the pastry, then fill it. Fold in the top and seal carefully so the singhara does not spring open.

FROM THAILAND

CHICKEN WRAPPED IN PANDANUS LEAF

PANDANUS LEAVES ACT AS BOTH A WRAPPING AND A FLAVOURING IN THIS DISH. LEAVING A LONG TAIL ON THE PARCELS WILL MAKE THEM PRETTIER AND EASIER TO HANDLE SO DON'T TRIM THE LEAVES. TO EAT, CAREFULLY UNWRAP THE PARCELS AND DIP THE CHICKEN IN THE SAUCE.

5 coriander (cilantro) roots, cleaned
    and roughly chopped
4–5 garlic cloves
1 teaspoon ground white pepper
¼ teaspoon salt
600 g (1 lb 5 oz) boneless, skinless
    chicken breasts, cut into 25
    cubes
2 tablespoons oyster sauce
1½ tablespoons sesame oil
1 tablespoon plain (all-purpose) flour
25 pandanus leaves, cleaned
    and dried
vegetable oil, for deep-frying

CONDIMENTS
plum sauce or sweet chilli sauce,
    to serve (see recipe on page 476)

MAKES 25

USING a pestle and mortar or a small blender, pound or blend the coriander roots, garlic, white pepper and salt into a paste.

IN a bowl, combine the paste with the chicken, oyster sauce, sesame oil and flour. Cover with plastic wrap and marinate in the refrigerator for at least 3 hours, or overnight.

FOLD one of the pandanus leaves, bringing the base up in front of the tip, making a cup. Put a piece of chicken in the fold and, moving the bottom of the leaf, wrap it around to create a tie and enclose the chicken. Repeat until you have used all the chicken.

HEAT the oil in a wok or deep frying pan over a medium heat.

WHEN the oil seems hot, drop a small piece of leaf into it. If it sizzles immediately, the oil is ready. Lower some parcels into the oil and deep-fry for 7–10 minutes or until the parcels feel firm. Lift out with a slotted spoon and drain on paper towels. Keep the cooked ones warm while deep-frying the rest. Transfer to a serving plate.

SERVE with plum sauce or a chilli sauce.

Pandanus leaves are used to enclose the chicken in an attractive tie shape.

Deep-fry the pakoras in batches of six or eight so that the oil temperature remains constant. Cooking too many at once will cool the oil.

FROM INDIA

PRAWN PAKORAS

600 g (1 lb 5 oz) prawns (shrimp)
50 g (1¾ oz/½ cup) besan (chickpea flour)
1 large red onion, finely chopped
1 teaspoon dried pomegranate seeds
4 green chillies, seeded and finely chopped
2 tablespoons finely chopped coriander (cilantro) leaves
pinch of bicarbonate of soda
ghee or oil for deep-frying

MAKES 30

PEEL and devein the prawns, then cut into small pieces.

PUT the besan in a bowl. Add 2 tablespoons of water, or enough to make a thick batter, mixing with a fork to beat out any lumps. Add all the remaining ingredients, except the oil, to the batter. Season with salt and mix well.

FILL a karhai or heavy-based saucepan one-third full with ghee or oil and heat to 180°C (350°F), or until a cube of bread browns in 15 seconds. Drop 1 heaped teaspoon of batter at a time into the ghee or oil and deep-fry in batches of six or eight pakoras until they are brown all over. Remove and drain on paper towels.

SERVE the pakoras hot.

GOLL BHAJI

GOLL BHAJI

90 g (3¼ oz/½ cup) rice flour
50 g (1¾ oz/⅓ cup) cashew nuts
75 g (2½ oz/⅔ cup) besan (chickpea flour)
pinch of bicarbonate of soda
10 curry leaves, chopped
4 green chillies, seeded and finely chopped
2 cm (¾ inch) piece of ginger, finely chopped
1 red onion, finely chopped
1 tablespoon ghee
oil for deep-frying

MAKES 20

PLACE a small frying pan over low heat and dry-roast the rice flour until it turns light brown. Dry-roast the cashew nuts in the same pan until they brown, then finely chop them.

MIX the rice flour with the besan, then add the bicarbonate of soda and a pinch of salt. Add the cashew nuts, curry leaves, green chilli, ginger, onion and ghee. Mix together well, adding a few drops of water, if necessary, to make a stiff dough. Form into 20 small balls.

FILL a karhai or heavy-based saucepan one-third full with ghee or oil and heat to 180°C (350°F), or until a cube of bread browns in 15 seconds. Fry five or six balls at a time until golden brown, then drain each batch on paper towels.

SERVE with a chutney.

FROM CHINA

JIAOZI

PERHAPS NO OTHER FOOD TYPIFIES THE HEARTY CHARACTERISTICS OF NORTHERN CHINESE HOME-STYLE COOKING MORE THAN THESE MEAT DUMPLINGS. YOU CAN BUY GOOD-QUALITY WHEAT DUMPLING WRAPPERS AT CHINESE GROCERS, WHICH MAKES THESE AN EASY SNACK TO PREPARE.

FILLING
300 g (10½ oz) Chinese cabbage,
    finely chopped
1 teaspoon salt
450 g (1 lb) minced (ground) pork
100 g (3 oz/3 bunches) Chinese
    garlic chives, finely chopped
2½ tablespoons light soy sauce
1 tablespoon Shaoxing rice wine
2 tablespoons roasted sesame oil
1 tablespoon finely chopped ginger
1 tablespoon cornflour (cornstarch)

50 round wheat dumpling wrappers

CONDIMENTS
red rice vinegar or a dipping sauce,
    to serve (see recipe on page 487)

MAKES 50

TO MAKE the filling, put the cabbage and salt in a bowl and toss lightly to combine. Leave for 30 minutes. Squeeze all the water from the cabbage and put the cabbage in a large bowl. Add the pork, garlic chives, soy sauce, rice wine, sesame oil, ginger and cornflour. Stir until combined and drain off any excess liquid.

PLACE a heaped teaspoon of the filling in the centre of each wrapper. Spread a little water along the edge of the wrapper and fold the wrapper over to make a half-moon shape. Use your thumb and index finger to form small pleats along the sealed edge. With the other hand, press the two opposite edges together to seal. Place the dumplings on a baking tray that has been lightly dusted with cornflour. Don't leave the dumplings to sit for too long or they will go soggy.

BRING a large saucepan of water to the boil. Add half the dumplings, stirring immediately to prevent them from sticking together, and return to the boil. For the traditional method of cooking dumplings, add 250 ml (9 fl oz/1 cup) cold water and continue cooking over high heat until the water boils. Add another 750 ml (26 fl oz/3 cups) cold water and cook until the water boils again. Alternatively, cook the dumplings in the boiling water for 8–9 minutes. Remove from the heat and drain the dumplings. Repeat with the remaining dumplings.

DUMPLINGS can also be fried. Heat 1 tablespoon oil in a frying pan, add a single layer of dumplings and cook for 2 minutes, shaking the pan to make sure they don't stick. Add 80 ml (2½ fl oz/⅓ cup) water and cover and steam for 2 minutes. Then uncover and cook until the water has evaporated. Repeat with the remaining dumplings.

SERVE with red rice vinegar or a dipping sauce.

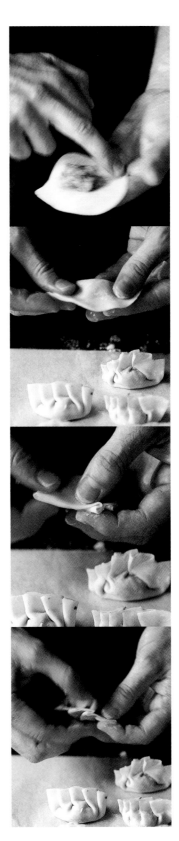

Fold the dumplings as shown above, handling the wrappers carefully so they don't tear and making sure they don't get too wet. Squeeze the pleats firmly or they will undo as they cook.

Fry the vegetable sticks in clumps. The batter will help them stick to each other and will set around them as they cook.

MASALA VADA

VEGETABLE BHAJI

125 g (4 oz) carrots
125g (4 oz) snowpeas (mangetout)
50 g (1¾ oz) thin eggplants
   (aubergines)
220 g (8 oz/2¼ cups) besan
   (chickpea flour)
1 teaspoon chilli powder
1 teaspoon ground turmeric
¼ teaspoon asafoetida
6 curry leaves
oil for deep-frying

MAKES 20

CUT the vegetables into thin sticks.

MIX together the besan, chilli powder, turmeric, asafoetida and a pinch of salt. Add enough water to make a thick batter that will hold the vegetables together.

MIX the vegetables and curry leaves into the batter.

FILL a karhai or heavy-based saucepan one-third full with oil and heat to 180°C/350°F (a cube of bread will brown in 15 seconds). Lift clumps of vegetables out of the batter and lower carefully into the oil. Fry until golden all over and cooked through, then drain on paper towels.

SPRINKLE with salt and serve hot with chutney or raita.

MASALA VADA

100 g (3½ oz) urad dal
120 g (4¼ oz) chana dal
2 green chillies, seeded and
   finely chopped
8 curry leaves, roughly chopped
½ teaspoon fennel seeds, crushed
1 red onion, finely chopped
½ teaspoon garam masala
   (see recipe on page 464)
3 tablespoons grated coconut
   (see recipe on page 468)
3 cm (1¼ inch) piece of ginger,
   grated
4 tablespoons chopped coriander
   (cilantro) leaves
3 tablespoons rice flour or
   urad dal flour
pinch of baking powder (optional)
oil for deep-frying

MAKES 18

SOAK the dal in cold water for 4 hours, then drain. Reserve 2 tablespoons of the soaked dal and coarsely grind the remainder in a food processor or pestle and mortar. Add the reserved dal to the ground dal for texture.

ADD the chillies, curry leaves, fennel, onion, garam masala, coconut, ginger and coriander leaves. Mix well and season with salt.

ADD the flour and baking powder, if using (it gives a crisper texture), then mix until the texture is soft but the dough can be shaped (you may need to add a little water).

DIVIDE the mixture into 18 portions and form each into a ball. Slightly flatten each ball to form a patty.

FILL a karhai or heavy-based saucepan one-third full with oil and heat to 180°C/350°F (a cube of bread will brown in 15 seconds). Fry the patties in the hot oil, in batches of four or five, until golden brown and crisp. Drain well on paper towels and serve hot with a chutney.

FROM INDIA

SAMBHAR

SAMBHAR IS OFTEN SERVED WITH DOSAS OR RICE FOR BREAKFAST OR LUNCH. DRUMSTICKS ARE A LONG, POD-LIKE VEGETABLE AND COME FRESH OR TINNED. TINNED ONES SHOULD BE ADDED AT THE END OF COOKING. TO EAT DRUMSTICKS, SCRAPE OUT THE FLESH AND DISCARD THE OUTER SHELL.

225 g (8 oz/¾ cup) toor dal
   (yellow lentils)
2 tablespoons coriander seeds
10 black peppercorns
½ teaspoon fenugreek seeds
2 tablespoons grated coconut
   (see recipe on page 468)
1 tablespoon roasted chana dal
6 dried chillies
2 drumsticks, cut into 5 cm (2 inch)
   pieces
2 carrots, cubed
1 onion, roughly chopped
125 g (4½ oz) eggplants
   (aubergines), cubed
50 g (1¾ oz) small okra, topped
   and tailed
1 tablespoon tamarind paste
   (see recipe on page 467)
2 tablespoons oil
1 teaspoon black mustard seeds
10 curry leaves
½ teaspoon ground turmeric
½ teaspoon asafoetida

SERVES 6

SOAK the dal in 500 ml (17 fl oz/2 cups) water for 2 hours. Drain the dal and put them in a saucepan with 1 litre (35 fl oz/4 cups) of water. Bring to the boil, then skim off any scum from the surface. Cover and simmer for 2 hours, or until the dal is cooked and tender.

PLACE a small frying pan over low heat and dry-roast the coriander, peppercorns, fenugreek, coconut, chana dal and chillies, stirring constantly until the coconut is golden brown. Grind the roasted mixture to a fine powder using a pestle and mortar or a spice grinder.

BRING 750 ml (26 fl oz/3 cups) water to the boil in a saucepan. Add the pieces of drumstick and the cubed carrot and bring back to the boil. Simmer for 10 minutes, then add the onion, eggplant and okra and more water if necessary. Simmer until the vegetables are almost cooked.

PUT the boiled dal and their liquid, the ground spices, the vegetables (with any vegetable water) and tamarind in a large saucepan and bring slowly to the boil. Reduce the heat and simmer for 30 minutes. Season with salt, to taste.

HEAT the oil in a small saucepan over medium heat, add the mustard seeds, cover and shake the pan until they start to pop. Add the curry leaves, turmeric, asafoetida and a little salt. Pour onto the simmering dal and stir until well mixed.

Eggplants (aubergines) and drumsticks are a common sight in most south Indian markets.

Sugar is sold loose in a market in Sichuan. This is slab sugar.

Chickens are bought live and prepared on the spot in a Beijing market to make sure they are really fresh.

FROM CHINA
BRAISED CHICKEN WINGS

THE CHINESE LOVE TO EAT EVERY PART OF THE CHICKEN, AND THE WINGS, DEEP-FRIED AND CRISP, ARE A FAVOURITE SNACK. THIS RECIPE IS A SIMPLE ONE THAT MAKES A GOOD SNACK OR FIRST COURSE. YOU'LL NEED TO HAND OUT FINGER BOWLS.

24 chicken wings
3 lumps rock (lump) sugar
1 tablespoon dark soy sauce
1 tablespoon light soy sauce
1 tablespoon Shaoxing rice wine
oil for deep-frying
2 teaspoons finely chopped ginger
1 spring onion (scallion), finely
  chopped
2 tablespoons hoisin sauce
125 ml (4 fl oz/½ cup) chicken
  stock (see recipe on page 491)

SERVES 6

DISCARD the tip of each chicken wing. Cut each wing into two pieces through the joint. Put the wing pieces in a bowl.

PUT the rock sugar, dark soy sauce, light soy sauce and rice wine in a small jug. Mix until combined, breaking the sugar down as much as you can. Pour the mixture over the chicken wings, then marinate in the fridge for at least 1 hour, or overnight.

DRAIN the chicken wings, reserving the marinade. Fill a wok one-quarter full of oil. Heat the oil to 180°C (350°F), or until a piece of bread fries golden brown in 15 seconds when dropped in the oil. Cook the chicken wings in batches for 2–3 minutes, or until they are well browned. Drain on paper towels.

CAREFULLY pour the oil from the wok, reserving 1 tablespoon. Reheat the wok over high heat, add the reserved oil and heat until very hot. Stir-fry the ginger and spring onion for 1 minute. Add the hoisin sauce, reserved marinade and chicken wings and cook for 1 minute, then add the stock and bring to the boil. Reduce the heat, cover the wok and cook gently for 8–10 minutes, or until the chicken wings are cooked through and tender. Increase the heat and bring the sauce to the boil, uncovered. Cook until the sauce reduces to a sticky coating.

FROM JAPAN

SUSHI CREPES

A PAPER-THIN EGG WRAP IS A DELICIOUS AND ATTRACTIVE VARIATION ON THE MORE USUAL NORI. THE CONTRAST OF ITS YELLOW WITH THE RED OF TUNA AND THE GREENS OF CUCUMBER AND AVOCADO MAKE THESE A VISUAL TREAT ON ANY SUSHI PLATTER.

4 eggs
½ quantity sushi rice
   (see recipe on page 460)
wasabi paste, for spreading
125 g (4½ oz) sashimi-grade tuna,
   cut into thin strips
1 small cucumber, peeled and cut
   into julienne strips
½ avocado, cut into julienne strips
3 tablespoons pickled ginger, cut
   into thin strips

CONDIMENTS
shoyu (Japanese soy sauce),
   to serve

MAKES ABOUT 40

TO MAKE the crepes, gently whisk the eggs with 2 tablespoons cold water and a pinch of salt in a bowl until combined. Heat and lightly oil a small crepe pan or heavy-based frying pan and pour enough of the egg mixture into the pan to lightly cover the base. Cook over low heat for 1 minute, being careful not to allow the crepe to brown. Turn the crepe over and cook for 1 minute. Transfer to a plate and repeat with the remaining mixture to make three more crepes.

PLACE one egg crepe on a bamboo mat. Spread 4 tablespoons of prepared sushi rice over the centre-third of the crepe, using a spatula or the back of a spoon. Spread a small amount of wasabi along the centre of the rice, then top with some tuna, cucumber, avocado and ginger.

USING the sushi mat to help you, fold the crepe over to enclose the filling and roll up firmly in the mat. Trim the ends using a sharp knife and cut the roll into 2 cm (¾ inch) rounds using a sharp knife.

SERVE immediately with shoyu for dipping.

Note: Unfilled crepes can be made ahead and stored in an airtight container in the refrigerator.

Cook the crepe over a low heat, taking care that it doesn't brown.

A traditional tea ceremony beneath blossoming cherry trees.

SUSHI CREPES

A traditional tea house in Hong Kong.

FROM CHINA

SIU MAI

SOME SIU MAI PURISTS CONSIDER THE ADDITION OF SEAFOOD TO THE TRADITIONAL ALL-MEAT FILLING TO BE OUTRAGEOUS. HOWEVER, THE PRAWNS (SHRIMP) ADD DEPTH AND CONTRAST TO THE FLAVOUR OF THE PORK AND IT IS NOW COMMON PRACTICE IN DIM SUM KITCHENS.

FILLING
180 g (6 oz) prawns (shrimp)
90 g (3 oz/½ cup) peeled water
  chestnuts
450 g (1 lb) minced (ground) pork
2 tablespoons light soy sauce
1½ tablespoons Shaoxing
  rice wine
2 teaspoons roasted sesame oil
¼ teaspoon freshly ground
  black pepper
2 tablespoons finely chopped ginger
1 spring onion (scallion), finely
  chopped
1 egg white, lightly beaten
2 tablespoons cornflour (cornstarch)

30 square or round egg dumpling
  wrappers
1 tablespoon shrimp roe (optional)

CONDIMENT
a dipping sauce, to serve
  (see recipes on page 487)

MAKES 30

TO MAKE the filling, peel and devein the prawns. Place in a tea towel (dish towel) and squeeze out as much moisture as possible, then roughly chop.

BLANCH the water chestnuts in a pan of boiling water for 1 minute, then refresh in cold water. Drain, pat dry and roughly chop them. Place the prawns, water chestnuts, minced pork and the remaining filling ingredients in a large bowl and stir until well combined.

PLACE 1 tablespoon of filling in the centre of a dumpling wrapper. Gather up the edges of the wrapper around the filling. Holding the dumpling between your thumb and index finger, lightly squeeze it to form a 'waist', while at the same time pushing up the filling from the bottom with the other hand to create a flat base. Smooth the surface of the filling with a knife dipped in water.

PLACE the dumplings well apart in four steamers lined with greaseproof paper punched with holes. Put a small dot of shrimp roe in the centre of the filling in each dumpling if using. Cover and steam over simmering water in a wok, reversing the steamers halfway through, for 15 minutes.

SERVE with a dipping sauce.

Hold the siu mai firmly in your hand and smooth the surface of the filling with a knife dipped in water to prevent it sticking.

GOLD BAGS

THIS DELICATE CHINESE-STYLE STARTER OR SNACK LOOKS EXACTLY AS IT IS DESCRIBED — A TINY GOLD BAG. BLANCHED CHIVES WILL ALSO WORK AS TIES FOR THE TOPS OF THE BAGS. IF YOU LIKE YOU CAN USE HALF PRAWNS (SHRIMP) AND HALF CHICKEN OR PORK FOR THE FILLING.

280 g (10 oz) raw prawns (shrimp), peeled, deveined and roughly chopped, or boneless, skinless chicken or pork fillet, roughly chopped
225 g (8 oz) tin water chestnuts, drained and roughly chopped
3–4 garlic cloves, finely chopped
3 spring onions (scallions), finely sliced
1 tablespoon oyster sauce
1 teaspoon ground white pepper
1 teaspoon salt
2–3 bunches of spring onions (scallions), or 40 chives, for ties
2 tablespoons plain (all-purpose) flour
40 spring roll sheets 13 cm (5 inch) square
peanut oil, for deep-frying

CONDIMENT
a chilli sauce, to serve (see recipe on page 488)

MAKES 40

USING a food processor or blender, whiz the prawns, chicken or pork to a fine paste. In a bowl, combine the minced prawn or meat, water chestnuts, garlic, spring onions, oyster sauce, white pepper and salt.

TO MAKE spring onion ties, cut each into 4 to 6 strips, using only the longest green parts, then soak them in boiling water for 5 minutes or until soft. Drain, then dry on paper towels.

TO MAKE the flour paste, mix the flour and 8 tablespoons cold water in a small saucepan until smooth. Stir and cook over a medium heat for 1–2 minutes or until thick.

PLACE 3 spring roll sheets in front of you and keep the remaining sheets in the plastic bag to prevent them drying out. Spoon 2 teaspoons of filling into the middle of each sheet. Brush around the filling with flour paste, then pull up into a bag and pinch together to enclose the filling. Place on a tray that is lightly dusted with plain (all-purpose) flour. Repeat until you have used all the filling and sheets. Tie a piece of spring onion twice around each bag and tie in a knot. Use chives if you prefer.

HEAT 7.5 cm (3 inches) oil in a wok or deep frying pan over a medium heat. When the oil seems hot, drop a small piece of spring roll sheet into it. If it sizzles immediately, the oil is ready. It is important not to have the oil too hot or the gold bags will cook too quickly and brown. Lower four bags into the oil and deep-fry for 2–3 minutes until they start to go hard. Lower another three or four bags into the oil and deep-fry them all together. To help cook the tops, splash the oil over the tops and deep-fry for 7–10 minutes or until golden and crispy. As each batch is cooked, lift the bags out with a slotted spoon and add another batch. Drain on paper towels. Keep the gold bags warm while deep-frying the rest.

SERVE with a chilli sauce.

Traditionally, Thais use spring onion greens for tying these bags but you may find it easier to use chives.

Roll up the nori on the diagonal to form a cone.

NORI CONES

NORI CONES FILLED WITH RICE AND VEGETABLES, SEASONED WITH WASABI AND AROMATIC SOUTHEAST ASIAN KECAP MANIS, MAKE A RATHER UNCOMMON, BUT DELICIOUS, SUSHI. SERVE THEM AS PART OF A SUSHI PLATTER ASSORTMENT OR AS ONE AMONG SEVERAL PARTY NIBBLES.

FILLING
3 dried shiitake mushrooms
1 quantity sushi rice
   (see recipe on page 460)
250 g (9 oz) choy sum (Chinese
   flowering cabbage), shredded,
   blanched
1 tablespoon pickled ginger,
   shredded
1 tablespoon sesame seeds,
   toasted
1 tablespoon kecap manis
½ teaspoon wasabi paste
2 teaspoons mirin
1 tablespoon shoyu (Japanese soy
   sauce)

10 nori sheets, toasted

CONDIMENT
ready-made sushi dipping sauce,
   to serve

MAKES 40

SOAK the shiitake in hot water for 30 minutes, then drain well. Discard the stems. Squeeze dry and roughly chop.

PUT the prepared sushi rice in a bowl and stir in the shiitake, choy sum, pickled ginger, sesame seeds and the combined kecap manis, wasabi, mirin and shoyu.

LAY the nori sheets, shiny side down, on the work surface and cut each one into four squares. Brush the joining edge with water and put 1 tablespoon of the mixture in the centre of the square. Roll up on the diagonal to form a cone and top up with 2 teaspoons of filling. Repeat with the remaining nori sheets and filling.

SERVE with the dipping sauce.

STARTERS & SALADS

FROM CHINA

STEAMED RICE NOODLE ROLLS

A DIM SUM FAVOURITE, THESE SILKY RICE NOODLES CAN BE FILLED WITH BARBECUE PORK (CHAR SIU), PRAWNS (SHRIMP) OR VEGETABLES. THE NOODLES ARE SOLD AS A LONG SHEET FOLDED INTO A ROLL. DON'T REFRIGERATE THEM. THEY MUST BE USED AT ROOM TEMPERATURE OR THEY'LL BREAK.

PORK FILLING
350 g (12 oz) barbecue pork
    (char siu), chopped
3 spring onions (scallions), chopped
2 tablespoons chopped coriander
    (cilantro)

OR

PRAWN FILLING
250 g (9 oz) small prawns (shrimp)
1 tablespoon oil
3 spring onions (scallions), chopped
2 tablespoons chopped coriander
    (cilantro)

OR

VEGETABLE FILLING
300 g (11 oz) Chinese broccoli
    (gai lan)
1 teaspoon light soy sauce
1 teaspoon roasted sesame oil
2 spring onions (scallions), chopped

4 fresh rice noodle rolls
oyster sauce, to serve

MAKES 4

TO MAKE the pork filling, combine the pork with the spring onion and coriander.

TO MAKE the prawn filling, peel and devein the prawns. Heat a wok over high heat, add the oil and heat until very hot. Stir-fry the prawns for 1 minute, or until they are pink and cooked through. Season with salt and white pepper. Add the spring onion and coriander and mix well.

TO MAKE the vegetable filling, wash the broccoli well. Discard any tough-looking stems and chop the rest of the stems. Put on a plate in a steamer, cover and steam over simmering water in a wok for 3 minutes, or until the stems and leaves are just tender. Combine the Chinese broccoli with the soy sauce, sesame oil and spring onion.

CAREFULLY unroll the rice noodle rolls (don't worry if they crack or tear a little at the sides). Trim each one into a neat rectangle about 15 x 18 cm (6 x 7 inches) (you may be able to get two out of one roll if they are very large). Divide the filling among the rolls, then re-roll the noodles. Put the rolls on a plate in a large steamer, cover and steam over simmering water in a wok for 5 minutes.

SERVE the rolls cut into pieces and drizzled with the oyster sauce.

Put the filling on the piece of noodle roll closest to you. Roll up carefully so you don't tear it, keeping the filling tucked inside.

DEEP FRIED PRAWNS WITH DIPPING SAUCE

FAMILIAR BREADED PRAWNS (SHRIMP) ARE ELEVATED HERE THROUGH THE USE OF PANKO, WHICH IS FAVOURED FOR ITS DELICATE FLAKINESS AND YIELDS A LIGHT AND CRISPY CRUST. PICKLED JAPANESE CUCUMBERS AND MITSUBA GIVE THE DIPPING SAUCE A PARTICULARLY EASTERN FLAVOUR.

The use of panko yields a light and crisp crust.

20 raw large prawns (shrimp)
30 g (1 oz/¼ cup) plain (all-purpose)
   flour, for coating
¼ teaspoon ground white pepper
1 egg
60 g (2¼ oz/1 cup) panko
   (Japanese breadcrumbs)
vegetable oil, for deep-frying
60 ml (2 fl oz/¼ cup) sesame oil

DIPPING SAUCE
170 g (6 oz/⅔ cup) Japanese
   mayonnaise
1½ tablespoons finely chopped
   pickled Japanese cucumber or
   dill pickles
1 tablespoon Japanese rice vinegar
1 spring onion (scallion), white part
   only, finely chopped
2 tablespoons mitsuba or flat-leaf
   (Italian) parsley, chopped
1 garlic clove, crushed
pinch of ground white pepper

lemon wedges, to serve

SERVES 4

PEEL and devein the prawns, leaving the tails intact. Make three cuts in the belly of the prawns. Turn the prawns over and, starting from the tail end, press down gently at intervals along the length of the prawn – this helps to break the connective tissue, preventing the prawns from curling up too much.

SEASON the flour with white pepper and ¼ teaspoon salt. Break the egg into a bowl, add 2 teaspoons water and lightly beat together. Holding the prawns by their tails so the tails remain uncoated, coat them lightly in flour, then into the egg, allowing any excess to drip off. Finally, coat with the panko, pressing on to help adhere. Refrigerate until you are ready to cook.

TO MAKE the dipping sauce, put all the ingredients in a small bowl and stir to combine. Season to taste with salt and white pepper. Refrigerate until ready to serve.

FILL a deep-fat fryer or large saucepan one-third full of vegetable oil and add the sesame oil. Heat to 180°C (350°F), or until a cube of bread dropped into the oil browns in 15 seconds. Deep-fry the prawns in batches for 2 minutes, or until golden. Drain on paper towels and serve immediately accompanied by the dipping sauce and lemon wedges.

FROM THAILAND

CRAB AND GREEN MANGO SALAD

DRESSING
2 tablespoons fish sauce
2 tablespoons lime juice
2 teaspoons palm sugar (jaggery)
2 green bird's eye chillies, chopped
2 red bird's eye chillies, chopped
1 teaspoon ground dried shrimp

300 g (10½ oz) fresh crabmeat
30 g (1 oz/⅔ cup) chopped mint
   leaves
20 g (¾ oz/⅓ cup) chopped
   coriander (cilantro) leaves
4 Asian shallots, finely sliced
1 green mango, flesh finely
   shredded
1 tomato, cut in half lengthways
   and thinly sliced
1 large green chilli, thinly sliced on
   an angle, to serve

SERVES 4

TO MAKE the dressing, put the fish sauce, lime juice, palm sugar, bird's eye chillies and dried shrimp in a small bowl and stir to dissolve the sugar.

JUST before serving, put the crabmeat, mint and coriander leaves, shallots, mango and tomato in a large bowl and toss gently.

POUR the dressing over the salad, then toss to combine and serve with the sliced chilli on top.

HOT AND SOUR GRILLED FISH SALAD

2 mackerel or whiting (about
   400 g/14 oz each fish), cleaned
   and gutted, with or without head,
   or firm white fish fillets
2 lemongrass stalks, white part only,
   finely sliced
2 Asian shallots, finely sliced
1 spring onion (scallion), finely sliced
2.5 cm (1 inch) piece of ginger,
   finely sliced
5 makrut (kaffir lime) leaves,
   finely sliced
20 g (1 cup) mint leaves
5 tablespoons lime juice
1 tablespoon fish sauce
4–5 bird's eye chillies, finely sliced
a few lettuce leaves
1 long red chilli, seeded and finely
   sliced, for garnish

SERVES 4

HEAT a barbecue or grill (broiler) to medium. If using a grill, line the tray with foil. Cook the fish for about 20 minutes on each side or until it is cooked and light brown. You can use a special fish-shaped griddle that opens out like tongs to make it easier to lift and turn on the barbecue.

USE your hands to remove the fish heads, backbone and other bones. Break all the fish, including the skin, into bite-sized chunks and put them in a bowl.

ADD the lemongrass, shallots, spring onion, ginger, makrut leaves, mint leaves, lime juice, fish sauce and chillies to the fish. Mix well, then taste and adjust the seasoning if necessary.

LINE a serving plate with lettuce leaves, then spoon the salad over the leaves. Sprinkle with chilli slices.

HOT AND SOUR GRILLED
FISH SALAD

CRAB AND GREEN MANGO SALAD

Mirin is pale gold in colour. It is a sweet spirit-based rice liquid sometimes referred to as sweet rice wine. Manufactured for use in cooking rather than drinking, it is commonly used in sauces, dressings and marinades. Look for bottles labelled hon mirin 'true mirin'.

FROM JAPAN

DEEP-FRIED MARINATED CHICKEN

A TENDERISING AND FLAVOUR-ENHANCING MARINADE USES A TRIO OF JAPANESE-STYLE LIQUID SEASONINGS FOR THE CHICKEN – SOY SAUCE, MIRIN AND SAKE. THE ADDITION OF GINGER AND GARLIC TO THE BLEND ADDS A FURTHER FLAVOUR BOOST TO THESE DEEP-FRIED CHICKEN MORSELS.

1 kg (2 lb 4 oz) chicken thigh cutlets
    or fillets, skin on
60 ml (2 fl oz/¼ cup) shoya
    (Japanese soy sauce)
60 ml (2 fl oz/¼ cup) mirin
1 tablespoon sake
2 teaspoons finely grated fresh
    ginger and its juice
3 garlic cloves, crushed
katakuriko or potato starch,
    for coating
oil, for deep-frying
lemon wedges, to serve

SERVES 6

REMOVE the bone from the cutlets and cut the chicken into 4 cm (1½ inch) squares.

COMBINE the soy sauce, mirin, sake, ginger and juice, and garlic in a non-metallic bowl and add the chicken. Stir to coat, cover with plastic wrap and marinate in the fridge for 1 hour.

FILL a deep-fat fryer or large saucepan one-third full of oil. Heat to 180°C (350°F), or until a cube of bread dropped into the oil browns in 15 seconds.

DRAIN the chicken pieces well, discarding the marinade. Lightly coat chicken in the katakuriko and shake off any excess. Deep-fry in batches for 6–7 minutes, or until golden and crisp and the chicken is just cooked through. Drain well on paper towels and sprinkle with salt.

SERVE with lemon wedges.

HOT AND SOUR VERMICELLI WITH MIXED SEAFOOD

ONE OF THE MILDER CLASSIC SALADS FOUND ALL OVER THAILAND, OFTEN MADE JUST WITH PRAWNS, BUT HERE MADE WITH SEAFOOD. THE VERMICELLI USED BECOMES ALMOST TRANSLUCENT WHEN SOAKED. AS THE DRESSING IS ABSORBED QUICKLY, DON'T MAKE THE SALAD TOO FAR AHEAD.

110 g (3¾ oz) mung bean vermicelli
175 g (6 oz) mixed raw medium
  prawns (shrimp), squid tubes and
  scallops
8 mussels
15 g (½ oz) dried black fungus
  (about half a handful)
1½ tablespoons vegetable oil
4–5 garlic cloves, finely chopped
3 tablespoons lime juice
1 tablespoon fish sauce
2 lemongrass stalks, white part only,
  finely sliced
3 Asian shallots, finely sliced
¼–½ teaspoon chilli powder
  or 2–3 bird's eye chillies,
  finely sliced
3 spring onions (scallions),
  finely chopped
a few lettuce leaves
1 long red chilli, seeded and
  finely sliced, for garnish

SERVES 4

SOAK the mung bean vermicelli in boiling water for 1–2 minutes, or until soft, then drain and roughly chop.

PEEL and devein the prawns and cut each prawn along the back so it opens like a butterfly (leave each prawn joined along the base and at the tail, leaving the tail attached). Peel off the skin from the squid tubes, rinse the insides and cut the tubes into 5 mm (¼ inch) rings. Remove any dark vein from the scallops. Scrub mussels and remove their hairy beards. Discard any open mussels and any that don't close when tapped on the work surface.

SOAK the black fungus in boiling water for 2–3 minutes or until soft, then drain and roughly chop them.

HEAT the oil in a small wok or frying pan and stir the garlic over a medium heat until light brown. Transfer the fried garlic to a small bowl.

IN a saucepan or wok, cook the prawns, squid rings and mussels over a medium heat with the lime juice and fish sauce for 1–2 minutes or until the prawns open and turn pink. Add the scallops and cook for 1 minute. Discard any unopened mussels. Add the vermicelli and mushrooms to the pan and cook for another 2 minutes or until the vermicelli is cooked. Remove from the heat.

ADD the lemongrass, shallots, chilli powder or chillies, and spring onions and mix well. Taste, then adjust the seasoning if necessary.

LINE a serving plate with lettuce leaves, then spoon the seafood over the leaves. Sprinkle with chilli slices and the fried garlic.

Add the mung bean vermicelli and mushrooms to the seafood, then the flavourings.

Unloading mussels in Pattaya.

A Punjabi dhaba in Mumbai (Bombay) sells speciality snacks.

Chapatis are cooked on a large tava at a street stall.

Cumin (jeera) seeds are the green or ochre, elongated ridged seeds of a plant of the parsley family. They have a peppery, slightly bitter flavour and are very aromatic.

FROM INDIA

PORK TIKKA

ENCRUSTED IN SPICES AND MOUTHWATERINGLY TENDER ON THE INSIDE, PORK TIKKA IS A POPULAR DISH IN PUNJABI DHABAS (ROADSIDE RESTAURANTS) AND AT STREET STALLS. IT IS OFTEN SERVED WITH CHAPATIS, ROTI OR NAAN AND CHUTNEY ON THE SIDE.

MARINADE
1 onion, roughly chopped
3 garlic cloves, roughly chopped
5 cm (2 inch) piece of ginger, roughly chopped
½ tablespoon ground cumin
1 teaspoon ground coriander
½ tablespoon garam masala (see recipe on page 464)
¼ teaspoon chilli powder
½ pinch ground black pepper
250 ml (9 fl oz/1 cup) thick plain yoghurt (see recipe on page 467)

500 g (1 lb 2 oz) pork tenderloin, centre cut, cut into 2.5 cm (1 inch) cubes

SAUCE
1 large red onion, roughly chopped
1 garlic clove, roughly chopped
2.5 cm (1 inch) piece of ginger, roughly chopped
1 green chilli, roughly chopped
25 g (1 oz/¾ cup) coriander (cilantro) leaves

125 ml (4 fl oz/½ cup) oil
1 tablespoon garam masala (see recipe on page 464)

SERVES 4

TO PREPARE the marinade, finely chop the onion, garlic and ginger in a food processor or, if you don't have a processor, with a knife. Add the spices and yoghurt to the paste and mix through.

PUT the pork in a bowl, add the marinade and mix well. Cover and marinate in the fridge for 2 hours or overnight.

TO MAKE the sauce, finely chop the onion, garlic, ginger, chilli and coriander in a food processor or, if you don't have a processor, with a knife.

HEAT the oil in a heavy-based frying pan, large enough to fit the meat in a single layer, until sizzling but not smoking. Add the sauce and stir over medium heat for 2 minutes, or until softened but not brown. Increase the heat to high and add the pork with the marinade. Stir constantly for 5 minutes, then reduce the heat to medium and let the meat and its juices bubble away for 15–20 minutes, or until the liquid has completely evaporated. The meat and the dryish sauce will be a rich dark brown.

SEASON with salt, to taste, and sprinkle with the garam masala. Cook for another 2 minutes to allow the added seasoning to be absorbed.

FROM JAPAN

PRESSED SUSHI

FRESH SWEET PRAWNS (SHRIMP) MAKE A LUXURIOUS AND APPEALING TOPPING FOR THIS EASY-TO-MAKE SUSHI. LAYERED BETWEEN DARK GREEN NORI AND RICE, THE CENTRE HIDES JEWEL-LIKE ORANGE FISH ROE, WHICH BURST WITH THE SALTY FLAVOUR OF THE SEA WITH EVERY BITE.

16 cooked king prawns (shrimp)
2 tablespoons Japanese rice
   vinegar, plus 1 tablespoon extra
1 teaspoon caster (superfine) sugar
wasabi paste, optional
1 quantity prepared sushi rice
   (see recipe on page 460)
125 g (4 oz) flying fish roe or
   salmon roe
4 toasted nori sheets

MAKES 16 PIECES

LINE a 26 x 16 cm (10½ x 6½ inch) baking tin about 4 cm (1½ inch) deep with two long pieces of plastic wrap so that it overhangs on all sides. You will also need another slightly smaller tin.

PEEL the prawns, then slit along their bellies, ensuring you don't cut all the way through. Carefully remove the vein.

MIX the vinegar with the sugar and a pinch of salt until the sugar is dissolved, then add the prawns and mix. Set aside for 15 minutes. Drain well, then neatly and snugly arrange the prawns in a single layer, belly-side up, in the baking tin. Flatten with your hands then smear a little wasabi over the cut side of each prawn, if you are using it.

FILL a bowl with warm water and mix in the extra rice vinegar. Dampen your hands with the water to prevent the rice sticking to your hands. Carefully spread half the rice over the prawns, without moving the prawns. Press down firmly. Smooth the rice over so that it forms an even layer, wetting your hands as needed.

SPREAD the roe over the rice in a thin even layer with the back of a spoon, then press down gently. Trim two sheets of the nori to fit the tin and cover the rice in a single layer. Press down to adhere. Add the second half of the rice, pressing and smoothing as before, then trim the remaining two sheets of nori to cover the rice and press down again to adhere.

FOLD the plastic wrap over the sides to enclose the rice. Put the smaller tin on top of the plastic and fill with cold water to weigh down the sushi. Leave for 30 minutes, then remove. Unfold the plastic wrap and invert the sushi onto a platter. Remove the plastic wrap carefully so the prawns stay in place. Use a knife to cut into 16 rectangles, each containing a prawn.

Spread the rice over the layer of prawns and press down firmly. Spread fish roe over the rice with the back of a spoon. Cover the rice in a single layer of nori.

FROM CHINA

SPICY SALT AND PEPPER SPARE RIBS

1 kg (2 lb 4 oz) Chinese-style pork
  spare ribs
1 egg, beaten
2–3 tablespoons plain (all-purpose)
  flour
oil for deep-frying
2 spring onions (scallions), finely
  chopped
2 small red chillies, finely chopped

MARINADE
½ teaspoon ground Sichuan
  peppercorns
½ teaspoon five-spice
½ teaspoon salt
1 tablespoon light soy sauce
1 tablespoon Shaoxing rice wine
¼ teaspoon roasted sesame oil

SERVES 4

ASK the butcher to cut the spare ribs crosswise into thirds that measure 4–5 cm (1½–2 inches) in length, or use a cleaver to do so yourself. Cut the ribs between the bones to separate them.

TO MAKE the marinade, combine the ingredients in a bowl. Add the ribs and toss lightly. Marinate in the fridge for at least 3 hours, or overnight.

MIX the egg, flour and a little water to form a smooth batter the consistency of thick cream.

FILL a wok one-quarter full of oil. Heat the oil to 180°C (350°F), or until a piece of bread fries golden brown in 15 seconds when dropped in the oil.

DIP the ribs in the batter and fry in batches for 5 minutes until they are crisp and golden, stirring to separate them, then remove and drain. Reheat the oil and fry the ribs for 1 minute to darken the colour. Remove and drain on paper towels.

SOAK the spring onion and chilli in the hot oil (with the heat off) for 2 minutes. Remove with a wire strainer or slotted spoon and sprinkle over the ribs.

A cleaver is the only knife heavy enough to easily cut through the bones of spare ribs.

BARBECUE SPARE RIBS

1.5 kg (3 lb 5 oz) Chinese-style pork
  spare ribs

MARINADE
125 ml (4 fl oz/½ cup) hoisin sauce
3 tablespoons light soy sauce
3 tablespoons Shaoxing rice wine
2 tablespoons sugar
3 tablespoons tomato sauce
  (ketchup)
4 garlic cloves, finely chopped
3 tablespoons finely chopped ginger

SERVES 6

ASK the butcher to cut the spare ribs crosswise into thirds that measure 4–5 cm (1½–2 inches) in length, or use a cleaver to do so yourself.

PLACE the spare ribs in a large clay pot, casserole or saucepan and cover with water. Bring to the boil, then reduce the heat to a simmer. Cook for 20 minutes, drain and allow the ribs to cool. Cut the ribs between the bones to separate them.

TO MAKE the marinade, combine the ingredients in a bowl. Add the ribs and toss lightly. Marinate in the fridge for at least 3 hours, or overnight.

PREHEAT the oven to 180°C (350°F/Gas 4). Put the ribs and marinade on a baking tray lined with foil. Bake for 45 minutes, turning once, until golden.

BARBECUE SPARE RIBS

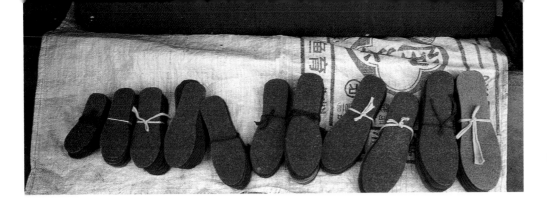

FROM CHINA

JELLYFISH AND CHICKEN SALAD

JELLYFISH ARE ONLY EVER EATEN ONCE THEY HAVE BEEN PRESERVED AND DRIED. THEY HAVE A CRUNCHY TEXTURE AND ARE NOT LIKE JELLY. YOU CAN BUY THEM DRIED, CUT INTO STRIPS OR WHOLE, AND ALSO ALREADY RECONSTITUTED IN VACUUM PACKS. THE LATTER ARE MUCH EASIER TO USE.

375 g (13 oz) dried or ready-prepared jellyfish
1.3 kg (3 lb) chicken
2 celery stalks, cut into 5 cm (2 inch) lengths and finely shredded
1 carrot, cut into 5 cm (2 inch) lengths and finely shredded
1 tablespoon oyster sauce
2 teaspoons light soy sauce
2 teaspoons roasted sesame oil
25 g (1 oz/¾ cup) coriander (cilantro) leaves
3 teaspoons sesame seeds

DRESSING
185 ml (6 fl oz/¾ cup) clear rice vinegar
55 g (2 oz/¼ cup) sugar
1 tablespoon finely chopped ginger
3 spring onions (scallions), thinly sliced

SERVES 8

TO PREPARE dried jellyfish, remove from the packet, cover with tepid water and soak overnight. Drain, then rinse to remove any sand and sediment. Drain well. Cut into strands using a pair of scissors, then cut any long strands into shorter lengths. If you are using ready-prepared jellyfish, remove it from the packet and rinse.

RINSE the chicken, drain, and remove any fat from the cavity opening and around the neck. Cut off and discard the parson's nose. Bring a large saucepan of water to the boil. Add the chicken and bring the water to a gentle simmer. Cook, covered, for 25–30 minutes, or until the chicken is cooked through. Remove the chicken from the saucepan and plunge into cold water. When cool enough to handle, remove the skin and bones from the chicken and finely shred the meat.

PLACE the chicken in a large bowl and add the jellyfish, celery, carrot, oyster sauce, soy sauce, sesame oil and coriander. Mix well to combine.

TO MAKE the dressing, place the vinegar and sugar in a bowl and stir until dissolved. Stir in the ginger and spring onion.

TOAST the sesame seeds by dry-frying in a pan until brown and popping. Sprinkle the salad with the sesame seeds and serve cold with the dressing alongside.

It is easiest to cut the jellyfish using a pair of scissors. Make sure you keep the strands roughly the same width.

As the tofu skins are rather thin, spread them out well before you roll them up.

FROM CHINA

TOFU ROLLS

THESE DELICATE ROLLS MAKE A CHANGE TO SPRING ROLLS AND ARE OFTEN SERVED AS DIM SUM. TOFU SKINS CAN BE PURCHASED EITHER VACUUM-PACKED AND READY TO USE, OR DRIED. THE DRIED TOFU SKINS NEED TO BE HANDLED CAREFULLY AS THEY BREAK EASILY.

4 dried Chinese mushrooms
100 g (3½ oz) fresh or tinned bamboo shoots, rinsed and drained
1 small carrot
3 tablespoons oil
300 g (10½ oz) firm tofu, drained and diced
200 g (7 oz) bean sprouts
½ teaspoon salt
½ teaspoon sugar
2 spring onions (scallions), finely shredded
1 tablespoon light soy sauce
1 teaspoon roasted sesame oil
1 tablespoon plain (all-purpose) flour
12 sheets soft or dried tofu skins
oil for deep-frying
red rice vinegar, soy sauce or a dipping sauce (see recipes on page 487), to serve

MAKES 12

SOAK the dried mushrooms in boiling water for 30 minutes, then drain and squeeze out any excess water. Remove and discard the stems and finely shred the caps. Cut the bamboo shoots and carrot into thin strips about the size of the bean sprouts. Heat a wok over high heat, add the oil and heat until very hot. Stir-fry carrot, tofu and bean sprouts for 1 minute. Add the mushrooms and bamboo shoots, toss, then add the salt, sugar and spring onion. Stir-fry for 1 minute. Add the soy sauce and sesame oil and blend well. Remove mixture from the wok and drain off excess liquid. Leave to cool.

COMBINE the flour with a little cold water to make a paste.

IF YOU are using dried tofu skins, soak them in cold water until they are soft. Peel off a sheet of tofu skin and trim to a 15 x 18 cm (6 x 7 inch) rectangle. Place 2 tablespoons of the filling at one end of the skin, and roll up to make a neat parcel, folding the sides in as you roll. Brush the skin with some of the flour paste to seal the flap firmly. Repeat with the remaining tofu skins and filling.

FILL a wok one-quarter full of oil. Heat the oil to 180°C (350°F), or until a piece of bread fries golden brown in 15 seconds when dropped in the oil. Cook rolls in batches for 3–4 minutes, or until golden.

SERVE with some red rice vinegar, soy sauce or a dipping sauce.

FROM JAPAN

CHILLED TOFU WITH GINGER AND SPRING ONION

ALTHOUGH DELICIOUS AT ANY TIME, CHILLED TOFU MAKES AN ESPECIALLY SUITABLE STARTER IN THE HEAT OF SUMMER. ITS DELICATE FLAVOUR AND CREAMY TEXTURE ARE WELL ACCENTED BY THE AROMATIC SHREDDED SHISO LEAVES, NUTTY SESAME SEEDS AND THE SALTINESS OF SOY SAUCE.

600 g (1 lb 5 oz) block silken firm
  tofu, chilled
1 tablespoon finely grated fresh
  ginger and its juice
2 spring onions (scallions), thinly
  sliced
2 teaspoons white or black sesame
  seeds, toasted
finely shredded shiso leaves,
  to garnish, optional
fine katsuobushi (bonito flakes),
  to garnish, optional
shoyu (Japanese soy sauce),
  for drizzling
sesame oil or chilli sesame oil,
  for drizzling

SERVES 4

BE very careful when working with the tofu – it is very soft and breaks easily. Cut the tofu into quarters, then put one piece of tofu in each of four small serving bowls.

TOP each serving with a little grated fresh ginger and juice, some spring onion and sesame seeds.

IF you like, sprinkle the tofu with shredded shiso leaves and katsuobushi. Drizzle with a little soy sauce and sesame oil, then serve immediately.

Tofu – also called beancurd, is made by soaking, crushing and boiling soya beans. The soya milk is squeezed out, strained and coagulated in moulds.

This tasty salad is made using a colourful combination with flavours that contrast well.

CRISPY FISH SALAD

THE FISH (TRADITIONALLY CATFISH) IN THIS RECIPE IS TURNED INTO AN ALMOST UNRECOGNISABLE FLUFFY, CRUNCHY AFFAIR THAT IS THEN FLAVOURED WITH A SWEET, HOT AND SOUR DRESSING. PINK SALMON IS SUITABLE TO USE AS A SUBSTITUTE FOR THE WHITE FISH.

DRESSING
1 lemongrass stalk, white part
  only, roughly chopped
4 bird's eye chillies,
  stems removed
1 garlic clove, chopped
1 tablespoon fish sauce
2 tablespoons lime juice
2 teaspoons palm sugar (jaggery)
¼ teaspoon ground turmeric

300 g (11 oz) skinless firm white
  fish fillets
1 tablespoon sea salt
peanut oil, for deep-frying
3 tomatoes or large cherry
  tomatoes, each cut into
  4 or 6 wedges
2 Asian shallots, thinly sliced
1 small red onion, sliced into
  thin wedges
15 g (½ oz/½ cup) coriander
  (cilantro) leaves
18–24 mint leaves
2 tablespoons roasted peanuts,
  roughly chopped

SERVES 4

TO MAKE the dressing, use a pestle and mortar or food processor to pound or blend the lemongrass, chillies and garlic to a paste. Transfer to a bowl and add the fish sauce, lime juice, sugar and turmeric. Stir until the sugar dissolves.

PREHEAT the oven to 180°C/350°F/Gas 4. Pat dry the fish fillets, then toss them in the sea salt. Place them on a rack in a baking tray and bake for 20 minutes. Remove, allow to cool, then transfer to a food processor and chop until the fish resembles large breadcrumbs.

HALF fill a wok with oil and heat over a high heat. Drop a small piece of fish into the oil. If it sizzles immediately, the oil is ready. Drop a large handful of the chopped fish into the hot oil. The fish will puff up and turn crisp. Cook for 30 seconds and carefully stir a little. Cook for another 30 seconds until golden brown. Remove with a slotted spoon and drain on paper towels. Repeat to cook all the fish.

PUT the tomatoes, shallots, red onion, coriander leaves, mint leaves and peanuts in a bowl with about half of the dressing.

TRANSFER the salad to a serving plate. Break the fish into smaller pieces if you wish and place on the salad. To ensure that the fish stays crispy, pour the remaining dressing over the salad just before serving.

FROM INDIA

KASHMIRI LAMB CUTLETS

1 kg (2 lb 4 oz) lamb cutlets
¾ teaspoon cumin seeds
1 teaspoon coriander seeds
¾ teaspoon black peppercorns
500 ml (17 fl oz/2 cups) milk
2 cinnamon sticks
10 cardamom seeds
10 cloves
2 cm (¾ inch) piece of ginger,
    grated
2 onions, finely chopped

75 g (2½ oz/⅔ cup) besan
    (chickpea flour)
2 teaspoons chilli powder
125 ml (4 fl oz/½ cup) thick plain
    yoghurt (see recipe on page 467)

oil for deep-frying

lime quarters, to serve

SERVES 6

TRIM the lamb of any fat and scrape the bone ends clean.

PLACE a small frying pan over low heat and dry-roast the cumin seeds until aromatic. Remove them and dry-roast the coriander seeds. Crush the coriander and cumin seeds with the peppercorns in a spice grinder or pestle and mortar. Transfer to a large, heavy-based saucepan and add the milk, cinnamon, cardamom, cloves, ginger and onion. Bring to the boil over medium heat, then add the chops to the pan and return to the boil. Reduce the heat and simmer for 30 minutes, or until the meat is tender and very little liquid remains. Remove the cutlets and drain them.

WHISK the besan and chilli powder into the yoghurt with 60 ml (2 fl oz/¼ cup) water, to make a batter.

FILL a karhai or heavy-based saucepan one-third full of oil and heat to 180°C/350°F (a cube of bread will brown in 15 seconds). Dip the cutlets in the batter, shake off any excess, then fry them in batches in the hot oil until they are crisp. Drain on paper towels and keep them warm.

SERVE sprinkled with a little lime juice and salt, to taste.

Chillies on display at the spice market in Delhi.

CHILLI LAMB CUTLETS

8 lamb cutlets

¼ teaspoon chilli powder
½ teaspoon ground turmeric
1 teaspoon garam masala
    (page 464)
2 cm (¾ inch) piece of ginger, grated
1 garlic clove, crushed
1 tablespoon thick plain yoghurt
    (see recipe on page 467)
3 tablespoons lemon juice

MAKES 8

TRIM the lamb of any fat and scrape the bone ends clean.

COMBINE the remaining ingredients to form a paste, adding a little lemon juice if necessary. Rub the paste over the chops, then cover and refrigerate for 2 hours or overnight.

PREHEAT the grill (broiler) to its highest setting. Sprinkle the chops with salt on both sides and grill (broil) them on each side for 2–3 minutes, or until they are browned and sizzling.

SQUEEZE the remaining lemon juice over them before serving.

CHILLI LAMB CUTLETS

Put 2 teaspoons of filling in the middle of the wrapper. Dampen the edge, then fold in half to form a semicircle. Fold pleats around the curved edge to form a dumpling.

GYOZA

THESE TASTY MORSELS MAKE A GREAT STARTER, EXCEPT FOR THE FACT THAT THOSE FEW BITES MAY LEAVE YOUR GUESTS LONGING FOR MORE. A LITTLE PRACTICE SOON YIELDS DEFTLY PLEATED EDGES, ALTHOUGH A LITTLE JAPANESE CRIMPING TOOL EXISTS PRECISELY TO SIMPLIFY THIS TASK.

FILLING
200 g (7 oz) Chinese cabbage, stems removed, finely chopped
200 g (7 oz) minced (ground) pork
2 teaspoons finely grated fresh ginger
3 garlic cloves, crushed
1½ tablespoons shoyu (Japanese soy sauce)
2 teaspoons sake
2 teaspoons mirin
¼ teaspoon ground white pepper
2 spring onions (scallions), finely chopped

DIPPING SAUCE
80 ml (2½ fl oz/⅓ cup) Japanese rice vinegar
80 ml (2½ fl oz/⅓ cup) shoyu (Japanese soy sauce)
2 teaspoons sesame oil or chilli sesame oil

200 g (7 oz) gyoza wrappers
vegetable oil, for pan-frying, plus an extra 2 teaspoons
2 teaspoons sesame oil
Japanese mustard, to serve, optional

MAKES 30

TO MAKE the filling, place cabbage in a colander, sprinkle with salt and stand for 30 minutes. Squeeze well, then mix with the rest of the filling ingredients.

MEANWHILE, to make the dipping sauce, put all the ingredients in a small bowl and stir to combine. Divide among small sauce dishes.

LAY a wrapper in the palm of your hand and put 2 teaspoons of the filling in the middle. Lightly dampen the edge of the wrapper with water, then fold the edges together to form a semicircle. Press firmly to enclose the filling. Lightly dampen the curved edge of the wrapper, then overlap around the edge to form a pleat. Put each dumpling on a tray lined with plastic wrap. Repeat with the remaining wrappers and filling. Refrigerate until ready to cook.

HEAT a little oil in a large, non-stick frying pan over medium–high heat. Put the dumpling in the pan, flat-side down, in a single layer, leaving a little space between each dumpling. (If your pan is not large enough to fit all the dumplings at once, cook them in batches.) Cook for 2 minutes, or until the bottoms are crisp and golden. Combine 125 ml (4 fl oz/½ cup) boiling water with 2 teaspoons of the vegetable oil and the sesame oil, then add to the pan. Cover, reduce the heat to low and cook for about 10 minutes. Remove the lid, increase the heat to high and cook until liquid has evaporated, making sure the dumplings don't catch and burn. Remove from the pan and drain on paper towels.

SERVE with the dipping sauce.

PRAWNS IN A BLANKET

THESE PRAWNS (SHRIMP), WHICH ARE PREPARED IN CHINESE STYLE, ARE AN APPEALING CANAPE. CHOOSE PLUMP BIG PRAWNS AND LEAVE THE TAILS ON FOR ATTRACTIVE PRESENTATION. YOU CAN MARINATE THE PRAWNS OVERNIGHT IN THE REFRIGERATOR IF YOU WANT TO PREPARE AHEAD.

12 raw large prawns (shrimp), peeled and deveined, tails intact
1 tablespoon plain (all-purpose) flour
2 garlic cloves, roughly chopped
3 coriander (cilantro) roots, finely chopped
1 cm (½ inch) piece of ginger, roughly sliced
1½ tablespoons oyster sauce or, for a hotter flavour, ½ teaspoon red curry paste (see recipe on page 472)
a sprinkle of ground white pepper
12 frozen spring roll sheets or filo sheets, 12 cm (5 inches) square, defrosted
peanut oil, for deep-frying
a chilli sauce, or plum sauce, to serve (see recipes on page 476)

SERVES 4

TO MAKE the prawns easier to wrap, you can make 3 or 4 shallow incisions in the underside of each, then open up the cuts to straighten the prawns.

MIX the flour and 3 tablespoons water in a small saucepan until smooth. Stir and cook over a medium heat for 1–2 minutes or until thick. Remove from the heat.

USING a pestle and mortar or a small blender, pound or blend the garlic, coriander roots and ginger together.

IN a bowl, combine the garlic paste with the prawns, oyster sauce, pepper and a pinch of salt. Cover with plastic wrap and marinate in the refrigerator for 2 hours, turning occasionally.

PLACE a spring roll or filo sheet on the work surface and keep all the remaining sheets in the plastic bag to prevent them drying out. Fold the sheet in half, remove a prawn from the marinade and place it on the sheet with its tail sticking out of the top. Fold the bottom up and then the sides in to tightly enclose the prawn. Seal the joins tightly with the flour paste. Repeat with the rest of the prawns and wrappers.

HEAT the oil in a wok or deep frying pan over a medium heat. When the oil seems hot, drop a small piece of spring roll sheet into it. If it sizzles immediately, the oil is ready. Deep-fry four prawns at a time for 3–4 minutes or until golden brown and crispy. Remove with a slotted spoon and drain on paper towels. Keep the prawns warm while deep-frying the rest.

TRANSFER to a serving plate. Serve hot with chilli sauce or plum sauce.

Large prawns are best for making these little bites. The attractive tails make them easier to pick up.

Soak cucumber slices in cold salted water for 10 minutes before draining and squeezing out excess moisture.

FROM JAPAN

CRAB, CUCUMBER AND WAKAME SALAD

THIS APPEALINGLY FRESH SUMMER SALAD COMBINES THREE CONTRASTING TEXTURES OF CRAB, CUCUMBER AND SEAWEED. THE LIGHT DRESSING ENHANCES THE NATURAL FLAVOURS OF THE INGREDIENTS WHILE NEVER OVERPOWERING THEM.

2 Lebanese (short) cucumbers
2 tablespoons dried wakame
   seaweed pieces
150 g (6 oz/1 cup) fresh, cooked
   crabmeat, picked over (or good-
   quality tinned crabmeat)

DRESSING
2 tablespoons Japanese rice
   vinegar
2 tablespoons dashi II (see recipe
   on page 483)
1 tablespoon shoyu (Japanese soy
   sauce)
2 teaspoons mirin
20 g (¾ oz) fresh ginger

SERVES 4

DISSOLVE 2 teaspoons of salt in 500 ml (17 fl oz/ 2 cups) cold water. Cut the cucumbers in half lengthways, scoop out the seeds, then slice the flesh very thinly. Put the cucumber flesh in the cold water and soak for 10 minutes. Drain well and gently squeeze out any excess moisture. Keep in the refrigerator until needed.

SOAK the wakame in a bowl of cold water for 5 minutes, or until rehydrated and glossy but not mushy. Drain well, then refrigerate until needed.

TO MAKE the dressing, combine the rice vinegar, dashi, shoyu and mirin in a small saucepan and bring to the boil over a high heat. Remove from the heat and cool to room temperature. Finely grate the ginger, then squeeze the grated ginger with your fingertips to release the juice (you will need 1½ teaspoons of ginger juice). Add the ginger juice to the dressing and stir well. Allow to cool completely. Refrigerate for 15 minutes, or until cold.

NEATLY arrange the cucumber, wakame and crabmeat into four small serving dishes, then carefully pour the dressing over the top.

FROM THAILAND

PRAWN AND POMELO SALAD

THIS NORTHERN THAI SALAD USES POMELO TO GIVE IT A SWEET/TART FLAVOUR. DIFFERENT VARIETIES OF POMELO ARE AVAILABLE IN THAILAND: SOME HAVE PINK FLESH AND OTHERS HAVE YELLOW. SERVE THE SALAD WITH STICKY RICE AND EAT IT AS SOON AS IT IS READY.

1 large pomelo

DRESSING
1 tablespoon fish sauce
1 tablespoon lime juice
1 teaspoon sugar
1 tablespoon chilli jam
    (see recipe on page 480)

300 g (10 oz) raw medium prawns
    (shrimp), peeled and deveined,
    tails intact
3 tablespoons shredded fresh
    coconut, lightly toasted until
    golden (if fresh unavailable, use
    shredded desiccated)
3 Asian shallots, finely sliced
5 bird's eye chillies, bruised
1 large handful mint leaves
2 small handfuls coriander (cilantro)
    leaves
1 tablespoon fried Asian shallots,
    to serve

SERVES 4

TO PEEL a pomelo, first, slice a circular patch off the top of the fruit, about 2 cm (¾ inch) deep (roughly the thickness of the skin). Next, score four deep lines from top to bottom, dividing the skin into four segments. Peel away the skin, one quarter at a time. Remove any remaining pith and separate the segments of the fruit. Peel the segments and remove any seeds. Crumble the segments into their component parts, without squashing them or releasing the juice.

TO MAKE the dressing, combine the fish sauce, lime juice, sugar and chilli jam in a small bowl and stir.

BRING a large saucepan of water to the boil. Add the prawns and cook for 2 minutes. Drain and allow the prawns to cool.

IN a large bowl, gently combine the pomelo, prawns, toasted coconut, shallots, chillies, mint and coriander. Just before serving, add the dressing and toss gently to combine all the ingredients.

SERVE sprinkled with fried shallots.

Slice off a section from the top of the pomelo before cutting it into sections and segmenting it.

Peeling pomelo in Pattaya.

Add the flour to the seafood, vegetables and mitsuba. Mix through the tempura batter. Drop into the hot oil and cook until crisp and golden.

FROM JAPAN

SEAFOOD AND VEGETABLE FRITTERS

HERE, QUANTITIES OF CHOPPED SEAFOOD AND VEGETABLES ARE TOSSED TOGETHER WITH BATTER AND THEN DEEP-FRIED BY THE SPOONFUL. THE SECRET IS TO HAVE THE FOOD AND BATTER AS COLD AS POSSIBLE AND TO MAKE THE BATTER JUST BEFORE YOU ARE READY TO USE IT.

300 g (11 oz) raw prawns (shrimp), peeled and deveined
100 g (4 oz) scallops, roe removed
1 small carrot, peeled
5 cm (2 inch) piece of daikon (about 60 g/2 oz), peeled
1 small onion
6 green beans
2 large handfuls mitsuba or flat-leaf (Italian) parsley with stems
1½ tablespoons plain (all-purpose) flour
vegetable oil, for deep-frying
60 ml (2 fl oz/¼ cup) sesame oil
1 quantity tempura batter (see recipe on page 439)
1 quantity tempura dipping sauce (see recipe on page 484), or ready-made

SERVES 6

CHOP the prawns and scallops into small pieces. Cut the carrot and daikon into 4 cm (1½ inch) lengths, then finely slice into matchsticks, using a very sharp knife or Japanese mandolin with a medium-tooth blade. Cut the onion in half and thinly slice. Thinly slice the beans on the diagonal. Roughly chop the mitsuba leaves and stems.

PUT the chopped seafood, julienned vegetables and chopped mitsuba in a bowl with the flour and mix to combine.

FILL a deep-fat fryer or large saucepan one-third full of vegetable oil, then add the sesame oil. Heat to 170°C (325°F), or until a cube of bread dropped into the oil browns in 20 seconds.

TO MAKE the tempura batter – see recipe on page 439.

LIGHTLY mix the seafood and vegetable mixture through the tempura batter. Working in batches, drop heaped tablespoons of the mixture into the hot oil and cook for 3–4 minutes, or until crisp, golden and cooked through. Drain on paper towels. Serve immediately with dipping sauce.

FROM JAPAN

TOFU DENGAKU

THIS NUTRITIOUS DISH CAME TO BE CALLED DENGAKU, NAMED FOR THE WOODEN SKEWERS ON WHICH IT WAS SOMETIMES COOKED. THESE LONG SKEWERS WERE REMINISCENT OF THE STILTS WORN IN AN ANCIENT DANCE OF THE SAME NAME.

700 g (1 lb 9 oz) firm (cotton) tofu
100 g (3½ oz/⅓ cup) red or white
    miso paste
1 egg yolk
1½ tablespoons dashi II
    (see recipe on page 483)
2 teaspoons mirin
2 teaspoons sugar
vegetable oil, for brushing

GARNISH (optional)
nori flakes
spring onion (scallion) thinly sliced
sesame seeds, lightly toasted

SERVES 4–6

TO WEIGHT the tofu, wrap it in a clean tea towel (dish towel). Put two plates on top of the tofu to extract any excess moisture and leave for 1 hour, or until the tofu is about half its original thickness. Remove from the towel. Pat dry with paper towels.

MEANWHILE, combine the miso, egg yolk, dashi, mirin and sugar in a bowl and whisk until smooth.

PREHEAT the grill (broiler) to high. Cut the tofu into six even slices and put on a foil-lined tray. Lightly brush the tofu blocks with a little vegetable oil and put under the grill for 2–3 minutes, or until lightly golden. Turn the tofu over and cook the other side.

THICKLY spread miso mixture onto one side of the tofu and place under the grill again, miso side up, for a few minutes, or until it is bubbling and golden in places.

SERVE immediately, sprinkled with one or a mixture of the garnishes.

Thickly spread the miso mixture onto one side of the tofu and grill again until bubbling and golden in places.

Miso, is a rich, earthy paste made from fermented soya beans. There are different grades and colours of miso. Generally the lighter the colour, the sweeter and less salty the taste. The names are a little misleading as white miso (shiromiso) is pale gold, while red miso (akamiso) is a mid caramel colour with a reddish tinge. Shinshu is an all-purpose yellowish miso that makes a good substitute in most circumstances. Hatcho miso is dark reddish brown with a very strong, salty flavour. It should be used sparingly.

TOFU DENGAKU

SOUPS

FROM THAILAND

CHICKEN, COCONUT AND GALANGAL SOUP

THIS IS ONE OF THE CLASSIC SOUPS OF THAILAND. THE THAI NAME MEANS 'BOILED GALANGAL CHICKEN'. ALTHOUGH USUALLY MADE WITH CHICKEN, YOU CAN MAKE THIS RECIPE USING PRAWNS, FISH OR VEGETABLES. DON'T WORRY WHEN THE COCONUT MILK SEPARATES – IT IS SUPPOSED TO.

750 ml (26 fl oz/3 cups) coconut
    milk
2 lemongrass stalks, white part only,
    each cut into a tassel
    or bruised
5 cm (2 inch) piece of galangal,
    cut into several pieces
4 Asian shallots, smashed with
    the flat side of a cleaver
400 g (14 oz) boneless, skinless
    chicken breast, cut into slices
2 tablespoons fish sauce
1 tablespoon palm sugar (jaggery),
    or soft brown sugar
200 g (7 oz) baby tomatoes, cut
    into bite-sized pieces if large
150 g (5½ oz) straw mushrooms
    or button mushrooms
3 tablespoons lime juice
6 makrut (kaffir lime) leaves,
    torn in half
3–5 bird's eye chillies, stems
    removed, bruised, or 2 long red
    chillies, seeded and finely sliced
a few coriander (cilantro) leaves,
    for garnish

SERVES 4

PUT the coconut milk, lemongrass, galangal and shallots in a saucepan or wok over a medium heat and bring to a boil.

ADD the chicken, fish sauce and palm sugar and simmer, stirring constantly for 5 minutes or until the chicken is cooked through.

ADD the tomatoes and mushrooms and simmer for 2–3 minutes. Add the lime juice, makrut leaves and chillies in the last few seconds, taking care not to let the tomatoes lose their shape. Taste, adjusting the seasoning, if necessary. This dish is not meant to be overwhelmingly hot, but to have a sweet, salty, sour taste.

SERVE garnished with coriander leaves.

It is best to carefully measure ingredients such as fish sauce as the flavour is quite strong.

Soup flavourings are often sold ready-prepared in bundles.

To see if they have been fertilised, eggs are checked at the market by placing them above a light.

Scalding the tomatoes in boiling water makes it very easy to slip off their skins.

TOMATO AND EGG SOUP

FROM CHINA

TOFU AND SPINACH SOUP

120 g (4 oz) soft tofu, drained
100 g (3½ oz) baby English
   spinach leaves
1 litre (35 fl oz/4 cups) chicken
   and meat stock (see recipe on
   page 491)
1 tablespoon light soy sauce

SERVES 4

CUT the tofu into small slices about 5 mm (¼ inch) thick.

CHOP the baby spinach leaves roughly if they are large.

BRING the stock to a rolling boil in a large clay pot or saucepan, then add the tofu slices and soy sauce. Return to the boil, then reduce the heat and simmer gently for 2 minutes. Skim any scum from the surface. Add the spinach and cook for 1–2 minutes. Season with salt and white pepper.

SERVE the soup hot.

TOMATO AND EGG SOUP

250 g (9 oz) firm ripe tomatoes
2 eggs
1 spring onion (scallion), finely
   chopped
1 tablespoon oil
1 litre (35 fl oz/4 cups) vegetable
   or chicken and meat stock
   (see recipe on page 491)
1 tablespoon light soy sauce
1 tablespoon cornflour (cornstarch)

SERVES 4

SCORE a cross in the bottom of each tomato. Plunge into boiling water for 20 seconds, then drain and peel the skin away from the cross. Cut into slices or thin wedges, trimming off the core.

BEAT the eggs with a pinch of salt and a few pieces of spring onion.

HEAT a wok over high heat, add the oil and heat until very hot. Stir-fry the spring onion for a few seconds to flavour the oil, then pour in the stock and bring to the boil. Add the tomato and return to the boil. Add soy sauce and very slowly pour in the beaten eggs, stirring as you pour. Return to the boil.

COMBINE the cornflour with enough water to make a paste, add to the soup and simmer until thickened.

FROM THAILAND

STUFFED TOFU SOUP WITH PRAWNS

THIS RECIPE IS QUITE FIDDLY BUT WELL WORTH THE EFFORT. DON'T OVERSTUFF THE TOFU OR IT MIGHT EXPLODE DURING COOKING. AS WITH OTHER 'BLAND' SOUPS, USE A GOOD-QUALITY STOCK. THE STUFFED TOFU CAN ALSO BE FRIED AND EATEN ON ITS OWN.

275 g (10 oz) raw prawns (shrimp)
2–3 coriander (cilantro) roots,
　roughly chopped
2 garlic cloves, roughly chopped
¼ teaspoon salt
1 tablespoon cornflour (cornstarch)
¼ teaspoon ground white pepper
320 g (11 oz) firm tofu (bean curd)
1.5 litres (52 fl oz/6 cups) vegetable
　stock
2.5 cm (1 inch) piece of ginger,
　sliced
4 tablespoons light soy sauce
1 tablespoon preserved radish
5 spring onions (scallions), cut into
　slivers, for garnish

SERVES 4

PEEL and devein the prawns. Set aside about 90 g (3 oz) of the prawns and cut the rest of them along their backs so they open like a butterfly (leave each prawn joined along the base and at the tail).

USING a food processor or blender, whiz the coriander roots and garlic until as smooth as possible. Add the prawns that are not butterflied, along with the salt, cornflour and white pepper, then blend until as smooth as possible. If you prefer, you can use a pestle and mortar to pound the coriander roots and garlic into a paste before processing with the prawns. This is more labour-intensive but gives a slightly better flavour.

DRAIN the tofu and cut it into 16 triangles. Cut a pocket into the long side of each piece of tofu with a knife. Spoon some prawn mixture into each pocket and gently press down on top. Repeat until you have used all the tofu and the mixture.

HEAT the stock to boiling point in a saucepan. Reduce the heat to low and add the ginger, light soy sauce and preserved radish. Lower the tofu envelopes into the stock and cook for 4–5 minutes or until cooked. Add the butterflied prawns and cook for another 1–2 minutes or until the prawns open and turn pink. Taste, then adjust the seasoning if necessary.

SERVE garnished with spring onions.

Spoon some of the prepared prawn mixture into each tofu pocket, then carefully lower them into the stock.

A spirit house in Damnoen Saduak.

Soak the dried shiitake mushrooms in hot water for 30 minutes.

Thin yellow ramen noodles are made from wheat flour and eggs.

RAMEN NOODLES WITH SOY BROTH

RAMEN ARE CHINESE WHEAT NOODLES, EATEN IN JAPAN SINCE THE 17TH CENTURY. SERVED IN A CLEAR BROWN BROTH PREPARED FROM PORK AND CHICKEN BONES, FLAVOURED WITH SOY SAUCE AND TOPPED WITH SLICED PORK AND VEGETABLES, IT MAKES A COMPLETE SOUP MEAL.

BROTH
1 kg (2 lb 4 oz) pork bones
1 kg (2 lb 4 oz) chicken bones
10 spring onions (scallions), bruised
10 cm (4 inch) piece of fresh ginger, sliced
1 bulb garlic, cut in half through the centre
2 carrots, peeled and chopped
10 cm (4 inch) square piece of konbu (kelp), wiped with a damp cloth

8 dried shiitake mushrooms
500 g (1 lb 2 oz) fresh ramen noodles
125–185 ml (4–6 fl oz/½–¾ cup) shoyu (Japanese soy sauce)
80 ml (2½ fl oz/⅓ cup) sake
100 g (3½ oz) bamboo shoots, sliced
125 g (4½ oz) Chinese barbecued pork, sliced
200 g (7 oz) bok choy (pak choy), sliced lengthways into wide strips, blanched
50 g (1¾ oz) bean sprouts, blanched
4 spring onions (scallions), cut into 4 cm (1½ inch) lengths
shichimi togarashi (seven-spice mix) to serve, optional
chilli sesame oil to serve, optional

SERVES 4

TO MAKE the broth, put the pork and chicken bones in a stockpot or large, deep saucepan and cover with cold water. Bring to the boil over high heat, then drain. Rinse the bones, then return them to a clean stockpot. Add the spring onions, ginger, garlic, carrot and konbu and pour in enough cold water to cover by about 5 cm (2 inches). Bring to the boil over high heat, remove the konbu, then reduce to a simmer, skimming any scum off the surface. Cook, uncovered, for about 6 hours, or until the liquid has reduced to about 1.5 litres (52 fl oz/6 cups). Cool slightly, remove the bones, then pour the stock through a fine strainer. Refrigerate for 6 hours, or until cold.

MEANWHILE, soak the shiitake in hot water for 30 minutes, then drain well. Discard the stems.

BRING a large saucepan of lightly salted water to the boil, add the noodles and separate with chopsticks. Cook for 1–2 minutes, or until tender. Drain well, then rinse under cold running water, rubbing the noodles together lightly with your hands to remove any excess starch.

SCOOP off any fat from the surface of the cooled broth, then pour the broth into a large saucepan. Add the shoyu and sake, bring to the boil over high heat, then reduce to a simmer. Pour a little broth into four large warmed bowls, then divide the noodles among the bowls. Ladle the broth over the noodles so that it just comes to the top of the noodles.

USING chopsticks, neatly arrange small piles of the shiitake, bamboo shoots, pork, bok choy, bean sprouts and spring onion on top of the noodles. Sprinkle with shichimi togarashi and drizzle with a little chilli sesame oil, if liked. Freeze any leftover broth for another time.

FROM INDIA

RASAM

3 tablespoons tamarind purée
   (see recipe on page 467)
1¹/₂ tablespoons coriander seeds
2 tablespoons cumin seeds
1 tablespoon black peppercorns
1 tablespoon oil
5 garlic cloves, skins on,
   roughly pounded
1 red onion, thinly sliced
2–3 dried chillies, torn into pieces
2 stalks curry leaves
200 g (7 oz) boneless, skinless
   chicken thighs, cut into
   small pieces

SERVES 4

MIX the tamarind purée with 750 ml (26 fl oz/3 cups) water.

PLACE a small frying pan over low heat and dry-roast the coriander seeds until aromatic. Remove, then dry-roast the cumin seeds, followed by the black peppercorns. Grind them together using a spice grinder or a pestle and mortar.

HEAT the oil in a large, heavy-based saucepan over low heat, add the garlic and onion and fry until golden. Add the chilli and the curry leaves and fry for 2 minutes, or until they are aromatic. Add the tamarind water, the ground spices and season with salt. Bring to the boil, reduce heat and simmer for 10 minutes.

ADD the chicken to the saucepan with 250 ml (9 fl oz/1 cup) water and simmer for 20 minutes, gradually adding another 250 ml (9 fl oz/1 cup) water as the soup reduces. Remove any garlic skin which has floated to the top. Season with salt, to taste.

SERVE with rice (see recipe on page 456).

Pepper, shown here in its fresh form, is indigenous to India.

TAMATAR SHORBA

2 tablespoons oil
1 onion, finely chopped
3 Indian bay leaves (cassia leaves)
5 cm (2 inch) cinnamon stick
12 peppercorns
2 teaspoons ground cumin
2 teaspoons garam masala
   (see recipe on page 464)
2 x 400 g (14 oz) tins chopped
   tomatoes
1 teaspoon sugar
250 ml (9 fl oz/1 cup) chicken stock
coriander (cilantro) leaves, to garnish

SERVES 2

HEAT the oil over low heat in a heavy-based saucepan and fry the onion, bay leaves, cinnamon and peppercorns until the onion is soft. Add the cumin, garam masala and the tomato, mashing the tomatoes with a fork to break them up. Add the sugar and stock and slowly bring to the boil. Simmer over low heat for 30 minutes.

STRAIN the soup by pushing it through a sieve, using the back of a metal spoon to push against the solids and extract as much of the liquid as possible. Discard what's left in the sieve. Reheat, then season with salt, to taste, and garnish with the coriander leaves before serving.

TAMATAR SHORBA

VERMICELLI SOUP WITH MINCED PORK

THIS IS A LIGHT, CLEAR SOUP FROM THE NORTH OF THAILAND. UNLIKE OTHER NOODLE RECIPES, THIS ONE IS ALWAYS EATEN WITH RICE. IT IS A WARMING 'COMFORT FOOD' AND IS VERY EASY TO PREPARE. THE NOODLES CONTINUE TO SOAK UP LIQUID AS THEY SIT, SO SERVE THE SOUP STRAIGHT AWAY.

15 pieces of dried black fungus
50 g (2 oz) mung bean vermicelli
2 tablespoons vegetable oil
3–4 large garlic cloves, finely
   chopped
450 g (1 lb) minced (ground) pork
20 coriander (cilantro) leaves,
   finely chopped
¼ teaspoon salt
¼ teaspoon ground white pepper
625 ml (21 ½ fl oz/2 ½ cups)
   vegetable or chicken stock
2 tablespoons light soy sauce
1 tablespoon preserved radish
a few coriander (cilantro) leaves,
   for garnish

SERVES 4

Coriander (cilantro) is sold in bunches with the root on. All parts of the plant are used.

SOAK the mushrooms in hot water for 5 minutes or until soft, then drain them and cut into smaller pieces if necessary.

SOAK the mung bean vermicelli in hot water for 5–7 minutes or until soft, then drain it well and cut it into small pieces.

HEAT the oil in a small wok or frying pan and stir-fry the garlic until light golden. Remove from the heat, lift out the garlic with a slotted spoon and drain on paper towels.

IN a bowl, combine the pork with the coriander leaves, salt and pepper. Use a spoon or your wet hands to shape the mixture into small balls about 1 cm (½ inch) across.

HEAT the stock to boiling point in a saucepan. Add the light soy sauce and preserved radish. Lower the pork balls into the stock and cook for 2 minutes over a medium heat. Add the mushrooms and noodles and cook for another 1–2 minutes, stirring frequently. Taste, then adjust the seasoning if necessary. Sprinkle with crispy garlic, garlic oil and coriander leaves.

Pedal power competes with cars in Chiang Mai.

FROM JAPAN

AGEDASHI TOFU

FOR THIS RECIPE, THE TOFU IS COATED WITH POTATO STARCH, THEN BRIEFLY DEEP-FRIED. THE OPTIONAL ADDITION OF SESAME OIL TO THE FRYING OIL WILL ENRICH THE FLAVOUR, WHILE THE FRESH, COOL GARNISHES PROVIDE A PLEASING CONTRAST TO THE WARM TOFU AND BROTH.

600 g (1 lb 5 oz) block silken firm tofu
vegetable oil, for deep-frying
60 ml (2 fl oz/¼ cup) sesame oil, optional
potato starch, for coating
70 g (2½ oz) daikon, peeled, finely grated, then squeezed to remove excess liquid
2 teaspoons fresh ginger, finely grated

SAUCE
170 ml (5½ fl oz/⅔ cup) dashi II (see recipe on page 483)
2 tablespoons shoyu (Japanese soy sauce)
1 tablespoon sake
1 tablespoon mirin

spring onion (scallion), thinly sliced, to garnish
nori flakes, to garnish

SERVES 4

BE VERY careful when working with tofu – it is very soft and breaks easily. To weight the tofu, first wrap it in a clean tea towel (dish towel). Put two plates on top and leave for about 30 minutes to extract any excess moisture. Remove the tofu from the tea towel, cut into eight pieces, then pat dry with paper towels.

TO MAKE the sauce, combine all the ingredients in a small saucepan. Bring to the boil over high heat, then reduce the heat to very low to keep the sauce warm until ready to use.

FILL a deep-fat fryer or large saucepan one-third full of vegetable oil, then add the sesame oil, if using. Heat to 180°C (350°F), or until a cube of bread dropped into the oil browns in 15 seconds.

LIGHTLY coat the tofu with the potato starch and then deep-fry in batches for about 3 minutes, or until the tofu just starts to become a pale golden colour around the edges. Drain well on paper towels, then divide the tofu among four individual bowls (or one large, wide bowl). Carefully pour the sauce into the bowl.

TOP the tofu with a little daikon and ginger and garnish with the spring onion and nori flakes. Eat with chopsticks and, if you need one, a spoon.

The tofu is first coated with potato starch and then briefly deep-fried.

Stripping corn cobs in Yunnan.

CANTONESE CORN SOUP

250 g (9 oz) boneless, skinless
   chicken breasts, minced (ground)
150 ml (5 fl oz) Shaoxing rice wine
400 g (14 oz) tinned creamed corn
1.5 litres (52 fl oz/6 cups) chicken
   stock (see recipe on page 491)
1 teaspoon salt
2½ tablespoons cornflour
   (cornstarch)
2 egg whites, lightly beaten
1 teaspoon roasted sesame oil

SERVES 6

PLACE the chicken in a bowl, add 3 tablespoons of the rice wine and stir to combine.

IN a large clay pot or saucepan, combine the creamed corn, stock, remaining rice wine and salt. Bring to the boil, stirring. Add the chicken and stir to separate the meat. Return to the boil and skim any scum from the surface.

COMBINE the cornflour with enough water to make a paste, add to the soup and simmer until thickened. Remove from the heat.

MIX 2 tablespoons water into the egg white, then slowly add to the clay pot or saucepan in a thin stream around the edge of the pan. Stir once or twice, then add the sesame oil. Check the seasoning, adding more salt if necessary.

SERVE immediately.

CHICKEN AND
MUSHROOM SOUP

CHICKEN AND MUSHROOM SOUP

2 tablespoons cornflour (cornstarch)
3–4 egg whites, beaten
1 teaspoon salt
100 g (3½ oz) boneless, skinless
   chicken breasts, thinly sliced
750 ml (26 fl oz/3 cups) chicken
   and meat stock (see recipe on
   page 491)
100 g (3½ oz) button or Chinese
   (shiitake) mushrooms, thinly sliced
1 teaspoon roasted sesame oil
chopped spring onion (scallion),
   to garnish

SERVES 4

COMBINE the cornflour with enough water to make a paste. Mix 1 teaspoon each of the egg white and cornflour paste and a pinch of salt with the chicken. Blend the remaining egg white and cornflour mixture to a smooth paste.

BRING the stock to a rolling boil in a large clay pot or saucepan. Add the chicken and return to the boil, then add the mushrooms and salt. Return to the boil then, very slowly, pour in the egg white and cornflour mixture, stirring constantly. As soon as the soup has thickened, add the sesame oil.

SERVE sprinkled with the spring onion.

FROM THAILAND

STUFFED SQUID SOUP

KAENG JEUT ARE ONE OF THE THREE MAIN TYPES OF SOUP COMMONLY FOUND IN THAILAND. THE NAME MEANS BLAND SOUP. THIS SOUP IS ANOTHER THAI DISH WITH A CHINESE INFLUENCE. BECAUSE THESE SOUPS ARE NOT HIGHLY FLAVOURED, BE SURE TO USE A GOOD-QUALITY STOCK.

280 g (10 oz) small squid
2 coriander (cilantro) roots,
    finely chopped
3–4 large garlic cloves, roughly
    chopped
280 g (10 oz) minced (ground) pork
    or chicken
¼ teaspoon salt
¼ teaspoon ground white pepper
2 litres (70 fl oz/8 cups) vegetable
    stock
2.5 cm (1 inch) piece of ginger,
    sliced
4 tablespoons light soy sauce
1 tablespoon preserved radish,
    sliced
5 spring onions (scallions), slivered,
    for garnish
a few coriander (cilantro) leaves,
    for garnish
ground white pepper, for sprinkling

SERVES 4

TO CLEAN each squid, grasp the squid body in one hand and pull away the head and tentacles from the body. Cut the head off the tentacles just above the eyes and discard the head. Clean out the body. Pull the skin off the squid and rinse well. Drain well.

USING a pestle and mortar, pound the coriander roots and garlic into a paste. In a bowl, combine the coriander paste with the pork or chicken and the salt and pepper.

SPOON some mixture into a squid sac until two-thirds full, being careful not to overfill it as the filling will swell during cooking. Squeeze the squid tube closed at the end. With a bamboo stick or sharp toothpick, prick several holes in the body of the squid. Place on a plate and repeat with the rest. Use a spoon or wet fingers to shape the remaining meat mixture into small balls about 1 cm (½ inch) in diameter.

HEAT the stock to boiling point in a saucepan. Reduce the heat to low and add the ginger, light soy sauce and preserved radish. Lower the meatballs into the stock, then gently drop in the stuffed squid and cook over a low heat for 4–5 minutes or until the meatballs and squid are cooked. Taste the broth and adjust the seasoning if necessary.

GARNISH with spring onions and coriander leaves. Sprinkle with ground white pepper.

Don't stuff too much of the mixture into the squid sac as it will swell during cooking.

Red and green 'bird's eye' or 'mouse dropping' *(phrik khii nuu)* chillies.

Delicious street food is available at the night markets.

HOT AND SOUR PRAWN SOUP

THIS SOUP IS PROBABLY THE MOST WELL-KNOWN THAI DISH OF ALL. ALTHOUGH IT IS USUALLY MADE WITH PRAWNS, IT WORKS EQUALLY WELL WITH FISH. TO ACHIEVE THE FAMOUS DISTINCTIVE AROMA AND FLAVOURS, USE ONLY THE FRESHEST GOOD-QUALITY INGREDIENTS.

350 g (12 oz) raw prawns (shrimp)
1 tablespoon oil
3 lemongrass stalks, white part only, bruised
3 thin slices of galangal
2 litres (70 fl oz/8 cups) chicken stock or water
5–7 bird's eye chillies, stems removed, bruised
5 makrut (kaffir lime) leaves, torn
2 tablespoons fish sauce
70 g (2 oz) straw mushrooms, or quartered button mushrooms
2 spring onions (scallions), sliced
3 tablespoons lime juice
a few coriander (cilantro) leaves, for garnish

SERVES 4

PEEL and devein the prawns, leaving the tails intact and reserving the heads and shells.

HEAT the oil in a large stockpot or wok and add the prawn heads and shells. Cook for 5 minutes or until the shells turn bright orange.

ADD one stalk of lemongrass to the pan with the galangal and stock or water. Bring to the boil, then reduce the heat and simmer for 20 minutes. Strain the stock and return to the pan. Discard the shells and flavourings.

FINELY slice the remaining lemongrass and add it to the liquid with the chillies, lime leaves, fish sauce, mushrooms and spring onions. Cook gently for 2 minutes.

ADD the prawns and cook for 3 minutes or until the prawns are firm and pink. Take off the heat and add the lime juice. Taste, then adjust the seasoning with extra lime juice or fish sauce if necessary.

GARNISH with coriander leaves.

Makrut (kaffir limes) *(luk ma-krut)* are knobbly skinned fruit that are used for their zest rather than their bitter juice. The leaves *(bai makrut)* are double leaves with a fragrant citrus oil. They are used very finely shredded or torn into large pieces.

FROM JAPAN

UDON NOODLES IN BROTH

NOODLES IN DASHI ARE AS MUCH A COMFORT FOOD FOR JAPANESE AS CHICKEN NOODLE SOUP IS FOR MANY WESTERNERS. WHILE SIMPLICITY ITSELF, THIS DISH OFFERS COMPLEX FLAVOURS AND TEXTURES – SWEET AND SALTY, SMOKY AND SPICY, AND SLIGHTLY CHEWY WITH A BIT OF CRUNCH.

1.5 litres (52 fl oz/6 cups) dashi II
 (see recipe on page 483)
3 spring onions (scallions),
 2 cut into 4 cm (1½ inch) lengths,
 1 thinly sliced on the diagonal
60 ml (2 fl oz/¼ cup) mirin
60 ml (2 fl oz/¼ cup) shoyu
 (Japanese soy sauce)
2 teaspoons sugar
400 g (14 oz) fresh udon noodles
shichimi togarashi (seven-spice
 mix), to serve, optional

SERVES 4

POUR the dashi into a large saucepan and bring to the boil over medium–high heat. Reduce to a simmer.

ADD the lengths of spring onion to the dashi along with the mirin, shoyu and sugar and stir to combine. Simmer over low heat for 5 minutes.

MEANWHILE, bring a large saucepan of lightly salted water to the boil, add the noodles and cook, stirring gently, for 5 minutes, or until tender. Drain well and rinse.

DIVIDE the noodles among four warmed serving bowls. Top with the thinly sliced spring onion. Ladle the broth over the top. If you like, pass around the shichimi togarashi for sprinkling.

Udon noodles are thick white Japanese noodles made from wheat flour. They are made in various widths.

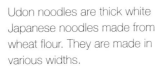

The delicious flavour of this soup comes from the melding of prawn, chicken and vegetables.

A huge woven basket used for threshing rice.

RICE SOUP WITH PRAWNS AND CHICKEN

ALTHOUGH DERIVED FROM CHINESE-STYLE 'CONGEE', THAI RICE SOUPS USE WHOLE RICE GRAINS RATHER THAN THE BROKEN GRAINS PREFERRED BY THE CHINESE. RICE SOUPS ARE ENJOYED AS A SNACK AT NIGHT OR AS A BREAKFAST DISH. THEY ARE SUSTAINING ENOUGH TO BE A MEAL.

110 g (4 oz) raw prawns (shrimp)
2 tablespoons vegetable oil
3–4 large garlic cloves, finely chopped
1 coriander (cilantro) root, finely chopped
1 garlic clove, extra, roughly chopped
a pinch of ground white pepper, plus extra, to sprinkle
75 g (2½ oz) minced (ground) chicken or pork
1 spring onion (scallion), finely chopped
935 ml (32 fl oz/3¾ cups) chicken or vegetable stock
2 tablespoons light soy sauce
2 teaspoons preserved radish
325 g (12 oz/1¾ cups) cooked jasmine rice
1 tablespoon finely sliced ginger
1 Chinese cabbage leaf, roughly chopped
2 spring onions (scallions), finely chopped, for garnish
a few coriander (cilantro) leaves, for garnish

SERVES 4

PEEL and devein the prawns and cut each prawn along the back so it opens like a butterfly (leave each prawn joined along the base and at the tail, leaving the tail attached).

HEAT the oil in a small wok or frying pan and stir-fry the finely chopped garlic until light golden. Remove from the heat and discard the garlic.

USING a pestle and mortar or a small blender, pound or blend the coriander root, roughly chopped garlic, pepper and a pinch of salt into a paste.

IN a bowl, combine the coriander paste with the chicken or pork and spring onion. Using a spoon or your wet hands, shape the mixture into small balls about 1 cm (½ inch) across.

HEAT the stock to boiling point in a saucepan. Add the light soy sauce, preserved radish and rice. Lower the meatballs into the stock over a medium heat and cook for 3 minutes or until the chicken is cooked. Add the prawns, ginger and Chinese cabbage to the stock. Cook for another 1–2 minutes or until the prawns open and turn pink. Taste, then adjust the seasoning if necessary.

GARNISH with spring onions and coriander leaves. Sprinkle with ground white pepper and the garlic oil.

FROM THAILAND

SOUR FISH SOUP WITH WATER SPINACH

SOUR CURRY PASTE
3 garlic cloves, roughly chopped
3 bird's eye chillies, stems removed
1 Asian shallot, chopped
1 teaspoon grated galangal
1 teaspoon grated turmeric
   (or a pinch of dried)
1 teaspoon shrimp paste
175 g (6 oz) boneless, skinless
   white fish fillets
3 tablespoons tamarind purée
175 g (6 oz) water spinach, cut into
   pieces, leaves separated
1 tablespoon fish sauce
1 tablespoon sugar

SERVES 4

TO MAKE the sour curry paste, use a pestle and mortar or food processor to pound or blend all the ingredients together until smooth.

REMOVE any remaining bones from the fish using tweezers, then cut the fish fillets into 5 cm (2 inch) pieces.

IN a saucepan, bring 625 ml (21½ fl oz/2½ cups) water to the boil. Stir in the sour curry paste and reduce the heat to medium. Add the tamarind, water spinach stems, fish sauce and sugar and cook for 2–3 minutes. Add the fish fillets and cook for another 1–2 minutes. Add the water spinach leaves and gently mix. Taste, then adjust the seasoning if necessary.

SPOON into a serving bowl and serve hot with rice.

RICE SOUP WITH FISH FILLET

2 tablespoons vegetable oil
3–4 large garlic cloves, finely chopped

1.25 litres (44 fl oz/5 cups)
   vegetable, chicken or fish stock
2½ tablespoons light soy sauce
2 teaspoons preserved radish,
   sliced
245 g (8½ oz/1⅓ cups) cooked
   jasmine rice
280 g (10 oz) boneless, skinless
   white fish fillets, cut into bite-sized
   pieces
1 tablespoon finely sliced ginger
1 spring onion (scallion), finely
   chopped, for garnish
a few coriander (cilantro) leaves,
   for garnish
ground white pepper, for sprinkling

SERVES 4

HEAT the oil in a small wok or frying pan and stir-fry the garlic until light golden. Remove from the heat and discard the garlic.

HEAT the stock to boiling point in a saucepan. Add the light soy sauce, preserved radish and rice and cook over a medium heat for 2–3 minutes. Add the fish and ginger and cook for another 1–2 minutes or until the fish is cooked. Season well, taste, then adjust seasoning again, if necessary.

GARNISH with spring onion and coriander leaves and sprinkle with ground pepper and the garlic oil.

RICE SOUP WITH FISH FILLET

FRAGRANT TOFU AND TOMATO SOUP

TOFU, OR BEAN CURD, COMES IN SEVERAL DIFFERENT VARIETIES, FROM SOFT TO QUITE FIRM. THE SOFTEST, CALLED SILKEN TOFU, HAS THE BEST TYPE OF TEXTURE FOR THIS RECIPE AND ITS MILD FLAVOUR IS IN PERFECT CONTRAST TO THE STRONG TASTE OF OTHER INGREDIENTS.

PASTE
½ teaspoon dried shrimp paste
1 teaspoon small dried prawns
  (shrimp)
4 Asian shallots, roughly chopped
½ teaspoon white peppercorns
2 coriander (cilantro) roots
1 garlic clove, chopped
2 teaspoons grated ginger

1 tablespoon vegetable oil
750 ml (26 fl oz/3 cups) chicken
  stock or water
3 tablespoons tamarind purée
1 tablespoon palm sugar (jaggery)
2 tablespoons fish sauce
3 cm (1¼ inch) piece of ginger,
  sliced into thin matchsticks
3 Asian shallots, smashed with the
  flat side of a cleaver
300 g (10 oz) silken tofu
  (bean curd), cut into 2 cm
  (¾ inch) cubes
2 tomatoes, each cut into 8 wedges
1 tablespoon lime juice
2 tablespoons coriander (cilantro)
  leaves, for garnish

SERVES 4

TO MAKE the paste, use a pestle and mortar or food processor to pound or blend the shrimp paste, dried prawns, shallots, peppercorns, coriander roots, garlic and ginger together.

HEAT the oil in a saucepan over a low heat, add the paste and cook for 10 to 15 seconds, stirring constantly.

ADD the stock or water, tamarind purée, palm sugar, fish sauce and ginger. Simmer for 5 minutes to soften the ginger.

ADD the shallots, tofu, tomatoes and lime juice to the pan and cook for 2–3 minutes to heat through.

GARNISH with coriander leaves.

FROM CHINA

TEN-TREASURE SOUP

THIS MEAL-IN-ONE SOUP IS A KIND OF STEW, WHERE THE INGREDIENTS ARE SIMMERED TOGETHER SO THAT THE FLAVOURS MELD. TRADITIONALLY, THIS SOUP HAS TEN MAIN INGREDIENTS, BUT THE EXACT NUMBER DOESN'T MATTER AND YOU CAN VARY THE INGREDIENTS DEPENDING ON WHAT'S AVAILABLE.

400 g (14 oz) Chinese cabbage
2 tablespoons oil
4 garlic cloves, smashed with the flat side of a cleaver
125 ml (4 fl oz/½ cup) Shaoxing rice wine
1.5 litres (52 fl oz/6 cups) chicken stock (see recipe on page 491)
1 teaspoon salt
250 g (9 oz) centre-cut pork loin, trimmed
2 teaspoons light soy sauce
½ teaspoon roasted sesame oil
450 g (1 lb) prawns (shrimp)
3 slices ginger, smashed with the flat side of a cleaver
30 g (1 oz) bean thread noodles
6 dried Chinese mushrooms
450 g (1 lb) firm tofu, drained and cut into 2.5 cm (1 inch) squares
2 carrots, cut into 2 cm (¾ inch) pieces
200 g (½ bunch) baby English spinach leaves
3 spring onions (scallions), green part only, cut diagonally into 1 cm (½ inch) lengths

SERVES 6

REMOVE the stems from the cabbage and cut the leaves into 5 cm (2 inch) squares. Separate the hard cabbage pieces from the leafy ones. Heat a wok over high heat, add the oil and heat until very hot. Add the hard cabbage pieces and the garlic. Toss lightly over high heat, adding 1 tablespoon of the rice wine. Stir-fry for several minutes, then add the leafy cabbage pieces. Stir-fry for 1 minute, then add 4 tablespoons of the rice wine, the stock and half of the salt. Bring to the boil, then reduce the heat to low and cook for 30 minutes. Transfer to a clay pot or saucepan.

CUT the pork across the grain into slices about 2 mm (⅛ inch) thick. Place the pork in a bowl, add the soy sauce and sesame oil, and toss lightly to coat. Marinate in the fridge for 20 minutes.

PEEL and devein the prawns, then place in a bowl with the ginger, remaining rice wine and salt and toss lightly. Marinate in the fridge for 20 minutes. Remove and discard the ginger.

SOAK the bean thread noodles in hot water for 10 minutes, then drain and cut into 15 cm (6 inch) lengths.

SOAK the dried mushrooms in boiling water for 30 minutes, then drain and squeeze out any excess water. Remove and discard the stems.

ARRANGE the pork slices, tofu, mushrooms, noodles and carrot in separate piles on top of the cabbage in the casserole, leaving some space in the centre for the prawns and spinach. Cover and cook over medium heat for 20 minutes. Arrange prawns and spinach in the centre and sprinkle with the spring onion. Cover and cook for 5 minutes, or until the prawns are pink and cooked through. Season with salt if necessary.

SERVE directly from the pot.

Use the flat side of a cleaver to smash the garlic cloves and the blade for cutting the carrots.

Adding the egg to the hot soup forms egg drops. Pour it in in an even stream.

HOT AND SOUR SOUP

4 dried Chinese mushrooms

2 tablespoons dried black fungus (wood ears)

100 g (3½ oz) lean pork, shredded

1 tablespoon cornflour (cornstarch)

120 g (4 oz) firm tofu, drained

60 g (2¼ oz/¼ cup) fresh or tinned bamboo shoots, rinsed and drained

1 litre (35 fl oz/4 cups) chicken and meat stock (see recipe on page 491)

1 teaspoon salt

1 tablespoon Shaoxing rice wine

2 tablespoons light soy sauce

1–2 tablespoons Chinese black rice vinegar

2 eggs, beaten

1–2 teaspoons freshly ground white pepper

1 chopped spring onion (scallion), for garnish

SERVES 4

SOAK the dried Chinese mushrooms in boiling water for 30 minutes, then drain and squeeze out any excess water. Remove and discard the stems and shred the caps.

SOAK the dried black fungus in cold water for 20 minutes, then drain and squeeze out any excess water. Shred the black fungus.

COMBINE the pork, a pinch of salt and 1 teaspoon of the cornflour.

THINLY shred the tofu and bamboo shoots to the same size as the pork.

BRING the stock to the boil in a large clay pot or saucepan. Add the pork and stir to separate the meat, then add the mushroom, fungus, tofu and bamboo. Return to the boil and add the salt, rice wine, soy and vinegar. Slowly pour in the egg, whisking to form thin threads, and cook for 1 minute. Combine the remaining cornflour with enough water to make a paste, add to the soup and simmer until thickened. Put the pepper in a bowl, pour in the soup and stir.

GARNISH with spring onion.

LAMB AND CUCUMBER SOUP

LAMB AND CUCUMBER SOUP

250 g (9 oz) lamb fillet

1 tablespoon Shaoxing rice wine

1 tablespoon light soy sauce

1 teaspoon roasted sesame oil

½ Lebanese (short) cucumber

750 ml (26 fl oz/3 cups) chicken and meat stock (see recipe on page 491)

2 teaspoons Chinese black rice vinegar, or to taste

coriander (cilantro) leaves, for garnish

SERVES 4

CUT the lamb into very thin slices and combine with the rice wine, soy sauce and sesame oil. Marinate in the fridge for at least 15 minutes.

HALVE the cucumber lengthways, discarding the seeds, and cut it into thin slices.

BRING the stock to a rolling boil in a large clay pot or saucepan. Add the lamb and stir to separate the meat. Return to the boil, then add the cucumber and rice vinegar, and season with salt and white pepper. Return to the boil.

SERVE garnished with the coriander leaves.

SEAFOOD

The Li River in Guangxi.

FROM CHINA
SMOKED FISH

IN FACT, THE FISH IN THIS DISH IS NOT SMOKED AT ALL. INSTEAD, IT ACQUIRES A SMOKY FLAVOUR FROM BEING MARINATED AND BRAISED IN A SPICY SAUCE, THEN BEING DEEP-FRIED AND MARINATED IN THE SAUCE ONCE MORE BEFORE SERVING.

2 tablespoons light soy sauce
1 tablespoon dark soy sauce
3 tablespoons Shaoxing rice wine
2 tablespoons rock (lump) sugar
2 teaspoons five-spice
1 spring onion (scallion), finely chopped
2 teaspoons finely chopped ginger
450 g (1 lb) firm white fish fillets, such as haddock, monkfish or sea bass, skin on
310 ml (17 fl oz/1¼ cups) chicken and meat stock (see recipe on page 491)
oil for deep-frying
coriander (cilantro) leaves, for garnish

SERVES 6

COMBINE the soy sauces, rice wine, sugar, five-spice, spring onion and ginger.

PAT dry the fish and leave in the marinade for 1 hour.

TRANSFER the fish and marinade to a clay pot or saucepan. Add the stock and bring to the boil. Reduce heat and simmer gently for 10 minutes, or until the fish is cooked through. Drain the fish, reserving the marinade.

FILL a wok one-quarter full of oil. Heat the oil to 190°C (375°F), or until a piece of bread fries golden brown in 10 seconds when dropped in the oil. Carefully cook the fish in batches for 3–4 minutes, or until golden and crisp (it will spit a little). Remove the fish from the oil and return it to the marinade. Leave to cool for 2–3 hours.

REMOVE the fish from the marinade and leave to dry for a few minutes. Cut the fish into thin slices and serve cold, sprinkled with coriander leaves.

Fishermen on the Li River use tame cormorants to catch fish.

FROM INDIA

PATRI NI MACCHI

THIS IS A DISH FROM THE PARSI PEOPLE, DESCENDANTS OF PERSIANS WHO MIGRATED TO THE WEST COAST OF INDIA, WHICH IS TYPICALLY SERVED AT WEDDINGS. THE LITTLE PARCELS ARE QUITE AROMATIC WHEN OPENED AND LOOK VERY APPEALING. YOU CAN USE ANY FIRM, WHITE FISH FOR THE RECIPE.

500 g (1 lb 2 oz) pomfret, sole or
    leatherjacket fillets, skinned
young banana leaves
1 teaspoon ground cumin
½ teaspoon sugar
150 g (5½ oz) grated coconut
    (see recipe on page 468)
4 green chillies, seeded and
    chopped
4 tablespoons chopped coriander
    (cilantro) leaves
a few mint leaves
6 garlic cloves, chopped
1 green unripe mango, diced
3 tablespoons oil or ghee
3 tablespoons lime or lemon juice
mint leaves, for garnish
whole green chillies, for garnish

SERVES 4

WASH the fish fillets, pat dry and cut into 8 cm (3 inch) pieces.

CUT banana leaves into as many 23 cm (9 inch) squares as there are pieces of fish (you should have six to eight). Soften the banana leaves by dipping them into a pan of very hot water. Wipe the pieces dry as they become pliant. If you can't get banana leaves, use foil.

GRIND the cumin, sugar, coconut, chilli, coriander, mint, garlic and green mango to a paste in a food processor, blender or pestle and mortar.

HEAT 1 tablespoon of the oil or ghee in a frying pan and cook the paste over low heat until aromatic. Season with salt.

PLACE the banana leaf squares on a work surface. Apply the paste liberally to both sides of each piece of fish. Sprinkle some lime or lemon juice on the fish. Place a piece of fish on each banana leaf and wrap up like a parcel, tying them firmly with kitchen string.

USING a large, heavy-based frying pan which has a lid, heat the remaining oil or ghee and shallow-fry the fish parcels together on one side. After about 5 minutes, turn the parcels over and fry for another 5 minutes. The leaves will darken and shrink. Cover the pan and cook the fish for a few more minutes.

OPEN out each fish parcel on its plate. Garnish with mint leaves and green chilli 'flowers' (do this by making slits down into the chilli from the top towards the stem so you form strips which fan out).

DEEP-FRIED FISH WITH THREE-FLAVOURED SAUCE

YOU CAN USE LIME JUICE IN THIS DISH IF YOU PREFER A CLEAR SAUCE, OR TAMARIND FOR A THICK OR DARKER-COLOURED SAUCE. USE TWO OR FOUR SMALLER FISH IF YOU CAN'T FIND ONE FISH LARGE ENOUGH. GARNISH WITH HOLY BASIL IF YOU CAN FIND IT.

1 x 350 g (12 oz) sea bream, red
   snapper or grey mullet
3 tablespoons plain (all-purpose)
   flour
pinch of ground black pepper
vegetable oil, for deep-frying

PASTE
4–5 garlic cloves, roughly chopped
5 long red chillies, seeded and
   roughly chopped
4–5 Asian shallots, roughly chopped
3 coriander (cilantro) roots, finely
   chopped

3 tablespoons palm sugar (jaggery),
   or soft brown sugar
2 tablespoons fish sauce
3 tablespoons tamarind purée or
   lime juice
a few holy basil or Thai sweet basil
   leaves, for garnish

SERVES 2

CLEAN and gut the fish, leaving the head on. Dry the fish thoroughly. Score it three or four times on both sides with a sharp knife. Rub inside and out with a pinch of salt. Put the flour and ground pepper on a plate or dish and press the fish lightly into it until coated with flour from head to tail. Shake off any excess.

HEAT 10 cm (4 inches) oil in a large wok or pan big enough to deep-fry the whole fish. When the oil seems hot, drop a piece of shallot into the oil. If it sizzles straight away, the oil is ready. Lower the heat to medium and gently slide the fish into the oil. Be careful as the hot oil may splash. Deep-fry the fish on just one side (but make sure the oil covers the whole fish) for about 15–20 minutes or until the fish is cooked and light brown (if you cook the fish until it is brown, it will be too dry). Drain, then put on paper towels before transferring to a warm plate. Keep warm.

WHILE the fish is cooking, use a pestle and mortar or a small blender to pound or blend the garlic, chillies, shallots and coriander roots together into a rough paste.

HEAT 1 tablespoon oil in a wok or frying pan and stir-fry the chilli paste over a medium heat for 2–3 minutes or until fragrant. Add the palm sugar, fish sauce and tamarind purée or lime juice, and cook for 2–3 minutes or until the sugar has dissolved. Pour the warm chilli sauce over the fish and garnish with basil leaves.

Deep-fry the whole floured fish on one side only, making sure the oil covers the fish.

Selling vegetables at the floating market.

LOBSTER FU RONG

THE WORDS 'FU RONG' MEAN EGG WHITES AND IN RECIPES DENOTE A CLASSIC CANTONESE COOKING METHOD, THOUGH THE TERM IS OFTEN ASSOCIATED WITH THE QUITE DIFFERENT EGG FOO YOUNG OF WESTERN CHINESE RESTAURANTS. THIS DISH CAN BE MADE WITH ANY KIND OF SEAFOOD.

450 g (1 lb) lobster meat
3 tablespoons Shaoxing rice wine
3 teaspoons finely chopped ginger
1½ teaspoons salt
12 egg whites
½ teaspoon cream of tartar
oil for deep-frying
125 ml (4 fl oz/½ cup) chicken
  stock (see recipe on page 491)
¼ teaspoon freshly ground white
  pepper
1 teaspoon roasted sesame oil
1 teaspoon cornflour (cornstarch)
2 spring onions (scallions), finely
  chopped

GARNISH
2 spring onions (scallions), green
  part only, sliced

SERVES 6

CUT the lobster meat into pieces, put in a bowl with 1 tablespoon of the rice wine, 1 teaspoon of the ginger and ½ teaspoon of the salt and toss lightly to coat.

BEAT the egg whites and cream of tartar using a balloon whisk or electric beaters until stiff. Fold the lobster into the egg white mixture.

FILL a wok one-quarter full of oil. Heat the oil to 190°C (375°F), or until a piece of bread fries golden brown in 10 seconds when dropped in the oil. Pour the lobster into the wok in batches – do not stir, otherwise it will scatter, but gently stir the oil from the bottom of the wok so that the 'fu rong' rises to the surface. Remove each batch as soon as it is set, without letting it go too brown, and drain well. Pour off the oil from the wok, leaving 2 tablespoons.

COMBINE the chicken stock, remaining rice wine and salt, white pepper, sesame oil and cornflour.

REHEAT the reserved oil over high heat until very hot and stir-fry the finely chopped spring onion and the remaining ginger for 10 seconds, or until fragrant. Add the stock mixture and cook, stirring constantly to prevent lumps, until thickened. Add the cooked lobster mixture and carefully toss it in the sauce.

TRANSFER to a serving platter, sprinkle with the sliced spring onion and serve.

FROM JAPAN

SCATTERED SUSHI

SCATTERED SUSHI IS NOT ONLY EASY TO PREPARE BUT WITH ITS ABUNDANT AND COLOURFUL TOPPINGS MAKES AN IMMENSELY APPETISING AND FESTIVE MEAL. THIS DISH IS TYPICALLY PRESENTED AT THE TABLE IN A HANDSOME WOOD OR LACQUERED BOWL.

1 quantity still-warm sushi rice (see recipe on page 460)

2 tablespoons white, black or mixed sesame seeds, toasted

2 spring onions (scallions), sliced

60 g (2¼ oz) simmered shiitake mushrooms, finely chopped

50 g (1¾ oz) bamboo shoots, finely chopped

60 g (2¼ oz) prepared kanpyo (gourd strip), finely chopped

2 tablespoons pickled ginger, finely chopped

1 tablespoon Japanese rice vinegar

4 thin crepe-like omelettes, cut into very thin strips (see recipe on page 356)

12 sugar snap peas, trimmed, blanched

80 g (2¾ oz/½ cup) fresh or frozen peas, cooked

100 g (3½ oz) sashimi-grade tuna or salmon, cut into short, thin strips

12 cooked king prawns (shrimp), peeled and deveined

2 toasted nori sheets, cut into thin strips

SERVES 4

COMBINE the sushi rice with the sesame seeds, spring onion, shiitake, bamboo shoots, kanpyo and pickled ginger in a large bowl.

SPREAD the mixture over the base of a large, wide shallow serving bowl or lacquerware tray with sides.

FILL a bowl with warm water and mix in the vinegar. Dampen your hands with the water to prevent the rice sticking to your hands. Smooth the rice mixture into the serving bowl, dampening your hands as needed.

SPRINKLE the omelette strips evenly over the top, then arrange or scatter the peas, sashimi strips, prawns and nori strips evenly over the top.

SERVE immediately. Use a wooden rice paddle or spoon to serve into small bowls.

Nori is paper-like sheets, the result of compressing and drying a particular marine algae found on the surface of the sea off Japan's coasts.

DEEP-FRIED FISH WITH CHILLIES AND BASIL

THIS IS ONE OF THE MOST POPULAR FISH DISHES IN THAILAND AND YOU CAN USE MOST TYPES OF FISH TO MAKE IT. THE FISH HAS A MILDLY SPICY FLAVOUR AND IS GARNISHED WITH DEEP-FRIED CHILLI AND BASIL LEAVES. THE DUSTING OF FLOUR ISN'T TRADITIONAL BUT IT HELPS CRISP THE SKIN.

Deep-fry the basil leaves in two batches until they are crisp.

1 large or 2 smaller red snapper
　(total weight about 1 kg/2 lb 4 oz)
3 tablespoons plain (all-purpose)
　flour
pinch of ground black pepper
1½ tablespoons vegetable oil
½ tablespoon red curry paste
　(see recipe on page 472) or
　bought paste
2 tablespoons palm sugar (jaggery),
　or soft brown sugar
2 tablespoons fish sauce
vegetable oil, for deep-frying
a handful of Thai sweet basil leaves
1 dried long red chilli, cut into
　5 mm (¼ inch) pieces,
　seeds discarded
3 makrut (kaffir lime) leaves,
　very finely sliced, for garnish

SERVES 4

CLEAN and gut the fish, leaving the head/s on. Thoroughly dry the fish. Score the fish three or four times on both sides with a sharp knife. Rub the fish inside and out with a pinch of salt. Place the flour and ground pepper on a plate and press the fish lightly into it until coated with flour from head to tail. Shake off any excess.

HEAT the oil in a small saucepan, add the red curry paste and stir over a medium heat for 1–2 minutes or until fragrant. Add the sugar, fish sauce and 2 tablespoons water and cook for another 1–2 minutes or until the sugar has dissolved. Remove from the heat.

HEAT 10 cm (4 inches) oil in a large wok or pan big enough to deep-fry the whole fish. When the oil is hot, drop a few basil leaves into it. If they sizzle immediately, the oil is ready. Deep-fry half of the basil leaves for 1 minute or until they are all crispy. Remove with a slotted spoon and drain on paper towels. Deep-fry the rest.

IN the same wok, deep-fry the dried chilli pieces for a few seconds over a medium heat until light brown. Be careful not to burn them. Remove with a slotted spoon and drain on paper towels. Lower the heat to medium and gently slide the fish into the oil. Be careful as the hot oil may splash. Deep-fry the fish on just one side (but make sure the oil covers the whole fish) for about 5–10 minutes or until the fish is cooked and light brown (if you cook the fish until it is very brown, it will be too dry). Drain off the oil and drain the fish on paper towels.

PUT the curry sauce in the wok and gently warm it. Add the fish and coat both sides with the sauce. Transfer the fish to a warm plate with any remaining sauce and sprinkle with crispy basil, fried chilli pieces and the makrut lime leaves.

Pattaya market.

FROM CHINA

WEST LAKE FISH

HANGZHOU IN THE EAST OF CHINA IS FAMOUS FOR ITS REFINED CUISINE AND EXQUISITE SCENERY. A SPECIALITY OF THIS REGION IS WEST LAKE FISH MADE WITH FRESHWATER CARP. THE POACHING METHOD IS UNIQUE AND QUITE INGENIOUS AS THE FISH IS COOKED OFF THE HEAT.

1 x 1.75 kg (4 lb) whole fish, such as carp, bream, grouper or sea bass

MARINADE
4 tablespoons Shaoxing rice wine
2 teaspoons salt
4 slices ginger, smashed with the flat side of a cleaver
4 spring onions (scallions), sliced and smashed with the flat side of a cleaver

1 tablespoon oil
2 tablespoons finely shredded ginger
1 spring onion (scallion), finely shredded
1 red chilli, seeded and finely shredded
½ teaspoon freshly ground white pepper
2½ tablespoons light soy sauce
2 tablespoons sugar
2 tablespoons Chinese black rice vinegar
1 tablespoon cornflour (cornstarch)

SERVES 6

IF YOU do manage to buy a swimming (live) fish, then ask the fishmonger to gut it through the gills. This is harder than gutting through the stomach, but leaves the fish looking whole. If you are gutting the fish yourself, make a cut from the throat to the tail and pull out the guts through the stomach. Remove any scales with a fish scaler or the back of a knife. Check that the gills have been cut out, then rinse the fish under cold, running water and drain thoroughly in a colander. Diagonally score both sides of the fish, cutting through as far as the bone at 2 cm (¾ inch) intervals.

TO MAKE the marinade, combine 1 tablespoon of the rice wine, 1 teaspoon of the salt, the ginger slices and smashed spring onions. Pinch the ginger slices and spring onions in the marinade repeatedly for several minutes to release their flavours into the marinade. Rub the marinade all over the outside of the fish and into the slits. Marinate fish in the refrigerator for 30 minutes.

BRING 4 litres (140 fl oz/16 cups) water to the boil in a wok with the oil and remaining rice wine. Gently lower the fish into the poaching liquid and return to the boil. Turn off the heat, cover, and leave for 20 minutes, or until the fish flakes when the skin is pressed firmly or the dorsal fin pulls out easily. If the fish is not cooked through, cook over low heat for 5 minutes. Using slotted spoons, carefully transfer the fish to a platter. Reserve 375 ml (13 fl oz/1½ cups) of the poaching liquid. Sprinkle the shredded ginger, shredded spring onion, chilli and white pepper over the fish.

ADD the soy sauce, remaining salt, sugar and black vinegar to the liquid. Heat the wok over high heat, add the liquid and bring to the boil. Combine the cornflour with enough water to make a paste, add to the sauce and simmer until thickened. Pour the sauce over the fish.

Rinse fish thoroughly, making sure that all the scales are washed off (any left on will be hard and unpalatable). Leaving the fish to marinate not only adds flavour but also makes it aromatic and less 'fishy' tasting.

The fish should be cut into bite-sized pieces and the bamboo shoots into matchsticks.

Bamboo shoots *(naw mai)* are available fresh when in season, and are otherwise preserved in jars or tinned. Fresh shoots should be blanched (possibly more than once) if they're bitter.

FROM THAILAND

RED CURRY WITH FISH AND BAMBOO SHOOTS

ALTHOUGH THERE ARE MANY STYLES IN THE LARGE RANGE OF THAI RED CURRIES, ALL HAVE THE DEFINING CHARACTERISTIC RED COLOUR. RED CURRIES ARE QUITE LIQUID COMPARED TO DRY CURRIES SUCH AS PANAENG. BE SURE TO USE A FIRM FISH THAT WON'T FALL APART.

60 ml (2 fl oz/¼ cup) coconut cream (see recipe on page 468)

2 tablespoons red curry paste (see recipe on page 472) or bought paste

440 ml (5¼ fl oz/1¾ cups) coconut milk (see recipe on page 468)

1½–2 tablespoons palm sugar (jaggery), or soft brown sugar

3 tablespoons fish sauce

350 g (12 oz) skinless firm white fish fillets, cut into 3 cm (1¼ inch) cubes

275 g (10 oz) tin bamboo shoots in water, drained, cut into matchsticks

50 g (2 oz) galangal, finely sliced

5 makrut (kaffir lime) leaves, torn in half

a handful of Thai sweet basil leaves, for garnish

1 long red chilli, seeded and finely sliced, for garnish

SERVES 4

PUT the coconut cream in a wok or saucepan and simmer over a medium heat for about 5 minutes, or until the cream separates and a layer of oil forms on the surface. Stir the cream if it starts to brown around the edges. Add the curry paste, stir well to combine and cook until fragrant.

STIR in the coconut milk, then add the sugar and fish sauce and cook for 2–3 minutes.

ADD the fish and bamboo shoots and simmer for about 5 minutes, stirring occasionally, until the fish is cooked.

ADD the galangal and makrut. Taste, then adjust the seasoning if necessary.

SPOON onto a serving plate and sprinkle with the basil leaves and sliced chilli.

FROM INDIA

PRAWNS WITH BITTER MELON

1 kg (2 lb 4 oz) bitter melon, peeled
300 g (10½ oz) tiger prawns
  (shrimp)
1 tablespoon oil
½ tablespoon ground turmeric
1 tablespoon ground coriander
1 tablespoon ground cumin
1 teaspoon chilli powder
4–5 green chillies
pinch of sugar
1 tablespoon ghee
4 curry leaves
¼ teaspoon cumin seeds
chopped coriander (cilantro) leaves
  (optional)

SERVES 4

SLICE the bitter melon in half and scoop out any seeds and membrane. Slice into half-moon shapes 5 mm (¼ inch) thick. Sprinkle with salt and degorge in a colander for 30 minutes. Rinse and drain, then dry in a tea towel (dish towel).

PEEL and devein the prawns.

HEAT the oil in a heavy-based frying pan, add the bitter melon, stir once or twice, then cover and cook for 3–4 minutes. The bitter melon will continue to sweat out liquid. Mix the turmeric, coriander, cumin and chilli powder to a paste with a small amount of water. Add to the pan and cook over high heat until liquid is reduced to almost dry. Add the prawns and green chillies and cook, tossing until dry. Season with the sugar and a little salt.

FOR the final seasoning (tarka), heat the ghee in a small pan, fry the curry leaves and cumin for 1 minute, then pour onto the bitter melon and stir in the coriander, if using.

When bitter melon is degorged, the bitterness is lessened. Paler or yellower ones are less bitter but more fibrous.

PRAWN CURRY WITH TAMARIND

500 g (1 lb 2 oz) tiger prawns
  (shrimp)
½ teaspoon fennel seeds
1 tablespoon oil
2 cinnamon sticks
3 cardamom pods
1 large onion, finely chopped
5 garlic cloves, crushed
2 cm (¾ inch) piece of ginger,
  grated
1 stalk of curry leaves
1 teaspoon turmeric
1 teaspoon chilli powder
1½ tablespoons tamarind purée
  (see recipe on page 467)

SERVES 4

PEEL and devein the prawns, leaving the tails intact.

PLACE a small frying pan over low heat and dry-roast the fennel seeds until aromatic.

HEAT the oil in a karhai or heavy-based frying pan and fry the fennel seeds, cinnamon, cardamom and onion until the onion is brown. Stir in the garlic, ginger and curry leaves, then add the prawns, turmeric, chilli powder and tamarind. Toss over high heat until the prawn tails turn pink and the prawns are cooked through. Remove from the heat and season with salt, to taste.

PRAWN CURRY WITH TAMARIND

Form mixture into balls about the size of a walnut – you should get about 18 – don't worry if they seem quite soft.

FROM JAPAN

SALMON AND TOFU BALLS

MOIST AND CRISP, THESE DEEP-FRIED CROQUETTE-LIKE MORSELS OF RED SALMON ARE LIGHTENED WITH MASHED TOFU. SERVED WITH COMPLEMENTARY SIDES, THEY MAKE A LIGHT MAIN DISH, BUT WOULD ALSO BE AN APPETISING STARTER OR AN ACCOMPANIMENT TO SAKE.

WASABI MAYONNAISE
DIPPING SAUCE
125 g (4½ oz/½ cup) Japanese
   mayonnaise
1 teaspoon shoyu (Japanese soy
   sauce)
1 teaspoon mirin
1 teaspoon Japanese rice vinegar
½ teaspoon wasabi paste

SALMON AND TOFU BALLS
200 g (7 oz) silken firm tofu
400 g (14 oz) tinned red salmon,
   well drained, to yield about 250 g
   (9 oz)
2 spring onions (scallions), finely
   chopped
2 teaspoons finely grated fresh
   ginger, squeezed to remove
   excess liquid
1 clove garlic, crushed
2 teaspoons mirin
1 tablespoon shoyu (Japanese
   soy sauce)
1 egg
2 tablespoons plain (all-purpose)
   flour
pinch ground white pepper

vegetable oil, for deep-frying
potato starch, for coating
lemon wedges, to serve

MAKES 18

TO MAKE the wasabi mayonnaise dipping sauce, put all the ingredients in a small bowl and combine well.

TO WEIGHT the tofu, wrap it in a clean tea towel (dish towel). Put two plates on top of the tofu and leave for about 2 hours to extract any excess moisture. Remove from the tea towel, then pat dry with paper towels. Put in a bowl and finely mash with a fork.

BREAK up the salmon with a fork, picking out any bones. Finely mash with a fork and add to the bowl with the tofu, along with the spring onion, ginger, garlic, mirin, shoyu, egg and flour and combine well. Season with salt and white pepper. If the mixture is still too wet, put in a fine colander and leave for 30 minutes to drain out the excess liquid.

WITH clean hands, form into balls about the size of a walnut and set aside – you should get about 18 balls. Don't worry if the balls seem quite soft.

FILL a deep-fat fryer or large saucepan one-third full of oil and heat to 180°C (350°F), or until a cube of bread dropped into the oil browns in 15 seconds. Lightly coat the balls with potato starch, then immediately lower into the hot oil. Cook in batches, turning occasionally, for about 2 minutes, or until golden all over and cooked through. Drain on paper towels and keep warm in a low oven while you repeat with the remaining mixture.

SERVE immediately with lemon wedges and the dipping sauce.

FROM INDIA

MOLEE

1 tablespoon oil
1 large onion, thinly sliced
3 garlic cloves, crushed
2 small green chillies, finely
  chopped
2 teaspoons ground turmeric
1 teaspoon ground coriander
1 teaspoon ground cumin
4 cloves
6 curry leaves
420 ml (15 fl oz/1⅔ cups) coconut
  milk (see recipe on page 468)
½ teaspoon salt
600 g (1 lb 5 oz) pomfret, sole or
  leatherjacket fillets, skinned
1 tablespoon chopped coriander
  (cilantro) leaves
curry leaves, for garnish

SERVES 6

HEAT the oil in a karhai or deep, heavy-based frying pan, add the onion and cook for 5 minutes. Add the garlic and chilli and cook for another 5 minutes, or until the onion has softened and looks translucent. Add the turmeric, coriander, cumin and cloves and stir-fry with the onion for 2 minutes. Stir in the curry leaves, coconut milk and salt and bring to just below boiling point. Reduce the heat and simmer for 20 minutes.

CUT each fish fillet into two or three large pieces and add them to the sauce. Bring sauce back to a simmer and cook for 5 minutes, or until the fish is cooked through and flakes easily. Check the seasoning, add more salt if necessary, then stir in the coriander leaves.

GARNISH with the curry leaves.

A truck waiting to be loaded with fresh fish at Sassoon Docks in Mumbai (Bombay).

BOMBAY-STYLE FISH

2 garlic cloves, crushed
3 small green chillies, seeded
  and finely chopped
½ teaspoon ground turmeric
½ teaspoon ground cloves
½ teaspoon ground cinnamon
½ teaspoon ground cayenne
  pepper
1 tablespoon tamarind purée
  (see recipe on page 467)
800 g (1 lb 12 oz) pomfret, sole or
  leatherjacket fillets, skinned
310 ml (11 fl oz/1¼ cups) coconut
  cream (see recipe on page 468)
2 tablespoons chopped coriander
  (cilantro) leaves, for garnish

SERVES 4

COMBINE the garlic, chilli, spices, tamarind and 125 ml (4 fl oz/½ cup) of the oil. Place the fish fillets in a shallow dish and spoon the marinade over them. Turnfish over, cover and refrigerate for 30 minutes.

HEAT the remaining oil in a large, heavy-based frying pan and add the fish in batches. Cook for 1 minute on each side. Return all the fish to the pan, then reduce the heat to low and add any remaining marinade and the coconut cream. Season with salt and gently cook for 3–5 minutes, or until the fish is cooked through and flakes easily. If the sauce is too runny, lift out the fish, simmer sauce for a few minutes, then pour it over the fish.

GARNISH with the coriander leaves.

BOMBAY-STYLE FISH

Tempura was not an original Japanese dish, but was inspired by the batter-fried fish meals of early Portuguese traders.

TEMPURA

THESE FEATHERLIGHT, CRISP PIECES OF SEAFOOD AND VEGETABLES MAKE A BEAUTIFULLY DELICATE DISH. TWO BATCHES OF TEMPURA BATTER ARE NEEDED HERE – MAKE EACH BATCH JUST BEFORE YOU NEED TO USE IT.

8 raw king prawns (shrimp), peeled, deveined, tails intact
200 g (7 oz) piece squid, opened out flat
200 g (7 oz) white fish fillet, cut into 4 even pieces
vegetable oil, for deep-frying
60 ml (2 fl oz/¼ cup) sesame oil
plain (all-purpose) flour, for coating

VEGETABLES
½ small onion, cut into 4 thin wedges, a toothpick securing each wedge
4 very thin slices jap (kent) pumpkin, unpeeled
4 fresh shiitake mushrooms, stems discarded
1 baby eggplant (aubergine), cut into 5 mm (¼ inch) thick slices on the diagonal
½ small green capsicum (pepper), cut lengthways into quarters
4 shiso leaves, optional

tempura dipping sauce (see recipe on page 484) or ready-made, to serve
70 g (2½ oz) daikon, peeled, finely grated, then squeezed to remove excess liquid, to serve
2 teaspoons finely grated fresh ginger, to serve

SERVES 4

MAKE two batches of the tempura batter (see recipe on page 439). One batch is for dipping the vegetables and one batch is for the seafood.

TO prepare the seafood, make three cuts in the belly of the prawns. Turn the prawns over and, starting from the tail end, press down gently at intervals along the length of the prawn – this helps to break the connective tissue, preventing the prawns from curling up too much. Finely score squid in a crisscross pattern on both sides, then cut into 4 x 3 cm (1½ x 1¼ inch) pieces. Arrange the seafood and vegetables on separate platters. Cover with plastic wrap. Refrigerate until using.

FILL a deep-fat fryer or large saucepan one-third full of vegetable oil, then add the sesame oil. Heat to 180°C (350°F), or until a cube of bread dropped into the oil browns in 15 seconds.

DIP each ingredient into the flour (except the shiso leaves) before dipping it into the batter. Dip the shiso directly into the batter. Starting with the onion and pumpkin, quickly dip into the tempura batter, allowing the excess to drip off, then lower into the oil. Cook for 2–3 minutes, or until cooked through and the batter is lightly golden and crispy. It should also look lacy and a little see-through – if the batter is too thick, add a little more iced water. Drain on paper towels. Keep warm in a low oven while you cook the rest of the vegetables. Skim off any bits of floating batter as you cook.

COOK seafood in small batches for 1–3 minutes, or until just cooked through and lightly golden and crisp. Keep warm in the oven.

SERVE with a small bowl of the tempura dipping sauce with grated daikon and ginger mixed in according to taste.

FROM THAILAND

PRAWNS WITH THAI SWEET BASIL LEAVES

600 g (1 lb 5 oz) raw prawns
(shrimp)
2 tablespoons vegetable oil
2 tablespoons dry curry paste
(see recipe on page 475)
or bought paste
185 ml (6 fl oz/¾ cup) coconut milk
(see recipe on page 468)
2 teaspoons fish sauce
2 teaspoons palm sugar (jaggery),
or soft brown sugar
a handful of Thai sweet basil leaves,
for garnish
1 long red chilli, seeded and finely
sliced, for garnish

SERVES 4

PEEL and devein the prawns and cut each prawn along the back so it opens like a butterfly (leave each prawn joined along the base and at the tail, leaving the tail attached).

HEAT the oil in a saucepan or wok and stir-fry the dry curry paste over a medium heat for 2 minutes or until fragrant.

ADD the coconut milk, fish sauce and palm sugar and cook for a few seconds. Add the prawns and cook for a few minutes or until the prawns are cooked through. Taste, then adjust the seasoning if necessary.

SPOON into a serving bowl and garnish with basil leaves and chillies.

PRAWN AND PINEAPPLE CURRY

SPICE PASTE
4 bird's eye chillies, seeded
6 Asian shallots
2 lemongrass stalks, white part only,
finely chopped
½ teaspoon shrimp paste
½ teaspoon ground turmeric
2 tablespoons oil
185 ml (6 fl oz/¾ cup) coconut milk
(see recipe on page 468)
300 g (10 oz) fresh pineapple,
cut into small wedges
2 tablespoons tamarind purée
3 makrut (kaffir lime) leaves
250 g (9 oz) raw prawns (shrimp)
2 teaspoons fish sauce
1 tablespoon palm sugar (jaggery)

SERVES 4

PEEL and devein the prawns and cut each prawn along the back so it opens like a butterfly (leave each prawn joined along the base and at the tail, leaving the tail attached).

PUT all the spice paste ingredients in a pestle and mortar and pound to a paste. Alternatively, use a food processor and add 2 tablespoons water. Blend until well combined.

HEAT the oil in a wok or saucepan. Add the spice paste and fry until fragrant. Stir in the coconut milk and cook for 2 minutes. Add the pineapple wedges, tamarind purée and makrut leaves and simmer for 5 minutes, or until the pineapple begins to soften.

ADD the prawns and stir well to cover them in the sauce. Simmer for 5–6 minutes until the prawns are cooked through.

STIR in the fish sauce and sugar before serving.

PRAWN AND PINEAPPLE
CURRY

FROM THAILAND

SPICY LOBSTER AND PINEAPPLE CURRY

EVEN THOUGH THIS RED CURRY IS EXPENSIVE BECAUSE OF THE LOBSTER, IT IS EXCELLENT FOR SPECIAL OCCASIONS. YOU CAN USE LARGE PRAWNS (SHRIMP) OR CRAB HALVES IF YOU LIKE. ALSO, YOU CAN MAKE THE SAUCE AND SERVE IT WITH BARBECUED LOBSTER HALVES.

60 ml (2 fl oz/¼ cup) coconut
   cream (see recipe on page 468)
2 tablespoons red curry paste
   (see recipe on page 472) or
   bought paste
1 tablespoon fish sauce
1 tablespoon palm sugar (jaggery)
250 ml (9 fl oz/1 cup) coconut milk
   (see recipe on page 468)
200 g (7 oz) fresh pineapple,
   cut into bite-sized wedges
300 g (10 oz) lobster tail meat
3 makrut (kaffir lime) leaves,
   2 roughly torn and 1 shredded
1 tablespoon tamarind purée
2 very large handfuls Thai sweet
   basil leaves
1 large red chilli, finely sliced,
   for garnish

SERVES 4

PUT the coconut cream in a wok or saucepan and simmer over a medium heat for about 5 minutes, or until the cream separates and a layer of oil forms on the surface. Stir the cream if it starts to brown around the edges.

ADD the curry paste, stir well to combine and cook until fragrant. Add the fish sauce and sugar and stir to combine. Cook for 4–5 minutes, stirring constantly. The mixture should darken.

STIR in the coconut milk and the pineapple. Simmer for 6–8 minutes to soften the pineapple.

ADD the lobster tail meat, makrut leaves, tamarind purée and basil leaves. Cook for another 5–6 minutes until the lobster is firm.

SERVE with sliced chilli on top.

When the mixture has darkened, stir in the pineapple pieces.

A stretch of beaches in Khao Sok National Park.

STIR-FRIED SCALLOPS WITH CHINESE GREENS

THIS DISH EMPHASISES THE FRESHNESS AND DELICATE SEASONING THAT GIVE CANTONESE CUISINE ITS REPUTATION. CHINESE BROCCOLI (GAI LAN) OR BOK CHOY (PAK CHOI) IS TRADITIONALLY USED, BUT YOU COULD USE REGULAR BROCCOLI.

350 g (12 oz) scallops, roe removed
2 tablespoons Shaoxing rice wine
1 tablespoon roasted sesame oil
1 teaspoon finely chopped ginger
½ spring onion (scallion), finely
    chopped
200 g (7 oz) Chinese broccoli
    (gai lan) or bok choy (pak choi)
80 ml (2½ fl oz/⅓ cup) chicken
    stock (see recipe on page 491)
½ teaspoon salt
¼ teaspoon sugar
¼ teaspoon freshly ground white
    pepper
1 teaspoon cornflour (cornstarch)
1 tablespoon oil
1 tablespoon finely shredded ginger
1 spring onion (scallion), finely
    shredded
1 garlic clove, very thinly sliced

SERVES 6

SLICE the small, hard white muscle off the side of each scallop and pull off any membrane. Rinse the scallops and drain. Holding a knife blade parallel to the cutting surface, slice each scallop in half horizontally. Place the scallops in a bowl with 1 tablespoon of the rice wine, ¼ teaspoon of the sesame oil and the chopped ginger and spring onion. Toss lightly, then leave to marinate for 20 minutes.

WASH the broccoli well. Discard any tough-looking stems and diagonally cut into 2 cm (¾ inch) pieces through the stem and the leaf. Blanch the broccoli in a pan of boiling water for 2 minutes, or until the stems and leaves are just tender, then refresh in cold water and dry thoroughly.

COMBINE the chicken stock, salt, sugar, white pepper, cornflour and the remaining rice wine and sesame oil.

HEAT a wok over high heat, add the oil and heat until very hot. Add the scallops and stir-fry for 30 seconds, then remove. Add the shredded ginger, shredded spring onion and the garlic and stir-fry for 10 seconds. Add the stock mixture and cook, stirring constantly, until the sauce thickens. Add the Chinese broccoli and scallops. Toss lightly to coat with the sauce.

Slice the white muscle off the side of each scallop – these will be hard and rubbery if left on and cooked. Stir-fry the scallops in the sauce for a few seconds, just to heat them through; if they overcook they can be tough.

FROM THAILAND

STEAMED FISH WITH PRESERVED PLUM

BUY AN APPROPRIATELY LARGE STEAMER FOR THIS RECIPE OR USE THE STEAMER RACK OF YOUR WOK. BOTH WILL WORK EQUALLY WELL. PRESERVED PLUMS ARE SOLD IN JARS IN ASIAN SUPERMARKETS AND, ONCE OPENED, WILL KEEP IN THE REFRIGERATOR FOR SOME TIME.

1 tablespoon light soy sauce
½ teaspoon sugar
1 large or 2 smaller pomfret, flounder, or turbot, (total weight about 1 kg/2 lb 4 oz)
50 g (2 oz) mushrooms, roughly sliced
2 small preserved plums, bruised
5 cm (2 inch) piece of ginger, cut into thin matchsticks
4 spring onions (scallions), sliced diagonally, for garnish
2 long red or green chillies, seeded and finely sliced, for garnish
a few coriander (cilantro) leaves, for garnish
a sprinkle of ground white pepper, for garnish

SERVES 4

IN a small bowl, mix the light soy sauce and sugar.

CLEAN and gut the fish, leaving the head/s on. Dry the fish thoroughly. Score the fish three or four times on both sides with a sharp knife. Place the fish on a deep plate slightly larger than the fish itself. Use a plate that will fit on the rack of a traditional bamboo steamer basket or on a steamer rack inside the wok.

SPRINKLE the mushrooms, preserved plums and ginger over the fish. Pour the light soy sauce mixture all over the fish.

FILL a wok or a steamer pan with water, cover and bring to a rolling boil over a high heat. Taking care not to burn your hands, set the rack or basket over the boiling water and put the plate with the fish on the rack. Reduce heat to a simmer. Cover and steam for 25–30 minutes (depending on the variety and size of the fish) or until the skewer will slide easily into the fish. Check and replenish the water every 10 minutes or so. Remove the fish from the steamer.

SERVE on the same plate. Sprinkle with spring onions, chillies, coriander leaves and pepper.

Fresh fish on display at Ranong fish market.

FROM JAPAN

SESAME TUNA STEAKS WITH NORI RICE

TUNA, SO TASTY WHEN SERVED AS SASHIMI OR AS A SUSHI TOPPING, IS ALSO VERY DELICIOUS COOKED. THESE STEAKS, COATED WITH CRUNCHY SESAME SEEDS, ARE SAUTEED ONLY UNTIL THE CRUST IS GOLDEN, BRINGING OUT THE NUTTY AROMA WHILE LEAVING THE TUNA RARE.

4 x 200 g (7 oz) tuna steaks
115 g (4 oz/¾ cup) sesame seeds
200 g (7 oz/1 cup) medium-grain rice
2½ tablespoons rice wine vinegar
1 tablespoon mirin
1 teaspoon sugar
¼ teaspoon salt
1 nori sheet, finely shredded
60 ml (2 fl oz/¼ cup) peanut oil

WASABI MAYONNAISE
125 g (4½ oz/½ cup) Japanese or whole-egg mayonnaise
2 teaspoons wasabi paste

pickled ginger, to serve, optional

SERVES 4

COAT the tuna steaks in the sesame seeds, pressing down to coat well. Refrigerate until needed.

WASH the rice until the water runs clear, then put in a saucepan with 500 ml (17 fl oz/2 cups) water. Bring to the boil, then reduce the heat to very low and cook, covered, for 10–12 minutes. Turn off the heat and leave, covered, for 5 minutes. While hot, pour on the combined rice wine vinegar, mirin, sugar and ¼ teaspoon salt. Stir with a fork to separate the grains, then fold in the shredded nori. Keep warm.

HEAT the oil in a large frying pan, add the tuna steaks and cook for 1–2 minutes on each side, or until the sesame seeds are crisp and golden. The tuna should still be a little pink in the middle. Drain on paper towels.

SPOON the rice into four lightly greased 125 ml (4 fl oz/½ cup) ramekins or cups, pressing down lightly, then invert onto each plate and remove the ramekins.

TO MAKE the wasabi mayonnaise, combine the Japanese mayonnaise and wasabi in a small bowl.

SERVE the tuna with the nori rice and with some wasabi mayonnaise on the side. Garnish with pickled ginger, if desired.

Spoon the nori rice into four lightly greased ramekins or cups.

Wasabi grows wild in and along clear mountain streams. This freshly grated knobbly root is used to add aroma and fire to dipping sauces, dressings, raw seafood and tofu.

SESAME TUNA STEAKS WITH NORI RICE

PRAWNS WITH GREEN MANGO

250 g (9 oz) tiger prawns (shrimp)

CURRY PASTE
1½ teaspoons chilli powder
1 teaspoon ground turmeric
½ teaspoon cumin seeds
½ teaspoon yellow mustard seeds
4 garlic cloves, roughly chopped
4 cm (1½ inch) piece of ginger,
   roughly chopped
1 red onion, roughly chopped

4 tablespoons oil
1 red onion, thinly sliced
1 green unripe mango, finely
   chopped

SERVES 4

PEEL and devein the prawns, leaving the tails intact.

TO MAKE the curry paste, put the chilli powder, turmeric, cumin, mustard, garlic, ginger and chopped red onion in a blender, food processor or pestle and mortar and process to form a paste. If necessary, add a little water.

HEAT the oil in a karhai or heavy-based frying pan and fry the sliced onion. When it starts to brown, add the curry paste and fry until aromatic.

ADD the prawns and 185 ml (6 fl oz/¾ cup) water to the pan, cover and simmer for about 3–4 minutes, until the prawns are cooked and start to curl up. Add the mango and cook for another minute or two to thicken the curry. Season with salt.

Green unripe mangoes, often used in Indian cookery, have a firm flesh and are used to give a tart flavour to recipes.

CREAMY PRAWN CURRY

500 g (1 lb 2 oz) tiger prawns
   (shrimp)
1½ tablespoons lemon juice
3 tablespoons oil
½ onion, finely chopped
½ teaspoon ground turmeric
5 cm (2 inch) cinnamon stick
4 cloves
7 cardamom pods
5 Indian bay leaves (cassia leaves)
2 cm (¾ inch) piece of ginger,
   grated
3 garlic cloves, chopped
1 teaspoon chilli powder
50 g (5½ fl oz/1¾ oz) creamed
   coconut mixed with 170 ml
   (5½ fl oz/⅔ cup) water, or 170 ml
   (⅔ cup) coconut milk (see recipe
   on page 468)

SERVES 4

PEEL and devein the prawns, leaving the tails intact. Put them in a bowl, add the lemon juice, then toss together and leave them for 5 minutes. Rinse the prawns under running cold water and pat dry with paper towels.

HEAT the oil in a karhai or heavy-based frying pan and fry the onion until lightly browned. Add the turmeric, cinnamon, cloves, cardamom, bay leaves, ginger and garlic, and fry for 1 minute. Add chilli powder, creamed coconut or coconut milk, and salt, to taste, and slowly bring to the boil. Reduce the heat and simmer for 2 minutes.

ADD the prawns to the pan, return to the boil, then reduce the heat and simmer for 5 minutes, or until the prawns are cooked through and the sauce is thick.

CREAMY PRAWN CURRY

CRACKED CRAB WITH CURRY POWDER

THIS CRAB RECIPE IS ONE OF THE FEW THAI DISHES TO USE CURRY POWDER AS A MAIN FLAVOURING.

BOUGHT CURRY POWDER (LOOK FOR A THAI BRAND) IS USUALLY VERY GOOD AND THIS IS WHAT THAI

COOKS WOULD USE BUT THERE IS A RECIPE ON PAGE 479 IF YOU NEED TO MAKE YOUR OWN.

1 live crab, 500 g (1 lb 2 oz)
170 ml (5½ fl oz/⅔ cup) coconut
  milk (see recipe on page 468)
1 tablespoon light soy sauce
½ tablespoon oyster sauce
2 teaspoons Thai curry powder
  (see recipe on page 479)
  or bought Thai curry powder
¼ teaspoon sugar
2 tablespoons vegetable oil
3–4 garlic cloves, finely chopped
1 small onion, cut into 3 wedges
2 spring onions (scallions),
  finely sliced
½ long red chilli, seeded and
  finely sliced, for garnish
a few coriander (cilantro) leaves,
  for garnish

SERVES 4

PUT the crab in the freezer for 1 hour. Leaving the legs attached, cut the crab in half through the centre of the shell from head to rear. Cut in half again from left to right (quartering the crab), with legs attached to each quarter. Twist off and remove upper shell pieces. Discard the stomach sac and the soft gill tissue. Using crackers or the back of a heavy knife, crack the crab claws to make them easier to eat. If the claws are too big, cut them in half.

MIX the coconut milk, light soy sauce, oyster sauce, curry powder and sugar in a bowl.

HEAT the oil in a wok or frying pan. Stir-fry the garlic over a medium heat until light brown. Add the crab and stir-fry for about 4–5 minutes. Add the coconut mixture and onion and continue stir-frying for another 5–7 minutes or until the crabmeat is cooked through and the sauce is reduced and very thick. Add the spring onions. Taste, then adjust the seasoning if necessary.

SPOON onto a serving plate and sprinkle with sliced chilli and coriander leaves.

Cut the crab into quarters, leaving the legs attached. Add the coconut milk mixture and onion after 5 minutes.

Snack seller in Bangkok.

Ready-cut banana leaves on sale in Chennai (Madras) market.

CURRIED SQUID

FISH IN BANANA LEAF

4 x 120 g (4 oz) pieces hilsa (elish) or blue-eye fillet, skinned
1½ tablespoons lemon juice
½ teaspoon salt

PASTE
3 tablespoons brown mustard seeds
5 cm (2 inch) piece of ginger, chopped
4 green chillies, chopped
3 teaspoons mustard oil
¼ teaspoon ground turmeric
1 teaspoon chilli powder

4 pieces young banana leaf, or foil, cut into neat pieces big enough to wrap the fish

SERVES 4

WASH the fish and pat dry with paper towels. Mix the lemon juice and salt and rub into the fish.

GRIND the mustard seeds to a fine powder in a spice grinder or pestle and mortar. Put the mustard, ginger, chilli, mustard oil, turmeric and chilli powder in a food processor or pestle and mortar and grind to a smooth paste.

SOFTEN the banana leaves by dipping them in very hot water. Wipe dry the pieces as they become pliant.

SMEAR the fish with the paste to thoroughly coat. Grease the leaves, or foil, with oil. Place a piece of fish and some marinade in the centre of each and loosely fold into a parcel. Tie with kitchen string and put in a steamer over a pan of simmering water. Cover and steam for 10–12 minutes. Open a parcel to check that the fish flakes easily with a fork and is cooked.

SERVE still in the banana leaves.

CURRIED SQUID

1 kg (2 lb 4 oz) fresh squid
1 teaspoon cumin seeds
1 teaspoon coriander seeds
1 teaspoon chilli powder
½ teaspoon ground turmeric
2 tablespoons oil
1 onion, finely chopped
10 curry leaves
½ teaspoon fenugreek seeds
4 garlic cloves, crushed
7 cm (2¾ inch) piece of ginger, grated
4 tablespoons coconut cream (see recipe on page 468)
3 tablespoons lime juice

SERVES 4

PULL squid heads and tentacles out of the bodies, along with any innards, and discard. Peel the skins. Rinse the bodies, pulling out the clear quills, then cut the bodies into 2.5 cm (1 inch) rings.

PLACE a small frying pan over low heat. Dry-roast the cumin until aromatic. Remove, then dry-roast the coriander. Grind both to a fine powder with the chilli and turmeric, using a spice grinder or pestle and mortar. Mix spices with squid.

HEAT the oil in a karhai or heavy-based frying pan and fry the onion until lightly browned. Add the curry leaves, fenugreek, garlic, ginger and coconut cream. Bring slowly to the boil. Add squid, then stir well. Simmer for 2–3 minutes, or until cooked and tender. Stir in lime juice, season and serve.

FROM THAILAND

DEEP-FRIED FISH WITH SWEET AND SOUR SAUCE

WHEN SERVING WHOLE FISH, LIFT OFF PORTIONS FROM THE TOP FILLETS AND THEN REMOVE THE BONES IN ONE PIECE SO YOU CAN ACCESS THE FILLETS UNDERNEATH. THE FLAVOUR OF SWEET AND SOUR SAUCE WORKS EXTREMELY WELL WITH ALL TYPES OF FISH.

400 g (14 oz) sea bream, red
    snapper or grey mullet
3½ tablespoons plain (all-purpose)
    flour
pinch of ground white pepper
vegetable oil, for deep-frying
225 g (8 oz) tin pineapple slices in
    juice, each slice cut into 4 pieces
    (reserve the juice)
1½ tablespoons plum sauce
    or ketchup
2½ teaspoons fish sauce
1 tablespoon sugar
1½ tablespoons vegetable oil
3–4 garlic cloves, finely chopped
1 medium onion, cut into 8 slices
½ red capsicum (pepper), cut into
    bite-sized pieces
1 small Lebanese cucumber (skin
    left on), cut into bite-sized pieces
1 medium tomato, cut into
    8 wedges, or 4 baby tomatoes
a few coriander (cilantro) leaves,
    for garnish

SERVES 2

CLEAN and gut fish, leaving the head on. Dry fish thoroughly and score it three or four times on both sides with a sharp knife. Rub the fish inside and out with a pinch of salt. Put 3 tablespoons of the flour and the pepper on a plate and press the fish lightly into it until coated with flour from head to tail. Shake off any excess.

HEAT 10 cm (4 inches) oil in a large wok or pan big enough to deep-fry the whole fish. Drop a small cube of bread into the oil and if it sizzles straight away, the oil is ready. Lower the heat to medium and gently slide the fish into the oil. Be careful as the hot oil may splash. Deep-fry the fish on just one side (but make sure the oil covers the whole fish) for about 15–20 minutes or until the fish is cooked and light brown (if you cook the fish until it is very brown, the fish will be too dry). Drain, then put on paper towels before transferring to a warm plate. Keep warm.

MEANWHILE, mix all the pineapple juice (about 6 tablespoons) with the remaining flour, plum sauce or ketchup, fish sauce and sugar in a small bowl until smooth.

REMOVE the oil from the wok or pan and heat 1½ tablespoons clean oil in the same wok or pan. Stir-fry the garlic over a medium heat for 1 minute or until light brown. Add the onion and capsicum and stir-fry for 1–2 minutes. Add the pineapple, cucumber, tomato and pineapple juice mixture. Stir together for another minute. Taste, then adjust the seasoning if necessary. Pour all over the warm fish and garnish with a few coriander leaves.

Fishing in Phang-nga.

The fish markets at Sassoon Dock, Mumbai (Bombay).

Pull off the large front claws, pull the body open and remove the gills. Crack the larger claws with the handle of a cleaver.

FROM INDIA

CHILLI CRAB

THIS RECIPE COMBINES SWEET-TASTING CRABMEAT WITH AROMATIC SPICES AND THE HEAT FROM CHILLIES. PROVIDE YOUR GUESTS WITH A CRAB CRACKER, PICKS, FINGER BOWLS AND PIECES OF ROTI TO MOP UP THE WONDERFUL JUICES. YOU CAN USE ANY KIND OF CRAB FOR THIS RECIPE.

4 x 250 g (9 oz) small live crabs
  or 2 x 500 g (1 lb 2 oz) live crabs

PASTE
125 ml (4 fl oz/½ cup) oil
2 garlic cloves, crushed
4 cm (1½ inch) piece of ginger,
  grated
½ teaspoon ground cumin
½ teaspoon ground coriander
¼ teaspoon ground turmeric
¼ teaspoon cayenne pepper
1 tablespoon tamarind purée
  (see recipe on page 467)
1 teaspoon sugar
2 small red chillies, finely chopped

2 tablespoons chopped coriander
  (cilantro) leaves, for garnish

SERVES 4

PUT the crabs in the freezer for 2 hours to immobilise them. Using a large, heavy-bladed knife or cleaver, cut off the large front claws from each crab, then twist off the remaining claws. Turn each body over and pull off each apron piece, then pull out the spongy grey gills and discard them. Cut each crab body in half (quarters if you are using the large crabs). Crack the large front claws with the handle of a cleaver or a rolling pin. Rinse off any chips of shell under cold running water and pat dry with paper towels.

MIX half the oil with the garlic, ginger, cumin, coriander, turmeric, cayenne pepper, tamarind, sugar, chilli and a generous pinch of salt until they form a paste. Heat the remaining oil in a karhai or large, heavy-based, deep frying pan over medium heat. Add the spice paste and stir for 30 seconds, or until aromatic.

ADD the crab portions to the pan and cook, stirring for 2 minutes, making sure the spice mix gets rubbed into the cut edges of the crab. Add 60 ml (2 fl oz/¼ cup) water, cover and steam the crabs, tossing them a couple of times during cooking, for another 5–6 minutes, or until cooked through. The crabs will turn pink or red when they are ready and the flesh will become opaque (make sure the large front claws are well cooked). Drizzle a little of the liquid from the pan over the crabs, then scatter with the coriander leaves and serve.

FROM THAILAND

SNAPPER WITH GREEN BANANA AND MANGO

GREEN BANANA IS VERY STARCHY, MUCH MORE LIKE A VEGETABLE THAN A FRUIT. HERE IT IS USED IN A YELLOW CURRY ALONGSIDE ANOTHER FRUIT, GREEN MANGO, WHICH ACTS AS A SOURING AGENT. RAW VEGETABLES ARE OFTEN SERVED AS AN ACCOMPANIMENT TO COUNTERACT THE CHILLI HEAT.

1 teaspoon salt

1 teaspoon ground turmeric

1 small green banana or plantain, thinly sliced

60 ml (2 fl oz/¼ cup) coconut cream (see recipe on page 468)

2 tablespoons yellow curry paste (see recipe on page 471) or bought paste

1 tablespoon fish sauce

1 teaspoon palm sugar (jaggery)

400 g (14 oz) snapper or other white fish fillets, cut into large cubes

315 ml (10¾ fl oz/1¼ cups) coconut milk (see recipe on page 468)

1 small green mango, cut into thin slices

1 large green chilli, finely sliced

12 Thai sweet basil leaves

SERVES 4

BRING a small saucepan of water to the boil. Add the salt, turmeric and banana slices and simmer for 10 minutes, then drain.

PUT the coconut cream in a wok or saucepan and simmer over a medium heat for about 5 minutes, or until the cream separates and a layer of oil forms on the surface. Stir the cream if it starts to brown around the edges. Add the curry paste, stir well to combine and cook until fragrant. Add the fish sauce and sugar and cook for another 2 minutes or until the mixture begins to darken.

ADD the fish pieces and stir well to coat the fish in the curry mixture. Slowly add the coconut milk until it has all been incorporated.

ADD the banana, mango, green chilli and most of the basil leaves to the pan and gently stir to combine all the ingredients, cooking for a minute or two.

GARNISH with the remaining basil.

The fruit is added towards the end of cooking.

Green mangoes.

A market stall in Sichuan.

Scrub off any barnacles from the mussels, then remove beards (byssus) by tugging them firmly.

FROM CHINA

STEAMED MUSSELS WITH BLACK BEAN SAUCE

1 kg (2 lb 4 oz) mussels
1 tablespoon oil
1 garlic clove, finely chopped
½ teaspoon finely chopped ginger
2 spring onions (scallions), finely
   chopped
1 red chilli, chopped
1 tablespoon light soy sauce
1 tablespoon Shaoxing rice wine
1 tablespoon salted, fermented
   black beans, rinsed and mashed
2 tablespoons chicken and meat
   stock (see recipe on page 491)
few drops of roasted sesame oil

SERVES 4

SCRUB the mussels with a stiff brush, remove any beards, and throw away any that do not close when tapped on the work surface.

PLACE the mussels in a large dish in a steamer. Steam over simmering water in a covered wok for 4 minutes, discarding any that do not open after this time.

MEANWHILE, heat the oil in a small saucepan. Add the garlic, ginger, spring onion and chilli and cook, stirring, for 30 seconds. Add the remaining ingredients, and blend well. Bring to the boil, then reduce the heat and simmer for 1 minute.

TO SERVE, remove and discard the top shell of each mussel, pour 2 teaspoons of sauce into each mussel and serve on the shell.

CLAMS IN YELLOW BEAN SAUCE

CLAMS IN YELLOW BEAN SAUCE

1.5 kg (3 lb 5 oz) hard-shelled
   clams (vongole)
1 tablespoon oil
2 garlic cloves, crushed
1 tablespoon grated ginger
2 tablespoons yellow bean sauce
125 ml (4 fl oz/½ cup) chicken
   stock (see recipe on page 491)
1 spring onion (scallion), sliced,
   for garnish

SERVES 4

WASH the clams in several changes of cold water, leaving them for a few minutes each time to remove any grit. Scrub the clams well, discarding any that remain open. Drain well.

HEAT a wok over high heat, add the oil and heat until very hot. Stir-fry the garlic and ginger for 30 seconds, then add the bean sauce and clams and toss together. Add stock. Stir for 3 minutes until the clams have opened, discarding any that do not open after this time. Season with salt and white pepper.

TRANSFER the clams to a plate and sprinkle with spring onion.

FROM JAPAN

CRUMBED SKEWERS

SKEWERED FOODS ARE CASUAL AND FUN TO EAT, AND THESE PORTIONS OF MEAT, SEAFOOD AND VEGETABLES, CRUMBED AND DEEP-FRIED, OFFER A GREAT TWIST ON CLASSIC YAKITORI. LIFT THE FLAVOUR ANOTHER NOTCH WITH FRUITY TONKATSU SAUCE AND SPICY JAPANESE MUSTARD.

SKEWERS

8 small scallops, roe removed

4 raw prawns (shrimp), peeled, deveined, tails intact

225 g (8 oz) pork fillet, cut into 3 x 2 cm (1¼ x ¾ inch) pieces about 1 cm (½ inch) thick

2 spring onions (scallions), white part only, cut into short lengths

4 small jap (kent) pumpkins, unpeeled, in slices 5 mm (¼ inch) thick

225 g (8 oz) beef fillet, cut into 3 x 2 cm (1¼ x ¾ inch) pieces about 1 cm (½ inch) thick

175 g (6 oz) firm fish fillets (such as snapper, salmon, tuna or swordfish) cut into 3 x 2 cm (1¼ x ¾ inch) pieces

pinch ground white pepper

plain (all-purpose) flour, for dusting

1 egg, lightly beaten

panko (Japanese breadcrumbs), for coating

vegetable oil, for deep-frying

60 ml (2 fl oz/¼ cup) sesame oil, optional

tonkatsu sauce ready-made, to serve

lemon wedges, to serve

Japanese mustard, to serve

English cabbage leaves, cut into 3 x 2 cm (1¼ x ¾ inch) pieces, to serve

SERVES 4

SOAK 24 bamboo skewers in water for 1 hour to prevent them burning.

USE four skewers for each group of ingredients. Use the following list as a guide to what should go on each skewer: two scallops and one prawn threaded lengthways so the tail is at the top of the skewer; alternating pieces of pork (three pieces) and spring onion (two pieces); one pumpkin slice and three pieces of beef; three pieces of fish.

LIGHTLY season each skewer with salt and white pepper, then coat with the flour, shaking off any excess. Dip into the beaten egg, allowing any excess to drip off, then press into the crumbs to coat well. Refrigerate until needed.

FILL a deep-fat fryer or large saucepan half-full with the vegetable oil and add the sesame oil, if using. Heat to 170°C (325°F), or until a cube of bread dropped into the oil browns in 20 seconds. Cook a few skewers at a time, lowering them into the oil and cooking until golden and crisp. Cooking time will vary with each ingredient but should take 1–3 minutes. Drain on paper towels.

SERVE with tonkatsu sauce, lemon wedges, mustard and a small bowl of the cabbage. For a more substantial meal, serve with rice, miso soup and pickles.

Press skewered food into the crumbs to coat thoroughly.

Score the fish, then prepare it
and wrap in the banana leaves.

GRILLED FISH WITH GARLIC AND CORIANDER

BANANA LEAVES ARE USED IN THIS RECIPE TO PROTECT THE FISH FROM DIRECT HEAT AS WELL AS TO

ADD A SUBTLE EXTRA FLAVOUR. THE LEAVES WILL CHAR AS THEY COOK. YOU WILL FIND BANANA

LEAVES IN ASIAN SUPERMARKETS, OFTEN IN THE FREEZER CABINETS.

4 red tilapa, grey/red mullet, or
    mackerel (about 300 g/
    10 oz each)

PASTE
8–10 garlic cloves, roughly chopped
6 coriander (cilantro) roots, chopped
1 teaspoon ground white pepper
1 teaspoon salt
1 tablespoon vegetable oil

8 pieces of banana leaf
chilli sauce of your choice, to serve

SERVES 4

CLEAN and gut the fish, leaving the heads on.
Dry the fish thoroughly. Score each fish three or
four times on both sides with a sharp knife.

USING a pestle and mortar or a small blender,
pound or blend the garlic, coriander roots,
ground pepper, salt and oil into a paste. Rub the
garlic paste inside the cavities and all over each
fish. Cover and marinate in the refrigerator for at
least 30 minutes.

TO soften the banana leaves and prevent
them from splitting, put them in a hot oven for
10 to 20 seconds, or blanch them briefly. Using
two pieces of banana leaf, each with the grain
running at right angles to the other, wrap each fish
like a parcel. Pin the ends of the banana leaves
together with toothpicks.

HEAT a grill (broiler) or barbecue to medium.
Barbecue or grill (broil) the fish for about
15 minutes on each side or until the fish is light
brown and cooked. To make the fish easier to lift
and turn during cooking, you can place the fish
in a fish-shaped griddle that opens out like tongs.
Transfer the fish to a serving plate.

SERVE with a chilli sauce.

FROM INDIA

FISH TIKKA

TIKKA IS THE HINDI WORD FOR CHUNK. HERE, FISH CHUNKS ARE MARINATED IN A BLEND OF SPICES AND YOGHURT AND COOKED. IN INDIA, A TANDOOR, A CHARCOAL-FIRED CLAY OVEN, WOULD BE USED. HOWEVER, BARBECUING IS A GOOD SUBSTITUTE AS IT ALSO IMPARTS A SMOKY FLAVOUR.

MARINADE
500 ml (17 fl oz/2 cups) thick plain
   yoghurt (see recipe on page 467)
½ onion, finely chopped
2 cm (¾ inch) piece of ginger,
   grated
4 garlic cloves, crushed
1 teaspoon ground coriander
2 tablespoons lemon juice
1½ tablespoons garam masala
   (see recipe on page 464)
1 teaspoon paprika
1 teaspoon chilli powder
2 tablespoons tomato paste (purée)
1 teaspoon salt

500 g (1 lb 2 oz) skinless firm white
   fish such as halibut, monkfish or
   blue-eye
2 onions, each cut into 8 chunks
2 small green or red capsicums
   (peppers), each cut into 8 chunks
50 g (1¾ oz) cucumber, peeled
   and diced
1 tablespoon chopped coriander
   (cilantro)
lemon wedges, to serve

SERVES 8

TO MAKE the marinade, mix half the yoghurt with all the other marinade ingredients in a shallow dish that is long enough and deep enough to take the prepared skewers. You will need eight metal skewers.

CUT the fish into about 24–32 bite-sized chunks. On each metal skewer, thread three or four pieces of fish and chunks of onion and capsicum, alternating them as you go. Put the skewers in the marinade and turn them so that all the fish and vegetables are well coated. Cover and marinate in the fridge for at least 1 hour, or until you are ready to cook.

PREHEAT the barbecue or grill (broiler). Lift the skewers out of the marinade. Cook on the barbecue, or under a grill on a wire rack set above a baking tray, for 5–6 minutes, turning once, or until the fish is cooked and firm and both the fish and the vegetables are slightly charred.

MEANWHILE, stir the cucumber and coriander into the other half of the yoghurt.

SERVE the fish with the yoghurt and lemon wedges.

Fish is sold fresh off the boats in the early hours of the morning all along India's coast.

A fish stall at Fort Kochi (Cochin), Kerala.

FISH TIKKA

SHANGHAI-STYLE FIVE-WILLOW FISH

THIS IS A VARIATION ON THE CLASSIC SWEET-AND-SOUR FISH. 'FIVE-WILLOW' REFERS TO THE FIVE SHREDDED VEGETABLES USED FOR THE SAUCE, WHILE THE AROMATICS TRADITIONALLY REMOVED ANY 'FISHY' TASTE FROM THE FRESHWATER FISH.

3–4 dried Chinese mushrooms
750 g–1 kg (1 lb 10 oz–2 lb 4 oz) whole fish, such as carp, bream, grouper or sea bass
1 teaspoon salt
oil for deep-frying
2 tablespoons oil, extra
1 tablespoon shredded ginger
2 spring onions (scallions), shredded
½ small carrot, shredded
½ small green capsicum (pepper), shredded
½ celery stalk, shredded
2 red chillies, seeded and finely shredded
2 tablespoons light soy sauce
3 tablespoons sugar
3 tablespoons Chinese black rice vinegar
1 tablespoon Shaoxing rice wine
125 ml (4 fl oz/½ cup) chicken and meat stock (see recipe on page 491)
1 tablespoon cornflour (cornstarch)
½ teaspoon roasted sesame oil

SERVES 4

SOAK the dried mushrooms in boiling water for 30 minutes. Drain and squeeze out excess water. Remove and discard stems. Finely shred the caps.

IF YOU do manage to buy a swimming (live) fish, then ask the fishmonger to gut it through the gills. This is harder than gutting through the stomach, but leaves the fish looking whole. If you are gutting the fish yourself, make a cut from the throat to the tail and pull out the guts through the stomach. Remove any scales with a fish scaler or the back of a knife. Check that the gills have been cut out, then rinse the fish under cold, running water and drain thoroughly in a colander.

DIAGONALLY score both sides of the fish, cutting through as far as the bone at intervals of 2 cm (¾ inch). Rub the salt all over the inside and outside of the fish and into the slits.

FILL a wok one-quarter full of oil. Heat the oil to 190°C (375°F), or until a piece of bread fries golden brown in 10 seconds when dropped in the oil. Holding the fish by its tail, gently and carefully lower it into the oil. Cook the fish for 3–4 minutes on each side, or until the fish flakes when the skin is pressed firmly or the dorsal fin pulls out easily. Remove from the wok and drain on paper towels, then place on a dish and keep warm in a low oven. Pour off the oil and wipe out the wok.

REHEAT the wok over high heat, add the extra oil and heat until very hot. Stir-fry the mushrooms, ginger, spring onion, carrot, green capsicum, celery and chilli for 1½ minutes. Add the soy sauce, sugar, rice vinegar, rice wine and stock, and bring to the boil. Combine the cornflour with enough water to make a paste, add to the sauce and simmer until thickened. Add the sesame oil, blend well and spoon over the fish.

The Oriental Pearl Tower in Pudong, Shanghai.

POULTRY

FROM JAPAN

SIMMERED CHICKEN MEATBALLS

CLASSIC JAPANESE SEASONING INGREDIENTS SUCH AS SAKE, SOY SAUCE AND MIRIN, ALONG WITH THE AROMATIC FLAVOURS OF FRESH GINGER AND SESAME OIL INFUSE THESE SIMMERED CHICKEN MEATBALLS. THE MEATBALLS ARE SERVED IN A SAUCE, WHICH HAS BEEN THICKENED WITH KUZU.

300 g (10½ oz) boneless, skinless
  chicken thighs
3 spring onions (scallions),
  2 chopped, 1 thinly sliced
1 teaspoon finely grated, fresh
  ginger and its juice
1 egg
1 teaspoon sake
1 tablespoon shoyu (Japanese soy
  sauce)
1 teaspoon mirin
20 g (¾ oz/⅓ cup) panko
  (Japanese breadcrumbs)
1 teaspoon sesame oil
1 tablespoon vegetable oil

SAUCE
500 ml (17 fl oz/2 cups) dashi II
  (see recipe on page 483)
80 ml (2½ fl oz/⅓ cup) mirin
60 ml (2 fl oz/¼ cup) sake
4 cm (1½ inch) length konbu (kelp),
  wiped with damp cloth, and cut
  into 1 cm (½ inch) strips
1½ tablespoons shoyu (Japanese
  soy sauce)
1 teaspoon kuzu starch or arrowroot

SERVES 4

PUT the chicken in a food processor and process until roughly minced (ground). Add the chopped spring onion, ginger and ginger juice, egg, sake, shoyu and mirin and process until finely chopped. Transfer to a bowl and add the panko, mixing well with your hands to combine well. Cover and refrigerate for 1 hour. Roll into balls about 3 cm (1 inch) in diameter.

HEAT the oils in a non-stick frying pan over medium heat and add the balls in batches. Cook for 5 minutes, or until golden all over. Remove the pan from the heat.

COMBINE all the sauce ingredients, except the kuzu, in a saucepan and bring to the boil over high heat. Remove the konbu and discard. Add the chicken balls and return sauce to the boil, then reduce to a simmer and cook for 5 minutes, or until cooked through. Remove the balls with a slotted spoon and set aside.

MIX the kuzu with a little of the hot liquid in a small bowl to form a loose paste, then stir into the pan – stir over high heat until the sauce boils and thickens to a light coating consistency.

PLACE the chicken balls in a serving bowl and pour the sauce over. Garnish with the thinly sliced spring onion.

Kuzu is a high-quality thickening starch made from the kudzu or kuzu vine. It is added to sauces to help them glaze well.

Dried jujubes, or Chinese dates, are thought to bring good luck because of their red colour.

YUNNAN POT CHICKEN

A YUNNAN POT IS AN EARTHENWARE SOUP POT WITH A CHIMNEY. THE POT COOKS FOOD BY 'CLOSED STEAMING', WHICH GIVES A CLEARER, MORE INTENSELY FLAVOURED STOCK THAN ORDINARY STEAMING. INSTEAD OF A YUNNAN POT, YOU CAN USE A CLAY POT OR CASSEROLE INSIDE A STEAMER.

25 jujubes (dried Chinese dates)
1.5 kg (3 lb 5 oz) chicken
6 wafer-thin slices dang gui (dried angelica)
6 slices ginger, smashed with the flat side of a cleaver
6 spring onions (scallions), ends trimmed, smashed with the flat side of a cleaver
60 ml (2 fl oz/¼ cup) Shaoxing rice wine
½ teaspoon salt

SERVES 6

SOAK the jujubes in hot water for 20 minutes, then drain and remove the stones.

RINSE chicken, drain, and remove any fat from the cavity opening and around the neck. Cut off and discard the parson's nose. Using a cleaver, cut the chicken through the bones into square 4 cm (1½ inch) pieces. Blanch the chicken pieces in a pan of boiling water for 1 minute, then refresh in cold water and drain thoroughly.

ARRANGE the chicken pieces, jujubes, dang gui, ginger and spring onions in a clay pot or casserole about 24 cm (9½ inches) in diameter. Pour rice wine and 1 litre (35 fl oz/4 cups) boiling water over the top and add the salt. Tightly cover the clay pot or casserole, adding a layer of wet muslin between the pot and lid to form a good seal, if necessary, and place it in a steamer.

STEAM over simmering water in a covered wok for about 2 hours, replenishing with boiling water during cooking.

REMOVE the pot from the steamer and skim any fat from the surface of the liquid. Discard dang gui, ginger and spring onions. Season, if necessary.

SERVE directly from the pot.

Chopping ginger outside a shop in Chengdu.

FROM THAILAND

GREEN CURRY WITH CHICKEN

THIS FAMILIAR CLASSIC, WHICH SHOULD NEVER BE EXTREMELY HOT, HAS AS ITS BASE A PASTE OF CHILLIES, GALANGAL AND LEMONGRASS. BITTER VEGETABLES SUCH AS THAI EGGPLANT OFFSET THE SWEETNESS OF THE COCONUT CREAM. TENDER STEAK CAN BE USED INSTEAD OF CHICKEN.

60 ml (2 fl oz/¼ cup) coconut
  cream (see recipe on page 468)
2 tablespoons green curry paste
350 g (12 oz) boneless, skinless
  chicken thighs, sliced
440 ml (15 fl oz/1¾ cups) coconut
  milk
2½ tablespoons fish sauce
1 tablespoon palm sugar (jaggery)
350 g (12 oz) mixed Thai eggplants
  (aubergines), cut into quarters,
  and pea eggplants (aubergines)
50 g (2 oz) galangal, sliced into thin
  matchsticks
7 makrut (kaffir lime) leaves,
  torn in half
a handful of Thai sweet basil leaves,
  for garnish
1 long red chilli, seeded and finely
  sliced, for garnish

SERVES 4

PUT the coconut cream in a wok or saucepan and simmer over a medium heat for about 5 minutes, or until the cream separates and a layer of oil forms on the surface. Stir the cream if it starts to brown around the edges. Add the curry paste, stir well to combine and cook until fragrant.

ADD the chicken and stir for a few minutes. Add nearly all of the coconut milk, the fish sauce and palm sugar and simmer over a medium heat for another 5 minutes.

ADD eggplants and cook, stirring occasionally, for about 5 minutes or until the eggplants are cooked. Add the galangal and makrut leaves. Taste, then adjust the seasoning if necessary.

SPOON into a serving bowl and sprinkle with the last bit of coconut milk, as well as the basil leaves and chilli slices.

Various types of eggplant are used in Thailand and the bitter taste is very popular. They don't take long to cook.

KASHMIRI CHICKEN

THIS CHICKEN DISH, COMBINING NUTS AND SAFFRON, IS DELICATELY FLAVOURED WITH A CREAMY SAUCE. TO MAKE THE SPICES MORE AROMATIC, IT IS BEST TO DRY-ROAST THEM AS SUGGESTED IN THE RECIPE, RATHER THAN USE READY-GROUND ONES.

1.5 kg (3 lb 5 oz) chicken or
   chicken pieces
6 cardamom pods
½ teaspoon coriander seeds
½ teaspoon cumin seeds
2 cm (¾ inch) cinnamon stick
8 peppercorns
6 cloves
100 g (⅔ cup) blanched almonds
75 g (½ cup) shelled pistachios
2 tablespoons ghee or oil
1 onion, finely chopped
4 garlic cloves, finely chopped
5 cm (2 inch) piece of ginger,
   finely chopped
125 ml (½ cup) chicken stock
250 ml (1 cup) thick plain yoghurt
   (page 280)
½ teaspoon saffron threads

SERVES 4

IF USING a whole chicken, cut it into eight pieces by removing both legs and cutting between the joint of the drumstick and thigh. Cut down either side of the backbone and remove the backbone. Turn the chicken over and cut through the cartilage down the centre of the breastbone. Remove the skin from the chicken and cut the flesh off the bones. Cut the chicken into bite-sized pieces. (You can reserve the carcass for making stock if you wish.)

REMOVE the seeds from the cardamom pods. Place a small frying pan over low heat and dry-roast the coriander seeds until aromatic. Remove and dry-roast the cumin seeds, then the piece of cinnamon stick. Grind the cardamom seeds, roasted spices, peppercorns and cloves to a fine powder using a spice grinder or pestle and mortar. Finely chop the almonds and pistachios in a food processor or spice grinder, or with a knife.

HEAT the ghee or oil in a karhai or casserole over low heat and fry the onion until golden brown. Add the garlic, ginger and chicken and fry rapidly for about 5 minutes. Add the ground spices and the chicken stock and simmer, covered tightly for 30 minutes.

STIR the ground nuts into the yoghurt. Mix the saffron with 1 teaspoon of hot water. Add the yoghurt and the saffron to the pan and bring to the boil. Simmer, uncovered, for 10 minutes. Season with salt, to taste.

Saffron from Kashmir is considered to be of a very high quality and is sold in small boxes.

FROM JAPAN

DEEP-FRIED CHICKEN WITH SEAWEED

MARINATED NUGGETS OF CHICKEN ARE TREATED TO AN UNCOMMON NORI COATING AND THEN DEEP-FRIED TO A CRISP GOLDEN BROWN. SET ATOP A BOWL OF RICE, THIS GINGERY CHICKEN IS PERFECT ACCOMPANIED BY A REFRESHING SALAD OR VEGETABLE DISH.

400 g (14 oz) boneless, skinless
    chicken breasts
60 ml (2 fl oz/¼ cup) shoyu
    (Japanese soy sauce)
60 ml (2 fl oz/¼ cup) mirin
4 cm (1½ inch) piece fresh ginger,
    very finely grated
1 nori sheet, finely chopped or
    crumbled into very small pieces
40 g (1½ oz/⅓ cup) cornflour
    (cornstarch)
vegetable oil, for deep-frying
steamed rice, to serve
pickled ginger, to serve
cucumber, thinly sliced, to serve

SERVES 4

CAREFULLY trim any sinew from the chicken. Cut the chicken into bite-sized pieces and discard any thin ends so that the pieces will be even in size. Place the chicken pieces in a bowl.

COMBINE the shoyu, mirin and ginger in a small bowl and pour the mixture over the chicken. Toss until the chicken pieces are evenly coated with the marinade. Set aside for 15 minutes, then drain off any excess marinade.

COMBINE nori and cornflour. With your fingertips, lightly coat each piece of chicken with the mixture.

FILL a deep-fat fryer or large saucepan one-third full of oil. Heat to 180°C (350°F), or until a cube of bread dropped into the oil browns in 15 seconds. Add the chicken, six to seven pieces at a time, and fry until golden, turning regularly. Drain on paper towels.

SERVE with steamed rice, pickled ginger and sliced cucumber.

A sign proclaims 'Thai-style chicken feet' for sale at an outdoor stall in Chengdu.

THREE-CUP CHICKEN

450 g (1 lb) boneless, skinless
    chicken thighs
1 tablespoon cornflour (cornstarch)
1 tablespoon oil
2 spring onions (scallions), chopped
4 small pieces ginger
3 tablespoons Shaoxing rice wine
3 tablespoons light soy sauce
125 ml (4 fl oz/½ cup) chicken
    and meat stock (see recipe on
    page 491)
½ teaspoon roasted sesame oil

SERVES 4

CUT the chicken into 2 cm (¾ inch) cubes.

COMBINE the cornflour with water to make a paste. Toss the chicken cubes in the paste to coat.

HEAT the oil in a small clay pot or casserole over a medium heat, lightly brown the chicken with the spring onion and ginger, then add the rice wine, soy and stock. Bring to the boil, then reduce the heat and simmer, covered, for 20–25 minutes. There should be a little liquid left. If there is too much, boil it off.

ADD the sesame oil and serve the chicken hot from the pot.

DRUNKEN CHICKEN

1.5 kg (3 lb 5 oz) chicken
150 ml (5 fl oz) Shaoxing rice wine
3 tablespoons Chinese spirit
    (Mou Tai) or brandy
3 slices ginger
3 spring onions (scallions), cut into
    short lengths
2 teaspoons salt
¼ teaspoon freshly ground
    black pepper
coriander (cilantro) leaves,
    for garnish

SERVES 4

RINSE the chicken, drain, and remove any fat from the cavity opening and around the neck. Cut off and discard the parson's nose. Blanch the chicken in a pan of boiling water for 2–3 minutes, then refresh in cold water.

PLACE the chicken, breast side down, in a bowl. Add the rice wine, Chinese spirit, ginger, spring onion and half the salt. Place the bowl in a steamer. Cover and steam over simmering water in a wok for 1½ hours, replenishing with boiling water during cooking. Transfer the chicken to a dish, breast side up, reserving the cooking liquid.

POUR half the liquid into a wok or saucepan and add the remaining salt and the pepper. Bring to the boil, then set aside. Using a cleaver, cut the chicken through the bones into bite-sized pieces. Place in a serving dish, pour the sauce over and garnish with the coriander.

DRUNKEN CHICKEN

FROM CHINA

CRISPY SKIN DUCK

NORTHERN CHEFS HAVE THEIR FAMOUS PEKING DUCK, BUT IN SICHUAN, CRISPY SKIN DUCK IS EQUALLY POPULAR. THIS DISH CAN ALSO BE MADE WITH BONELESS DUCK BREASTS. JUST ADJUST THE COOKING TIMES. SERVE THE DUCK WITH MANDARIN PANCAKES OR STEAMED FLOWER ROLLS.

2.25 kg (5 lb) duck

MARINADE
8 spring onions (scallions), ends
    trimmed, smashed with the flat
    side of a cleaver
8 slices ginger, smashed with the
    flat side of a cleaver
3 tablespoons Shaoxing rice wine
2 tablespoons salt
2 teaspoons Sichuan peppercorns
1 star anise, smashed with the flat
    side of a cleaver

2 tablespoons light soy sauce
125 g (4½ oz/1 cup) cornflour
    (cornstarch)
oil for deep-frying
hoisin sauce, optional, to serve
Mandarin pancakes (see recipe on
    page 455), optional, to serve
steamed breads, optional, to serve

SERVES 6

RINSE the duck, drain, and remove any fat from the cavity opening and around the neck. Cut off and discard the parson's nose.

TO MAKE the marinade, combine the spring onion, ginger, rice wine, salt, Sichuan peppercorns and star anise. Rub the marinade all over the inside and outside of the duck. Place the duck, breast side down, in a bowl with the remaining marinade and leave in the fridge for at least 1 hour.

PUT the marinated duck, breast side up, on a heatproof plate in a steamer, or cut into halves or quarters and put in several steamers.

STEAM over simmering water in a covered wok for 1½ hours, replenishing with boiling water during cooking. Remove the duck, discard the marinade and let cool.

RUB the soy sauce over the duck and then dredge in the cornflour, pressing lightly to make it adhere to the skin. Let the duck dry in the fridge for several hours until very dry.

FILL a wok one-quarter full of oil. Heat the oil to 190°C (375°F), or until a piece of bread fries golden brown in 10 seconds when dropped in the oil. Lower the duck into the oil and fry, ladling the oil over the top, until the skin is crisp and golden.

REMOVE duck from the wok and drain. Using a cleaver, cut it through the bones into pieces.

SERVE plain or with hoisin sauce and pancakes or steamed breads.

Note: For serving, poultry is traditionally chopped into bite-sized pieces, rather than jointed, so that the pieces can be picked up with chopsticks.

Steaming the duck and then frying it keeps the meat very moist and allows the flavours of the marinade to penetrate.

Cook the skewers, turning
regularly, for 3–4 minutes,
then baste with the sauce.

YAKITORI

YAKI MEANS GRILLED (BROILED) AND *TORI* MEANS CHICKEN, BUT ALTHOUGH *YAKITORI* REFERS TO ALL SORTS OF SKEWERED FOODS, CHICKEN REMAINS AMONG THE MOST POPULAR. THESE DELICIOUS MORSELS CAN MAKE A MEAL WITH SIDES, OR PROVIDE A SNACK FOR DRINKS, PARTICULARLY SAKE.

SAUCE
500 g (1 lb 2 oz) chicken wings,
  cut into pieces at the joints
375 ml (13 fl oz/1½ cups) mirin
250 ml (9 fl oz/1 cup) sake
375 ml (13 fl oz/1½ cups) shoyu
  (Japanese soy sauce)
55 g (2 oz/¼ cup) caster (superfine)
  sugar
3 teaspoons kuzu starch rocks or
  arrowroot

500 g (1 lb 2 oz) large boneless
  chicken thighs, skinless
4 baby leeks or thick spring onions
  (scallions), white part only, cut into
  4 pieces

MAKES 8

SOAK eight small bamboo skewers in water for 1 hour.

TO MAKE the sauce, preheat the grill (broiler) to high. Cook chicken wings, turning occasionally, for 15 minutes, or until dark golden and starting to blacken slightly. Remove and set aside. Pour the mirin and sake into a saucepan over high heat and bring to the boil. Add the shoyu and sugar and stir until the sugar has dissolved. Add the wings and bring liquid to the boil, then reduce to a simmer for 30 minutes. Remove the pan from the heat and allow to cool for 30 minutes. Strain the sauce (you can serve the wings as a snack). Pour a little of the sauce into a small dish and add the kuzu. Crush the rocks and stir into the sauce until dissolved, then return to the pan. Put the pan over high heat and stir until mixture boils and becomes thick and glossy. Remove from the heat and allow to cool before using.

CUT each chicken thigh into 12 even pieces. Starting with a piece of chicken, and alternating with the leek, thread three pieces of chicken and two pieces of leek onto each skewer.

POUR a little of the sauce into a dish for basting and reserve the rest for serving.

HEAT the grill to high and cook the skewers, turning regularly, for 3–4 minutes, then baste with the sauce. Cook on each side for a further 1–2 minutes, basting again, until well glazed and the chicken is cooked through.

SERVE with a drizzle of the sauce.

FROM THAILAND

SPICY GROUND DUCK

LAAP MEANS 'GOOD FORTUNE'. THIS VERSION USING DUCK IS A SPECIALITY FROM AROUND UBON RACHATHANI, BUT YOU CAN USE MINCED CHICKEN INSTEAD OF DUCK. LAAP IS SERVED WITH RAW VEGETABLES SUCH AS SNAKE BEANS, CABBAGE AND FIRM, CRISP LETTUCE.

1 tablespoon jasmine rice
280 g (10 oz) minced (ground) duck
3 tablespoons lime juice
1 tablespoon fish sauce
2 lemongrass stalks, white part
   only, finely sliced
50 g (2 oz) Asian shallots,
   finely sliced
5 makrut (kaffir lime) leaves,
   finely sliced
5 spring onions (scallions),
   finely chopped
¼–½ teaspoon roasted chilli
   powder, according to taste
a few lettuce leaves
a few mint leaves, for garnish
raw vegetables such as snake
   (yard-long) beans, cut into
   lengths, cucumber slices, thin
   wedges of cabbage, halved baby
   tomatoes, to serve

SERVES 4

DRY-FRY the rice in a small pan over a medium heat. Shake the pan to move the rice around, for 6–8 minutes, or until the rice is brown. Using a pestle and mortar or a small blender, pound or blend the rice until it almost forms a powder.

IN a saucepan or wok, cook the duck with the lime juice and fish sauce over a high heat. Crumble and break the duck until the meat has separated into small pieces. Cook until light brown, then remove from the heat.

ADD rice powder, lemongrass, shallots, makrut leaves, spring onions and chilli powder to the duck and stir together. Taste, then adjust the seasoning if necessary.

LINE a serving plate with lettuce leaves. Spoon the duck over the leaves, then garnish with mint leaves. Arrange vegetables on a separate plate.

Pound the dry-fried rice in a pestle and mortar until it forms a powder. Alternatively, you can use a small blender.

Paddy fields are a common sight in Thailand where farmers help each other with planting and harvesting by growing crops in rotation.

Cook the spinach for just a short amount of time so that it keeps its rich colour.

KUNG PAO CHICKEN

KUNG PAO IS ONE OF THE MOST CLASSIC HOT-AND-SOUR SICHUANESE SAUCES, AND CAN BE STIR-FRIED WITH SEAFOOD, PORK OR VEGETABLES AS WELL AS CHICKEN. THE SEASONINGS ARE FRIED IN OIL OVER HIGH HEAT, INTENSIFYING THE SPICINESS AND FLAVOURING THE OIL.

350 g (12 oz) boneless, skinless chicken breast,
3 tablespoons light soy sauce
3 tablespoons Shaoxing rice wine
2 teaspoons roasted sesame oil
1 tablespoon cornflour (cornstarch)
120 g (4½ oz/¾ cup) peeled water chestnuts
3 tablespoons oil
450 g (1 lb) baby English spinach leaves
½ teaspoon salt
3 garlic cloves, finely chopped
120 g (4½ oz/¾ cup) unsalted peanuts
1 spring onion (scallion), finely chopped
1 tablespoon finely chopped ginger
1 teaspoon chilli sauce
1 tablespoon sugar
1 teaspoon Chinese black rice vinegar
60 ml (2 fl oz/¼ cup) chicken stock

SERVES 6

CUT the chicken into 2.5 cm (1 inch) cubes. Place the cubes in a bowl, add 2 tablespoons of the soy sauce, 2 tablespoons of rice wine, 1 teaspoon of sesame oil and 2 teaspoons of cornflour, and toss lightly. Marinate in the fridge for 20 minutes.

BLANCH the water chestnuts in a pan of boiling water, then refresh in cold water. Drain, pat dry and cut into thin slices.

HEAT a wok over high heat, add 1 teaspoon of oil until very hot. Stir-fry spinach, salt, 2 teaspoons garlic and 2 teaspoons of rice wine, turning constantly, until the spinach is just becoming limp. Remove spinach from the wok, arrange around the edge of a platter, cover and keep warm.

REHEAT wok over high heat, add 1 tablespoon oil and heat until very hot. Stir-fry half the chicken pieces, turning constantly until cooked. Remove with a slotted spoon and drain. Repeat with 1 tablespoon of oil and the remaining chicken. Wipe out the pan.

DRY-FRY the peanuts in the wok until browned, remove and set aside.

REHEAT the wok over a high heat, add remaining oil and heat until very hot. Stir-fry the spring onion, ginger, the remaining garlic and the chilli sauce for 10 seconds, or until fragrant. Add the sliced water chestnuts and stir-fry for 15 seconds, or until heated through.

COMBINE the sugar, black vinegar, chicken stock and remaining soy sauce, rice wine, sesame oil and cornflour, add to the wok and simmer until thickened. Add cooked chicken and the peanuts. Toss lightly to coat with the sauce. Transfer to the centre of the platter and serve.

Roasting sesame oil outside a shop in Chengdu.

FROM CHINA

PEKING DUCK

THIS DISH OWES ITS REPUTATION NOT SO MUCH TO THE WAY IT IS COOKED, BUT TO THE WAY IT IS THEATRICALLY CARVED AND EATEN ROLLED INTO PANCAKES. IN RESTAURANTS, THE DUCK IS COOKED IN A SPECIAL OVEN, BUT THIS RECIPE HAS BEEN MODIFIED FOR THE HOME KITCHEN.

2.5 kg (5 lb 8 oz) duck
2 tablespoons maltose or honey, dissolved in 2 tablespoons water
125 ml (4 fl oz/½ cup) hoisin sauce or plum sauce
24 Mandarin pancakes (see recipe on page 455)
6–8 spring onions (scallions), shredded
½ Lebanese (short) cucumber, shredded

SERVES 6

CUT the wing tips off the duck with poultry shears. Rinse the duck, drain, and remove any fat from the cavity opening and around the neck. Cut off and discard the parson's nose. Plunge the duck into a pot of boiling water for 2–3 minutes to tighten the skin. Remove and drain, then dry thoroughly.

WHILE the skin is still warm, brush the duck all over with the maltose or honey and water solution, then hang it up to dry in a cool and airy place for at least 6 hours, or overnight, or leave it uncovered in the fridge.

PREHEAT the oven to 200°C (400°F/Gas 6). Place the duck, breast side up, on a rack in a roasting tin, and cook without basting or turning for 1½ hours. Check to make sure the duck is not getting too dark and, if it is, cover it loosely with foil.

Remove the crisp duck skin in small slices by using a sharp carving knife, then carve the meat, or carve both together. Arrange on a serving plate.

TO SERVE, spread about 1 teaspoon of the hoisin sauce or plum sauce in the centre of a pancake, add a few strips of spring onion, cucumber, duck skin and meat, roll up the pancake and turn up the bottom edge to prevent the contents from falling out.

Carve the duck so that each slice has some crisp skin and tender meat. The skin can also be eaten separately, wrapped in the pancakes, while the meat is used in a stir-fry.

Commercially made pancakes are available in Asian shops, fresh or frozen, or from restaurants that sell take-away ducks and barbecued meat.

Bicycles are a common form of transport all over India.

FROM INDIA

BUTTER CHICKEN

BUTTER CHICKEN, OR MURGH MAKHNI, IS A MOGHUL DISH THAT HAS MANY VERSIONS. THE BUTTER IN THE TITLE REFERS TO GHEE, A TYPE OF CLARIFIED BUTTER. RICE IS AN IDEAL ACCOMPANIMENT AND PIECES OF ROTI OR NAAN CAN BE USED TO MOP UP THE DELICIOUS JUICES.

2 cm (¾ inch) piece of ginger, roughly chopped
3 garlic cloves, roughly chopped
80 g (2½ oz/½ cup) blanched almonds
170 ml (6 fl oz/⅔ cup) thick plain yoghurt
½ teaspoon chilli powder
¼ teaspoon ground cloves
¼ teaspoon ground cinnamon
1 teaspoon garam masala (see recipe on page 464)
4 cardamom pods, lightly crushed
400 g (14 oz) tin chopped tomatoes
1¼ teaspoons salt
1 kg (2 lb 4 oz) boneless, skinless chicken thigh fillets, cut into fairly large pieces
5 tablespoons ghee or clarified butter
1 large onion, thinly sliced
6 tablespoons finely chopped coriander (cilantro) leaves
4 tablespoons thick (double/heavy) cream

SERVES 6

BLEND the ginger and garlic to a paste in a food processor or pestle and mortar, or crush the garlic and finely grate the ginger and combine them. Grind the almonds in a food processor or finely chop with a knife. In a bowl, combine the paste and almonds with the yoghurt, chilli powder, cloves, cinnamon, garam masala, cardamom pods, tomato and salt.

ADD chicken pieces and stir to coat thoroughly. Cover and marinate for 2 hours, or overnight, in the refrigerator.

PREHEAT the oven to 180°C (350°F/Gas 4).

HEAT the ghee or clarified butter in a karhai or deep, heavy-based frying pan, add the onion and fry until softened and brown. Add the chicken mixture and fry for 2 minutes. Mix in the fresh coriander. Put the mixture into a shallow baking dish, pour in the cream and stir with a fork.

BAKE for 1 hour. If the top is browning too quickly during cooking, cover with a piece of foil. Leave to rest for 10 minutes before serving. The oil will rise to the surface. Just before serving, place the dish under a hot grill (broiler) for about 2 minutes to brown the top. Before serving, slightly tip the dish and spoon off any extra oil.

FROM CHINA

SOY CHICKEN

1.5 kg (3 lb 5 oz) chicken
1 tablespoon ground Sichuan
 peppercorns
2 tablespoons grated ginger

MARINADE
2 tablespoons sugar
3 tablespoons Shaoxing rice wine
310 ml (10¾ fl oz/1¼ cups) dark
 soy sauce
185 ml (6 fl oz/¾ cup) light soy
 sauce

625 ml (2½ fl oz/2½ cups) oil
440 ml (15¼ fl oz/1¾ cups)
 combined chicken and meat
 stock (see recipe on page 491)
2 teaspoons roasted sesame oil

SERVES 4

RINSE the chicken, drain, and remove any fat from the cavity opening and around the neck. Cut off and discard the parson's nose.

RUB the Sichuan peppercorns and ginger all over the inside and outside of the chicken.

TO MAKE the marinade, combine the sugar, rice wine and soy sauces. Add the chicken and coat with the marinade. Leave in the fridge for at least 3 hours, turning occasionally.

HEAT a wok over high heat, add the oil and heat until very hot. Drain the chicken, reserving the marinade, and fry for 8 minutes until browned.

PUT the chicken in a clay pot or casserole with the reserved marinade and stock. Place over moderate heat and bring to the boil. Reduce heat, simmer, covered, for 35–40 minutes. Leave off the heat for 2 hours. Drain the chicken, reserving the cooking liquid. Brush with sesame oil. Refrigerate for 1 hour.

USING a cleaver, chop the chicken through the bones into bite-sized pieces, pour over a couple of tablespoons of heated reserved cooking liquid.

The soy sauce and sugar in the marinade turn the chicken skin a rich dark brown when cooked.

RED-COOKED CHICKEN

RED-COOKING LIQUID
2 cinnamon or cassia sticks
1½ star anise
2 pieces dried tangerine or orange
 peel, about 5 cm (2 inches) long
½ teaspoon fennel seeds
375 ml (13 fl oz/1½ cups) dark soy
 sauce
90 g (3½ oz) sugar
125 ml (4 fl oz/½ cup) Shaoxing rice
 wine

1.5 kg (3 lb 5 oz) chicken
1 tablespoon roasted sesame oil

SERVES 6

TO MAKE the red-cooking liquid, place all the ingredients in a clay pot or casserole with 1.5 litres (52 fl oz/6 cups) water, bring to the boil. Reduce the heat and simmer for 30 minutes.

RINSE the chicken, drain, and remove any fat from the cavity opening and around the neck. Cut off and discard the parson's nose. Place the chicken, breast side down, in the cooking liquid and cook for 1½ hours, turning two or three times. Turn off the heat and leave in the liquid for 30 minutes.

BRUSH chicken with the sesame oil. Cut the chicken through the bones into bite-sized pieces. Spoon over a little of the red-cooking liquid and serve hot or cold.

RED-COOKED CHICKEN

YELLOW CHICKEN CURRY WITH PEPPERCORNS

FRESH PEPPERCORNS HAVE A FRAGRANT, PUNGENT QUALITY THAT LIFTS THE FLAVOUR OF ANY CURRY IN WHICH THEY ARE USED. YOU SHOULD BEWARE OF EATING A WHOLE SPRIG IN ONE GO THOUGH AS, JUST LIKE THE PEPPER THEY BECOME, THEY ARE EXTREMELY HOT.

60 ml (2 fl oz/¼ cup) coconut
   cream (see recipe on page 468)
2 tablespoons yellow curry paste
   (see recipe on page 471) or
   bought paste
1 tablespoon fish sauce
2 teaspoons palm sugar (jaggery)
¼ teaspoon turmeric
600 g (1 lb 5 oz) boneless, skinless
   chicken thighs, cut into thin slices
440 ml (15¼ fl oz/1¾ cups)
   coconut milk
100 g (3 oz) bamboo shoots,
   thinly sliced
4 sprigs fresh green peppercorns
4–6 makrut (kaffir lime) leaves
12 Thai sweet basil leaves

SERVES 4

PUT the coconut cream in a wok or saucepan and simmer over a medium heat for about 5 minutes, or until the cream separates and a layer of oil forms on the surface. Stir the cream if it starts to brown around the edges.

ADD the curry paste, stir well to combine and cook until fragrant. Add the fish sauce, palm sugar and turmeric and stir well. Cook for 2–3 minutes, stirring occasionally, until the mixture darkens.

ADD the chicken to the pan and stir to coat all the pieces evenly in the spice mixture. Cook over a medium heat for 5 minutes, stirring occasionally and adding the coconut milk a tablespoon at a time to incorporate.

ADD the bamboo shoots, peppercorns, lime and basil leaves and cook for another 5 minutes.

Curry pastes *(khreuang kaeng)* are made at home using a granite pestle and mortar. They have a more intense flavour than those made by machine because the ingredients are crushed rather than chopped.

FROM CHINA

BANG BANG CHICKEN

THIS CLASSIC SICHUANESE COLD PLATTER IS MADE FROM CHICKEN, CUCUMBER AND BEAN THREAD NOODLES, MIXED IN A SESAME OR PEANUT SAUCE. THE SESAME DRESSING IS THE AUTHENTIC ONE BUT THE PEANUT VERSION IS ALSO VERY GOOD.

1½ cucumbers
1 teaspoon salt
30 g (1 oz) bean thread noodles
1 teaspoon roasted sesame oil
250 g (9 oz) cooked chicken,
    cut into shreds
2 spring onions (scallions), green
    part only, finely sliced

SESAME DRESSING
¼ teaspoon Sichuan peppercorns
3 garlic cloves
2 cm (¾ inch) piece ginger
½ teaspoon chilli sauce
3 tablespoons toasted sesame
    paste
2 tablespoons roasted sesame oil
2½ tablespoons light soy sauce
1 tablespoon Shaoxing rice wine
1 tablespoon Chinese black
    rice vinegar
1 tablespoon sugar
3 tablespoons chicken stock

OR

PEANUT DRESSING
60 g (2¼ oz/¼ cup) smooth peanut
    butter
1 teaspoon light soy sauce
1½ tablespoons sugar
2 teaspoons Chinese black
    rice vinegar
1 tablespoon Shaoxing rice wine
1 tablespoon roasted sesame oil
1 spring onion (scallion), finely
    chopped
1 tablespoon finely chopped ginger
1 teaspoon chilli sauce
2½ tablespoons chicken stock

SERVES 6

TO MAKE the sesame dressing, put Sichuan peppercorns in a frying pan and cook over medium heat, stirring occasionally, for about 8 minutes, or until golden brown and very fragrant. Cool slightly, then crush into a powder. Combine garlic, ginger, chilli sauce, sesame paste, sesame oil, soy sauce, rice wine, vinegar, sugar and stock in a blender, food processor or mortar and pestle. Blend to a smooth sauce the consistency of thick cream. Stir in the Sichuan peppercorn powder. Pour into a bowl and set aside.

TO MAKE the peanut dressing, combine peanut butter, soy sauce, sugar, vinegar, rice wine, sesame oil, spring onion, ginger, chilli sauce and stock in a blender, food processor or mortar and pestle. Blend until the mixture is the consistency of thick cream, adding a little water if necessary. Pour into a bowl and set aside.

SLICE the cucumbers lengthways and remove most of the seeds. Cut each half crossways into thirds, then cut each piece lengthways into thin slices that are 5 cm (2 inches) long and 1 cm (½ inch) wide. Place the slices in a bowl, add the salt, toss lightly, and set aside for 20 minutes. Pour off the water that has accumulated.

SOAK the bean thread noodles in hot water for 10 minutes, then drain and cut into 8 cm (3 inch) lengths. Blanch the noodles in a pan of boiling water for 3 minutes, then refresh in cold water and drain again. Toss the noodles in the sesame oil and arrange them on a large platter. Arrange the cucumber slices on top. Place the chicken shreds on top of the cucumber.

JUST before serving, pour the sesame or peanut dressing over the chicken. Sprinkle with the spring onion and serve.

PARSI CHICKEN WITH APRICOTS

IN THIS DELICIOUS PARSI DISH FROM MUMBAI (BOMBAY), THE USE OF DRIED APRICOTS, JAGGERY AND VINEGAR GIVE A SWEET SOUR FLAVOUR. THE POTATO STRAWS MAKE AN UNUSUAL GARNISH AND ADD A CONTRASTING CRUNCHY TEXTURE TO ENHANCE THE RECIPE.

1.5 kg (3 lb 5 oz) chicken or
  chicken pieces
3 tablespoons oil
2 large onions, finely sliced
1 clove garlic, finely chopped
4 cm (1½ inch) piece of ginger,
  finely chopped
3 dried chillies
1½ teaspoons garam masala
  (see recipe on page 464)
2 tablespoons tomato paste (purée)
1 teaspoon salt
2 tablespoons clear vinegar
1½ tablespoons palm sugar
  (jaggery) or soft brown sugar
12 dried apricots

POTATO STRAWS
1 large waxy potato
1 tablespoon salt
oil for deep-frying

SERVES 4

IF USING a whole chicken, cut it into eight pieces by removing both legs and cutting between the joint of the drumstick and thigh. Cut down either side of the backbone and remove the backbone. Turn chicken over and cut through the cartilage down the centre of the breastbone. Cut each breast in half, leaving the wing attached to the top half. Trim off the wing tips.

HEAT the oil in a karhai or casserole. Add the onion and stir over medium heat until softened and starting to brown. Stir in the garlic, ginger, dried chillies and garam masala, then add all the chicken pieces. Stir and brown the chicken for 5 minutes, taking care not to burn the onion. Add the tomato paste, salt and 250 ml (8 fl oz/1 cup) water. Bring to the boil, then reduce the heat, cover and simmer gently for 20 minutes.

ADD vinegar, palm sugar and dried apricots to the pan, cover and simmer for another 15 minutes.

TO MAKE the potato straws, grate the potato on the largest holes of a grater, then put in a large bowl with about 1.5 litres (53 fl oz/6 cups) water and the salt. Stir and remove some potato a handful at a time, squeezing and patting it dry on a tea towel (dish towel). Fill a karhai or deep, heavy-based saucepan one-third full with oil. Heat the oil slowly to 160°C (315°F), or until a cube of bread browns in 30 seconds). Add a small handful of potato. Be careful not to add too much as it will make the oil bubble and rise up the pan at first. When the potato is golden and crisp, remove it and drain on paper towels. Cook all the potato straws in the same way.

SERVE the chicken pieces garnished with the potato straws.

Street decorations on a busy street in Mumbai (Bombay) during the festival of Divali.

FROM THAILAND

RED CURRY WITH ROASTED DUCK AND LYCHEES

IN THAILAND, THIS SPECIALITY DISH IS OFTEN SERVED DURING THE TRADITIONAL FAMILY FEASTING
THAT ACCOMPANIES CELEBRATIONS INCLUDING THE ORDINATION OF BUDDHIST MONKS, WEDDINGS
AND NEW YEAR. THIS IS VERY RICH, SO SERVE IT ALONGSIDE A SALAD TO CUT THROUGH THE SAUCE.

60 ml (2 fl oz/¼ cup) coconut
   cream
2 tablespoons red curry paste
   (see recipe on page 472) or
   bought paste
½ roasted duck, boned and
   chopped
440 ml (15¼ fl oz/1¾ cups)
   coconut milk
2 tablespoons fish sauce
1 tablespoon palm sugar (jaggery)
225 g (8 oz) tin lychees, drained
110 g (4 oz) baby tomatoes
7 makrut (kaffir lime) leaves,
   torn in half
a handful of Thai sweet basil leaves,
   for garnish
1 long red chilli, seeded and
   finely sliced, for garnish

SERVES 4

PUT the coconut cream in a wok or saucepan and
simmer over a medium heat for about 5 minutes,
or until the cream separates and a layer of oil
forms on the surface. Stir the cream if it starts to
brown around the edges.

ADD the curry paste, stir well to combine and
cook until fragrant.

ADD the roasted duck and stir for 5 minutes.

ADD the coconut milk, fish sauce and palm sugar
and simmer over a medium heat for another
5 minutes.

ADD the lychees and baby tomatoes and cook for
1–2 minutes. Add the makrut leaves. Taste, then
adjust the seasoning if necessary.

SPOON into a serving bowl and sprinkle with the
basil leaves and sliced chilli.

This curry, with its combination
of coconut milk, duck and fruit,
is very rich. Cook the lychees
for only a few minutes.

FROM CHINA

LEMON CHICKEN

LEMON CHICKEN IS A POPULAR CANTONESE DISH OF FRIED CHICKEN GLAZED WITH A TART, LEMONY SAUCE. HERE THE LEMON SAUCE IS HOME-MADE AND QUITE UNLIKE THE GLUGGY SAUCES OFTEN SERVED WITH THIS DISH. CHICKEN WINGS OR DUCK ARE ALSO DELICIOUS PREPARED IN THIS WAY.

500 g (1 lb 2 oz) boneless, skinless chicken breasts
1 tablespoon light soy sauce
1 tablespoon Shaoxing rice wine
1 spring onion (scallion), finely chopped
1 tablespoon finely chopped ginger
1 garlic clove, finely chopped
1 egg, lightly beaten
90 g (3¼ oz/¾ cup) cornflour (cornstarch)
oil for deep-frying

LEMON SAUCE
2 tablespoons lemon juice
2 teaspoons sugar
½ teaspoon salt
½ teaspoon roasted sesame oil
3 tablespoons chicken stock or water
½ teaspoon cornflour (cornstarch)

SERVES 6

CUT the chicken into slices. Place in a bowl, add the soy sauce, rice wine, spring onion, ginger and garlic, and toss lightly. Marinate in the fridge for at least 1 hour, or overnight.

ADD the egg to the chicken mixture and toss lightly to coat. Drain any excess egg and coat the chicken pieces with the cornflour. The easiest way to do this is to put the chicken and cornflour in a plastic bag and shake it.

FILL a wok one-quarter full of oil. Heat the oil to 190°C (375°F), or until a piece of bread fries golden brown in 10 seconds when dropped in the oil. Add half the chicken, a piece at a time, and fry, stirring constantly, for 3½–4 minutes, or until golden brown. Remove with a wire sieve or slotted spoon and drain. Repeat with the remaining chicken. Reheat the oil and return all the chicken to the wok. Cook until crisp and golden brown. Drain the chicken. Pour off the oil and wipe out the wok.

TO MAKE the lemon sauce, combine the lemon juice, sugar, salt, sesame oil, stock and cornflour.

REHEAT the wok over medium heat until hot, add the lemon sauce and stir constantly until thickened. Add the chicken and toss lightly in the sauce.

Peeling garlic in Sichuan.

Elderly men take their songbirds out with them to the park when they meet their friends. The cages are hung up so the birds can sing together while their owners chat.

The significance of rice in Japan is immense. Cultivated for more than 2,000 years, it has come to form the absolute foundation of the diet.

FROM JAPAN

STEAMED SAKE CHICKEN

ALTHOUGH GRAPE WINE IS MORE FAMILIAR TO MOST WESTERN COOKS, SAKE, JAPAN'S BELOVED RICE BREW, CAN BE A WONDERFUL MARINADE BASE. ENHANCED WITH A VARIETY OF ASIAN SEASONINGS, IT GIVES THESE STEAMED CHICKEN BREASTS A PARTICULARLY INVITING TENDERNESS AND FLAVOUR.

500 g (1 lb 2 oz) chicken breasts, with skin on
80 ml (2½ fl oz/⅓ cup) sake
2 tablespoons lemon juice
4 cm (1½ inch) piece fresh ginger, thinly sliced
2 tablespoons shoyu (Japanese soy sauce)
1 tablespoon mirin
1 teaspoon sesame oil
1 spring onion (scallion), sliced on the diagonal, plus extra to garnish
½ small red capsicum (pepper), skin removed, flesh cut into thin 3 cm (1¼ inch) long strips, for garnish

SERVES 4

USE a fork to prick the skin on the chicken in several places. Place the chicken, skin side up, in a shallow dish, then pour over the combined sake, lemon juice, ginger and 1 teaspoon salt. Cover and marinate in the refrigerator for 30 minutes.

COMBINE the shoyu, mirin, sesame oil and spring onion in a small bowl and set aside.

LINE a steamer with baking paper. Place chicken, skin side up, in the steamer. Fill a saucepan with 500 ml (17 fl oz/2 cups) water and sit the steamer over the top. Cover and cook over simmering water for 20 minutes, or until cooked.

CUT the chicken into bite-sized pieces, put into a serving bowl and drizzle with the shoyu mixture. Garnish with the capsicum strips and extra spring onion.

SERVE with rice.

Sake is made by fermenting cooked, ground rice mash. It has a dry flavour, somewhere between vodka and dry sherry.

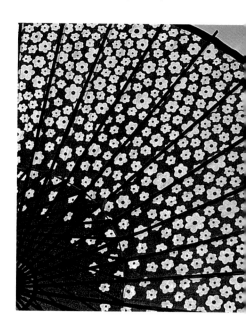

Holy basil *(bai ka-phrao)* has a hot sharp flavour and comes in both white (above) and red varieties. Used with seafood and stir-fries.

Floating markets at Damnoen Saduak.

FROM THAILAND

CHICKEN WITH CRISPY HOLY BASIL LEAVES

THIS IS ONE OF THE MOST COMMON DISHES YOU WILL COME ACROSS IN THAILAND. HOLY BASIL COMES IN TWO COLOURS, RED AND GREEN. IT HAS A HOT, SLIGHTLY SHARP FLAVOUR AND IS OFTEN USED IN CONJUNCTION WITH CHILLIES IN STIR-FRIES. SERVE WITH PLENTY OF RICE.

500 g (1 lb 2 oz) boneless, skinless chicken breasts, thinly sliced
4–5 garlic cloves, finely chopped
4–5 small red or green bird's eye chillies, lightly crushed
1 tablespoon fish sauce
2 tablespoons oyster sauce
vegetable oil, for deep-frying
2 handfuls of holy basil leaves
2 tablespoons vegetable or chicken stock, or water
½ teaspoon sugar
1 red capsicum (pepper), cut into bite-sized pieces
1 medium onion, cut into thin wedges

SERVES 4

Mix the chicken, garlic, chillies, fish sauce and oyster sauce in a bowl. Cover with plastic wrap and marinate in the refrigerator for at least 30 minutes.

HEAT 5 cm (2 inches) oil in a wok or deep frying pan over a medium heat. When the oil seems hot, drop a few basil leaves into it. If they sizzle immediately, the oil is ready. Deep-fry three-quarters of the basil leaves for 1 minute or until they are all crispy. Lift out with a slotted spoon and drain on paper towels. Discard the remaining oil.

HEAT 2 tablespoons oil in the same wok or frying pan and stir-fry half the chicken over a high heat for 3–4 minutes. Remove from the pan and repeat with the remaining chicken. Return all the chicken to the wok.

ADD the stock and sugar to the wok, then the capsicum and onion, and stir-fry for another 1–2 minutes. Stir in the fresh basil leaves. Taste, then adjust the seasoning if necessary.

GARNISH with the crispy basil leaves.

DEEP-FRIED QUAILS WITH SPICY SALT

4 quails
1 teaspoon spicy salt and pepper
  (see recipe on page 488)
1 teaspoon sugar
1 tablespoon light soy sauce
1 tablespoon Shaoxing rice wine
2–3 tablespoons plain (all-purpose)
  flour
oil for deep-frying
1 spring onion (scallion), finely
  chopped
1 red chilli, finely chopped

SERVES 4

SPLIT each quail in half down the middle and clean well.

MARINATE with the spicy salt and pepper, the sugar, soy sauce and rice wine for 2–3 hours in the fridge, turning frequently.

COAT each quail piece in the flour.

FILL a wok one-quarter full of oil. Heat the oil to 190°C (375°F), or until a piece of bread fries golden brown in 10 seconds when dropped in the oil. Reduce the heat and fry the quail for 2–3 minutes on each side. Remove from the wok and drain on paper towels.

SOAK the spring onion and chilli in the hot oil (with the heat turned off) for 2 minutes. Remove with a wire sieve or slotted spoon and drain, then sprinkle over the quail pieces.

Marinate the quail for long enough for the flavours to penetrate the meat.

LACQUERED QUAIL

4 x 500 g (1 lb 2 oz) quail
4 slices ginger
4 spring onions (scallions), chopped
4 tablespoons light soy sauce
3 tablespoons dark soy sauce
3 tablespoons Shaoxing rice wine
4 tablespoons rock (lump) sugar
1 teaspoon salt
2 cinnamon sticks
2 star anise
1 litre (35 fl oz/4 cups) chicken
  stock (see recipe on page 491)
oil for deep-frying

SERVES 4

BLANCH the quail in a pan of boiling water for 2 minutes, then remove and drain.

COMBINE the remaining ingredients except the oil in a clay pot or casserole and bring to a simmer.

ADD the quail, cover and simmer for 20 minutes. Remove from the heat, take out the quail and leave to dry for at least 1 hour.

FILL a wok one-quarter full of oil. Heat the oil to 190°C (375°F), or until a piece of bread fries golden brown in 10 seconds when dropped in the oil. Fry the quail until they are very crisp and brown. Drain well and sprinkle with salt. Using a cleaver, cut the quails through the bones into bite-sized pieces and serve.

LACQUERED QUAIL

Just before serving, stir in the snowpeas and cook until wilted.

FROM JAPAN

CHICKEN AND VEGETABLE HOTPOT

DIFFERENT FROM THE MORE COMMON STEW-LIKE HOTPOT, THIS CHICKEN AND VEGETABLE RECIPE IS A JUICY DISH MEANT TO BE EATEN ALONGSIDE A BOWL OF RICE. GOBO, LOTUS ROOT AND BAMBOO SHOOTS ARE JUST SEVERAL AMONG ITS MIX OF APPEALING VEGETABLES.

100 g (3½ oz) fresh or frozen gobo
   (burdock root)
1 teaspoon Japanese rice vinegar
100 g (3½ oz) fresh or frozen
   lotus root
2 teaspoons sesame oil
1 tablespoon vegetable oil
750 g (1 lb 10 oz) boneless,
   skinless chicken thighs, cut into
   2.5 cm (1 inch) squares
150 g (5½ oz) taro, peeled and cut
   into 2 cm (¾ inch) squares
1 carrot, cut on the diagonal into
   1.5 cm (⅝ inch) thick slices
125 g (4 oz) bamboo shoots, sliced
125 g (4 oz) fresh shiitake
   mushrooms, stems discarded,
   large caps halved
500 ml (17 fl oz/2 cups) dashi II
   (see recipe on page 483)
80 ml (2½ fl oz/⅓ cup) shoyu
   (Japanese soy sauce)
60 ml (2 fl oz/¼ cup) mirin
1 tablespoon caster (superfine)
   sugar
125 g (4 oz) snowpeas (mangetout),
   trimmed
shichimi togarashi (seven-spice
   mix), to serve, optional

SERVES 4

IF USING fresh gobo, roughly scrape the skin with a sharp knife, then rinse. Cut into 2 cm (¾ inch) pieces on the diagonal. Put in a bowl with 500 ml (17 fl oz/2 cups) water and the vinegar. Leave for about 15 minutes to remove some bitterness from the gobo. If using frozen gobo, this step is not necessary as the gobo has been scraped and cut, ready for use.

IF USING fresh lotus root, peel it, cut into 5 mm (¼ inch) slices, then put in cold water. This step is not necessary if using frozen lotus.

HEAT the sesame and vegetable oil in a large saucepan over medium–high heat and cook the chicken in batches until lightly golden. Remove from the pan and set aside.

DRAIN the gobo and lotus.

ADD the gobo and taro to the pan and cook, stirring frequently, for 2 minutes. Add lotus and carrot and cook for a further 2 minutes, or until lightly golden. Add bamboo shoots and shiitake and cook for a further 2 minutes. Pour in dashi, shoyu and mirin, add the sugar and bring to the boil, then reduce to a simmer. Add the chicken and simmer for a further 10–15 minutes.

JUST before serving, add the snowpeas and stir until just wilted.

SERVE in deep bowls with rice. Sprinkle with shichimi togarashi, if desired.

FROM INDIA

TANDOORI CHICKEN

TRADITIONALLY COOKED IN A TANDOOR (CLAY OVEN), THIS IS PERHAPS THE MOST POPULAR CHICKEN DISH FROM NORTHERN INDIA, WHERE IT IS SERVED WITH NAAN AND LACCHA. YOU CAN NEVER GET EXACTLY THE SAME RESULTS AT HOME BUT THIS IS A VERY GOOD APPROXIMATION.

1.5 kg (3 lb 5 oz) chicken or skinless chicken thighs and drumsticks

MARINADE
2 teaspoons coriander seeds
1 teaspoon cumin seeds
1 onion, roughly chopped
3 garlic cloves, roughly chopped
5 cm (2 inch) piece of ginger, roughly chopped
250 ml (8 fl oz/1 cup) thick plain yoghurt
grated rind of 1 lemon
3 tablespoons lemon juice
2 tablespoons clear vinegar
1 teaspoon paprika
2 teaspoons garam masala (see recipe on page 464)
½ teaspoon tandoori food colouring (optional)

2 tablespoons ghee
onion rings
lemon wedges

SERVES 4

REMOVE the skin from the chicken and cut the chicken in half. Using a sharp knife, make 2.5 cm (1 inch) long diagonal incisions on each limb and breast, taking care not to cut through to the bone. If using thighs and drumsticks, trim away any excess fat and make an incision in each piece.

TO MAKE the marinade, place a frying pan over low heat and dry-roast the coriander seeds until aromatic. Remove and dry-roast the cumin seeds. Grind the roasted seeds to a fine powder using a spice grinder or pestle and mortar. Blend all the marinade ingredients in a food processor to form a smooth paste. Season with salt, to taste. If you don't have a food processor, chop the onion, garlic and ginger more finely and mix with the rest of the ingredients in a bowl.

MARINATE chicken in the spicy yoghurt marinade for at least 8 hours, or overnight. Turn the chicken occasionally in the marinade to ensure that all sides are soaked.

HEAT oven to 200°C (400°F/Gas 6). Place chicken on a wire rack on a baking tray. Cover with foil and roast on the top shelf for about 45 minutes or until cooked through (test by inserting a skewer into a thigh – the juices should run clear). Baste chicken with the marinade once during cooking. Remove the foil 15 minutes before the end of cooking, to brown the tandoori mixture. Preheat grill (broiler) to its highest setting.

HEAT the ghee, prior to serving, while the chicken is still on the rack, and pour it over the chicken halves. Cook under the grill (broiler) for 5 minutes to blacken the edges of the chicken like a tandoor.

SERVE the chicken garnished with onion rings and lemon wedges. The chicken pieces can also be grilled (broiled), barbecued or spit-roasted.

Freshly made yoghurt is left to set in porous earthenware bowls, which help to drain and thicken it.

SHANGHAI SOY DUCK

THIS DUCK, SIMILAR TO CANTONESE SOY CHICKEN, IS TRADITIONALLY SERVED AT ROOM TEMPERATURE AS A FIRST COURSE. HOWEVER, THERE IS NO REASON WHY IT CAN'T BE A MAIN COURSE, HOT OR COLD. YOU CAN ALSO USE JOINTED PIECES OR DUCK BREASTS, JUST REDUCE THE COOKING TIME.

2.25 kg (5 lb) duck
2 teaspoons salt
4 spring onions (scallions), each tied in a knot
4 x 1 cm (½ inch) slices ginger, smashed with the flat side of a cleaver
6 star anise
3 cinnamon or cassia sticks
1 tablespoon Sichuan peppercorns
100 ml (3½ fl oz) Shaoxing rice wine
200 ml (7 fl oz) light soy sauce
100 ml (3½ fl oz) dark soy sauce
100 g (3½ oz) rock (lump) sugar

SERVES 4

RINSE the duck, drain, and remove any fat from the cavity opening and around the neck. Cut off and discard the parson's nose. Blanch the duck in a pan of boiling water for 2–3 minutes, then refresh in cold water, pat dry and rub the salt inside the cavity.

PLACE the duck, breast side up, in a clay pot or casserole, and add the spring onion, ginger, star anise, cinnamon, peppercorns, rice wine, soy sauces, rock sugar and enough water to cover. Bring to the boil, then reduce the heat and simmer, covered, for 40–45 minutes. Turn off the heat and leave the duck to cool in the liquid for 2–3 hours, transferring the clay pot to the fridge once it is cool enough. Leave in the fridge until completely cold (you can keep the duck in the liquid overnight and serve it the next day).

TO SERVE, remove the duck from the liquid and drain well. Using a cleaver, cut the duck through the bones into bite-sized pieces.

TRADITIONALLY, this dish is served at room temperature, but if you want to serve it hot, put the pot with the duck and the liquid back on the stove and bring to the boil. Simmer 10 minutes, or until the duck is completely heated through.

Ducks hanging up to dry after they have been plucked.

Soya beans are rarely eaten whole, but when made into soy sauce, tofu, soy milk, vegetable oil, fermented beans, bean pastes or shaped into noodles, they then become one of the essential ingredients of Chinese cooking.

MEAT

Harvesting bok choy in Liugan.

Roll the mixture into balls using the palms of your hands, then dust with cornflour (cornstarch) to prevent them from sticking when you cook them.

FROM CHINA

LION'S HEAD MEATBALLS

THIS DISH IS SO NAMED BECAUSE THE LARGE MEATBALLS ARE SAID TO LOOK LIKE LION'S HEADS SURROUNDED BY A MANE OF BOK CHOY (PAK CHOI). ORIGINALLY THE MEATBALLS TENDED TO BE MADE FROM PORK AND PORK FAT AND WERE COARSER IN TEXTURE.

450 g (1 lb) minced (ground) pork
1 egg white
4 spring onions (scallions), finely chopped
1 tablespoon Shaoxing rice wine
1 teaspoon grated ginger
1 tablespoon light soy sauce
2 teaspoons sugar
1 teaspoon roasted sesame oil
300 g (10½ oz) bok choy (pak choi)
1 tablespoon cornflour (cornstarch)
oil for frying
500 ml (2 cups) chicken and meat stock (see recipe on page 491)

SERVES 4

PUT the pork and egg white in a food processor and process briefly until you have a fluffy mixture, or mash the pork in a large bowl and gradually stir in the egg white, beating the mixture well until it is fluffy. Add the spring onion, rice wine, ginger, soy sauce, sugar and sesame oil, season with salt and white pepper, and process or beat again briefly. Fry a small portion of the mixture and taste it, reseasoning if necessary. Divide the mixture into walnut-size balls.

SEPARATE the boy choy leaves and place in the bottom of a clay pot or casserole dish.

DUST the meatballs with cornflour.

HEAT a wok over high heat, add 1 cm (½ inch) oil and heat until very hot. Cook the meatballs in batches until they are browned all over. Drain well and add to the clay pot in an even layer. Pour off the oil and wipe out the wok.

REHEAT the wok over high heat until very hot, add the chicken stock and heat until it is boiling. Pour over the meatballs. Cover and bring very slowly to the boil. Simmer gently with the lid slightly open for 1½ hours, or until the meatballs are very tender.

SERVE the meatballs in the dish they were cooked in.

FROM INDIA

PORK WITH CAPSICUM AND POTATOES

THIS IS A FAVOURITE IN SIMLA IN THE NORTH OF INDIA. THE 'POTATO OF THE MOUNTAIN' AND THE GREEN CAPSICUM ARE COOKED WITH PORK. THIS DISH IS IDEAL SERVED WITH ANY INDIAN BREADS SUCH AS PARATHAS, PURIS OR CHAPATIS.

125 ml (4 fl oz/½ cup) oil

1 large onion, chopped

4 garlic cloves, crushed

8 cm (3 inch) piece of ginger, chopped

2 Indian bay leaves (cassia leaves)

600 g (1 lb 5 oz) pork spare rib chops, bones removed, meat cut into 2 cm (¾ inch) cubes

pinch of asafoetida

1 teaspoon chilli powder

½ teaspoon ground turmeric

1½ tablespoons ground cumin

1½ tablespoons ground coriander

½ teaspoon garam masala (see recipe on page 464)

1½ tablespoons lemon juice

4 dried chillies

1 teaspoon kalonji (nigella seeds)

1 teaspoon yellow mustard seeds

2 tomatoes, finely chopped

4 green chillies

2 teaspoons paprika

2 red capsicums (peppers), cut into 2.5 cm (1 inch) pieces

2 green capsicums (peppers), cut into 2.5 cm (1 inch) pieces

1 tablespoon salt

1 teaspoon ground black pepper

500 g (1 lb 2 oz) potatoes, cut into 3 cm (1 inch) cubes

10 curry leaves

1 teaspoon garam masala (see recipe on page 464) extra

SERVES 6

HEAT about 80 ml (2 fl oz/⅓ cup) of the oil in a karhai or casserole over medium heat. Add half of each of the onion, garlic and ginger, along with the bay leaves and fry for about 2 minutes, until the onion is soft. Increase the heat to high, add the meat and asafoetida and fry for 2 minutes, stirring until all the meat is brown. Reduce the heat to medium and cook for 10 minutes. Remove from the heat, lift out the meat with a spatula and place in a large bowl.

ADD the chilli powder, turmeric, 1¼ tablespoons cumin, 2 teaspoons coriander and the garam masala to the meat, stirring in while meat is still warm. Stir in the lemon juice.

HEAT the remaining oil in the same pan over medium heat and fry the remaining onion, garlic and ginger for a few minutes until the onion is soft. Add dried chillies, kalonji, yellow mustard seeds and the remaining coriander and cumin. Fry for about 2 minutes, or until the seeds start to pop. Add the chopped tomato and fry for 1 minute. Reduce heat to a simmer and cook for 5 minutes, or until the liquid from the tomato has reduced.

STIR in the green chillies and the paprika. Add the meat and stir over medium heat for 2 minutes, or until all the sauce has been absorbed by the meat. Add the red and green capsicum, reduce the heat to simmering and cover pan. The capsicum will release its own water so no extra water is needed. Cook 10 minutes, then add the salt, pepper and cubed potato. Add 125 ml (4 fl oz/½ cup) water, cover and simmer for 1 hour, stirring occasionally. Add curry leaves and cook for another 15 minutes. The meat and potato should be very tender, but if not, cook for a further 15 minutes. Add the extra garam masala and season with salt, to taste.

The spice market in Delhi houses offices and dwellings on its upper floors.

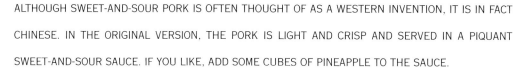

A pickle stall in Sichuan.

Deep-frying the pork gives it a crispy, well-browned outside while keeping the meat inside very tender.

FROM CHINA

SWEET AND SOUR PORK

ALTHOUGH SWEET-AND-SOUR PORK IS OFTEN THOUGHT OF AS A WESTERN INVENTION, IT IS IN FACT CHINESE. IN THE ORIGINAL VERSION, THE PORK IS LIGHT AND CRISP AND SERVED IN A PIQUANT SWEET-AND-SOUR SAUCE. IF YOU LIKE, ADD SOME CUBES OF PINEAPPLE TO THE SAUCE.

600 g (1 lb 5 oz) centre-cut pork loin, trimmed
1 egg
100 g (3½ oz) cornflour (cornstarch)
1 tablespoon oil
1 onion, cubed
1 red capsicum (pepper), cubed or cut into small triangles
2 spring onions (scallions), cut into 2 cm (¾ inch) lengths
150 g (5 oz) Chinese pickles
250 ml (1 cup) clear rice vinegar
60 ml (2 fl oz/¼ cup) tomato sauce (ketchup)
300 g (1⅓ cups) sugar
oil for deep-frying

SERVES 4

CUT the pork into 2 cm (¾ inch) cubes and put it in a bowl with the egg, 75 g (2½ oz) of the cornflour and 2 teaspoons water. Stir to coat all of the pieces of pork.

HEAT a wok over high heat, add the oil and heat until very hot. Stir-fry the onion for 1 minute. Add the capsicum and spring onion and cook for 1 minute. Add the pickles and toss together to combine. Add the rice vinegar, tomato sauce and sugar and stir over low heat until the sugar dissolves. Bring to the boil, then simmer for 3 minutes.

COMBINE the remaining cornflour with about 80 ml (3 fl oz/⅓ cup) water, add to sweet-and-sour mixture. Simmer until thickened. Set aside.

FILL a wok one-quarter full of oil. Heat the oil to 180°C (350°F), or until a piece of bread fries golden brown in 15 seconds when dropped in the oil. Cook pork in batches until golden brown and crisp. Return all of the pork to the wok, cook until crisp again, then remove with a wire sieve or slotted spoon and drain well. Add pork pieces to the sauce, stir to coat, and reheat until bubbling.

FROM JAPAN

TONKATSU

ALTHOUGH TONKATSU ACTUALLY COUNTS AS *YOSHOKU*, A WESTERN DISH, SINCE IT WAS FIRST TASTED IN THE LATE 19TH CENTURY, THE JAPANESE HAVE ADOPTED IT AS THEIR OWN. THEIR VERSION HAS A CRISP, LIGHT PANKO CRUST, AND IS SERVED SLICED TO ENABLE EATING WITH CHOPSTICKS.

4 x 150 g (51/2 oz) or 700 g pork
   schnitzels (1 lb 9 oz) pork fillets
plain (all-purpose) flour, for coating
1 egg, lightly beaten
panko (Japanese breadcrumbs),
   for coating
vegetable oil, for deep-frying
60 ml (2 fl oz/1/4 cup) sesame oil

TONKATSU SAUCE
60 ml (2 fl oz/1/4 cup) worcestershire
   sauce
2 tablespoons tamari or shoyu
   (Japanese soy sauce)
2 tablespoons caster (superfine)
   sugar
2 tablespoons tomato sauce
   (ketchup)
1/2 teaspoon Japanese mustard
1 tablespoon sake
1 tablespoon Japanese rice vinegar
1 clove garlic, bruised

1/4 white cabbage, very finely
   shredded, to serve
lemon wedges, to serve
Japanese mustard, to serve,
   optional

SERVES 4

USING a meat mallet or the back of a large, heavy knife, pound the pork schnitzel until 5 mm (1/4 inch) thick, then lightly score around the edges with the point of the knife to prevent it from curling during cooking. If using pork fillets, trim any skinny ends and cut into 5 cm (2 inch) lengths. Do not pound.

SEASON the flour with salt and pepper. Lightly coat the pork with the seasoned flour. Dip pork pieces into the egg, allowing any excess to drip off, then coat in panko, pressing down on both sides to help the crumbs adhere. Transfer to a plate, cover and refrigerate for 15 minutes.

MEANWHILE, to make the tonkatsu sauce, combine all the ingredients in a small saucepan and bring to the boil over high heat. Reduce to a simmer and cook for 20 minutes, or until glossy and thickened slightly.

FILL a deep heavy-based saucepan or deep-fat fryer one-third full of vegetable oil and add the sesame oil. Heat to 170°C (325°F), or until a cube of bread dropped in the oil browns in 20 seconds. Cook schnitzels one at a time, or the fillet a few pieces at a time, turning once or twice for about 4 minutes, or until golden brown all over and cooked through. The fillet will take a little longer, about 6–8 minutes. Drain on crumpled paper towels, then keep warm in a low oven while you cook the rest.

SLICE the pork schnitzel, then lift it onto serving plates, arranging the fillet in its original shape. Serve with a pile of cabbage and lemon wedges, and pass around the sauce. If you like, serve with mustard. For a hearty meal, serve with rice and miso soup.

Cook the schnitzels, one at a time, until golden brown.

Palm sugar (jaggery) on sale.

BARBECUED PORK SPARE RIBS

2–3 garlic cloves, chopped
1 tablespoon chopped coriander (cilantro) roots or ground coriander
6 tablespoons palm sugar (jaggery)
7 tablespoons plum sauce or tomato ketchup
2 tablespoons light soy sauce
2 tablespoons oyster sauce
1 teaspoon ground pepper
½ teaspoon ground star anise (optional)
900 g (2 lb) pork spare ribs, chopped into 13–15 cm (5–6 inch) long pieces (baby back, if possible – ask your butcher to prepare it)

SERVES 4

USING a pestle and mortar or a small blender, pound or blend the garlic and coriander roots into a paste. In a large bowl, combine all the ingredients and rub marinade all over the ribs with your fingers. Cover with plastic wrap and marinate in the refrigerator for at least 3 hours, or overnight.

PREHEAT oven to 180°C/350°F/Gas 4 or heat a barbecue or grill (broiler). If cooking in the oven, place the ribs with all the marinade in a baking dish. Bake for 45–60 minutes, basting several times during cooking. If barbecuing, put the ribs on the grill, cover and cook for 45 minutes, turning and basting a couple of times. If the ribs do not go sufficiently brown, grill (broil) them for 5 minutes on each side until well browned and slightly charred. If using a grill, line the grill tray with foil. Cook the pork, turning several times and brushing frequently with the remaining sauce, until the meat is cooked through and slightly charred.

DEEP-FRIED PORK SPARE RIBS

DEEP-FRIED PORK SPARE RIBS

5 coriander (cilantro) roots, chopped
3 garlic cloves, finely chopped
1 tablespoon fish sauce
1½ tablespoons oyster sauce
½ teaspoon ground white pepper
900 g (2 lb) pork spare ribs, chopped into 4–5 cm (1½–2 inch) long pieces (baby back, if possible, ask your butcher to prepare it)
vegetable oil, for deep-frying
sweet chilli sauce (see recipe on page 476), to serve

SERVES 4

USING a pestle and mortar or a small blender, pound or blend the coriander roots and garlic into a paste. In a large bowl, combine the coriander paste, fish sauce, oyster sauce and ground pepper. Rub the marinade into the pork ribs using your fingertips, then cover and marinate in the refrigerator for at least 3 hours, or overnight.

HEAT 6 cm (2½ inches) oil in a wok or deep frying pan over a medium heat. When the oil seems hot, drop a small piece of garlic into it. If it sizzles at once, the oil is ready. It's important not to have the oil too hot or the spare ribs will burn. Deep-fry half the ribs at a time for about 15 minutes or until golden brown and cooked. Drain on paper towels.

SERVE with sweet chilli sauce.

RED PORK CURRY WITH GREEN PEPPERCORNS

PEPPERCORNS ADD A DISTINCTIVE, VERY FRESH AND SPICY, NOT TOO HOT, TASTE TO THIS DISH. YOU CAN USE PORK, AS SUGGESTED, OR FINELY SLICED CHICKEN THIGH FILLETS. COOKED BABY POTATOES AND BAMBOO SHOOTS ARE A POPULAR ADDITION TO THIS CURRY.

60 ml (2 fl oz/¼ cup) coconut
   cream (see recipe on page 468)
2 tablespoons red curry paste
   (see recipe on page 472) or
   bought paste
3 tablespoons fish sauce
1½ tablespoons palm sugar
   (jaggery)
500 g (1 lb 2 oz) lean pork,
   finely sliced
440 ml (15 fl oz/1¾ cups) coconut
   milk (see recipe on page 468)
280 g (10 oz) Thai eggplants
   (aubergines), cut in halves
   or quarters, or 1 eggplant
   (aubergine), cubed
75 g (3 oz) fresh green
   peppercorns, cleaned
7 makrut (kaffir lime) leaves,
   torn in half
2 long red chillies, seeded
   and finely sliced, for garnish

SERVES 4

PUT the coconut cream in a wok or saucepan and simmer over a medium heat for about 5 minutes, or until the cream separates and a layer of oil forms on the surface. Stir the cream if it starts to brown around the edges.

ADD the curry paste, stir well to combine and cook until fragrant.

ADD the fish sauce and palm sugar and cook for another 2 minutes or until the mixture begins to darken.

ADD the pork and stir for 5–7 minutes.

ADD the coconut milk to the saucepan or wok and simmer over a medium heat for another 5 minutes.

ADD the eggplants and green peppercorns and cook for 5 minutes.

ADD the makrut leaves. Taste, then adjust the seasoning if necessary.

TRANSFER to a serving bowl. Top with chillies.

Thai cuisine is built on a large number of highly flavoured aromatic ingredients. These are used, despite their diversity, to produce an overall effect of some sophistication, balance and subtlety.

This slow-cooked dish results in the most tender, succulent pork.

OKINAWAN SLOW COOKED PORK

PORK IS EXTREMELY POPULAR ON THE ISLANDS OF OKINAWA, WHERE THE CULTURE AND CUISINE HAVE BEEN INFLUENCED BY THEIR PROXIMITY TO CHINA. THIS TENDER, GINGER-FLAVOURED DISH IS SLOW-COOKED FOR SEVERAL HOURS, AND BLACK SUGAR LENDS A PARTICULARLY CARAMELY GLAZE.

2 teaspoons vegetable oil
1 kg (2 lb 4 oz) pork belly, boneless, cut into 5 cm (2 inch) cubes
100 g (3½ oz) fresh ginger, peeled and cut into thick slices
500 ml (17 fl oz/2 cups) dashi II (see recipe on page 483)
170 ml (5½ fl oz/⅔ cup) sake
60 ml (2 fl oz/¼ cup) mirin
80 g (2¾ oz/⅓ cup firmly packed) black or dark brown sugar
125 ml (4 fl oz/½ cup) shoyu (Japanese soy sauce)
Japanese mustard, to serve, optional

SERVES 4–6

HEAT the oil in a large, heavy-based saucepan or small flameproof casserole dish over high heat. Add pork in two batches and cook for 5 minutes, or until browned all over.

RINSE the pork under hot water to remove excess oil. Remove any excess fat from the pan and return the pork to the pan, adding enough cold water to cover well. Add ginger slices and bring to the boil over high heat. Reduce to a simmer and cook 2 hours. Top up with water, if needed. Strain, discarding the liquid and ginger. Set the pork aside.

PUT the dashi, sake, mirin, sugar and shoyu in a clean, heavy-based saucepan and stir over high heat until the sugar has dissolved. Add the pork and return to the boil, then reduce to a simmer and cook, turning occasionally, for 1 hour, or until the pork is very tender. Remove from the heat and leave the pork to rest in the liquid for 20 minutes. Place the pork in a serving dish, cover and keep warm while you reduce the sauce.

SIT the saucepan over high heat, bring the liquid to the boil and cook for 5 minutes, or until the sauce has reduced to a slightly syrupy glaze. Return the pork to the sauce and stir to combine before arranging in a serving dish. Pour over any remaining sauce and serve immediately, with a little Japanese mustard on the side, if using.

SERVE with rice and Asian greens.

FROM THAILAND

CHIANG MAI PORK CURRY

THIS BURMESE-STYLE CURRY IS TYPICAL OF THE CHIANG MAI AREA. UNLIKE FRAGRANT THAI CURRIES, THIS HAS A SPICIER, ALMOST INDIAN FLAVOUR. NEARLY ALWAYS MADE WITH PORK, YOU WILL OCCASIONALLY FIND IT MADE WITH CHICKEN. THIS CURRY IMPROVES IF MADE IN ADVANCE.

500 g (1 lb 2 oz) pork belly,
  cut into cubes
2 tablespoons oil
2 garlic cloves, crushed
2 tablespoons Chiang Mai curry
  paste (see recipe on page 475)
  or bought paste
4 Asian shallots, smashed with the
  blade of a cleaver
4 cm (1½ inch) piece of ginger,
  shredded
4 tablespoons roasted unsalted
  peanuts
3 tablespoons tamarind purée
2 tablespoons fish sauce
2 tablespoons palm sugar (jaggery)

SERVES 4

BLANCH the pork cubes in boiling water for 1 minute, then drain well.

HEAT the oil in a wok or saucepan and fry the garlic for 1 minute.

ADD the curry paste and stir-fry until fragrant.

ADD the pork, shallots, ginger and peanuts and stir briefly. Add 500 ml (17 fl oz/2 cups) water and the tamarind purée and bring to a boil.

ADD the fish sauce and sugar and simmer for about 1½ hours or until the pork is very tender. Add more water as the pork cooks, if necessary. The meat is ready when it is very tender.

As soon as the curry paste is fragrant, stir in the pork, Asian shallots, ginger and peanuts.

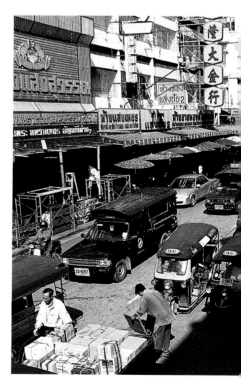

Songathews and tuk tuks in Chiang Mai.

Hanging the char siu to roast above a tray of water creates a steamy atmosphere which helps keep the meat moist. Generally in China, char siu is bought from take-aways as most homes do not have an oven.

CHAR SIU

CHAR SIU, OR BARBECUE PORK, IS A CANTONESE SPECIALITY THAT CAN BE SEEN HANGING IN CHINESE RESTAURANTS. CHAR SIU MEANS 'SUSPENDED OVER FIRE' AND IS TRADITIONALLY DYED A RED COLOUR.

MARINADE
1 tablespoon rock (lump) sugar
1 tablespoon yellow bean sauce
1 tablespoon hoisin sauce
1 tablespoon oyster sauce
1 tablespoon red fermented tofu
1 tablespoon Chinese spirit
    (Mou Tai) or brandy
1/2 teaspoon roasted sesame oil

750 g (1 lb 10 oz) centre-cut pork
    loin, trimmed and cut into four
    20 cm (8 inch) strips
2 tablespoons maltose or honey,
    dissolved with a little water

SERVES 4

TO MAKE the marinade, combine the ingredients. Add the pork to the marinade and leave in the fridge for at least 6 hours.

PREHEAT the oven to 220°C (425°F/Gas 7). Put a baking dish with 625 ml (21 fl oz//2½ cups) boiling water in the bottom of the oven. Drain pork, reserving marinade. Put an S-shaped meat hook through one end of each strip and hang from the top rack.

COOK for 10–15 minutes, then baste with the marinade. Reduce the heat to 180°C (350°F/Gas 4) and cook for 8–10 minutes. Cool for 2–3 minutes, then brush with the maltose and lightly brown under a grill (broiler) for 4–5 minutes, turning to give a charred look around the edges.

CUT the meat into slices. Add 185 ml (6 fl oz/¾ cup) cooking liquid to the marinade. Bring to the boil and cook for 2 minutes. Strain and pour over the pork.

SPICY CRISPY PORK

750 g (1 lb 10 oz) belly pork, rind on
1 teaspoon salt
1 teaspoon five-spice powder

DIPPING SAUCE
2 tablespoons light soy sauce
1 tablespoon dark soy sauce
1 tablespoon chilli sauce (optional)

SERVES 6

SCRAPE the pork rind to make sure it is free of any bristles. Dry, then rub with the salt and five-spice powder. Leave uncovered in the fridge for at least 2 hours.

TO MAKE the dipping sauce, combine all of the ingredients.

PREHEAT the oven to 240°C (475°F/Gas 9). Place the pork, skin side up, on a rack in a roasting tin. Roast for 20 minutes, reduce the heat to 200°C (400°F/Gas 6) and cook for 40–45 minutes until crispy. Cut into pieces and serve with the sauce.

SPICY CRISPY PORK

SHABU SHABU

INSPIRED BY MONGOLIAN HOTPOT COOKERY, SHABU SHABU IS ONE OF THE MOST ENJOYABLE OF WINTER DISHES. THE ARRAY OF INGREDIENTS IS PREPARED IN ADVANCE, MAKING IT POSSIBLE FOR THE HOSTS TO RELAX AND ENJOY A CONVIVIAL MEAL WITH THEIR GUESTS.

750 g (1 lb 10 oz) scotch fillet
   (rib eye), partially frozen
15 spring onions (scallions)
3 carrots
400 g (14 oz) button mushrooms
½ Chinese cabbage
150 g (5½ oz) firm (cotton) tofu
2 litres (70 fl oz/8 cups) chicken
   stock (see notes)
ready-made shabu-shabu sauce,
   to serve
220 g (7 oz/1 cup) Japanese short-
   grain rice, cooked

SERVES 4

CUT the steak into very thin slices and set aside.

CUT the firm section of the spring onions into 4 cm (1½ inch) lengths and discard the dark green tops. Slice the carrots very thinly. Slice the mushrooms. Chop the cabbage into bite-sized pieces and discard any tough parts. Cut the tofu into bite-sized cubes.

ARRANGE the prepared vegetables, tofu and meat in separate piles on a serving platter. Cover with plastic wrap and refrigerate until about 30 minutes before cooking time.

SET the table with individual place settings, each with a serving bowl, a bowl of shabu-shabu sauce, a bowl of rice, chopsticks, soup spoons (if desired) and napkins. Position the serving platter and cooking vessel (see note) so they are within easy reach of each diner.

WHEN all the diners are seated, pour the stock into the cooking vessel, cover and bring to a simmer. Each diner then picks up an ingredient or two with their chopsticks, and places it in the simmering stock for about 1 minute, or until just cooked. (Do not overcook – vegetables should be just tender and the steak still pink in the centre.) The food is dipped into the shabu shabu sauce and eaten with the rice. The remaining stock can be served as soup at the end of the meal.

Note: Dashi, made from dashi granules, can be substituted for the chicken stock. The cooking vessel can be an electric wok, a frying pan or flameproof casserole dish on a burner, or a steamboat.

The dish is prepared by submerging a very thin slice of meat or a piece of vegetable in a pot of boiling water or dashi (broth) made with kombu (kelp) and swishing it back and forth several times. The familiar swishing sound is where the dish gets its name. Shabu shabu roughly translates to 'swish-swish'.

Rice growing in paddy fields near Kochi (Cochin), Kerala.

GOAN BEEF CURRY

FRIED BEEF KERALA

oil for deep-frying
1 potato, cut into small cubes
500 g (1 lb 2 oz) rump steak, thinly sliced
3 garlic cloves, crushed
1 teaspoon ground black pepper
1 tablespoon ginger juice (page 488)
2 tablespoons oil, extra
2 onions, sliced in rings
60 ml (2 fl oz/$1/4$ cup) beef stock
2 tablespoons tomato paste (purée)
$1/2$ tablespoon soy sauce
1 teaspoon chilli powder
3 tablespoons lemon juice
3 tomatoes, chopped
90 g (3 oz/$1/2$ cup) fresh or frozen peas
coriander (cilantro) leaves (optional)

SERVES 4

FILL a deep, heavy-based saucepan one-third full with oil and heat to 180°C (350°F); it is hot enough when a cube of bread browns in it in 15 seconds. Deep-fry potato cubes until golden brown. Drain on paper towels.

PUT the steak in a bowl, add the garlic, pepper and ginger juice and toss well.

HEAT the oil and fry the beef quickly in batches over high heat. Keep each batch warm as you remove it. Reduce the heat, fry the onion until golden, then remove.

PUT stock, tomato paste, soy sauce, chilli powder and lemon juice in pan. Cook over medium heat until reduced. Add fried onion, cook 3 minutes, add chopped tomato and peas, then stir well and cook for 1 minute. Add beef and potato. Toss well until heated through. Garnish with coriander.

GOAN BEEF CURRY

8 cardamom pods
1 teaspoon fennel seeds
8 cloves
10 cm (4 inch) cinnamon stick
$1/2$ teaspoon fenugreek seeds
$1/2$ teaspoon ground black pepper
3 teaspoons coriander seeds
3 teaspoons cumin seeds
125 ml (4 fl oz/$1/2$ cup) oil
2 onions, finely chopped
6 garlic cloves, finely chopped
10 cm (4 inch) piece of ginger, grated
1 kg (2 lb 4 oz) braising or stewing steak, cut into 2.5 cm (1 inch) cubes
$1/2$ teaspoon ground turmeric
2 teaspoons chilli powder
100 g ($3 1/2$ oz) creamed coconut, dissolved in 310 ml (10 fl oz/$1 1/4$ cups) water

SERVES 6

REMOVE the seeds from the cardamom pods and grind them in a spice grinder or pestle and mortar with the fennel seeds, cloves, cinnamon stick, fenugreek seeds, black pepper and the coriander and cumin seeds, until they form a fine powder.

HEAT the oil in a karhai, heavy-based frying pan or casserole over medium heat and fry the onion, garlic and ginger until lightly browned. Add the meat and fry until brown all over. Add all the spices and fry for 1 minute. Add creamed coconut and bring slowly to the boil. Cover, reduce the heat. Simmer for about 1 hour, or until meat is tender.

IF the liquid evaporates during cooking, add about 185 ml (6 fl oz/$3/4$ cup) boiling water and stir to make a thick sauce. If the sauce is still too liquid at the end of the cooking time, simmer with the lid off until it evaporates. Season with salt, to taste.

FROM JAPAN

STEAK IN ROASTED SESAME SEED MARINADE

THE RICH ESSENCE OF A SESAME AND SOY MARINADE SPIKED WITH GINGER AND GARLIC PERMEATES THESE JUICY STEAKS. A HEAP OF CRISP SPRING ONION (SCALLION) CURLS MAKES AN ATTRACTIVE GARNISH, WHILE A SPICY DIPPING SAUCE ADDS STILL MORE FLAVOUR AT THE TABLE.

2 tablespoons sesame seeds
1 clove garlic, crushed
3 cm (1¼ inch) piece fresh ginger, grated
2 tablespoons shoyu (Japanese soy sauce)
1 tablespoon sake
1 teaspoon caster (superfine) sugar
500 g (1 lb 2 oz) scotch fillet (rib eye), cut into 4 steaks
3 spring onions (scallions)
1 tablespoon oil

DIPPING SAUCE
4 cm (1½ inch) piece fresh ginger
½ teaspoon shichimi togarashi (seven-spice mix)
125 ml (4 fl oz/½ cup) shoyu (Japanese soy sauce)
2 teaspoons dashi granules

SERVES 4

ROAST the sesame seeds in a dry frying pan over low heat for 2 minutes, shaking the pan constantly, until the seeds begin to pop. Crush the toasted seeds in a mortar and pestle.

PLACE the crushed sesame seeds, garlic, ginger, shoyu, sake and sugar in a bowl and whisk until the sugar has dissolved.

PLACE the steaks in a shallow dish, spoon the marinade over the top and marinate for 30 minutes.

TO MAKE dipping sauce, cut ginger lengthways into very fine strips about 4 cm (1½ inch) long. Put sliced ginger, shichimi togarashi, shoyu, dashi and 2 tablespoons water in a small bowl and whisk lightly until well combined.

CUT the spring onions lengthways into very fine strips about 4 cm (1½ inch) long. Place the strips in a bowl of iced water and leave until they are crisp and curled, then drain.

REMOVE the steaks from the marinade and lightly brush them with the oil. Grill (broil) or fry them in a frying pan or chargrill pan for 4–6 minutes on each side – don't overcook or they will become tough. Set the steaks aside for 5 minutes, then cut into diagonal slices.

ARRANGE the slices on serving plates and drizzle over a little of the dipping sauce. Garnish with the spring onion curls and serve with steamed rice and the remaining dipping sauce.

Arrange the steak slices on serving plates and drizzle over a little of the dipping sauce. Garnish with spring onion curls and serve with steamed rice and the remaining dipping sauce.

As with many Thai curries, this one cooks relatively quickly. Keep the meat moving around the wok until you add the liquid.

Busy bustling Bangkok.

FROM THAILAND

PANAENG BEEF CURRY

PANAENG CURRY IS A DRY, RICH, THICK CURRY MADE WITH SMALL AMOUNTS OF COCONUT MILK AND A DRY (PANAENG) CURRY PASTE, WHICH HAS RED CHILLIES, LEMONGRASS, GALANGAL AND PEANUTS. IT IS NOT TOO HOT AND HAS A SWEET AND SOUR TASTE. YOU CAN USE ANY TENDER CUT OF BEEF.

2 tablespoons vegetable oil
2 tablespoons dry curry paste (see recipe on page 475) or bought paste
700 g (1 lb 9 oz) beef flank steak, sliced into strips
185 ml (6 fl oz/¾ cup) coconut milk (see recipe on page 468)
1 tablespoon fish sauce
1 tablespoon palm sugar (jaggery)
3 tablespoons tamarind purée
2 makrut (kaffir lime) leaves, finely sliced, for garnish
½ long red chilli, seeded and finely sliced, for garnish
cucumber relish (see recipe on page 479), to serve

SERVES 4

HEAT the oil in a saucepan or wok and stir-fry the curry paste over a medium heat for 2 minutes or until fragrant.

ADD beef and stir for 5 minutes. Add nearly all of the coconut milk, the fish sauce, palm sugar and tamarind purée and reduce to a low heat. Simmer, uncovered, for 5–7 minutes. Although this is meant to be a dry curry, you can add a little more water during cooking if you feel it is drying out too much. Taste and adjust the seasoning, if needed.

SPOON the curry into a serving bowl, spoon the last bit of coconut milk over the top and sprinkle with makrut leaves and chilli slices.

SERVE with cucumber relish.

BEEF WITH OYSTER SAUCE

300 g (11 oz) rump or sirloin steak, trimmed
1 teaspoon sugar
1 tablespoon dark soy sauce
2 teaspoons Shaoxing rice wine
2 teaspoons cornflour (cornstarch)
4 dried Chinese mushrooms
oil for deep-frying
4 slices ginger
1 spring onion (scallion), cut into short lengths
75 g (2¹/₂ oz) snowpeas (mangetout), ends trimmed
1 small carrot, thinly sliced
¹/₂ teaspoon salt
2–3 tablespoons chicken and meat stock (see recipe on page 491)
2 tablespoons oyster sauce

SERVES 4

CUT beef across the grain into thin bite-size slices. Combine with half the sugar, the soy sauce, rice wine, cornflour and 2 tablespoons water. Marinate in the fridge for several hours, or overnight.

SOAK the dried mushrooms in boiling water for 30 minutes, then drain and squeeze out any excess water. Remove and discard stems and cut the caps in half, or quarters if large.

FILL a wok one-quarter full of oil. Heat the oil to 180°C (350°F), or until a piece of bread fries golden brown in 15 seconds when dropped in the oil. Cook the beef for 45–50 seconds, stirring to separate the pieces, and remove as soon as the colour changes. Drain well in a colander. Pour the oil from the wok, leaving 2 tablespoons.

REHEAT the reserved oil over high heat until very hot and stir-fry the ginger and spring onion for 1 minute. Add the snowpeas, mushrooms and carrot and stir-fry for 1 minute, then add the salt, stock and remaining sugar. Stir-fry for 1 minute. Toss with the beef and oyster sauce.

STEAMED BEEF WITH RICE FLOUR

450 g (1 lb) rump or sirloin steak
2 tablespoons soy sauce
1 tablespoon chilli bean paste (toban jiang)
1 tablespoon Shaoxing rice wine
1 tablespoon finely chopped ginger
¹/₄ teaspoon freshly ground white pepper
1 tablespoon oil
125 g (4 oz) glutinous rice flour
¹/₂ teaspoon ground cinnamon
1 teaspoon roasted sesame oil
1 spring onion (scallion), shredded

SERVES 4

CUT the beef into 2 mm (¹/₈ inch) slices and cut the slices into bite-size pieces. Combine with the soy sauce, chilli bean paste, rice wine, ginger, pepper and oil. Marinate in fridge for 30 minutes.

DRY-FRY the rice flour in a wok until it is brown and smells roasted. Add the cinnamon. Drain the beef and toss in the rice flour to coat the slices.

PLACE the beef slices in a steamer lined with greaseproof paper punched with holes. Cover and steam over simmering water in a wok for 20 minutes. Sprinkle with the sesame oil and garnish with the spring onion.

STEAMED BEEF WITH RICE FLOUR

FROM THAILAND

MASSAMAN CURRY WITH BEEF

THIS CURRY HAS MANY CHARACTERISTICS OF SOUTHERN THAI COOKING. THE SWEET FLAVOURS AND SPICES DOMINATE, EVEN THOUGH THE CURRY IS MODERATELY HOT. IT ALSO HAS A SOUR TASTE FROM THE TAMARIND. THIS DISH IS ONE OF THE FEW THAI DISHES WITH POTATOES AND PEANUTS.

2 pieces of cinnamon stick
10 cardamom seeds
5 cloves
2 tablespoons vegetable oil
2 tablespoons massaman curry paste (see recipe on page 472) or bought paste
800 g (1 lb 12 oz) beef flank or rump steak, cut into 5 cm (2 inch) cubes
410 ml (14 fl oz/1⅔ cups) coconut milk (see recipe on page 468)
250 ml (8 fl oz/1 cup) beef stock
2 or 3 potatoes, cut into 2.5 cm (1 inch) pieces
2 cm (¾ inch) piece of ginger, shredded
3 tablespoons fish sauce
3 tablespoons palm sugar (jaggery)
110 g (⅔ cup) ready-made roasted salted peanuts, without skin
3 tablespoons tamarind purée

SERVES 4

DRY-FRY the cinnamon stick, cardamom seeds and cloves in a saucepan or wok over a low heat. Stir all the ingredients around for 2–3 minutes or until fragrant. Remove from the pan.

HEAT the oil in the same saucepan or wok and stir-fry the massaman paste over a medium heat for 2 minutes or until fragrant.

ADD the beef to the pan and stir for 5 minutes.

ADD the coconut milk, stock, potatoes, ginger, fish sauce, palm sugar, three-quarters of the roasted peanuts, tamarind purée and the dry-fried spices. Reduce the heat to low and gently simmer for 50–60 minutes until the meat is tender and the potatoes are just cooked. Taste, then adjust the seasoning if necessary.

SPOON into a serving bowl and garnish with the rest of the roasted peanuts.

Floating vendor.

FROM JAPAN

GLAZED BEEF AND VEGETABLE ROLLS

THE CLASSIC IDEA OF 'MEAT AND VEGETABLES' IS REDEFINED BY THESE FLAVOURFUL ROLLS. ASPARAGUS SPEARS AND SPRING ONION (SCALLION) STALKS ARE WRAPPED IN THIN SLICES OF BEEF, BROWNED IN A LITTLE OIL, AND ENRICHED WITH A SLIGHTLY SWEET SOY GLAZE.

400 g (14 oz) sirloin steak, cut into
   3 cm (1¼ inch) thick slices,
   trimmed
2½ teaspoons potato starch, for
   sprinkling
6 spring onions (scallions), cut into
   twelve 6 cm (2½ inch) lengths
6 thin asparagus spears, trimmed,
   cut in half and lightly blanched
vegetable oil, for cooking
80 ml (2½ fl oz/⅓ cup) sake
80 ml (2½ fl oz/⅓ cup) mirin
80 ml (2½ fl oz/⅓ cup) shoyu
   (Japanese soy sauce)
1½ tablespoons caster (superfine)
   sugar

MAKES 12 ROLLS

FREEZE the beef for 3 hours, or until partially frozen. Use a sharp knife to slice very thinly along the length of the steak to make long, thin strips – you should have about 24 slices. Lay one strip of beef on a clean work surface with the short end towards you. Lay another strip alongside it so that it just overlaps along its length, forming one strip of meat about 6 cm (2½ inch) wide at the short end. Sprinkle with a little seasoned potato starch. Repeat with the rest of the meat – you should have 12 strips in total. Put a piece of spring onion and asparagus along the edge of the beef closest to you, then roll up and secure with kitchen string. Repeat with the remaining beef and vegetables. Heat a little vegetable oil in a large frying pan over medium–high heat, then, working in batches, cook the rolls for 5–7 minutes, or until browned all over. Remove from the pan.

COMBINE the sake, mirin, shoyu and caster sugar with 80 ml (2½ fl oz/⅓ cup) water, then add to the pan, stirring until the sugar dissolves. Bring to the boil for 1 minute, then reduce to a simmer. Add beef rolls and cook for 5 minutes, or until cooked through, turning occasionally. Remove from the pan. Carefully cut the string from the rolls, transfer beef rolls to a plate, cover with foil and set aside until needed.

POUR any meat juices from the resting meat into the pan, then sit the pan over medium–high heat and bring to the boil. Cook for 5–7 minutes, or until liquid is slightly thickened and glossy. Return beef rolls to the pan immediately and cook for a further minute, turning continuously to coat and glaze well. Remove from the heat. Cut each roll into thirds if serving with chopsticks, and drizzle with remaining glaze before serving at once.

SERVE with a crisp green salad and rice.

Roll up the beef to enclose the vegetables and tie with string.

STIR-FRIED BEEF WITH SPRING ONIONS

500 g (1 lb 2 oz) rump or sirloin steak
2 garlic cloves, finely chopped
2 tablespoons light soy sauce
1 tablespoon Shaoxing rice wine
2 teaspoons sugar
1 tablespoon cornflour (cornstarch)
3 tablespoons oil
5 spring onions (scallions), green
    part only, cut into thin strips

SAUCE
3 tablespoons light soy sauce
2 teaspoons sugar
½ teaspoon roasted sesame oil

SERVES 6

CUT the beef across the grain into 2 mm (⅛ inch) thick slices. Cut into bite-sized pieces. Combine with the garlic, soy, rice wine, sugar and cornflour. Marinate in the fridge for at least 1 hour. Drain.

TO MAKE the sauce, combine all the ingredients.

HEAT a wok over high heat, add the oil and heat until very hot. Cook the beef in two batches for 1½ minutes, or until brown. Remove and drain. Pour the oil from the wok, leaving 1 tablespoon.

REHEAT the reserved oil over high heat until very hot and stir-fry the spring onion for 1 minute. Add the beef and the sauce. Toss to coat the meat and spring onion with the sauce.

CRISPY SHREDDED BEEF

CRISPY SHREDDED BEEF

400 g (14 oz) rump or sirloin steak,
    trimmed
2 eggs, beaten
½ teaspoon salt
4 tablespoons cornflour (cornstarch)
oil for deep-frying
2 carrots, finely shredded
2 spring onions (scallions), shredded
1 garlic clove, finely chopped
2 red chillies, shredded
80 g (2½ oz/⅓ cup) caster
    (superfine) sugar
3 tablespoons Chinese black
    rice vinegar
2 tablespoons light soy sauce

SERVES 4

CUT the beef into thin shreds. Combine the eggs, salt and cornflour, then coat the shredded beef with the batter. Mix well.

FILL a wok one-quarter full of oil. Heat the oil to 180°C (350°F), or until a piece of bread fries golden brown in 15 seconds when dropped in the oil. Cook beef for about 4 minutes, stirring to separate, then remove and drain. Cook the carrot for 1½ minutes, then remove and drain. Pour the oil from the wok, leaving 1 tablespoon.

REHEAT the reserved oil over high heat until very hot and stir-fry the spring onion, garlic and chilli for a few seconds. Add the beef, carrot, sugar, vinegar and soy and stir to combine.

FROM JAPAN

TEPPANYAKI

STEAK AND VEGETABLES PREPARED ON A HOT *TEPPAN*, AN IRON PLATE OR SHEET, ARE A REAL TASTE TREAT, BUT NEVER MORE SO THAN WHEN THEY ARE COOKED RIGHT AT THE TABLE WHERE DINERS NOT ONLY ENJOY THE COLOURS AND AROMAS BUT ALSO SHARE COMPANIONSHIP AND CONVERSATION.

350 g (12 oz) scotch fillet (rib eye), partially frozen
4 small slender eggplants (aubergines)
100 g (3½ oz) fresh shiitake mushrooms
100 g (3½ oz) small green beans
6 yellow or green baby (pattypan) squash
1 red or green capsicum (pepper), seeded
6 spring onions (scallions)
200 g (7 oz) tinned bamboo shoots, drained
60 ml (2 fl oz/¼ cup) oil
sesame seed sauce (see recipe on page 484) or ready-made, to serve

SERVES 4

SLICE the steak into very thin pieces. Place the meat slices in a single layer on a large serving platter and season thoroughly with plenty of salt and freshly ground black pepper. Set aside.

TRIM the ends from the eggplants and cut the flesh into long, very thin diagonal slices. Trim any hard stems from the mushrooms. Top and tail the beans. If beans are longer than 7 cm (3 inches), cut them in half. Quarter, halve or leave the baby squash whole, depending on the size. Cut the capsicum into thin strips. Remove the outer layer of the spring onions and slice into lengths about 7 cm (3 inches) long, discarding the tops. Arrange the vegetables in separate bundles on the platter.

WHEN the diners are seated, heat a portable tabletop grill or electric frying pan until very hot, then lightly brush it with the oil.

QUICKLY fry a quarter of the meat, searing on both sides, and then push it over to the edge of the pan. Add about a quarter of the vegetables and quickly stir-fry, adding a little more oil as needed.

SERVE a small portion of the meat and vegetables to the diners, along with the sesame seed sauce, for dipping. Repeat the process with the remaining meat and vegetables, cooking in batches as extra helpings are required. Serve with steamed rice.

The word *teppanyaki* is derived from *teppan*, which means iron plate, and *yaki*, which means fried or broiled.

Tying the spring onions (scallions) into knots bruises the flesh and allows more flavour to come out.

FROM CHINA

FIVE-SPICE BEEF

750 g (1 lb 10 oz) shin of beef or stewing or braising beef, trimmed
2 spring onions (scallions), each tied in a knot
3 slices ginger, smashed with the flat side of a cleaver
4 tablespoons Chinese spirit (Mou Tai) or brandy
1.5 litres (52 fl oz/6 cups) chicken and meat stock (see recipe on page 491)
1 teaspoon salt
4 tablespoons light soy sauce
3 tablespoons dark soy sauce
1 tablespoon five-spice powder
150 g (5½ oz) rock (lump) sugar
1 spring onion (scallion), finely sliced
1 teaspoon roasted sesame oil

SERVES 8

CUT the beef into two to three long strips and place in a clay pot or casserole with the spring onions, ginger, Chinese spirit and stock. Bring to the boil and skim off any scum. Simmer, covered, for 15–20 minutes.

ADD the salt, soy sauces, five-spice powder and sugar to the beef, return to the boil, then simmer, covered, for 25–30 minutes.

LEAVE the beef in the liquid to cool for 1 hour, then remove, drain, and cool for 3–4 hours. Just before serving, slice thinly across the grain and sprinkle with the spring onion and sesame oil.

RED-COOKED BEEF

500 g (1 lb 2 oz) shin of beef or stewing or braising beef, trimmed
3 tablespoons Shaoxing rice wine
3 slices ginger
3 tablespoons dark soy sauce
60 g (2 oz) rock (lump) sugar
300 g (10 oz) carrots
1 teaspoon salt

SERVES 4

CUT the beef into 1.5 cm (½ inch) cubes and put in a clay pot or casserole with enough water to cover. Add the rice wine and ginger, bring to the boil, skim off any scum, then simmer, covered, for 35–40 minutes. Add the soy and sugar and simmer for 10–15 minutes.

CUT the carrots into pieces roughly the same size as the beef, add to the saucepan with the salt and cook for 20–25 minutes.

RED-COOKED BEEF

BEEF WITH THAI SWEET BASIL LEAVES

THAI SWEET BASIL IS ONE OF THE TROPICAL HERBS WITH A DISTINCTIVE FLAVOUR AND PERFUME THAT
INSTANTLY EVOKES THAI CUISINE. NO OTHER HERB WILL DO AS A SUBSTITUTE FOR THIS RECIPE. YOUR
WOK SHOULD BE VERY HOT AND THE DISH SHOULD TAKE NO MORE THAN 7 OR 8 MINUTES TO COOK.

1 tablespoon fish sauce
3 tablespoons oyster sauce
4 tablespoons vegetable or
  chicken stock, or water
½ teaspoon sugar
2 tablespoons vegetable oil
4 garlic cloves, finely chopped
3 bird's eye chillies, lightly crushed
  with the side of a cleaver
500 g (1 lb 2 oz) tender rump or
  fillet steak, finely sliced
1 medium onion, cut into thin
  wedges
2 handfuls of Thai sweet basil
  leaves

SERVES 4

MIX the fish sauce, oyster sauce, stock and sugar
in a small bowl.

HEAT the oil in the wok or frying pan and
stir-fry half the garlic over a medium heat until
light brown.

ADD half the crushed chillies and half the meat
and stir-fry over a high heat for 2–3 minutes or
until the meat is cooked. Remove from the wok
and repeat with the remaining garlic, chillies and
meat. Return all the meat to the wok.

ADD the onion and the fish sauce mixture and
stir-fry for another minute.

ADD the basil leaves and stir-fry until the basil
begins to wilt. Taste, then adjust the seasoning if
necessary. Spoon onto a serving plate.

Thai sweet basil (bai horapha)
is often used in curries and
soups. It has a very intense
aniseed fragrance, instantly
recognisable as Thai.

BEEF WITH THAI SWEET BASIL LEAVES

Amaranth is a green or red leafy vegetable used in India instead of spinach. It is interchangeable with spinach in all saag recipes.

Domestic stoves in India are usually wood-fired. Cooking pots are placed over the opening at the top and fuel is lit from below.

SAAG GOSHT

THIS IS A RICHLY FLAVOURED, TRADITIONAL DISH FROM THE NORTHERN PART OF INDIA. IT IS COOKED UNTIL THE SAUCE IS VERY THICK. IT CAN BE SERVED WITH EITHER RICE OR BREADS. IF YOU CAN'T BUY FRESH SPINACH, YOU CAN USE DEFROSTED, DRAINED, FROZEN SPINACH INSTEAD.

2 teaspoons coriander seeds
1½ teaspoons cumin seeds
3 tablespoons oil
1 kg (2 lb 4 oz) boneless leg or shoulder of lamb, cut into 2.5 cm (1 inch) cubes
4 onions, finely chopped
6 cloves
6 cardamom pods
10 cm (4 inch) cinnamon stick
10 black peppercorns
4 Indian bay leaves (cassia leaves)
3 teaspoons garam masala (see recipe on page 464)
¼ teaspoon ground turmeric
1 teaspoon paprika
8 cm (3 inch) piece of ginger, grated
4 garlic cloves, crushed
185 ml (6 fl oz/¾ cup) thick plain yoghurt (see recipe on page 467)
450 g (1 lb) English spinach or amaranth leaves, roughly chopped

SERVES 6

PLACE a small frying pan over low heat and dry-roast the coriander seeds until aromatic. Remove them and dry-roast the cumin seeds. Grind the roasted seeds to a fine powder using a spice grinder or pestle and mortar.

HEAT the oil in a karhai or casserole over low heat. Fry a few pieces of meat at a time until browned. Remove from the pan. Add more oil to the pan and fry the onion, cloves, cardamom pods, cinnamon stick, peppercorns and bay leaves until the onion is lightly browned. Add the cumin and coriander, garam masala, turmeric and paprika and fry for 30 seconds. Add the meat, ginger, garlic, yoghurt and 420 ml (14 fl oz/1⅔ cups) water and bring to the boil. Reduce the heat to a simmer, cover and cook for 1½–2 hours, or until the meat is very tender. At this stage, most of the water should have evaporated. If it hasn't, remove the lid, increase the heat and fry until the moisture has evaporated. Season with salt, to taste.

COOK spinach briefly in a little simmering water until it is just wilted, then refresh in cold water. Drain thoroughly, then finely chop. Squeeze out any extra water by putting the spinach between two plates and pushing them together.

ADD the spinach to the lamb and cook for 3 minutes, or until the spinach and lamb are well mixed and any extra liquid has evaporated.

FROM INDIA
MEMSAHIB'S LAMB RAAN

THIS DISH LOOKS VERY IMPRESSIVE EVEN THOUGH IT CAN BE MADE WITHOUT MUCH FUSS. IT IS EXCELLENT FOR DINNER OR A SPECIAL LUNCH, BUT IT DOES NEED TO BE MARINATED OVERNIGHT SO THE FLAVOURS CAN PERMEATE THE LAMB. SERVE IT WITH A COUPLE OF VEGETABLE DISHES AND SOME RICE.

1.7 kg (3 lb 12 oz) leg of lamb

MARINADE
1 teaspoon cardamom seeds
1 onion, roughly chopped
4 garlic cloves, roughly chopped
2 cm (¾ inch) piece of ginger,
  roughly chopped
3 green chillies, seeded
2 teaspoons ground cumin
½ teaspoon ground cloves
1½ tablespoons lemon juice
250 ml (8 fl oz/1 cup) thick plain
  yoghurt (see recipe on page 467)

ALMOND COATING
3 tablespoons blanched almonds
1 tablespoon palm sugar (jaggery)
  or soft brown sugar
125 ml (4 fl oz/½ cup) thick plain
  yoghurt
½ teaspoon red food colouring
  (optional)

coriander (cilantro) leaves (optional)

SERVES 6

TRIM the excess fat from the lamb and stab the meat all over with a sharp skewer so that the marinade will penetrate.

TO MAKE the marinade, grind the cardamom seeds to a fine powder using a spice grinder or pestle and mortar. Chop onion, garlic and ginger to a paste with the green chillies in a blender or food processor. If you don't have a processor, finely chop them with a knife, then grind to a paste in a pestle and mortar. Mix in ground cardamom seeds, cumin and cloves. Add the lemon juice and yoghurt and mix well.

COAT the lamb thickly all over, using half the marinade. Cover with plastic wrap and marinate in the fridge overnight. Cover remaining marinade and refrigerate it.

TO MAKE the almond coating, preheat the oven to 190°C (375°F/Gas 5). Finely chop the almonds in a food processor or with a knife. Mix reserved marinade with the ground almonds, palm sugar, yoghurt and food colouring, if using. Uncover lamb and coat it all over with the mixture, especially on the top and sides.

TRANSFER the lamb to a shallow roasting tin and cover loosely with oiled foil. Bake for 1 hour, then remove the foil and bake for another 30 minutes, or until the lamb is cooked and the coating set and browned. Test meat nearest the bone to see if it's cooked – a skewer should come out very hot.

CAREFULLY press on any yoghurt and almond coating that has dropped off during cooking, so that the finished product looks neat.

CARVE meat at the table for full effect. Garnish with coriander. Top servings with almond coating.

The High Court in Kolkata (Calcutta), was built in 1872. The design copied that of the Staadhaus in Ypres, Belgium.

A hand-painted film poster in Chennai (Madras).

Fresh, aromatic curry leaves are bought from market vendors on a daily basis.

FROM INDIA
LAMB MADRAS

TRADITIONALLY IN INDIA, HOGGET (SHEEP) OR GOAT MEAT IS OFTEN THE ONLY MEAT AVAILABLE. AS GOAT CAN BE TOUGH WHEN COOKED THIS WAY, WE HAVE USED LAMB. IT IS COOKED SLOWLY SO THE SAUCES ARE ABSORBED AND THE CURRY MATURES TO A FULL FLAVOUR. BEEF CAN ALSO BE USED.

1 kg (2 lb 4 oz) boneless leg or
    shoulder of lamb, cut into 2.5 cm
    (1 inch) cubes
1½ teaspoons ground turmeric
2 tablespoons coriander seeds
2 teaspoons cumin seeds
10 dried chillies
12 curry leaves
10 garlic cloves, roughly chopped
5 cm (2 inch) piece of ginger,
    roughly chopped
1 teaspoon fennel seeds
1 tablespoon tamarind purée
    (see recipe on page 467)
4 tablespoons oil or ghee
3 large onions, sliced
625 ml (20 fl oz/2½ cups) coconut
    milk (see recipe on page 468)
8 cm (3 inch) cinnamon stick
6 cardamom pods
extra curry leaves, for garnish

SERVES 6

RUB the cubed lamb with the ground turmeric. Place a small frying pan over low heat and dry-roast the coriander seeds until aromatic. Remove and dry-roast the cumin seeds, then repeat with the chillies. Grind them all to a powder in a pestle and mortar or spice grinder. Add six curry leaves, the garlic and ginger and grind to a paste.

DRY-ROAST the fennel seeds in the pan until they brown and start to pop. Dissolve the tamarind in 125 ml (4 fl oz/½ cup) hot water.

HEAT the oil or ghee in a karhai or casserole over low heat and fry the onion for 5–10 minutes until soft. Add the chilli paste and cook for a few minutes or until aromatic. Add the meat and toss well to mix with the paste. Add 500 ml (16 fl oz/2 cups) coconut milk and 60 ml (2 fl oz/¼ cup) water. Bring to the boil and simmer over medium heat for 10 minutes, or until liquid has reduced.

WHEN the liquid has reduced, add the remaining coconut milk, the cinnamon stick, cardamom pods and whole fennel seeds. Season with salt and pepper. Cover and cook, partially covered over medium heat, for 1 hour or until the meat is tender, stirring occasionally. When meat is tender, add tamarind and check the seasoning. Stir until the oil separates out from the meat, then spoon or blot it off before removing the pan from the heat.

STIR well and add the remaining six curry leaves. Garnish with more curry leaves.

FROM CHINA

MONGOLIAN LAMB

300 g (10½ oz) lamb fillet
2 teaspoons finely chopped ginger
1 spring onion (scallion), chopped
2 teaspoons ground Sichuan
  peppercorns
1 teaspoon salt
2 tablespoons light soy sauce
1 tablespoon yellow bean sauce
1 tablespoon hoisin sauce
1 teaspoon five-spice
2 tablespoons Shaoxing rice wine
oil for deep-frying
crisp lettuce leaves
80 ml (2 fl oz/⅓ cup) hoisin sauce,
  extra
½ cucumber, shredded
6 spring onions (scallions), chopped

SERVES 4

CUT the lamb along the grain into six long strips. Combine with the ginger, spring onion, pepper, salt, soy, yellow bean and hoisin sauces, five-spice powder and rice wine. Marinate in the fridge for at least 2 hours. Put the lamb and marinade in a heatproof dish in a steamer. Cover and steam for 2½–3 hours over simmering water in a wok, replenishing with boiling water during cooking. Remove the lamb from the liquid and drain well.

FILL a wok one-quarter full of oil. Heat the oil to 180°C (350°F), or until a piece of bread fries golden brown in 15 seconds when dropped in the oil. Cook the lamb for 3–4 minutes, then remove and drain. Cut the lamb into bite-size shreds.

TO SERVE, place some lamb in the lettuce leaves with some hoisin sauce, cucumber and spring onion and roll up into a parcel.

Making bread and pancakes at a street stall in Beijing.

STIR-FRIED LAMB AND LEEKS

300 g (10½ oz) lamb fillet
¼ teaspoon ground Sichuan
  peppercorns
½ teaspoon sugar
1 tablespoon light soy sauce
2 teaspoons Shaoxing rice wine
2 teaspoons cornflour (cornstarch)
½ teaspoon roasted sesame oil
3 tablespoons dried black fungus
  (wood ears)
625 ml (21 fl oz/2½ cups) oil
4 small pieces ginger
200 g (7 oz) young leeks, white part
  only, cut into short lengths
2 tablespoons yellow bean sauce

SERVES 4

CUT the lamb into thin slices and combine with the Sichuan peppercorns, sugar, soy sauce, rice wine, cornflour and sesame oil. Marinate in the fridge for at least 2 hours.

SOAK the dried black fungus in cold water for 20 minutes, then drain and squeeze out any excess water.

HEAT a wok over high heat, add the oil and heat until very hot. Stir-fry the lamb for 1 minute, or until the colour changes. Remove and drain. pour the oil from the wok, leaving 2 tablespoons.

REHEAT reserved oil over high heat until very hot and stir-fry the ginger, leek and black fungus for 1 minute, then add the yellow bean sauce, blend well, and add lamb. Continue stirring for 1 minute.

STIR-FRIED LAMB AND LEEKS

The remains of an ancient college built in 1354 in Haus Khas village, Delhi.

FROM INDIA
MOGHUL-STYLE LAMB

FOR THIS DISH, THE LAMB IS MARINATED, PREFERABLY OVERNIGHT, BEFORE IT IS COOKED. THIS ENSURES THAT THE MEAT IS TENDER AND FULL OF FLAVOUR. THE CREAM IS ADDED TO TEMPER THE STRONG COMBINATION OF SPICES.

6 garlic cloves, roughly chopped
4 cm (1½ inch) piece of ginger, roughly chopped
60 g (2 oz/⅓ cup) blanched almonds
2 onions, thinly sliced
750 g (1 lb 10 oz) boneless leg or shoulder of lamb, cut into 2.5 cm (1 inch) cubes
2 teaspoons coriander seeds
40 g (1½ oz) ghee
7 cardamom pods
5 cloves
1 cinnamon stick
1 teaspoon salt
310 ml (10 fl oz/1¼ cups) cream
½ teaspoon cayenne pepper
½ teaspoon garam masala (see recipe on page 464)
flaked toasted almonds

SERVES 4

BLEND garlic, ginger, almonds and 50 g (1¾ oz) of the onion in a blender or food processor. If you don't have a blender, finely chop them with a knife or grind them in a pestle and mortar. Add a little water, if necessary, to make a smooth paste, then put in a bowl with the lamb and mix thoroughly to coat the meat. Cover and marinate in the fridge for 2 hours, or overnight.

PLACE a small frying pan over low heat, dry-roast coriander seeds until aromatic, then grind to a fine powder using a spice grinder or pestle and mortar.

HEAT the ghee in a karhai or casserole. Add the cardamom pods, cloves and cinnamon stick and, after a few seconds, add the remaining onion and fry until it is soft and starting to brown. Transfer the onion to a plate.

FRY the meat and the marinade in the pan until the mixture is quite dry and has started to brown a little. Add 170 ml (6 fl oz/⅔ cup) hot water to the pan, cover tightly and cook over low heat for 30 minutes, stirring occasionally.

ADD the ground coriander, salt, cream, cayenne pepper and cooked onion to the pan, cover and simmer for another 30 minutes, or until the lamb is tender. Stir occasionally to prevent the lamb from sticking to the pan.

REMOVE the cardamom pods, cloves and cinnamon stick, then stir in the garam masala. Sprinkle with flaked almonds.

FROM INDIA

LAMB KORMA

THIS MILD DISH, WHICH COMES IN MANY GUISES, NEEDS TO BE COOKED VERY SLOWLY TO LET THE SUBTLE FLAVOURS EMERGE. THIS VERSION USES WHITE POPPY SEEDS AND CASHEW NUTS TO THICKEN THE SAUCE AND YOGHURT TO MAKE IT CREAMY.

1 kg (2 lb 4 oz) boneless leg or shoulder of lamb, cut into 2.5 cm (1 inch) cubes

2 tablespoons thick plain yoghurt (see recipe on page 467)

1 tablespoon coriander seeds

2 teaspoons cumin seeds

5 cardamom pods

2 onions

2 tablespoons grated coconut (see recipe on page 468)

1 tablespoon white poppy seeds (khus khus)

3 green chillies, roughly chopped

4 garlic cloves, crushed

5 cm (2 inch) piece of ginger, grated

25 g (1 oz) cashew nuts

6 cloves

¼ teaspoon ground cinnamon

2 tablespoons oil

SERVES 4

PUT the meat in a bowl, add the yoghurt and mix to coat thoroughly.

PLACE a small frying pan over low heat and dry-roast coriander seeds until aromatic. Remove and dry-roast the cumin seeds. Grind the roasted mixture to a fine powder using a spice grinder or pestle and mortar. Remove the seeds from the cardamom pods and grind them.

ROUGHLY chop one onion and finely slice the other. Put just the roughly chopped onion with the ground spices, coconut, poppy seeds, chilli, garlic, ginger, cashew nuts, cloves and cinnamon in a blender, add 170 ml (6 fl oz/⅔ cup) water and process to a smooth paste. If you don't have a blender, crush them in a pestle and mortar, or finely chop with a knife, before adding the water.

HEAT the oil in a karhai or casserole over medium heat. Add the finely sliced onion and fry until lightly browned. Pour blended mixture into pan, season with salt and cook over low heat for 1 minute, or until the liquid evaporates and the sauce thickens. Add the lamb with the yoghurt and slowly bring to the boil. Cover tightly and simmer for 1½ hours, or until the meat is very tender. Stir meat occasionally to prevent it from sticking to the pan. If the water has evaporated during the cooking time, add another 125 ml (4 fl oz/½ cup) of water to make a sauce. The sauce should be quite thick.

The poppy seeds used in Indian cuisine are white rather than black. They are used to thicken kormas and are usually ground, then mixed into a wet paste.

A shop selling freshly made yoghurt in Hyderabad.

FROM INDIA
ROGAN JOSH

THERE ARE MANY CURRY PASTES AVAILABLE FOR MAKING THIS CLASSIC. HOWEVER, NOTHING COMPARES WITH A VERSION MADE WITH FRESHLY GROUND SPICES. THE COLOUR COMES FROM THE CHILLI POWDER AND PAPRIKA. IN KASHMIR, RED COCKSCOMB FLOWERS ARE TRADITIONALLY USED FOR COLOUR.

8 garlic cloves, crushed

6 cm (2½ inch) piece of ginger, grated

2 teaspoons ground cumin

1 teaspoon Kashmiri chilli powder

2 teaspoons paprika

2 teaspoons ground coriander

1 kg (2 lb 4 oz) boneless leg or shoulder of lamb, cut into 3 cm (1¼ inch) cubes

5 tablespoons ghee or oil

1 onion, finely chopped

6 cardamom pods

4 cloves

2 Indian bay leaves (cassia leaves)

8 cm (3 inch) cinnamon stick

185 ml (¾ cup) thick plain yoghurt (see recipe on page 467)

4 strands saffron, mixed with 2 tablespoons milk

¼ teaspoon garam masala (see recipe on page 464)

SERVES 6

MIX the garlic, ginger, cumin, chilli powder, paprika and coriander in a large bowl. Add the meat and stir thoroughly to coat the meat cubes well. Cover and marinate for at least 2 hours, or overnight, in the fridge.

HEAT the ghee or oil in a karhai or casserole over low heat. Add the onion and cook for about 10 minutes, or until the onion is lightly browned. Remove from the pan.

ADD the cardamom pods, cloves, bay leaves and cinnamon to the pan and fry for 1 minute. Increase the heat to high, add the meat and onion, then mix well and fry for 2 minutes. Stir well, then reduce the heat to low, cover and cook for 15 minutes.

UNCOVER and fry for another 3 minutes, or until the meat is quite dry. Add 125 ml (½ cup) water, cover and cook for 5–7 minutes, until the water has evaporated and the oil separates out and floats on the surface. Fry meat for 1–2 minutes, then add 250 ml (1 cup) water. Cover and cook for 40–50 minutes, gently simmering until the meat is tender. The liquid will reduce quite a bit.

STIR in the yoghurt when the meat is almost tender, taking care not to allow the meat to catch on the base of the pan. Add the saffron and milk. Stir the mixture a few times to mix in the saffron. Season with salt, to taste. Remove from the heat and sprinkle with the garam masala.

The Indian version of the pestle and mortar. The base is the *sil* and the crushing stone the *nora*.

FROM JAPAN

JAPANESE CURRY

CURRY, OF INDIAN ORIGIN, WAS INTRODUCED VIA THE ENGLISH, MEANING THAT IT WAS A LITTLE TRANSFORMED, NOT ONCE BUT TWICE. JAPANESE CURRY, SUITED WELL TO JAPANESE TASTES, IS A POPULAR RESTAURANT LUNCH-ON-THE-RUN AS WELL AS A FAVOURITE FAMILY DISH.

25 g (1 oz) butter

1 teaspoon sesame oil

2 tablespoons vegetable oil

1 large onion, cut in half, then sliced into 1 cm (½ inch) wedges

750 g (1 lb 10 oz) pork or lamb shoulder or chuck steak, cut into 3 cm (1¼ inch) cubes

pinch ground white pepper

2 cloves garlic, crushed

1½ tablespoons Japanese curry powder

375 ml (13 fl oz/1½ cups) dashi II (see recipe on page 483)

2 tablespoons mirin

1 tablespoon shoyu (Japanese soy sauce)

3 tablespoons white miso paste

2 large all-purpose potatoes, cut into 2 cm (¾ inch) cubes

2 carrots, cut in half lengthways, then cut into 3 cm (1¼ inch) pieces

100 g (3½ oz) green beans, trimmed and cut into 4 cm (1½ inch) lengths

pickles, to serve

SERVES 4

HEAT butter, sesame oil and half the vegetable oil in a large saucepan over medium heat. Add onion and cook, stirring regularly, for 10–15 minutes, or until golden. Remove from the pan and set aside.

POUR the remaining vegetable oil into the pan. Season the meat with salt and white pepper, then cook in batches for 5–7 minutes, or until browned all over. Remove from the pan and set aside.

ADD the garlic and curry powder to the pan and stir for 1 minute, or until fragrant. Return the onion and meat to the pan and stir to coat with the curry.

POUR in the dashi, mirin, shoyu and 500 ml (17 fl oz/2 cups) water, then stir in the miso. Bring to the boil, then reduce to a simmer and cook for 1 hour.

ADD the potato and carrot and cook for a further 50 minutes. Add the beans and cook for 10 minutes, or until all the vegetables are very tender. Season to taste and serve with rice or noodles, accompanied by pickles of your choice.

Cook the meat for 1 hour, then add the potato and carrot and cook for 50 minutes. Add beans last and continue cooking until all the vegetables are tender.

TOFU, LEGUMES & VEGETABLES

Fresh tofu and chilli pastes are readily available at the markets in China.

MA PO TOFU

A QUINTESSENTIAL SICHUANESE DISH, SUPPOSEDLY NAMED AFTER AN OLD WOMAN WHO SERVED THIS IN HER RESTAURANT AND WHOSE POCKMARKED COMPLEXION LED TO THE DISH BEING CALLED MA PO TOFU, 'POCKMARKED GRANDMOTHER'S TOFU'. SOFT TOFU IS TRADITIONALLY USED.

750 g (1 lb 10 oz) soft or firm tofu, drained
250 g (9 oz) minced (ground) beef or pork
2 tablespoons dark soy sauce
1½ tablespoons Shaoxing rice wine
½ teaspoon roasted sesame oil
2 teaspoons Sichuan peppercorns
1 tablespoon oil
2 spring onions (scallions), finely chopped
2 garlic cloves, finely chopped
2 teaspoons finely chopped ginger
1 tablespoon chilli bean paste (toban jiang), or to taste
250 ml (8 fl oz/1 cup) chicken and meat stock (see recipe on page 491)
1½ teaspoons cornflour (cornstarch)
1 spring onion (scallion), finely shredded

SERVES 6

CUT the tofu into cubes. Place the meat in a bowl with 2 teaspoons of the soy sauce, 2 teaspoons of the rice wine and the sesame oil, and toss lightly. Dry-fry peppercorns in a wok or pan until brown and aromatic, then crush lightly.

HEAT a wok over high heat, add the oil and heat until very hot. Stir-fry the meat until browned, mashing and chopping to separate the pieces. Remove the meat with a wire sieve or slotted spoon and heat the oil until any liquid from the meat has evaporated. Add the spring onion, garlic and ginger and stir-fry for 10 seconds, or until fragrant. Add the chilli bean paste and stir-fry for 5 seconds.

COMBINE the stock with the remaining soy sauce and rice wine. Add to the wok, bring to the boil, then add the tofu and meat. Return to the boil, reduce the heat to medium and cook for 5 minutes, or until the sauce has reduced by a quarter. If you are using soft tofu, do not stir or it will break up.

COMBINE the cornflour with enough water to make a paste, add to the sauce and simmer until thickened. Season, if necessary. Serve sprinkled with the spring onion and Sichuan peppercorns.

Selling snacks in Yunnan.

FROM INDIA

SPINACH KOFTA IN YOGHURT SAUCE

THIS IS A TYPICAL GUJARATI DISH AND IS MORE SUBSTANTIAL THAN SOME VEGETARIAN DISHES. YOU CAN EAT THE YOGHURT SAUCE AND THE SPINACH KOFTA AS SEPARATE DISHES BUT THEY GO VERY WELL TOGETHER AS IN THIS RECIPE.

YOGHURT SAUCE

375 ml (12 fl oz/1½ cups) thick plain yoghurt (see recipe on page 467)
4 tablespoons besan (chickpea flour)
1 tablespoon oil
2 teaspoons black mustard seeds
1 teaspoon fenugreek seeds
6 curry leaves
1 large onion, finely chopped
3 garlic cloves, crushed
1 teaspoon ground turmeric
½ teaspoon chilli powder

SPINACH KOFTAS

1 bunch English spinach (about 450 g/1 lb), leaves picked off the stems, or 500 g (1 lb 2 oz) frozen spinach, thawed and drained
180 g (6 oz/1½ cups) besan (chickpea flour)
1 red onion, finely chopped
1 ripe tomato, finely diced
2 garlic cloves, crushed
1 teaspoon ground cumin
2 tablespoons coriander (cilantro) leaves

oil for deep-frying
coriander (cilantro) leaves (optional)

SERVES 6

TO MAKE the yoghurt sauce, whisk the yoghurt, besan and 750 ml (25 fl oz/3 cups) water to a smooth paste. Heat oil in a heavy-based saucepan or deep frying pan over low heat. Add mustard and fenugreek seeds and the curry leaves. Cover pan and allow seeds to pop for 1 minute. Add the onion and cook for 5 minutes, or until soft and starting to brown. Add garlic and stir 1 minute, or until soft. Add the turmeric and chilli powder and stir for 30 seconds. Add the yoghurt mixture, bring to the boil and simmer over low heat for 10 minutes. Season with salt, to taste.

TO MAKE the spinach koftas, blanch the spinach in boiling water for 1 minute and refresh in cold water. Drain, squeeze out any extra water by putting the spinach between two plates and pushing them together. Finely chop the spinach. Combine with the remaining kofta ingredients and up to 60 ml (2 fl oz/¼ cup) of water, a little at a time, adding enough to make the mixture soft but not sloppy. If it becomes too sloppy, add more besan. Season with salt, to taste. (To test the seasoning, fry a small amount of the mixture and taste it.) Shape mixture into balls by rolling it in dampened hands, using 1 tablespoon of mixture for each.

FILL a karhai or heavy-based saucepan one-third full with oil and heat to 180°C (350°F), or until a cube of bread browns in the oil in 15 seconds. Lower the koftas into the oil in batches and fry until golden and crisp. Don't overcrowd the pan. Remove the koftas as they cook, shake off any excess oil and add them to the yoghurt sauce.

GENTLY reheat the yoghurt sauce and sprinkle with the coriander leaves if using.

STIR-FRIED SNAKE BEANS

2 tablespoons vegetable oil
2 teaspoons red curry paste
   (see recipe on page 472)
   or bought paste
350 g (12 oz) boneless, skinless
   chicken breasts, finely sliced
350 g (12 oz) snake (yard long)
   beans, cut diagonally into 2.5 cm
   (1 inch) pieces
1 tablespoon fish sauce
25 g (1 oz) sugar
4 makrut (kaffir lime) leaves,
   very finely shredded, to serve

SERVES 4

HEAT the oil in a wok or frying pan and stir-fry the red curry paste over a medium heat for 2 minutes or until fragrant.

ADD the chicken and stir for 4–5 minutes or until the chicken is cooked. Add the beans, fish sauce and sugar. Stir-fry for another 4–5 minutes.

TRANSFER to a serving plate and sprinkle with the makrut leaves.

PUMPKIN WITH CHILLI AND BASIL

PUMPKIN WITH CHILLI AND BASIL

3 tablespoons dried shrimp
½ teaspoon shrimp paste
2 coriander (cilantro) roots
10–12 white peppercorns
2 garlic cloves, chopped
2 Asian shallots, chopped
125 ml (4 fl oz/½ cup) coconut
   cream (see recipe on page 468)
300 g (10 oz) butternut pumpkin
   (squash), cut into 4 cm (1½ inch)
   cubes
2 large red chillies, cut lengthways
125 ml (4 fl oz/½ cup) coconut milk
   (see recipe on page 468)
1 tablespoon fish sauce
1 tablespoon palm sugar (jaggery)
2 teaspoons lime juice
12 Thai sweet basil leaves

SERVES 4

SOAK 2 tablespoons of the dried shrimp in a small bowl of water for 20 minutes, then drain.

PUT the remaining dried shrimp, shrimp paste, coriander roots, peppercorns, garlic and shallots in a pestle and mortar or food processor and pound or blend to a paste.

BRING the coconut cream to a boil in a saucepan and simmer for 5 minutes. Add the paste and stir to combine. Cook for another 2–3 minutes, then add the pumpkin, chillies, rehydrated shrimp and coconut milk. Stir to combine all the ingredients and simmer for 10–15 minutes, until pumpkin is just tender. Don't let the pumpkin turn to mush.

ADD the fish sauce, palm sugar and lime juice to the pan and cook for another 2–3 minutes.

STIR in the basil leaves before serving.

BRAISED TOFU WITH CHINESE MUSHROOMS

300 g (10½ oz) firm tofu, drained
60 g (2 oz) dried Chinese
    mushrooms
4 tablespoons oil
1 teaspoon salt
1 teaspoon sugar
1 tablespoon Shaoxing rice wine
½ teaspoon roasted sesame oil
1 teaspoon cornflour (cornstarch)
1 tablespoon light soy sauce

SERVES 4

CUT the drained tofu into strips. Soak the dried mushrooms in boiling water for 30 minutes, then drain, reserving the soaking liquid, and squeeze out any excess water. Remove and discard the stems. Cut the caps in half.

HEAT a wok over high heat, add the oil and heat until very hot. Stir-fry the mushrooms for 35 seconds, then add 125 ml (4 fl oz/½ cup) of the reserved liquid and bring to the boil. Add the tofu, salt, sugar and rice wine to the wok, and stir very gently to blend well. Braise for 2 minutes, making sure there is enough liquid to prevent the tofu from sticking to the wok, then sprinkle with the sesame oil.

COMBINE the cornflour and soy with enough of the reserved liquid to make a paste. Add to the sauce and simmer to form a clear, light glaze.

FERMENTED TOFU WITH ASIAN GREENS

600 g (1 lb 5 oz) choy sum
250 g (9 oz) bok choy (pak choi)
1 tablespoon oil
3 garlic cloves, crushed
3 tablespoons fermented white tofu
1 teaspoon light soy sauce
3 tablespoons oyster sauce
2 teaspoons sugar
1 teaspoon roasted sesame oil

SERVES 4

CUT the choy sum horizontally into thirds and the bok choy into thirds and then quarters. Trim off any roots that may hold the pieces together, then wash well and dry thoroughly.

HEAT a wok over high heat, add the oil and heat until very hot. Stir-fry the garlic and tofu for 1 minute. Add the choy sum stems and stir-fry for 1 minute, then add the leaves and bok choy and stir-fry for 1–2 minutes, or until the vegetables just start to wilt. Add the soy and oyster sauces, sugar and sesame oil and toss everything together.

FERMENTED TOFU WITH
ASIAN GREENS

Asafoetida is used as a pungent seasoning in many dishes. It is also used in dishes made with pulses because it helps to dissipate the gasses they create. Powdered versions like this often contain rice flour and turmeric as well.

Pulses are on sale all over India, in their uncooked form and also fried as snacks.

CHANA MASALA

CHANA MASALA IS SERVED UP BY TRAVELLING VENDORS, IN BAZAARS OR ON THE STREETS OF INDIA, AND EATEN WITH PURIS. IT IS ENJOYED BY EVERYBODY AT ALL TIMES OF THE DAY AS A SNACK OR A LIGHT MEAL AND MAKES A GOOD ACCOMPANIMENT TO ANY INDIAN MEAL.

250 g (9 oz) chickpeas
1 large onion, roughly chopped
2 garlic cloves, roughly chopped
5 cm (2 inch) piece of ginger, roughly chopped
1 green chilli, chopped
170 ml (6 fl oz/2/3 cup) oil
1 tablespoon ground cumin
1 tablespoon ground coriander
1 teaspoon chilli powder
pinch of asafoetida
2 tablespoons thick plain yoghurt (see recipe on page 467)
2¼ tablespoons garam masala (see recipe on page 464)
2 teaspoons tamarind purée (see recipe on page 467)
½ lemon
3 green chillies, extra
¼ teaspoon ground black pepper
3 teaspoons salt
2 teaspoons chaat masala (see recipe on page 464)
½ red onion, sliced into thin rings
2 cm (¾ inch) piece of ginger, cut into thin strips
coriander (cilantro) leaves, roughly chopped (optional)

SERVES 6

SOAK the chickpeas overnight in 2 litres (70 fl oz/ 8 cups) of water. Drain, then put the chickpeas in a large saucepan with another 2 litres (8 cups) water. Bring to the boil, spooning off any scum from the surface, then simmer over low heat for 1–1½ hours, until soft. It is important the chickpeas are soft at this stage as they won't soften once the sauce has been added. Drain, reserving the cooking liquid.

BLEND the onion, garlic, ginger and chopped chilli to a paste in a food processor or very finely chop them together with a knife.

HEAT the oil in a heavy-based saucepan over medium heat and fry the onion mixture until golden brown. Add cumin, coriander, chilli powder and asafoetida, then stir for 1 minute. Add the yoghurt and stir for 1 minute. Stir in 2 tablespoons of the garam masala and pour in 1.25 litres (42 fl oz/ 5 cups) of the reserved cooking liquid, a little at a time, stirring after each addition. Bring to the boil, then reduce the heat to simmering point.

ADD the tamarind purée, lemon, whole chillies, chickpeas, pepper and the salt. Partially cover the pan, simmer for 30 minutes, then remove the lemon. Cook for another 30 minutes, or until all the liquid has reduced, leaving softened chickpeas coated in a rich dark brown sauce.

ADD the chaat masala and remaining garam masala and stir in the raw onion rings, ginger and coriander leaves if using.

FROM THAILAND

MUSHROOMS WITH TOFU

TOFU AND MUSHROOMS ARE COMMONLY USED TOGETHER IN CHINESE DISHES, JUST AS THEY ARE HERE IN THIS THAI DISH. THE BLANDNESS OF THE TOFU IS A CONTRAST TO BOTH THE TEXTURE AND FLAVOUR OF THE MUSHROOMS. FOR THE BEST FLAVOUR, USE THE TYPE OF MUSHROOMS SUGGESTED.

350 g (12 oz) firm tofu (bean curd)
1 teaspoon sesame oil
2 teaspoons light soy sauce
¼ teaspoon ground black pepper, plus some to sprinkle
1 tablespoon finely shredded ginger
5 tablespoons vegetable stock or water
2 tablespoons light soy sauce
2 teaspoons cornflour (cornstarch)
½ teaspoon sugar
1½ tablespoons vegetable oil
2 garlic cloves, finely chopped
200 g (7 oz) oyster mushrooms, hard stalks removed, cut in half if large
200 g (7 oz) shiitake mushrooms, hard stalks removed
2 spring onions (scallions), sliced diagonally, for garnish
1 long red chilli, seeded and finely sliced, for garnish

SERVES 2

DRAIN each block of tofu and cut into 2.5 cm (1 inch) pieces. Put them in a shallow dish and sprinkle with the sesame oil, light soy sauce, ground pepper and ginger. Leave to marinate for 30 minutes.

MIX the stock with the light soy sauce, cornflour and sugar in a small bowl until smooth.

HEAT the oil in a wok or frying pan and stir-fry the garlic over a medium heat until light brown.

ADD all the mushrooms and stir-fry for about 4 minutes or until the mushrooms are cooked.

ADD the cornflour liquid, then carefully add the pieces of tofu and gently mix for 1–2 minutes. Taste, then adjust the seasoning if necessary.

SPOON onto a serving plate and sprinkle with spring onions, chilli slices and ground pepper.

The mushrooms and tofu are cut into similarly sized pieces so that they cook evenly in the wok.

Ringing the bells at Wat Phra That Doi Tung.

MUSHROOMS WITH TOFU

Add the egg yolk to the miso mixture and whisk until glossy.

MISO TOFU STICKS WITH CUCUMBER AND WAKAME SALAD

THESE DENSE AND DELICIOUS GRILLED (BROILED) TOFU STICKS, WITH THEIR GOLDEN GLAZE OF MISO AND EGG YOLK, MAKE AN UNCOMMON TOPPING FOR THIS VEGETARIAN SALAD. THE CUCUMBERS AND BEAN SPROUTS OFFER A CRISPY FRESHNESS, AND THE WAKAME GIVES A HINT OF THE SEA.

3 Lebanese (short) cucumbers, thinly sliced
20 g (¾ oz/½ cup) dried wakame seaweed pieces
500 g (1 lb 2 oz) silken firm tofu, well drained
3 tablespoons white miso paste
1 tablespoon mirin
1 tablespoon sugar
1 tablespoon rice vinegar
1 egg yolk
100 g (4 oz) bean sprouts, blanched
2 tablespoons sesame seeds, toasted

DRESSING
60 ml (2 fl oz/¼ cup) rice vinegar
¼ teaspoon shoyu (Japanese soy sauce)
1½ tablespoons sugar
1 tablespoon mirin
½ teaspoon salt

SERVES 4

SPRINKLE the cucumber generously with salt and set aside for 20 minutes, or until very soft, then rinse and drain. Squeeze out any excess water. Refrigerate until needed.

SOAK the wakame in cold water for 5 minutes, or until rehydrated and glossy but not mushy. Drain well, then refrigerate until needed.

PLACE the tofu in a colander, put two plates on top of the tofu and leave for about 30 minutes to extract any excess moisture.

PUT the miso, mirin, sugar, rice vinegar and 2 tablespoons water in a saucepan and stir over low heat for 1 minute, or until the sugar dissolves. Remove from the heat, add the egg yolk and whisk until glossy. Cool slightly.

CUT the tofu into thick sticks and put on a non-stick baking tray. Brush miso mixture over the tofu and cook under a hot grill (broiler) for 6 minutes each side, or until the tofu is light golden.

TO MAKE the dressing, put all the ingredients in a bowl and whisk together well.

TO ASSEMBLE, place the cucumber in the centre of a plate, top with the bean sprouts and wakame, drizzle with the dressing, then top with tofu and serve sprinkled with sesame seeds.

FROM INDIA

BLACK-EYED BEANS WITH MUSHROOMS

BLACK-EYED BEANS OR LOBHIA ARE SOMETIMES CALLED BLACK-EYED PEAS. THE EARTHY FLAVOUR OF THE LOBHIA COMBINED WITH MUSHROOMS AND TOMATOES MAKES THIS AN EXCELLENT VEGETARIAN MAIN COURSE. THE DISH IS ALSO SUITABLE FOR SERVING ON THE SIDE WITH MEAT OR VEGETABLES.

200 g (7 oz) black-eyed beans
400 g (14 oz) ripe tomatoes
   or 400 g (14 oz) tin chopped
   tomatoes
125 ml (½ cup) oil
1 teaspoon cumin seeds
3 cm (1¼ inch) cinnamon stick
150 g (5½ oz) onion, chopped
4 garlic cloves, finely chopped
250 g (9 oz) mushrooms, sliced
2 teaspoons ground coriander
1 teaspoon ground cumin
½ teaspoon ground turmeric
¼ teaspoon cayenne pepper
2 tablespoons chopped coriander
   (cilantro) leaves

SERVES 6

When the beans are soaked sufficiently, they will be creamy in colour and plump.

PUT the black-eyed beans in a large saucepan with 1 litre (4 cups) of water and bring to the boil. Cover and simmer 2 minutes. Remove from the heat and leave to stand for 1 hour. Alternatively, if you prefer, you can soak the black-eyed beans overnight in the cold water.

SCORE a cross in the top of each ripe tomato. Plunge them into boiling water for 20 seconds, then drain and peel away from the cross. Chop the tomatoes roughly, discarding the cores and seeds and reserving any juices.

BRING the black-eyed beans back to the boil, then simmer for 20–30 minutes, until tender. Drain well.

MEANWHILE, heat the oil in a karhai or deep, heavy-based frying pan or saucepan. Add cumin seeds and cinnamon stick, let them sizzle for 10 seconds, then add the onion and garlic. Stir over medium heat until soft and starting to brown. Add mushrooms and fry for 2–3 minutes. Add the tomato, ground coriander, cumin, turmeric and cayenne pepper. Cover and cook over low heat for 10 minutes.

COMBINE the black-eyed beans with the tomato and mushroom mixture and season with salt, to taste. Stir in the coriander leaves and simmer, uncovered, for 30 minutes.

Push the stuffing fairly firmly into the slit in the tofu – the pocket should be open at one end and the stuffing showing.

STIR-FRIED TOFU IN YELLOW BEAN SAUCE

FROM CHINA

STUFFED TOFU

6 x 5 cm (2 inch) square cakes firm tofu, drained
2 dried Chinese mushrooms
50 g (1¾ oz) prawns (shrimp)
50 g (1¾ oz) minced (ground) pork
a pinch of salt
½ egg white, beaten
1 teaspoon Shaoxing rice wine
1 teaspoon light soy sauce
1–2 teaspoons cornflour (cornstarch)
3–4 tablespoons oil
2½ tablespoons chicken and meat stock (see recipe on page 491)
2 tablespoons oyster sauce
1 spring onion (scallion), sliced

SERVES 4

PARBOIL the tofu cakes in a pan of lightly salted boiling water for 2–3 minutes to harden them, then drain. Cut each cake into two triangular pieces and make a slit at the base of each triangle.

SOAK the dried mushrooms in boiling water for 30 minutes, then drain and squeeze out any excess water. Remove and discard the stems and finely chop the caps. Peel and devein the prawns and chop them finely until they are almost a paste. Place mushrooms and prawns in a bowl with the pork, salt, egg white, rice wine, soy sauce and enough cornflour to hold mixture together. Fill the slit of each tofu piece with stuffing (the pieces will gape open and show the stuffing).

HEAT a wok over high heat, add the oil and heat until very hot. Cook the stuffed tofu for 2 minutes on each side, or until golden. Pour off any excess oil. Add the stock and oyster sauce, bring to the boil and braise for 5–6 minutes. Sprinkle with the spring onion.

STIR-FRIED TOFU IN YELLOW BEAN SAUCE

400 g (14 oz) firm tofu, drained
2 tablespoons oil
1 garlic clove, crushed
1½ tablespoons yellow bean sauce
2 teaspoons oyster sauce
2 teaspoons sugar
2 teaspoons cornflour (cornstarch)
1 spring onion (scallion), cut into 2 cm (¾ inch) lengths
5 coriander (cilantro) sprigs, to serve

SERVES 4

CUT the drained tofu into bite-size pieces. Heat the wok over medium heat, add the oil and heat until hot. Cook the tofu until it is golden brown on both sides.

ADD the garlic, yellow bean sauce, oyster sauce and sugar and toss until well combined. Combine the cornflour with 170 ml (6 fl oz/⅔ cup) water, add to the sauce with the spring onion and simmer until sauce has thickened and the spring onion has softened slightly. If the sauce is still a little thick, add a little water.

GARNISH with coriander sprigs to serve.

FROM THAILAND

STIR-FRIED MIXED VEGETABLES

CARROTS, SNOWPEAS AND ASPARAGUS ARE NOT TYPICALLY THAI BUT THEY ARE NOW WIDELY GROWN AND EATEN. THE NORTH-WEST OF THAILAND HAS THE RIGHT CLIMATE FOR GROWING COLDER WEATHER VEGETABLES, PARTICULARLY PLACES LIKE THE KING'S PROJECT NORTH OF CHIANG MAI.

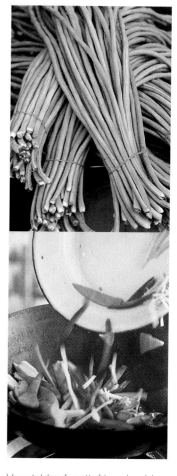

4 thin asparagus spears
4 baby sweet corn
50 g (2 oz) snake (yard long) beans
110 g (4 oz) mixed red and yellow
    capsicums (peppers)
½ small carrot
50 g (2 oz) Chinese broccoli,
    chopped, or broccoli florets
25 g (1 oz) snowpeas (mangetout),
    topped and tailed
2 cm (¾ inch) piece of ginger,
    finely sliced
1 tablespoon fish sauce
1½ tablespoons oyster sauce
2 tablespoons vegetable stock
    or water
½ teaspoon sugar
1½ tablespoons vegetable oil
3–4 garlic cloves, finely chopped
2 spring onions (scallions), sliced

SERVES 4

CUT off the tips of the asparagus and slice each spear into 5 cm (2 inch) lengths. Cut the sweet corn in halves lengthways and the beans into 2.5 cm (1 inch) lengths. Cut both on an angle. Halve the capsicums and discard the seeds, then cut into bite-sized pieces. Peel the carrot and cut into batons.

BLANCH the asparagus stalks, sweet corn, beans and broccoli florets in boiling salted water for 30 seconds. Remove and place in a bowl of iced water to ensure a crisp texture. Drain and place in a bowl with the capsicum, carrot, snowpeas, asparagus tips and ginger.

MIX the fish sauce, oyster sauce, stock and sugar in a small bowl.

HEAT the oil in a wok or frying pan and stir-fry the garlic over a medium heat until light brown. Add the mixed vegetables and the sauce mixture, then stir-fry over a high heat for 2–3 minutes. Taste, then adjust the seasoning if necessary.

ADD the spring onions and toss.

Vegetables for stir-fries should be cut into a uniform size.

FROM INDIA

CABBAGE WITH SPLIT PEAS

125 g (4½ oz) split peas
450 g (1 lb) green cabbage
3 tablespoons oil
¼ teaspoon black mustard seeds
2 teaspoons cumin seeds
8 curry leaves
2 dried chillies
pinch of asafoetida
¼ teaspoon ground turmeric
coriander (cilantro) leaves,
    to serve (optional)

SERVES 4

SOAK the split peas in 750 ml (25 fl oz/3 cups) boiling water for 2 hours. Drain thoroughly.

SHRED the cabbage.

HEAT the oil in a karhai or deep, heavy-based frying pan over low heat. Add the mustard and cumin seeds, cover and allow to pop briefly. Add curry leaves, dried chillies and split peas and fry for 5 minutes, stirring often. Add the asafoetida, turmeric and cabbage and fry over low heat until the cabbage is cooked through and tender. Season with salt, to taste.

SERVE garnished with coriander leaves.

PUNJABI CABBAGE

PUNJABI CABBAGE

½ onion, roughly chopped
1 garlic clove, roughly chopped
2.5 cm (1 inch) piece of ginger,
    chopped
2 green chillies, seeded and chopped
4 tablespoons oil
1 teaspoon cumin seeds
1 teaspoon ground turmeric
500 g (1 lb 2 oz) green cabbage,
    finely shredded
1 teaspoon salt
½ teaspoon ground black pepper
2 teaspoons ground cumin
1 teaspoon ground coriander
¼ teaspoon chilli powder
1 tablespoon unsalted butter

SERVES 4

PUT the onion, garlic, ginger and chilli in a food processor and chop until finely chopped but not a paste, or chop together with a knife.

HEAT the oil in a karhai or heavy-based frying pan over low heat and fry the onion mixture until softened but not browned. Add the cumin seeds and turmeric to the pan and stir for 1 minute. Mix in the cabbage, stirring thoroughly until all the leaves are coated in the yellow paste. Add the salt, pepper, ground cumin, coriander and chilli powder. Stir to coat the cabbage, then cook for 10 minutes with the pan partially covered, stirring occasionally until cabbage is soft. If the cabbage becomes too dry and starts sticking to the pan, add 1–2 tablespoons water. Stir in the butter and season with salt, to taste.

FROM INDIA

TOOR DAL

IN SOME PARTS OF INDIA IT IS COMMON TO COMBINE A SWEET AND SOUR TASTE, PARTICULARLY IN LENTIL CURRIES SUCH AS THIS ONE. PLAN IN ADVANCE WHEN YOU WANT TO MAKE THIS DISH AS THE DAL HAS TO BE SOAKED BEFORE YOU COOK IT.

500 g (1 lb 2 oz) toor dal (yellow lentils)
5 x 5 cm (2 inch) pieces of kokum
2 teaspoons coriander seeds
2 teaspoons cumin seeds
2 tablespoons oil
2 teaspoons black mustard seeds
10 curry leaves
7 cloves
10 cm (4 inch) cinnamon stick
5 green chillies, finely chopped
½ teaspoon ground turmeric
400 g (14 oz) tin chopped tomatoes
20 g (½ oz) jaggery or 10 g (¼ oz) molasses
coriander (cilantro) leaves

SERVES 8

SOAK the lentils in cold water for 2 hours.

RINSE the kokum, remove any stones and put the kokum in a bowl with cold water for a few minutes to soften.

DRAIN the lentils and put them in a heavy-based saucepan with 1 litre (35 fl oz/4 cups) of water and the pieces of kokum. Bring slowly to the boil, then simmer for about 40 minutes, or until the lentils feel soft when pressed between the thumb and index finger.

PLACE a small frying pan over low heat and dry-roast the coriander seeds until aromatic. Remove and dry-roast the cumin seeds. Grind the roasted seeds to a fine powder using a spice grinder or pestle and mortar.

FOR the final seasoning (tarka), heat the oil in a small pan over low heat. Add the mustard seeds and allow to pop. Add the curry leaves, cloves, cinnamon, chilli, turmeric and the roasted spice mix and cook for 1 minute. Add the tomato and cook for 2–3 minutes until the tomato is soft and can be broken up easily and incorporated into the sauce. Add the jaggery, then pour the spicy mixture into the simmering lentils and cook for another 10 minutes. Season with salt, to taste. Garnish with coriander leaves.

Test to see if the toor dal are cooked by gently squeezing them between your thumb and index finger. They should be soft.

A Hindu shrine.

TOOR DAL

Lighting candles at a Buddhist temple.

Tiger lily buds, or golden needles, are dried unopened lilies. When reconstituted they resemble limp bean sprouts.

FROM CHINA

BUDDHA'S DELIGHT

THE ORIGINAL RECIPE FOR THIS WELL-KNOWN DISH USED NO FEWER THAN EIGHTEEN DIFFERENT INGREDIENTS TO REPRESENT THE EIGHTEEN BUDDHAS. NOWADAYS, ANYTHING BETWEEN SIX TO EIGHT INGREDIENTS IS USUAL PRACTICE.

25 g (1 oz) tiger lily buds (golden needles)
6–8 dried Chinese mushrooms
10 g (1 cup) dried black fungus (wood ears)
150 g (5½ oz) ready-made braised gluten, drained
50 g (1¾ oz) tofu puffs (deep-fried cubes of tofu)
100 g (3 oz/1 cup) bean sprouts
1 carrot
4 tablespoons oil
60 g (2 oz/½ cup) snowpeas (mangetout), ends trimmed
1 teaspoon salt
½ teaspoon sugar
4 tablespoons vegetable stock (see recipe on page 491)
2 tablespoons light soy sauce
½ teaspoon roasted sesame oil

SERVES 4

SOAK the tiger lily buds in boiling water for 30 minutes. Rinse and drain the tiger lily buds, and trim off any roots if they are hard.

SOAK the dried mushrooms in boiling water for 30 minutes, then drain and squeeze out any excess water. Remove and discard the stems and cut the caps in half (or quarters if large).

SOAK the dried black fungus in cold water for 20 minutes, then drain and squeeze out any excess water. Cut any large pieces of fungus in half.

CUT the gluten and tofu into small pieces. Wash the bean sprouts, discarding any husks and straggly end pieces, and dry thoroughly. Diagonally cut the carrot into thin slices.

HEAT a wok over high heat, add the oil and heat until very hot. Stir-fry the carrot for 30 seconds, then add the snowpeas and bean sprouts. Stir-fry for 1 minute, then add the gluten, tofu, lily buds, mushrooms, black fungus, salt, sugar, stock and soy sauce. Toss everything together, then cover and braise for 2 minutes at a gentle simmer.

ADD the sesame oil, toss it through the mixture and serve hot or cold.

FROM INDIA

SWEET AND SOUR CHICKPEAS

500 g (1 lb 2 oz/2¼ cups)
  chickpeas
2 tablespoons oil or ghee
2 large red onions, thinly sliced
2 cm (¾ inch) piece of ginger, finely
  chopped
2 teaspoons sugar
2 teaspoons ground coriander
2 teaspoons ground cumin
pinch of chilli powder (optional)
1 teaspoon garam masala (see recipe
  on page 464)
3 tablespoons tamarind purée
  (see recipe on page 467)
4 ripe tomatoes, chopped
4 tablespoons coriander (cilantro) or
  mint leaves, finely chopped

SERVES 6

SOAK the chickpeas overnight in 2 litres (70 fl oz/ 8 cups) water. Drain, then put the chickpeas in a large saucepan with 2 litres (70 fl oz/8 cups) water. Bring to the boil, spooning off any scum from the surface. Cover and simmer over low heat for 1–1½ hours, until soft. It is important they are soft at this stage as they won't soften once the sauce is added. Drain.

HEAT the oil in a karhai or heavy-based frying pan. Fry the onion until soft and brown, then stir in the ginger. Add chickpeas, sugar, coriander, cumin, chilli powder, garam masala and a pinch of salt. Stir, then add the tamarind and tomato and simmer for 2–3 minutes. Add 500 ml (17 fl oz/ 2 cups) water, bring to the boil and cook until the sauce has thickened. Stir in the coriander leaves.

SERVE with rotis.

CHOLE CHAAT

220 g (8 oz/1 cup) chickpeas
2 tablespoons oil
½ onion, chopped
1 teaspoon ground coriander
1 teaspoon ground cumin
¼ teaspoon ground turmeric
1 teaspoon garam masala
  (see recipe on page 464)
2 cm (¾ inch) piece of ginger,
  grated
2 red chillies, finely chopped
200 g (7 oz) tin chopped tomatoes,
  drained

SERVES 4

SOAK the chickpeas overnight in 2 litres (70 fl oz/ 8 cups) water. Drain, then put the chickpeas in a large saucepan with 2 litres (70 fl oz/8 cups) water. Bring to the boil, spooning off any scum from the surface. Simmer over low heat for 1–1½ hours, until soft. It is important the chickpeas are soft at this stage as they won't soften any more once the sauce has been added. Drain, reserving the cooking liquid. Remove 6 tablespoons of the chickpeas and thoroughly mash them with a fork.

HEAT the oil in a heavy-based saucepan over low heat and cook the onion until golden brown. Add the coriander, cumin, turmeric and garam masala and fry for 1 minute. Add ginger, chilli, tomato and salt, to taste. Stir until well mixed. Add chickpeas and their cooking liquid, and also the mashed chickpeas. Bring to the boil, reduce the heat and simmer, uncovered, for 5 minutes.

CHOLE CHAAT

SMOKY SPICED EGGPLANT

WHEN EGGPLANTS (AUBERGINES) ARE IN SEASON IN INDIA, THEY ARE OFTEN PLACED ON THE DYING EMBERS OF A CHARCOAL FIRE AND LEFT TO SMOKE OVERNIGHT, READY TO BE FRIED AND BLENDED WITH SPICES THE FOLLOWING MORNING. SERVE THIS DISH WITH BREADS OR AS A COLD RELISH.

600 g (1 lb 5 oz) eggplants
  (aubergines)
1 red onion, chopped
1 garlic clove, chopped
2.5 cm (1 inch) piece of ginger,
  chopped
1 green chilli, chopped
90 ml (3 fl oz/⅓ cup) oil
¼ teaspoon chilli powder
½ teaspoon garam masala
  (see recipe on page 464)
2 teaspoons ground cumin
2 teaspoons ground coriander
2 teaspoons salt
½ teaspoon ground black pepper
2 ripe tomatoes, chopped
3–4 tablespoons coriander (cilantro)
  leaves, finely chopped

SERVES 4

SCORCH the eggplants by holding them over a medium gas flame, or heating them under a grill (broiler) or on an electric hotplate. Keep turning them until the skin is blackened on all sides. Set aside until cool, then peel off the charred skin. Roughly chop the flesh. Don't worry if black specks remain on the flesh because they add to the smoky flavour.

COMBINE the onion, garlic, ginger and chilli in a blender and process until chopped together but not a paste. Alternatively, chop finely with a knife and mix in a bowl.

HEAT the oil in a deep, heavy-based frying pan over medium heat, add the onion mixture and cook until slightly browned. Add all the spices, and the salt and pepper, and stir for 1 minute. Add the chopped tomato and simmer until the liquid has reduced. Put the eggplants in the pan and mash them with a wooden spoon, stirring around with the spices. Simmer for 10 minutes, or until the eggplants are soft.

STIR in the chopped coriander leaves and season with salt, to taste.

Using a pair of tongs, hold the eggplant (aubergine) in the gas flame until it is charred all over. The skin will then peel away quite easily.

SOFT TOFU WITH CHILLI AND SPRING ONION

250 g (9 oz) soft tofu, drained
2 spring onions (scallions), sliced
1 red chilli, thinly sliced
2 tablespoons chopped coriander
   (cilantro)
2 tablespoons soy sauce
90 ml (3 fl oz/⅓ cup) oil
1 teaspoon roasted sesame oil

SERVES 4

CUT the drained tofu into cubes and put it on a heatproof plate.

SCATTER the spring onion, chilli, coriander and soy sauce over the tofu.

PUT the oils in a small saucepan and heat until they are smoking, then immediately pour the oils over the tofu.

Soft tofu is sold by shops and travelling carts and is eaten as a snack. Here it is dressed with honey.

BRAISED TOFU

8 dried Chinese mushrooms
150 g (5½ oz) Chinese cabbage or
   choy sum
225 g (8 oz) firm tofu, drained
125 g (4 oz) carrots
125 g (4 oz) baby corn
3–4 tablespoons oil
2 tablespoons light soy sauce or
   oyster sauce
1 teaspoon salt
½ teaspoon sugar
1 tablespoon Shaoxing rice wine
2 spring onions (scallions), cut into
   short lengths
1 teaspoon roasted sesame oil

SERVES 4

SOAK the dried mushrooms in boiling water for 30 minutes, then drain, reserving the liquid, and squeeze out any excess water. Remove and discard the stems and cut the caps in half.

CUT the cabbage into large pieces and the tofu into 12 cubes. Diagonally cut the carrots. Leave the corn whole if small, or cut into pieces.

LINE a clay pot, casserole or saucepan with the Chinese cabbage and pour in 2½ tablespoons of the reserved liquid. Heat a wok over high heat, add half the oil and heat until very hot. Lightly brown the tofu for 2–3 minutes, transfer to the pot and add the soy or oyster sauce.

REHEAT wok over high heat, add the remaining oil and heat until very hot. Stir-fry the carrot, corn and mushrooms for 1 minute. Add salt, sugar and rice wine, blend well, then transfer to the pot. Bring to the boil, place spring onion on top, then simmer, covered, for 15–20 minutes. Sprinkle with the sesame oil.

BRAISED TOFU

Make sure that the stuffing fills the capsicums (peppers) adequately, but don't pack it in too firmly or it may spill out as it cooks.

STUFFED CAPSICUMS

STUFFING VEGETABLES IS A COOKING METHOD USED FOR SPECIAL OCCASIONS. THESE STUFFED CAPSICUMS (PEPPERS) ARE SIMMERED IN A COCONUT-FLAVOURED SAUCE. THE CAPSICUMS SHOULD BE THE SMALL VARIETY USUALLY USED IN INDIA. RED OR YELLOW ONES CAN ALSO BE USED.

400 g (14 oz) potatoes, quartered
6 small green capsicums (peppers)
2 tablespoons oil
2 onions, finely chopped
2 teaspoons ground cumin
2 teaspoons ground coriander
½ teaspoon ground turmeric
½ teaspoon chilli powder

SAUCE
½ onion, finely chopped
6 cloves
6 cardamom pods
2 garlic cloves, finely chopped
2 cm (¾ inch) piece of ginger, finely chopped
1 cinnamon stick
1 teaspoon ground coriander
1 teaspoon ground cumin
¼ teaspoon ground turmeric
½ teaspoon chilli powder
50 g (1¾ oz) creamed coconut, mixed with 250 ml (8 fl oz/1 cup) water, or 250 ml (8 fl oz/1 cup) coconut cream (see recipe on page 468)

SERVES 6

COOK the potato in a saucepan of simmering water for 15 minutes, or until tender, then drain and cut into small cubes.

BRING a large saucepan of water to the boil, add the capsicums and blanch for 5 minutes. Refresh the capsicums in cold water, cut round the stem and remove both it and the seeds. Drain well upside-down.

HEAT the oil in a small frying pan and cook the onion over medium heat until soft but not browned. Add the cumin, coriander, turmeric and chilli and mix thoroughly. Mix in the potato and season with salt. Remove from the heat and leave until cool.

DIVIDE into six portions and fill each capsicum.

TO MAKE the sauce, combine all the ingredients in a deep, heavy-based frying pan and bring slowly to the boil. Reduce the heat to low, cover and simmer for 20 minutes. Season with salt, to taste. Add the stuffed capsicums to the pan, arranging them so that they stand upright in a single layer, and cook for another 5 minutes, or until the sauce is thick. Serve the capsicums with a little sauce spooned over the top.

AVIAL

½ teaspoon ground turmeric

200 g (7 oz) carrots, cut into batons

200 g (7 oz) sweet potato, cut into batons

200 g (7 oz) green beans, topped and tailed and cut in half

50 g (1¾ oz) grated coconut (see recipe on page 468)

5 cm (2 inch) piece of ginger, grated

3 green chillies, finely chopped

1½ teaspoons ground cumin

420 ml (14 fl oz/1⅔ cups) thick plain yoghurt (see recipe on page 467)

1 tablespoon oil

10 curry leaves

SERVES 4

BRING 500 ml (2 cups) water to the boil in a saucepan, add the turmeric and carrot, reduce the heat and simmer for 5 minutes. Add sweet potato and the beans, return to the boil, then reduce the heat and simmer for 5 minutes, or until the vegetables are almost cooked.

PUT the coconut, ginger and chilli in a blender or pestle and mortar, with a little water, and blend or grind to a paste. Add to the vegetables with the cumin and some salt and simmer for 2 minutes. Stir in the yoghurt and heat through.

FOR the final seasoning (tarka), heat the oil over low heat in a small saucepan. Add the curry leaves and allow to crisp. Pour the hot oil and the leaves over the vegetables.

A depiction of a Hindu deity painted on a door in Hyderabad.

CAULIFLOWER BHAJI

1 teaspoon cumin seeds

3–4 tablespoons oil

¼ teaspoon black mustard seeds

250 g (9 oz) potatoes, cut into small cubes

750 g (1 lb 10 oz) cauliflower, broken into florets

½ teaspoon ground cumin

½ teaspoon ground coriander

¼ teaspoon ground turmeric

½ teaspoon garam masala (see recipe on page 464)

2 garlic cloves, finely chopped

2 green chillies, seeded and finely chopped

5 curry leaves

SERVES 4

PLACE a small frying pan over low heat and dry-roast ¼ teaspoon of the cumin seeds until aromatic. Grind the roasted seeds to a fine powder using a pestle and mortar.

HEAT the oil over low heat in a karhai or heavy-based saucepan. Add the mustard seeds and remaining cumin seeds, cover and allow to pop for a couple of seconds. Uncover, add the diced potato and fry for 1 minute, stirring occasionally to prevent the potato from sticking to the pan. Add the cauliflower, all the remaining spices, garlic, chilli and curry leaves and stir to combine. Add 60 ml (¼ cup) water and bring to the boil. Cover and simmer for 5–7 minutes, or until cauliflower is cooked and tender. Season with salt, to taste.

CAULIFLOWER BHAJI

FROM INDIA

PARIPPU

A DISH THAT INCLUDES LENTILS OF SOME SORT IS A MUST AS PART OF ANY INDIAN MEAL. THIS RECIPE IS FROM THE SOUTH AND IS FLAVOURED WITH COCONUT AS WELL AS A TARKA OF FRIED ONION, CUMIN SEEDS, MUSTARD SEEDS AND CURRY LEAVES WHICH IS MIXED IN TOWARDS THE END OF COOKING.

225 g (8 oz) masoor dal (red lentils)
1 onion, roughly chopped
1 ripe tomato, roughly chopped
50 g (1¾ oz) creamed coconut, mixed with 250 ml (8 fl oz/1 cup) water, or 250 ml (8 fl oz/1 cup) coconut milk (see recipe on page 468)
2 green chillies, chopped
¼ teaspoon ground turmeric
½ teaspoon ground cumin
½ teaspoon ground coriander
2 tablespoons oil
1 teaspoon cumin seeds
½ teaspoon black mustard seeds
1 onion, very finely chopped
10 curry leaves

SERVES 4

PUT the lentils in a heavy-based saucepan with 500 ml (17 fl oz2 cups) water. Add the roughly chopped onion, tomato, creamed coconut or coconut milk, green chilli, turmeric, ground cumin and coriander, and bring to the boil. Simmer and cook, stirring occasionally, until lentils are cooked to a soft mush (masoor dal does not hold its shape when it cooks). Allow about 25 minutes. If all the water has evaporated before the lentils are cooked, add 125 ml (½ cup) boiling water.

FOR the final seasoning (tarka), heat the oil in a small saucepan over low heat. Add the cumin seeds and mustard seeds, cover and allow the seeds to pop. Add the finely chopped onion and curry leaves and fry over low heat until the onion is golden brown.

POUR the seasoned onions into the simmering lentils. Season with salt, to taste, and cook for another 5 minutes.

A woman binds curry leaves into neat bundles in the market.

BABY EGGPLANT AND CHERRY TOMATO STIR-FRY

12 small round Thai eggplants
(aubergines), green, yellow
or purple
1 teaspoon fish sauce,
plus 1 tablespoon
1 tablespoon vegetable oil
1 small red chilli, chopped
1 tablespoon finely sliced ginger
2 Asian shallots, finely chopped
1 garlic clove, chopped
150 g (5 oz) cherry tomatoes
2 tablespoons black vinegar
2 tablespoons palm sugar (jaggery)
12–18 Thai sweet basil leaves

SERVES 4

CUT each eggplant in half and toss them in a bowl
with 1 teaspoon fish sauce.

PUT about 8 cm (3 inches) of water in a wok and
bring to the boil. Place the eggplants in a bamboo
steamer, place the steamer over the boiling water
and steam the eggplants for 15 minutes.

HEAT the oil in a wok, add the chilli, ginger,
shallots and garlic and cook for 15 seconds.

ADD the eggplants and tomatoes and toss well.

ADD the black vinegar, sugar and remaining fish
sauce and cook for 2–3 minutes, until the sauce
thickens.

STIR in the basil leaves and serve.

STIR-FRIED BROCCOLI WITH OYSTER SAUCE

350 g (12 oz) Chinese broccoli,
cut into pieces
1 tablespoon vegetable oil
2 garlic cloves, finely chopped
1 tablespoon oyster sauce
1 tablespoon light soy sauce

SERVES 4

BLANCH the Chinese broccoli in boiling salted
water for 2–3 minutes, then drain thoroughly.

HEAT the oil in a wok or frying pan and stir-fry
the garlic over a medium heat until light brown.

ADD the Chinese broccoli and half of the oyster
sauce and the light soy sauce. Stir-fry over a high
heat for 1–2 minutes until the stems are just
tender. Drizzle with the remaining oyster sauce.

STIR-FRIED BROCCOLI
WITH OYSTER SAUCE

BABY EGGPLANT AND CHERRY TOMATO STIR-FRY

A Buddhist temple in Sichuan.

FROM CHINA

MOCK DUCK

GLUTEN IS USED IN VEGETARIAN CHINESE COOKING TO TAKE THE PLACE OF MEAT IN RECIPES. RATHER THAN RESEMBLING DUCK, THIS DISH IS COOKED AS DUCK WOULD BE COOKED. YOU CAN MAKE THE GLUTEN OR USE READY-MADE GLUTEN – PLAIN OR SHAPED LIKE PIECES OF DUCK.

Incense and temple offerings are on sale at shops in the streets around temples.

1 kg (2 lb 4 oz) plain (all-purpose) flour
1 teaspoon salt
1½ tablespoons cornflour (cornstarch)
2 tablespoons oil
1 green capsicum (pepper), diced
125 ml (4 fl oz/½ cup) vegetable stock (see recipe on page 491)
2 tablespoons light soy sauce
2 teaspoons Shaoxing rice wine
1 teaspoon sugar
1 teaspoon roasted sesame oil

SERVES 4

SIFT the flour into a bowl with salt and gradually add 560 ml (19 fl oz/2¼ cups) warm water to make a dough. Knead until smooth, then cover with a damp cloth and leave in a warm place for 55–60 minutes.

RINSE the dough under cold water and wash off all the starch by pulling, stretching and squeezing the dough with your hands. You should have about 300 g (11 oz) gluten after 10–15 minutes of washing and squeezing. Extract as much water as you can by squeezing the dough hard, then cut the dough into bite-size pieces. Dry thoroughly.

TOSS the gluten in 1 tablespoon of the cornflour. Heat a wok over high heat, add the oil and heat until very hot. Quickly stir-fry the gluten until it is browned all over, then remove from the wok. Stir-fry the capsicum until it starts to brown around the edges, then remove. Pour off any excess oil.

ADD the stock, soy sauce, rice wine and sugar to the wok and bring to the boil. Return the gluten and capsicum and simmer for 1 minute.

COMBINE the remaining cornflour with enough water to make a paste, add to the sauce and simmer until thickened.

SPRINKLE with the sesame oil and serve.

FROM INDIA

GAJAR MATAR

1 small onion, roughly chopped
1 garlic clove, roughly chopped
2.5 cm (1 inch) piece of ginger, chopped
125 ml (4 fl oz/½ cup) oil
1 teaspoon cumin seeds
1½ teaspoons ground turmeric
350 g (12 oz) carrots, diced
1 teaspoon ground cumin
1 teaspoon ground coriander
250 g (8 oz/1⅔ cups) peas
3 teaspoons salt
¼ teaspoon sugar
¼ teaspoon chilli powder
4 teaspoons pomegranate seeds (optional)
½ teaspoon garam masala (see recipe on page 464)

SERVES 6

PUT the onion, garlic and ginger in a food processor and blend until finely chopped, or chop them with a knife and mix together.

HEAT the oil in a karhai or frying pan, then add the onion mixture and stir over high heat for 2 minutes, or until softened. Reduce the heat to medium and add the cumin seeds and turmeric.

WHEN the seeds are sizzling, add the carrot and stir for 2 minutes. Add the ground cumin and coriander and fry for 2 minutes.

STIR in the peas and then the salt, sugar and chilli powder. Add 2 tablespoons of water if using frozen peas, or 4 tablespoons if using fresh peas. Reduce the heat to a simmer, add pomegranate seeds, if using, and stir before partially covering the pan. Simmer for 15 minutes, or until the carrot and peas are tender. Stir in the garam masala.

SAAG BHAJI

200 g (7 oz) small turnips, finely chopped
1 kg (2 lb 4 oz) mixed English spinach and amaranth leaves, finely shredded
½ teaspoon chilli powder
1 tablespoon ghee or oil
2 cm (¾ inch) piece of ginger, grated
1 onion, finely chopped
1½ tablespoons lemon juice

SERVES 4

SAAG BHAJI

BRING 125 ml (4 fl oz/½ cup) water to the boil in a large heavy-based saucepan over medium heat. Add the turnip, cook for 1–2 minutes, then add the spinach and amaranth. Stir in the chilli powder and a pinch of salt and cook for 2–3 minutes, or until almost all the water has evaporated. Mash the mixture well and remove from the heat.

HEAT the ghee or oil in a heavy-based saucepan over low heat and fry the ginger and onion for 2–3 minutes.

ADD the mashed vegetables, mix well and keep tossing until everything is well mixed. Season with salt, to taste.

SERVE warm with a dash of lemon juice.

The dal used for this recipe can be split but not skinned as shown here, or can be both split and skinned.

URAD DAL

250 g (9 oz) unskinned urad dal
¼ teaspoon ground turmeric
4 ripe tomatoes, chopped
1 small onion, roughly chopped
2 tablespoons oil
½ teaspoon cumin seeds
1 teaspoon fennel seeds
5 cm (2 inch) piece of ginger, grated
2 dried chillies, broken into pieces
pinch of asafoetida
coriander (cilantro) leaves

SERVES 4

PUT the dal in a heavy-based saucepan and add 1 litre (35 fl oz/4 cups) water, the turmeric, chopped tomato and onion. Bring to the boil, then reduce heat, cover and simmer for 40 minutes, or until the dal is cooked and feels soft when pressed between the thumb and index finger.

FOR the final seasoning (tarka), heat oil in a small saucepan, add the cumin and fennel seeds and allow to pop. Add the ginger, chilli and asafoetida and fry over low heat for 30 seconds. Pour into the hot dal and simmer for another 5 minutes. Season with salt, to taste.

GARNISH with coriander leaves before serving.

DAL SAAG

DAL SAAG

225 g (8 oz) moong dal
2–3 tablespoons oil
1 teaspoon black mustard seeds
8 curry leaves
¼ teaspoon asafoetida
¼ teaspoon ground turmeric
1 teaspoon ground cumin
1 teaspoon ground coriander
3 cm (1¼ inch) piece of ginger, grated
2 green chillies, seeded and cut into 1 cm (½ inch) pieces
125 g (4 oz) English spinach leaves, roughly chopped
5 spring onions (scallions), finely chopped

SERVES 4

PUT the moong dal in a heavy-based saucepan, add 750 ml (26 fl oz/3 cups) water and bring to the boil. Reduce heat and simmer for 30 minutes, or until the moong dal are soft and breaking up. Moong dal tend to soak up most of the liquid so you may need to add a little more.

FOR the final seasoning (tarka), heat the oil in a saucepan, add the mustard seeds, cover and allow to pop. Stir in the curry leaves, asafoetida, turmeric, cumin, coriander, ginger and chilli, then pour into the cooked dal.

STIR in the spinach and spring onion and cook for about 2 minutes, or until the spinach is just cooked. Season with salt, to taste.

NOODLES & RICE

Stir the paste into the coconut cream before adding the chicken, soy sauce, sugar, stock and coconut milk.

FROM THAILAND

CHIANG MAI NOODLES

ONE OF CHIANG MAI'S WELL KNOWN DISHES, THIS IS FOUND ON RESTAURANT MENUS AND AT HAWKER STALLS, PARTICULARLY THOSE NEAR THE MOSQUE. SERVE WITH THE ACCOMPANIMENTS SUGGESTED AS THEY COMPLEMENT THE NOODLES PARTICULARLY WELL.

PASTE
3 dried long red chillies
4 Asian shallots, chopped
4 garlic cloves, crushed
2 cm (¾ inch) piece of turmeric, grated
5 cm (2 inch) piece of ginger, grated
4 tablespoons chopped coriander (cilantro) roots
1 teaspoon shrimp paste
1 teaspoon curry powder

5 tablespoons coconut cream (see recipe on page 468)
2 tablespoons palm sugar (jaggery)
2 tablespoons soy sauce
4 chicken drumsticks and 4 chicken thighs, with skin and bone
500 ml (17 fl oz/2 cups) chicken stock or water
410 ml (14 fl oz/1⅔ cups) coconut milk (see recipe on page 468)
400 g (14 oz) fresh flat egg noodles
chopped or sliced spring onions (scallions), for garnish
a handful of coriander (cilantro) leaves, for garnish
lime wedges, to serve
pickled mustard greens or cucumber, to serve
roasted chilli sauce (see recipe on page 480), to serve
Asian shallots, quartered, to serve

SERVES 4

TO MAKE the paste, soak the dried chillies in hot water for 10 minutes, then drain and chop the chillies into pieces, discarding the seeds. Put the chillies in a pestle and mortar with the shallots, garlic, turmeric, ginger, coriander roots and shrimp paste and pound to a fine paste. Add the curry powder and a pinch of salt and mix well.

PUT coconut cream in a wok or saucepan and simmer over a medium heat for about 5 minutes, or until the cream separates and a layer of oil forms on the surface. Stir the cream if it starts to brown around the edges.

ADD the paste and stir until fragrant. Add the palm sugar, soy sauce and chicken and stir well, then add the stock and coconut milk and bring to the boil. Reduce the heat and simmer for 30 minutes or until the chicken is cooked and tender.

MEANWHILE, cook 100 g (3 oz) of the egg noodles by deep-frying them in very hot oil in a saucepan until they puff up. Drain on paper towels. Cook the remaining noodles in boiling water according to the packet instructions.

PUT the boiled noodles in a large bowl and spoon the chicken mixture over the top. Garnish with the crispy noodles, spring onions and coriander leaves. Serve the accompaniments alongside.

FROM JAPAN

YAKISOBA

YAKISOBA IS EASY TO MAKE AT HOME IN A WOK. STIR-FRY THE MEAT AND VEGETABLES WITH THE NOODLES AND THEN MELD THEM ALL TOGETHER WITH A SAVOURY SAUCE. THIS NOODLE DISH IS ALSO A POPULAR STREET STALL FOOD IN JAPAN.

4 dried shiitake mushrooms

300 g (11 oz) beef fillet steak or pork fillet, thinly sliced across the grain

3 garlic cloves, finely chopped

3 teaspoons fresh ginger, finely chopped

500 g (1 lb 2 oz) yakisoba noodles

6 slices bacon, cut into 3 cm (1¼ inch) squares

2 tablespoons vegetable oil

1 teaspoon sesame oil

6 spring onions (scallions), cut into 3 cm (1¼ inch) lengths

1 carrot, thinly sliced on the diagonal

1 small green capsicum (pepper), cut into thin strips

250 g (9 oz) Chinese cabbage, thinly sliced

125 g (4 oz) bamboo shoots, thinly sliced

1 tablespoon pickled ginger, thinly sliced

nori flakes or strips, to serve, optional

fine katsuobushi (bonito flakes), to serve, optional

SAUCE

60 ml (2 fl oz/¼ cup) shoyu (Japanese soy sauce)

2 tablespoons worcestershire sauce

1½ tablespoons Japanese rice vinegar

1 tablespoon sake

1 tablespoon mirin

1 tablespoon tomato sauce

1 tablespoon oyster sauce

2 teaspoons black or dark brown sugar

SERVES 4

SOAK the shiitake in hot water for 30 minutes. Drain, reserving 2 tablespoons of the soaking liquid. Discard stems and thinly slice the caps.

MEANWHILE, put beef in a large bowl with half the garlic and half the fresh ginger and mix well. Put the yakisoba noodles in a colander and pour boiling water over them. Drain the noodles and separate them.

TO MAKE the sauce, combine all the ingredients in a bowl with the reserved mushroom liquid and the remaining garlic and ginger.

HEAT a wok over medium–high heat, add the bacon and stir-fry for 3 minutes, or until starting to soften and brown. Set aside in a large bowl.

COMBINE the vegetable and sesame oils in a bowl. Increase the heat to high and add a little of the oil mixture, then stir-fry the beef for 1 minute, or until it starts to change colour all over. Add to the bacon. Add a little more oil to the wok, then stir-fry the shiitake, spring onion, carrot, capsicum, cabbage and bamboo shoots for 1–2 minutes, or until the vegetables are just cooked but still crisp. Add to the bowl with the meat. Add the remaining oil to the wok and stir-fry the noodles for 1 minute. Return the meat and vegetables to the wok, add the sauce and pickled ginger and stir-fry for 2–3 minutes, or until heated through.

SERVE garnished with nori and katsuobushi, if using.

Yakisoba, literally meaning 'fried noodles', is a dish often sold at festivals in Japan, but originated in China.

Roll the meatballs so they are completely coated in the glutinous rice, then press the rice on firmly so it sticks.

FROM CHINA

PEARL BALLS

THIS FAMOUS DISH ORIGINATED IN HUNAN PROVINCE, ONE OF CHINA'S MAJOR RICE BASINS. ONCE STEAMED, THE STICKY RICE THAT FORMS THE COATING FOR THESE MEATBALLS TURNS INTO PEARL-LIKE GRAINS. TRADITIONALLY, GLUTINOUS OR SWEET RICE IS USED, BUT YOU COULD USE RISOTTO RICE.

330 g (12 oz) glutinous or
    sweet rice
8 dried Chinese mushrooms
160 g (5 oz/1 cup) peeled water
    chestnuts
450 g (1 lb) minced (ground) pork
1 small carrot, grated
2 spring onions (scallions),
    finely chopped
1½ tablespoons finely chopped
    ginger
2 tablespoons light soy sauce
1 tablespoon Shaoxing rice wine
1½ teaspoons roasted sesame oil
2½ tablespoons cornflour
    (cornstarch)
soy sauce

SERVES 6

PUT the rice in a bowl and, using your fingers as a rake, rinse under cold running water to remove any dust. Drain the rice in a colander, then place it in a bowl with enough cold water to cover. Set aside for 1 hour. Drain the rice and transfer it to a baking tray in an even layer.

SOAK the dried mushrooms in boiling water for 30 minutes, then drain and squeeze out any excess water. Remove and discard the stems and chop the caps.

BLANCH the water chestnuts in a pan of boiling water for 1 minute, then refresh in cold water. Drain, pat dry and finely chop them.

PLACE the pork in a bowl, add the mushrooms, water chestnuts, carrot, spring onion, ginger, light soy sauce, rice wine, sesame oil and cornflour. Stir the mixture vigorously to combine.

ROLL the mixture into 2 cm (¾ inch) balls, then roll each meatball in the glutinous rice so that it is completely coated. Lightly press the rice to make it stick to the meatball. Place the pearl balls well apart in three steamers lined with greaseproof paper punched with holes or some damp cheesecloth or muslin. Cover and steam over simmering water in a wok, reversing the steamers halfway through, for 25 minutes. If the rice still has a bite to it, continue to cook for a little longer until it softens. Serve with the soy sauce.

FROM JAPAN

JAPANESE FRIED RICE

CALLED *YAKIMESHI* OR *CHAHAN* IN JAPAN, WHERE IT IS PARTICULARLY POPULAR AMONG THE YOUNGER GENERATIONS. FRIED RICE IS AN ENTICING WAY TO USE UP LEFTOVER RICE AND WHATEVER ELSE MIGHT BE ON HAND IN THE REFRIGERATOR AND PANTRY.

300 g (10 oz/1¼ cups) Japanese short-grain rice

2 eggs

2 tablespoons dashi II (see recipe on page 483)

2 teaspoons sake

1 teaspoon sugar

pinch ground white pepper

1 tablespoon shoyu (Japanese soy sauce)

vegetable oil, for pan-frying

2 teaspoons sesame oil

3 spring onions (scallions), 2 chopped, 1 sliced on the diagonal

4 fresh shiitake mushrooms, stems discarded, caps sliced

60 g (2 oz) bamboo shoots, thinly sliced

60 g (2 oz) sliced ham, cut into strips

40 g (1½ oz/¼ cup) frozen green peas, thawed

1 teaspoon pickled ginger, finely chopped

SERVES 4

RINSE the rice several times in cold water until the water runs clear, then drain in a colander for 1 hour. Put in a saucepan with 375 ml (13 fl oz/ 1½ cups) water. Bring to the boil, then cover with a tight-fitting lid, reduce the heat to low and simmer for 15 minutes. Turn off the heat but leave the pan on the hotplate. Working quickly, remove the lid, lay a clean tea towel (dish towel) over the top, then put the lid on and set aside for 15 minutes. Cool completely, then rinse well.

PUT the eggs, dashi, sake, sugar, white pepper and 2 teaspoons of the shoyu in a bowl and mix well.

HEAT a little of the vegetable oil in a small non-stick frying pan over medium heat, then pour in the egg mixture. Drag the egg mixture into the centre of the pan with a wooden spoon a couple of times, and allow the mixture to flow back to the edges. Cook for 1 minute, or until almost set, then flip over and cook for a further 30 seconds. Remove and allow to cool. Roll the omelette up, then slice thinly.

POUR a little more vegetable oil and half the sesame oil into a wok or large frying pan and heat over medium heat. Add the chopped spring onion, shiitake and bamboo shoots. Stir-fry for 2 minutes, then add ham and peas and stir-fry for a further 2 minutes. Remove from the wok.

ADD a little more vegetable oil and the remaining sesame oil to the wok and add the rice. Stir-fry for 2 minutes, then return the mushroom mixture to the wok, along with the remaining shoyu and the pickled ginger and stir to combine and heat through. Scoop into a bowl and top with the egg and remaining sliced spring onion and serve.

Life in industrial Japan does mean that for most Japanese, rice no longer comes directly from the field, but from a shop or even a vending machine.

FROM INDIA

UPAMA

2 tablespoons chana dal
4 tablespoons ghee or oil
75 g (½ cup) cashew nuts
1 teaspoon black mustard seeds
15 curry leaves
½ onion, finely chopped
140 g (1½ cups) coarse semolina
lime juice

SERVES 4

SOAK the dal in plenty of water for 3 hours. Drain, then put in a saucepan with 500 ml (2 cups) water. Bring to the boil and cook for 2 minutes. Drain the dal, then dry in a tea towel (dish towel). Brush a little of the ghee onto the cashew nuts and toast them in a frying pan over low heat until golden.

HEAT the remaining ghee in a heavy-based frying pan and add the mustard seeds and dal. Cook until the seeds start to pop, add the curry leaves and onion and cook until the onion softens. Add the semolina. Toss everything together and when the semolina is hot and the grains are brown and coated in oil, sprinkle with 500 ml (17 fl oz/2 cups) boiling water, 125 ml (4 fl oz/½ cup) at a time, tossing and stirring after each addition, until absorbed. Season with salt. Sprinkle with lime juice and cashews.

KHICHHARI

60 g (2 oz/¼ cup) toor dal (yellow
    lentils)
300 g (10 oz/1½ cups) basmati rice
3 tablespoons ghee
1 teaspoon cumin seeds
6 cloves
½ cinnamon stick
2 onions, finely chopped
2 garlic cloves, finely chopped
2 cm (¾ inch) piece of ginger, finely
    chopped
1 teaspoon garam masala
    (see recipe on page 464)
3 tablespoons lemon juice
1 teaspoon salt

SERVES 6

SOAK the dal in 500 ml (17 fl oz/2 cups) water in a large saucepan for 2 hours. Wash the rice in a sieve under cold water until the water from the rice runs clear. Drain.

HEAT the ghee in a heavy-based saucepan over low heat and fry the cumin seeds, cloves and cinnamon for a few seconds. Increase the heat to medium, add the onion, garlic and ginger and cook until they soften and begin to brown.

ADD the rice and dal and toss to thoroughly coat in ghee. Add the garam masala, lemon juice, salt and 750 ml (25 fl oz/3 cups) boiling water. Bring to the boil, then reduce the heat to very low, cover tightly and cook for 15 minutes. Remove from the heat and gently fluff up with a fork. Cover the pan with a clean cloth and leave for 10 minutes. Fluff up again and season with salt, to taste.

KHICHHARI

FROM JAPAN

OMELETTES FILLED WITH RICE

YOSHOKU MEANS 'WESTERN FOOD' BUT IT ACTUALLY REFERS TO THOSE NEW DISHES OF THE LATE 19TH AND EARLY 20TH CENTURIES WHICH THE JAPANESE ADAPTED TO SUIT THEMSELVES. AMONG THEM IS *OMURAISU*, A SOY- AND MIRIN-SEASONED OMELETTE WRAPPED AROUND FLAVOURED RICE.

300 g (10 oz/1¼ cups) Japanese short-grain rice
25 g (1 oz) butter
a few drops sesame oil
1 onion, finely chopped
2 cloves garlic, crushed
2 teaspoons fresh ginger, finely chopped
250 g (9 oz) boneless, skinless chicken thighs, diced
60 g (2 oz) peas frozen, thawed
125 ml (4 fl oz/½ cup) tomato sauce, plus extra to serve
Japanese mayonnaise, to serve, optional

OMELETTES
8 eggs
2 teaspoons shoyu (Japanese soy sauce)
1 tablespoon mirin
1 teaspoon caster (superfine) sugar

SERVES 4

RINSE the rice several times in cold water until the water runs clear, then drain in a colander for 1 hour. Put in a saucepan with 375 ml (13 fl oz/ 1½ cups) water. Bring to the boil, then cover with a tight-fitting lid, reduce heat to low and simmer for 15 minutes. Turn off the heat but leave the pan on the hotplate. Working quickly, remove the lid, lay a clean tea towel (dish towel) over the top, replace the lid and set aside for 15 minutes. Cool completely, then rinse well.

MELT the butter in a large frying pan, add the sesame oil and onion and cook over medium heat for 8–10 minutes, or until golden. Add the garlic, ginger and diced chicken and cook, stirring, for 1 minute, or until the chicken starts to change colour. Add the peas and tomato sauce and mix well. Add the rice and mix again until the rice is evenly pink from the tomato sauce. Continue cooking, stirring occasionally, for about 5 minutes, or until the chicken is cooked and the rice is completely heated through. Season, then cover and set aside while you make the omelettes.

LIGHTLY oil a Japanese omelette pan or non-stick frying pan and put over medium heat. Combine all the omelette ingredients in a bowl and lightly beat. Pour one-quarter of the egg mixture into the pan. Using chopsticks or a soft spatula, gently drag the outside edges of the egg into the centre until it just starts to set, then leave to cook for 1 minute. Spoon a quarter of the rice mixture along the centre line of the egg, then very carefully fold two sides towards the centre, over the rice, so you have a rectangular omelette. Put a serving plate over the top and very carefully invert the omelette onto the plate so the seam is on the bottom. Repeat with the remaining mixture to make three more omelettes.

SERVE with extra tomato sauce and a little mayonnaise, if you like.

Japanese mayonnaise has a slightly salty-sweet egg flavour and contains soya bean oil.

FROM THAILAND

HOT AND SOUR NOODLES WITH PRAWNS

200 g (7 oz) mung bean vermicelli
100 g (3 oz) minced (ground) pork
2 tablespoons oil
8 cooked prawns (shrimp), peeled
4 pickled garlic cloves, chopped
2 Asian shallots, finely sliced
4 bird's eye chillies, finely sliced
2 tablespoons fish sauce
1 tablespoon lime juice
2 tomatoes, seeded and cut into
   thin wedges
handful of Thai sweet basil leaves
handful of coriander (cilantro) leaves

SERVES 4

SOAK the noodles in hot water for 10 minutes or until soft. Drain the noodles and cut them into shorter lengths using a pair of scissors.

COOK the pork in boiling water for 2 minutes, breaking it up into small pieces, then drain.

HEAT the oil in a wok and add all the ingredients except the basil and coriander. Toss together for a minute or two.

ADD the herbs, toss briefly and serve.

Toss all the ingredients together before adding the herbs.

STIR-FRIED NOODLES WITH HOLY BASIL

450 g (1 lb) wide fresh flat rice
   noodles (sen yai)
2 teaspoons soy sauce
4 garlic cloves
4 bird's eye chillies, stems removed
4 tablespoons vegetable oil
20 g (7 oz) boneless, skinless
   chicken breasts, cut in thin strips
2 tablespoons fish sauce
2 teaspoons palm sugar (jaggery)
handful of holy basil leaves

SERVES 4

PUT the noodles in a bowl with the soy sauce and rub the sauce through the noodles, separating them out as you do so.

POUND the garlic and chillies together with a pestle and mortar until you have a fine paste.

HEAT the oil in a wok and add the garlic and chilli paste and fry until fragrant.

ADD the chicken and toss until cooked. Add the fish sauce and palm sugar and cook until the sugar dissolves. Add the noodles and basil leaves, toss together and serve.

STIR-FRIED NOODLES WITH
HOLY BASIL

FIVE-FLAVOURED RICE

THIS SATISFYING DISH, CALLED *TAKIKOMI GOHAN* IN JAPANESE, IS POPULAR AND NUTRITIOUS FARE.

THE RICE AND ASSORTED ADDED INGREDIENTS, WITH THEIR INDIVIDUAL TEXTURES AND TASTES, ARE

COOKED TOGETHER IN SEASONED DASHI TO YIELD A DEEPLY FLAVOURFUL MEAL-IN-A-BOWL.

440 g (16 oz/2 cups) Japanese
   short-grain rice
5 dried shiitake mushrooms
25 g (1 oz) abura-age (deep-fried
   tofu sheets)
100 g (3½ oz) konnyaku (yam
   cake), optional
1 small carrot, peeled
60 g (2 oz) bamboo shoots
500 g (1 lb 2 oz) boneless, skinless
   chicken thighs, cut into bite-sized
   pieces
500 ml (17 fl oz/2 cups) dashi II
   (see recipe on page 483)
80 ml (2½ fl oz/⅓ cup) shoyu
   (Japanese soy sauce)
2 tablespoons mirin
2 tablespoons mitsuba or flat-leaf
   (Italian) parsley, chopped, optional

SERVES 4–6

RINSE the rice several times in cold water until the water runs clear, then soak in fresh water for 1 hour.

MEANWHILE, soak the shiitake in 375 ml (13 oz/1½ cups) hot water for 30 minutes, then drain well, reserving the liquid. Discard the stems and thinly slice the caps.

PUT the abura-age in a heatproof bowl and cover with boiling water for a few minutes. Drain and squeeze the sheets gently between paper towels to remove the excess oil.

CUT the konnyaku, carrot, bamboo shoots and abura-age into 3 cm x 5 mm (1¼ x ¼ inch) strips and put in a bowl with the shiitake. Add the chicken pieces to the bowl.

COMBINE the reserved mushroom liquid, dashi, shoyu, mirin and 1 teaspoon salt in a bowl, then pour the liquid over the chicken and vegetables and set aside for about 20 minutes.

DRAIN the rice and spread over the base of a large saucepan. Pour the chicken and vegetable mixture over the rice but do not stir. Sit the saucepan over high heat and bring to the boil, then cover, reduce the heat to low and cook for 15 minutes. Turn off the heat, leaving the pan on the stove, and leave to stand for 10 minutes before stirring to combine all the ingredients. If using it, stir in the mitsuba and serve.

Stir the rice after it has been left to stand for 10 minutes.

Rice is a staple across most of India. Hundreds of varieties exist, each with its own flavour, aroma and texture.

YAKHNI PULAO

THIS RICE DISH IS PARTICULARLY DELICIOUS WHEN COOKED IN HOME-MADE STOCK (YAKHNI) BUT YOU CAN, OF COURSE, USE READY-MADE STOCK. YAKHNI PULAO IS DELICATELY FLAVOURED WITH WHOLE SPICES AND GOES WELL NOT ONLY WITH INDIAN DISHES, BUT WITH OTHER CASSEROLES.

225 g (8 oz) basmati rice
500 ml (17 fl oz/2 cups) chicken
   stock
6 tablespoons ghee or oil
5 cardamom pods
5 cm (2 inch) cinnamon stick
6 cloves
8 black peppercorns
4 Indian bay leaves (cassia leaves)
1 onion, finely sliced

SERVES 4

WASH the rice in a sieve under cold running water until the water from the rice runs clear. Drain. Heat the stock to near boiling point in a saucepan.

MEANWHILE, heat 2 tablespoons of the ghee or oil over medium heat in a large, heavy-based saucepan. Add the cardamom, cinnamon, cloves, peppercorns and bay leaves and fry for 1 minute. Reduce the heat to low, add the rice and stir constantly for 1 minute. Add the heated stock and some salt to the rice and bring rapidly to the boil. Cover and simmer over low heat for 15 minutes. Leave the rice to stand for 10 minutes before uncovering. Lightly fluff up the rice before serving.

MEANWHILE, heat the remaining ghee or oil in a frying pan over low heat and fry the onion until soft. Increase the heat and fry until onion is dark brown. Drain on paper towels and use as garnish.

PRAWN PULAO

PRAWN PULAO

200 g (1 cup) basmati rice
320 g (11 oz) small prawns (shrimp)
3 tablespoons oil
1 onion, finely chopped
2.5 cm (1 inch) cinnamon stick
6 cardamom pods
5 cloves
4 Indian bay leaves (cassia leaves)
1 stalk lemongrass, finely chopped
4 garlic cloves, crushed
5 cm (2 inch) piece of ginger,
   grated
¼ teaspoon ground turmeric

SERVES 4

WASH the rice in a sieve under cold running water until the water from the rice runs clear. Drain. Peel and devein the prawns, then wash thoroughly and pat dry with paper towels.

HEAT the oil in a karhai or heavy-based frying pan over low heat and fry the onion, cinnamon, cardamom, cloves, bay leaves and lemongrass until the onion is lightly browned. Stir in the garlic, ginger and turmeric. Add the prawns and stir until they turn pinkish. Add rice and fry over medium heat for 2 minutes. Add 500 ml (17 fl oz/2 cups) boiling water and some salt and bring to the boil. Reduce heat and simmer 15 minutes. Remove from the heat, cover tightly with a lid and leave 10 minutes. Lightly fluff up rice before serving.

Making noodle dishes at a market in Yunnan.

FROM CHINA

RAINBOW NOODLES

THIS DISH OF PRAWNS (SHRIMP), BEAN SPROUTS AND THIN RICE NOODLES IS ENLIVENED WITH A TOUCH OF CHINESE CURRY POWDER. MUCH MILDER THAN ITS INDIAN COUNTERPART AND SIMILAR TO FIVE-SPICE POWDER, YOU COULD USE A MILD INDIAN CURRY POWDER INSTEAD.

225 g (8 oz) prawns (shrimp)
1 tablespoon Shaoxing rice wine
2½ tablespoons finely chopped
 ginger
1 teaspoon roasted sesame oil
300 g (10 oz) rice vermicelli
2 leeks, white part only
4 tablespoons oil
1½ tablespoons Chinese
 curry powder
200 g (7 oz/2¼ cups) bean sprouts
60 ml (2 fl oz/¼ cup) chicken stock
 or water
2 tablespoons light soy sauce
1 teaspoon salt
½ teaspoon sugar
½ teaspoon freshly ground
 black pepper

SERVES 4

PEEL the prawns, leaving the tails intact. Using a sharp knife, score lengthways along the back and remove the vein. Place in a bowl, add the rice wine, 2 teaspoons of the ginger and the sesame oil, and toss to coat.

SOAK the noodles in hot water for 10 minutes, then drain. Cut the leeks into 5 cm (2 inch) lengths and shred finely. Wash well and dry thoroughly.

HEAT a wok over high heat, add 1 tablespoon of the oil and heat until very hot. Stir-fry the prawns in batches for 1½ minutes, or until they turn opaque. Remove with a wire sieve or slotted spoon and drain. Pour off the oil and wipe out the wok.

REHEAT the wok over high heat, add the remaining oil and heat until very hot. Stir-fry the curry powder for a few seconds, or until fragrant. Add the leek and remaining ginger and stir-fry for 1½ minutes. Add the bean sprouts and cook for 20 seconds, then add the prawns, stock or water, soy sauce, salt, sugar and pepper, and stir to combine.

ADD the noodles and toss until they are cooked through and have absorbed all the sauce.

TRANSFER to a serving dish and serve.

Cook the meat and then put the rice and saffron mixture on top. Use a rope of dough to seal on the lid and keep in the flavours.

FROM INDIA

LAMB BIRYANI

THIS IS A RICE AND LAMB DISH IN WHICH BOTH INGREDIENTS ARE COOKED TOGETHER IN A SEALED CONTAINER. YOU CAN COOK THE LAMB WITHOUT BROWNING IT FIRST AND, IN FACT, THIS IS THE TRADITIONAL METHOD. HOWEVER, BROWNING THE MEAT ADDS EXTRA FLAVOUR.

1 kg (2 lb 4 oz) boneless lamb leg or shoulder, cut into 3 cm (1¼ inch) cubes
8 cm (3 inch) piece of ginger, grated
2 garlic cloves, crushed
2 tablespoons garam masala (see recipe on page 464)
½ teaspoon chilli powder
½ teaspoon ground turmeric
4 green chillies, finely chopped
30 g (1 oz/⅔ cup) chopped coriander (cilantro) leaves
15 g (¼ cup) chopped mint leaves
500 g (2½ cups) basmati rice
4 onions, thinly sliced
¼ teaspoon salt
125 ml (4 fl oz/½ cup) oil
125 g (4 oz) unsalted butter, melted
250 ml (8 fl oz/1 cup) thick plain yoghurt (see recipe on page 467)
½ teaspoon saffron strands, soaked in 2 tablespoons hot milk
3 tablespoons lemon juice

SEALING DOUGH
200 g (7 oz/1⅓ cups) wholewheat flour
1 teaspoon salt

SERVES 6

MIX lamb in a bowl with ginger, garlic, garam masala, chilli powder, turmeric, chilli, coriander and mint. Cover and marinate in the fridge overnight.

WASH the rice in a sieve under cold, running water until the water from the rice runs clear. Put the sliced onion in a sieve, sprinkle with the salt and leave for 10 minutes to drain off any liquid that oozes out. Rinse and pat dry.

HEAT the oil and butter in a large, heavy-based saucepan, add the onion and fry for about 10 minutes or until golden brown. Drain through a sieve, reserving the oil and butter.

REMOVE the lamb from the marinade, reserving the marinade, and fry in batches in a little of the oil and butter until the lamb is well browned all over. Transfer to a 'degchi' (thick-based pot) or heavy casserole and add the browned onion, any remaining marinade and the yoghurt, and cook everything over low heat for 30–40 minutes, or until the lamb is tender.

IN A separate saucepan, boil enough water to cover the rice. Add the rice to the pan. Return the water to the boil, cook the rice for 5 minutes, then drain well and spread the rice evenly over the meat. Pour 2 tablespoons of leftover oil and ghee over the rice and drizzle with the saffron and milk.

TO MAKE the sealing dough, preheat the oven to 220°C (425°F/Gas 7). Make a dough by mixing the flour and salt with a little water. Roll the dough into a sausage shape and use to seal the lid onto the rim of the pot or casserole, pressing it along the rim where the lid meets the pot. Put the pot over high heat for 5 minutes to bring the contents to the boil, then transfer it to the oven for 40 minutes. Remove the pot and break the seal of dough.

Fishermen in longtail boats fish near Phang-nga.

FROM THAILAND

EGG NOODLES WITH SEAFOOD

BA-MII ARE WHEAT FLOUR NOODLES, USUALLY MADE WITH EGG. STALLS SPECIALISING IN BA-MII CAN
BE FOUND ALL OVER THAILAND. NOODLE DISHES LIKE THIS ARE USUALLY EATEN AS A SNACK. SERVE
WITH SLICED CHILLIES IN FISH SAUCE, DRIED CHILLI AND WHITE SUGAR FOR SEASONING.

8 raw prawns (shrimp)
2 squid tubes
250 g (9 oz) egg noodles
1 tablespoon vegetable oil
4 Asian shallots, smashed with the
    side of a cleaver
4 spring onions (scallions), cut into
    lengths and smashed with the
    side of a cleaver
2 cm (¾ inch) piece of ginger,
    finely shredded
2 garlic cloves, finely sliced
1 tablespoon preserved cabbage,
    rinsed and chopped (optional)
4 scallops, cut in half horizontally
1 tablespoon oyster sauce
2 teaspoons soy sauce
2 teaspoons fish sauce
small handful holy basil leaves

SERVES 4

PEEL and devein the prawns and cut each prawn
along the back so it opens like a butterfly (leave
each prawn joined along the base and at the tail,
leaving the tail attached).

OPEN out the squid tubes and score the insides
in a criss-cross pattern. Cut the squid tubes into
squares.

COOK the egg noodles in boiling water, then drain
and rinse.

HEAT the oil in a wok and add the shallots, spring
onions, ginger, garlic and cabbage and stir-fry for
2 minutes.

ADD the prawns, squid and scallops one after the
other, tossing after each addition, and cook for
3 minutes.

ADD the oyster and soy sauces and noodles and
toss together.

ADD the fish sauce and holy basil and serve.

Score the insides of the squid
tubes in a crisscross pattern.

Peel and devein the prawns and
cut each along the back of each
one so it opens like a butterfly.

YANGZHOU FRIED RICE WITH PRAWNS

125 g (4½ oz) cooked prawns
  (shrimp)
150 g (1 cup) fresh or frozen peas
1 tablespoon oil
3 spring onions (scallions), chopped
1 tablespoon finely chopped ginger
2 eggs, lightly beaten
1 quantity cooked rice (see recipe
  on page 463)
1½ tablespoons chicken stock
  (see recipe on page 491)
1 tablespoon Shaoxing rice wine
2 teaspoons light soy sauce
½ teaspoon salt, or to taste
½ teaspoon roasted sesame oil
¼ teaspoon ground black pepper

SERVES 4

PEEL the prawns and cut then in half through the back, removing the vein.

COOK the peas in a pan of simmering water for 3–4 minutes for fresh or 1 minute for frozen.

HEAT a wok over high heat, add the oil and heat until hot. Stir-fry the spring onion and ginger for 1 minute. Reduce the heat, add the egg and lightly scramble. Add the prawns and peas and toss lightly to heat through, then add the rice before the egg is set too hard, increase the heat and stir to separate the rice grains and break the egg into small bits.

ADD the stock, rice wine, soy sauce, salt, sesame oil and pepper, and toss lightly.

EGG FRIED RICE

EGG FRIED RICE

4 eggs
1 spring onion (scallion), chopped
60 g (2 oz/⅓ cup) fresh or frozen
  peas (optional)
3 tablespoons oil
1 quantity cooked rice (see recipe
  on page 463)

SERVES 4

BEAT the eggs with a pinch of salt and 1 teaspoon of spring onion. Cook peas in simmering water for 3–4 minutes for fresh or 1 minute for frozen.

HEAT a wok over high heat, add the oil and heat until very hot. Reduce the heat, add the egg and lightly scramble. Add the rice before the egg is set too hard, increase the heat and stir to separate the rice grains and break the egg into small bits.

ADD the peas and the remaining spring onion and season with salt. Stir constantly for 1 minute.

FROM CHINA

CROSSING-THE-BRIDGE NOODLES

LEGEND HAS IT THAT THIS DISH WAS INVENTED BY A WOMAN WHO HAD TO TAKE HER HUSBAND'S FOOD TO HIM EACH DAY. TO KEEP THE SOUP HOT FOR THE LONG JOURNEY, SHE FLOATED OIL ON TOP TO KEEP IN THE HEAT. THE SOUP MUST BE SERVED CLOSE TO BOILING AS YOU COOK THE FOOD IN IT.

125 g (4 oz) prawns (shrimp)

125 g (4 oz) boneless, skinless chicken breasts

125 g (4 oz) squid tubes

125 g (4 oz) Chinese ham, thinly sliced

8 dried Chinese mushrooms

125 g (4 oz/1⅓ cups) bean sprouts

350 g (12 oz) fresh rice noodles or 250 g (9 oz) rice stick noodles

chilli sauce

light soy sauce

1 litre (35 fl oz/4 cups) chicken stock (see recipe on page 491)

4 spring onions (scallions), finely chopped

SERVES 4

PEEL the prawns and cut them in half through the back, removing the vein. Slice prawns and chicken breast thinly on the diagonal.

OPEN up the squid tubes by cutting down one side, scrub off any soft jelly-like substance and slice thinly on the diagonal. Arrange the prawns, chicken, squid and ham on a plate, cover and refrigerate until needed.

SOAK the dried mushrooms in boiling water for 30 minutes, then drain and squeeze out any excess water. Remove and discard the stems. Add the mushrooms to the plate. Wash the bean sprouts and drain thoroughly. Add to the plate.

SEPARATE the rice noodles into four bundles. If you are using dried rice noodles, soak in hot water for 10 minutes, then drain.

GIVE each guest a small saucer of chilli sauce and a saucer of soy sauce. Place the ingredients and dipping sauces on the table. Heat four soup bowls either in a low oven or by running them under very hot water for a few minutes.

PUT the chicken stock in a clay pot, casserole or saucepan with the spring onion and bring to the boil. When the stock has reached a rolling boil, fill the soup bowls.

GIVE each guest a hot bowl filled with stock and let them cook the meat, vegetables and noodles in the stock. You can be authentic and add a dash of oil to each bowl to seal in the heat, but it isn't really necessary.

A canal running through Lijiang.

STIR-FRIED EGG NOODLES WITH VEGETABLES

2 tablespoons oyster sauce
1 tablespoon light soy sauce
1 teaspoon sugar
2 tablespoons vegetable oil
4 garlic cloves, finely chopped
225 g (8 oz) mixed Chinese broccoli
　florets, baby sweet corn,
　snake (yard long) beans cut into
　lengths, snowpeas (mangetout)
　cut into bite-sized pieces
250 g (9 oz) fresh egg noodles
60 g (2 oz/½ cup) bean sprouts
3 spring onions (scallions), finely
　chopped
½ long red or green chilli, seeded
　and finely sliced
a few coriander (cilantro) leaves,
　for garnish

SERVES 4

COMBINE the oyster sauce, light soy sauce and sugar in a small bowl.

HEAT the oil in a wok or frying pan and stir-fry the garlic over a medium heat until lightly brown. Add all the mixed vegetables and stir-fry over a high heat for 1–2 minutes. Add the egg noodles and oyster sauce mixture to the wok and stir-fry for 2–3 minutes.

ADD the bean sprouts and spring onions. Taste, then adjust the seasoning if necessary.

SPOON onto a serving plate. Garnish with chilli and coriander leaves.

FRIED RICE WITH PRAWNS AND CHILLI JAM

225 g (8 oz) raw prawns (shrimp)
3 tablespoons vegetable oil
4 garlic cloves, finely chopped
1 small onion, sliced
3 teaspoons chilli jam (see recipe on
　page 480)
450 g (1 lb) cooked jasmine rice,
　refrigerated overnight
1 tablespoon light soy sauce
½ teaspoon sugar
1 long red chilli, seeded and
　finely sliced
2 spring onions (scallions),
　finely sliced
ground white pepper, for sprinkling
a few coriander (cilantro) leaves,
　for garnish

SERVES 4

PEEL and devein the prawns and cut each prawn along the back so it opens like a butterfly (leave each prawn joined along the base and at the tail, leaving the tail attached).

HEAT the oil in a wok or frying pan and stir-fry the garlic and onion over a medium heat until light brown. Add the chilli jam and stir for a few seconds or until fragrant.

ADD the prawns and stir-fry over a high heat for 2 minutes or until the prawns open and turn pink.

ADD the cooked rice, light soy sauce and sugar and stir-fry for 3–4 minutes. Add chilli and spring onions and mix well. Adjust seasoning, if needed.

SPOON onto a serving place and sprinkle with white pepper and coriander leaves.

FRIED RICE WITH PRAWNS
AND CHILLI JAM

Soba noodles are made from buckwheat flour and have a slightly nutty flavour.

CHILLED SOBA NOODLES

THIS BUCKWHEAT NOODLE DISH WITH ITS EARTHY FLAVOUR AND SAVOURY DIP IS A HOT WEATHER FAVOURITE IN JAPAN. OFTEN SERVED ON BASKET-WEAVE TRAYS CALLED ZARU, THESE COLD NOODLES ARE EQUALLY ATTRACTIVE DISHED UP INTO BOWLS.

250 g (9 oz) dried soba (buckwheat) noodles

4 cm (1½ inch) piece fresh ginger, cut into thin matchsticks

1 carrot, cut into 4 cm (1½ inch) lengths, then cut into thin matchsticks

4 spring onions (scallions), thinly sliced

1 nori sheet, toasted, cut into thin strips

pickled ginger, to garnish

pickled daikon, thinly sliced, to garnish

DIPPING SAUCE

3 tablespoons dashi granules

125 ml (4 fl oz/½ cup) shoyu (Japanese soy sauce)

80 ml (2½ fl oz/⅓ cup) mirin

SERVES 4

HALF-FILL a large saucepan with lightly salted water and bring to the boil over high heat, then gradually lower the noodles into the water. Stir so the noodles don't stick together. Pour in 250 ml (9 fl oz/1 cup) cold water and return to the boil. Repeat this step another two to three times, or until the noodles are tender. This cooking method helps to cook this delicate noodle more evenly. The noodles should be al dente with no hard core in the centre but not completely soft all the way through. Drain the noodles, then rinse well under cold running water, lightly rubbing the noodles together with your hands to remove any excess starch. Drain thoroughly and set aside.

BRING a pan of water to the boil and add ginger, carrot and spring onion. Blanch 30 seconds, then drain and put in a bowl of iced water. Drain again when the vegetables are cool.

TO MAKE the dipping sauce, combine 375 ml (13 fl oz/1½ cups) water, dashi granules, shoyu, mirin and a good pinch each of salt and pepper in a small pan. Bring to the boil; cool completely. To serve, pour sauce into four small, wide bowls.

TOSS the noodles and vegetables to combine and arrange in four serving bowls. Scatter the nori strips over the noodles and garnish with a little pickled ginger and daikon.

SERVE the noodles with the dipping sauce. Dip the noodles into the sauce before eating them.

Toast the nori sheet over low heat for a few seconds, then cut into thin strips using scissors.

Fresh water chestnuts and fresh market eggs.

FRIED RICE WITH CRAB

FRIED RICE IS BEST MADE WITH DAY-OLD RICE, IN OTHER WORDS LEFTOVERS, THOUGH THE LIKELIHOOD OF THERE BEING LEFTOVER RICE IN THAILAND IS REMOTE. USE A WOK FOR THE BEST RESULTS. CRAB, PREFERABLY FRESH IF POSSIBLE, GOES PARTICULARLY WELL WITH THE RICE.

2 tablespoons vegetable oil
4 garlic cloves, finely chopped
2 eggs
450 g (15 oz/2½ cups) cooked
    jasmine rice, refrigerated overnight
110 g (4 oz) crabmeat
    (drained well if tinned)
½ small onion, sliced
175 g (6 oz) tin water chestnuts,
    drained and sliced
2 tablespoons finely julienned ginger
    (optional)
1 tablespoon light soy sauce
1 teaspoon sugar
4 cooked crab claws, for garnish
½ long red chilli, seeded and finely
    sliced, for garnish
2 spring onions (scallions), finely
    chopped, for garnish

SERVES 4

HEAT the oil in a wok or frying pan and stir-fry the garlic over a medium heat until light brown. Using a spatula, move the fried garlic to the outer edges of the wok. Add the eggs and stir to scramble for 1–2 minutes.

ADD the cooked rice, crabmeat and onion, stirring for 1–2 minutes.

ADD the water chestnuts, ginger, light soy sauce and sugar and stir together for 1 minute. Taste, then adjust the seasoning if necessary.

SPOON onto a serving plate and garnish with the crab claws. Sprinkle with sliced chilli and spring onions.

Detail from a Wat in Ratchaburi.

DAN DAN MIAN

1 tablespoon Sichuan peppercorns

200 g (7 oz) minced (ground) pork

60 g (2 oz) preserved turnip, rinsed
and finely chopped

2 tablespoons light soy sauce

2 tablespoons oil

2 garlic cloves, crushed

2 tablespoons grated ginger

4 spring onions (scallions), finely
chopped

2 tablespoons sesame paste or
smooth peanut butter

2 tablespoons light soy sauce

2 teaspoons chilli oil

185 ml (6 fl oz/¾ cup) chicken
stock (see recipe on page 491)

400 g (14 oz) thin wheat flour noodles

SERVES 4

DRY-FRY the Sichuan peppercorns in a wok or
pan until brown and aromatic, then crush lightly.

COMBINE the pork with the preserved turnip and
soy sauce and leave to marinate for a few minutes.

HEAT a wok over high heat, add the oil and heat
until very hot. Stir-fry the pork until crisp and
browned. Remove and drain well.

ADD the garlic, ginger and spring onion to the wok
and stir-fry for 30 seconds, then add the sesame
paste, soy sauce, chilli oil and stock and simmer
for 2 minutes.

COOK the noodles in a pan of salted boiling water
for 4–8 minutes, then drain well. Divide among
four bowls, ladle the sauce over the noodles, then
top with the crispy pork and Sichuan peppercorns.

Making wheat noodles by pulling
them by hand. The noodles are
made fresh for each customer
and cooked immediately.

SINGAPORE NOODLES

2 tablespoons dried shrimp

300 g (10 oz) rice vermicelli

100 g (3 oz) barbecue pork
(char siu)

100 g (3 oz/1 cup) bean sprouts

4 tablespoons oil

2 eggs, beaten

1 onion, thinly sliced

1 teaspoon salt

1 tablespoon Chinese curry powder

2 tablespoons light soy sauce

2 spring onions (scallions),
shredded

2 red chillies, shredded

SERVES 4

SOAK the dried shrimp in boiling water for 1 hour,
then drain.

SOAK noodles in hot water for 10 minutes, drain.

THINLY slice pork. Wash and drain bean sprouts.

HEAT a wok over high heat, add 1 tablespoon
of the oil and heat until very hot. Pour in the
egg and make an omelette. Remove from the
wok and cut into small pieces.

REHEAT the wok over high heat, add remaining oil
and heat until very hot. Stir-fry the onion and bean
sprouts with the pork and shrimp for 1 minute,
then add the noodles, salt, curry powder and soy
sauce, blend well and stir for 1 minute. Add the
omelette, spring onion and chilli. Toss to combine.

SINGAPORE NOODLES

Scallops, or *hotate-gai*, thrive in cold, clean waters such as those off the coast of Hokkaido, and northern Honshu.

Drain the noodles, then rinse under cold running water, lightly rubbing the noodles together with your hands to remove any excess starch.

FROM JAPAN

SCALLOPS WITH SOBA NOODLES AND DASHI BROTH

AS DELICIOUS AS A SIMPLE BOWL OF BUCKWHEAT NOODLES IN BROTH CAN BE, THE ADDITION OF LIGHTLY COOKED FRESH SCALLOPS AND ASIAN BLACK FUNGUS TURN IT INTO A SUBSTANTIAL MEAL. SLIVERS OF SHREDDED NORI PROVIDE AN ELEGANT GARNISH.

250 g (9 oz) dried soba (buckwheat) noodles
3 tablespoons mirin
60 ml (2 fl oz/¼ cup) shoyu (Japanese soy sauce)
2 teaspoons rice wine vinegar
1 teaspoon dashi granules
2 spring onions (scallions), sliced on the diagonal
1 teaspoon fresh ginger, finely chopped
24 large scallops, roe removed
5 fresh black fungus, chopped (see note)
1 nori sheet, shredded, for garnish

SERVES 4

COOK the soba noodles in a large saucepan of boiling water for 5 minutes, or until tender. Drain and rinse under cold water.

Put the mirin, shoyu, vinegar, dashi granules and 750 ml (26 fl oz/ 3 cups) water in a saucepan. Bring to the boil, then reduce the heat and simmer for 3–4 minutes.

ADD the spring onion and ginger and keep at a gentle simmer until needed.

HEAT a chargrill pan or plate until very hot and sear the scallops on both sides, in batches, for 1 minute. Remove.

DIVIDE the noodles and black fungus among four deep serving bowls. Pour 185 ml (6 fl oz/¾ cup) broth into each bowl and top with six scallops each. Garnish with the shredded nori and serve.

Note: If fresh black fungus is not available, use dried instead. Soak in warm water for 15–20 minutes before use.

SEVIAN KHEEMA

1 teaspoon cumin seeds

3 tablespoons ghee or oil

1 red onion, finely chopped

3 garlic cloves, crushed

2 cm (¾ inch) piece of ginger, grated

225 g (8 oz) minced (ground) lamb or beef

1 teaspoon ground black pepper

225 g (8 oz) sevian, broken into small pieces

3 tablespoons lime or lemon juice

SERVES 4

PLACE a small frying pan over low heat, dry-roast the cumin until aromatic, then grind to a fine powder using a spice grinder or pestle and mortar.

HEAT 1 tablespoon ghee in a karhai or heavy-based frying pan and fry the onion, garlic and ginger for 3–4 minutes. Add the cumin, cook for 1 minute, then add the meat and cook for 8 minutes, or until the meat is dry, breaking up any lumps with the back of a fork. Season with the black pepper and salt, to taste, and remove from the pan.

HEAT the remaining ghee and fry the sevian for 1–2 minutes. Add the meat and fry for 1 minute. Add 170 ml (⅔ cup) water and cook until the sevian are tender, adding more water if necessary. The dish should be dry, so don't add too much at once. When cooked, sprinkle with the juice.

Sevian or vermicelli made from wheat flour are available as skeins of noodles or as bunches of straight lengths. Sometimes they are sold toasted.

IDIYAPPAM

225 g (8 oz) rice sticks or vermicelli

4 tablespoons oil

60 g (2 oz/⅓ cup) cashew nuts

½ onion, chopped

3 eggs

150 g (5 oz/1 cup) fresh or frozen peas

10 curry leaves

2 carrots, grated

2 leeks, finely shredded

1 red capsicum (pepper), diced

2 tablespoons tomato sauce (ketchup)

1 tablespoon soy sauce

1 teaspoon salt

SERVES 4

SOAK the rice sticks in cold water for 30 minutes, then drain and put them in a saucepan of boiling water. Remove from the heat and leave in the pan for 3 minutes. Drain and refresh in cold water.

HEAT 1 tablespoon oil in a frying pan and fry the cashews until golden. Remove, add the onion to the pan, fry until dark golden, then drain on paper towels. Cook eggs in boiling water for 10 minutes to hard-boil, then cool them immediately in cold water. When cold, peel and cut into wedges. Cook peas in boiling water until tender.

HEAT the remaining oil in a frying pan and briefly fry the curry leaves. Add the carrot, leek and red capsicum and stir for 1 minute. Add the tomato sauce, soy sauce, salt and rice sticks. Mix, stirring constantly to prevent sticks from sticking to pan.

SERVE on a platter and garnish with the peas, cashews, fried onion and egg.

IDIYAPPAM

ACCOMPANIMENTS & SIDE DISHES

FROM CHINA

CHINESE BROCCOLI IN OYSTER SAUCE

CHINESE BROCCOLI DIFFERS FROM ITS WESTERN RELATIVE IN THAT THE STEMS ARE LONG, THE FLORETS ARE TINY, AND THE FLAVOUR IS SLIGHTLY BITTER. SOME VERSIONS ARE PURPLE. CHINESE BROCCOLI IS AVAILABLE IN CHINESE GROCERS.

1 kg (2 lb 4 oz) Chinese broccoli (gai lan)
1½ tablespoons oil
2 spring onions (scallions), chopped
1½ tablespoons grated ginger
3 garlic cloves, finely chopped
3 tablespoons oyster sauce
1½ tablespoons light soy sauce
1 tablespoon Shaoxing rice wine
1 teaspoon sugar
1 teaspoon roasted sesame oil
125 ml (4 fl oz/½ cup) chicken stock (see recipe on page 491)
2 teaspoons cornflour (cornstarch)

SERVES 6

WASH the broccoli well. Discard any tough stems and diagonally cut into 2 cm (¾ inch) pieces through the stem and the leaf. Blanch the broccoli in a pan of boiling water for 2 minutes, or until the stems and leaves are just tender, then refresh in cold water and dry thoroughly.

HEAT a wok over high heat, add the oil and heat until very hot. Stir-fry the spring onion, ginger and garlic for 10 seconds, or until fragrant. Add the broccoli and cook until the broccoli is heated through. Combine the remaining ingredients, add to the wok, stirring until the sauce has thickened, and toss to coat the broccoli.

SICHUAN-STYLE SPICY EGGPLANT

THE CHINESE EGGPLANT (AUBERGINE) IS LONG, THIN AND ABOUT THE SIZE OF A ZUCCHINI (COURGETTE). ITS TENDER FLESH ABSORBS FLAVOURS AND IT IS THE PERFECT CARRIER FOR BOTH SPICY AND DELICATE SAUCES. IF THEY ARE UNAVAILABLE, USE SMALL, TENDER WESTERN ONES.

500 g (1 lb 2 oz) Chinese eggplants (aubergines) or thin eggplants
½ teaspoon salt
3 tablespoons light soy sauce
1 tablespoon Shaoxing rice wine
1 tablespoon roasted sesame oil
2 teaspoons clear rice vinegar
1 teaspoon sugar
1 spring onion (scallions), chopped
2 garlic cloves, finely chopped
1 teaspoon chilli bean paste (toban jiang)

SERVES 6

PEEL the eggplants and trim off the ends. Cut the eggplants in half lengthways and cut each half into strips 2 cm (¾ inch) thick. Cut the strips into 5 cm (2 inch) lengths. Place the eggplant in a bowl, add the salt and toss lightly, then set aside for 1 hour. Pour off any water that has accumulated.

ARRANGE the eggplant on a heatproof plate and place in a steamer. Cover and steam over simmering water in a wok for 20 minutes, or until tender. Combine the remaining ingredients in a bowl, then pour the sauce over the eggplant, tossing lightly to coat.

SICHUAN-STYLE
SPICY EGGPLANT

FROM THAILAND

SHRIMP PASTE DIPPING SAUCE

THAI HOT DIPPING SAUCE IS USED TO ACCOMPANY GRILLED OR DEEP-FRIED FISH, PIECES OF OMELETTE, AND FRESH VEGETABLES AND FRUIT SUCH AS EGGPLANT, CUCUMBER, WING BEANS AND SNAKE BEANS. YOU CAN VARY THE NUMBER OF CHILLIES, DEPENDING ON HOW HOT YOU LIKE IT.

3–4 garlic cloves
2 teaspoons shrimp paste
2–3 small red and green chillies
3–4 Thai eggplants (aubergines)
    (optional)
1 teaspoon sugar
1 tablespoon fish sauce
2 tablespoons lime juice
mixed raw vegetables and fruit
    such as pieces of Thai eggplant
    (aubergine), cucumber batons,
    wing beans, pieces of snake (yard
    long) beans, spring onions
    (scallions), pomelo segments,
    pieces of rose apple, to serve

SERVES 4

USING a pestle and mortar, pound the garlic into a rough paste. Add the shrimp paste and grind together. Add the chillies and lightly bruise to release the hot taste. (Do this gently so the liquid won't splash.) Add the eggplants and lightly pound. Add the sugar, fish sauce and lime juice and lightly mix in. Taste the sauce, then adjust the seasoning if necessary.

TO MAKE without a pestle and mortar, put the finely chopped garlic in a bowl and, using the back of a spoon, scrape the garlic into a paste. Add the shrimp paste and mix well. Add the chillies and break them up with a fork. Add the eggplant and squash it gently against the side of the bowl. Add the sugar, fish sauce and lime juice and lightly mix.

SPOON into a small serving bowl and serve with the mixed vegetables.

When you have pounded the ingredients together, stir in the sugar, fish sauce and lime juice.

BEANS WITH SESAME MISO DRESSING

INGEN, OR GREEN BEANS, ARE NAMED AFTER THE CHINESE BUDDHIST PRIEST WHO IS SAID TO HAVE INTRODUCED THEM INTO JAPAN SEVERAL CENTURIES AGO. THEIR FRESH, SLIGHTLY CRISP TASTE IS COMPLEMENTED HERE BY THE CREAMY, SOMEWHAT NUTTY FLAVOUR OF THE DRESSING.

250 g (9 oz) green beans, trimmed
   and cut into 5 cm (2 inch) lengths

DRESSING
50 g (1¾ oz/⅓ cup) sesame seeds
1 teaspoon sugar
2 tablespoons red or white miso
   paste
2 tablespoons mirin

SERVES 4

BRING a saucepan of lightly salted water to the boil. Add the beans and cook for 2 minutes, or until just tender. Drain, plunge into iced water until cool, then drain well.

TO MAKE the dressing, dry-fry the sesame seeds over medium heat, stirring regularly, for 5 minutes, or until lightly golden and aromatic. Immediately scoop the sesame seeds into a mortar or a suribachi (Japanese ribbed mortar), reserving 1 teaspoon of whole seeds for the garnish, and grind with a pestle until very finely crushed. Gradually incorporate the sugar, miso and mirin to form a thickish paste.

PUT the beans in a bowl with the dressing and toss to combine.

SERVE in a mound in a bowl or on a plate and sprinkle with the reserved sesame seeds.

Black, white or golden in colour, sesame seeds, *goma*, are used to add a nutty flavour and aroma to dishes.

FROM CHINA

STIR-FRIED TWIN WINTER

THIS SIMPLE DISH IS CALLED 'TWIN WINTER' BECAUSE BOTH MUSHROOMS AND BAMBOO SHOOTS ARE AT THEIR BEST IN THE WINTER MONTHS. ANOTHER VERSION OF THIS DISH, TRIPLE WINTER, USES BAMBOO SHOOTS AND MUSHROOMS WITH CABBAGE.

Fresh bamboo shoots.

12 dried Chinese mushrooms
300 g (10½ oz) fresh or tinned
   bamboo shoots, rinsed and
   drained
3 tablespoons oil
2 tablespoons light soy sauce
2 teaspoons sugar
2 teaspoons cornflour (cornstarch)
½ teaspoon roasted sesame oil

SERVES 4

SOAK the dried mushrooms in boiling water for 30 minutes, then drain, reserving the liquid, and squeeze out any excess water. Remove and discard the stems and cut the caps in half (or quarters if large). Cut the bamboo shoots into small pieces the same size as the mushrooms.

HEAT a wok over high heat, add the oil and heat until very hot. Stir-fry the mushrooms and bamboo shoots for 1 minute. Add the soy sauce and sugar, stir a few times, then add 125 ml (4 fl oz/½ cup) of the reserved liquid. Bring to the boil and braise for 2 minutes, stirring constantly.

COMBINE the cornflour with enough water to make a paste, add to the sauce and simmer until thickened.

SPRINKLE with the sesame oil, blend well and serve.

STIR-FRIED CHINESE CABBAGE

CHINESE CABBAGE IS A COOL-WEATHER CROP, BUT IT CAN NOW BE BOUGHT ALL YEAR ROUND. THERE ARE TWO KINDS; ONE HAS A PALE-GREEN, FINE LEAF, THE OTHER IS PALE YELLOW.

STIR-FRIED CHINESE CABBAGE

30 g (1 oz) dried shrimp
1 tablespoon oil
400 g (14 oz) Chinese cabbage,
   cut into 1 cm (½ inch) strips
1 tablespoon light soy sauce
2 teaspoons sugar
1 tablespoon clear rice vinegar
2 teaspoons roasted sesame oil

SERVES 4

SOAK the dried shrimp in boiling water for 1 hour, then drain.

HEAT a wok over high heat, add the oil and heat until very hot. Toss the Chinese cabbage for 2 minutes, or until wilted. Add the shrimp, soy sauce, sugar and rice vinegar and cook for 1 minute. Sprinkle with the sesame oil and serve.

Pickles (achar) and chutneys (chatnis) are popular all over India. Shops and stalls usually sell a bewildering variety.

FROM INDIA

POUSSIN PICKLE

THIS RECIPE USES SPATCHCOCKS (POUSSIN OR BABY CHICKENS). HOWEVER, IN NORTHERN INDIA, WHEN THE GAME SEASON IS UNDER WAY, PARTRIDGE WOULD BE USED. THE PICKLE IS AN IDEAL ACCOMPANIMENT TO MOST DISHES OR CAN BE EATEN WITH BREADS.

2 x 900 g (2 lb) spatchcocks (poussin) or 1 partridge
6 garlic cloves, roughly chopped
5 cm (2 inch) piece of ginger, roughly chopped
420 ml (1⅔ cups) mustard oil or oil
2 Indian bay leaves (cassia leaves)
12 dried chillies
20 black peppercorns
1 teaspoon kalonji (nigella seeds)
3 teaspoons coriander seeds
1 teaspoon cumin seeds
2 teaspoons yellow mustard seeds
¼ teaspoon ground turmeric
1 teaspoon garam masala (see recipe on page 464)
pinch of asafoetida
1 tablespoon salt
125 g (4 oz) jaggery or soft brown sugar
420 ml (1⅔ cups) dark vinegar

MAKES 1 LITRE (35 FL OZ/4 CUPS)

CUT each spatchcock or partridge into six pieces by removing both legs and cutting between the joint of the drumstick and thigh. Cut down one side of each backbone, leaving it attached to one side. Turn each poussin or partridge over and cut through the cartilage down the centre of each breastbone. Trim off all the wing tips. Trim off any excess fat or skin.

CHOP the garlic and ginger in a food processor until finely chopped, or grate the ginger and crush the garlic and mix them together. Heat the mustard oil in a heavy-based saucepan over medium heat until smoking. Reduce the heat to low, then add the garlic and ginger mixture, bay leaves, dried chillies, peppercorns, kalonji, coriander, cumin and mustard seeds, turmeric, garam masala and asafoetida to the pan. Gently shake the pan until the seeds start to sizzle and pop. Add the spatchcock pieces and salt, stir well and fry over medium heat for 20 minutes, stirring occasionally until the spatchcocks are browned all over and cooked through. Remove spatchcock pieces from the pan with a slotted spoon and place in a bowl. Leave pan of spiced oil to cool.

PUT the jaggery and vinegar in a saucepan and bring to the boil, reduce the heat and cook over medium heat for 10–15 minutes, until the jaggery has completely dissolved and the vinegar has reduced by a third. Leave to cool.

WHEN the vinegar has cooled, mix it with the cooled oil, stir in the spatchcock pieces and mix well. Store the pickle in special ceramic pickling pots or sterilised jars (wash the jars in boiling water and dry in a warm oven). Marinate for 3–5 days, shaking the bottle gently at least twice daily so that poussin can absorb the flavours. Store in a cool place, or in the fridge after opening.

FLASH-COOKED PEA SHOOTS WITH GARLIC

PEA SHOOTS ARE THE DELICATE LEAVES AT THE TOP OF PEA PLANTS. THEY ARE PARTICULARLY GOOD WHEN STIR-FRIED SIMPLY WITH A LITTLE OIL AND GARLIC. IF UNAVAILABLE, SPINACH OR ANY OTHER LEAFY GREEN MAY BE SUBSTITUTED.

350 g (12 oz) pea shoots
1 teaspoon oil
2 garlic cloves, finely chopped
1½ tablespoons Shaoxing
   rice wine
¼ teaspoon salt

SERVES 6

TRIM the tough stems and wilted leaves from the pea shoots. Wash well and dry thoroughly.

HEAT a wok over high heat, add the oil and heat until very hot. Add the pea shoots and garlic and toss lightly for 20 seconds, then add the rice wine and salt, and stir-fry for 1 minute, or until the shoots are slightly wilted, but still bright green.

TRANSFER to a platter, leaving behind most of the liquid. Serve hot, at room temperature, or cold.

STIR-FRIED LOTUS ROOT

THE LOTUS IS A SYMBOL OF PURITY IN BUDDHIST CULTURE AS THE ROOTS, WHICH GROW IN MUD, ARE CLEAN AND PURE DESPITE THEIR MUDDY ORIGINS. LOTUS ROOT CAN BE EATEN RAW OR COOKED AND HAS A CRISP, CRUNCHY TEXTURE.

450 g (1 lb) fresh lotus root or
   350 g (12 oz) ready-prepared
   lotus root
1 tablespoon oil
1 garlic clove, thinly sliced
10 very thin slices ginger
2 spring onions (scallions), finely
   chopped
60 g (2 oz) Chinese ham, rind
   removed, diced
1 tablespoon Shaoxing rice wine
1 tablespoon light soy sauce
1 teaspoon sugar

SERVES 4

IF USING fresh lotus root, peel, cut into slices, wash well and drain thoroughly. Ready-prepared lotus root just needs to be washed, sliced and drained thoroughly.

HEAT a wok over high heat, add the oil and heat until very hot. Stir-fry the garlic and ginger for 30 seconds. Add the spring onion, ham and lotus root and stir-fry for 1 minute, then add the rice wine, soy sauce and sugar and cook for 2–3 minutes, or until the lotus root is tender but still crisp.

STIR-FRIED LOTUS ROOT

FROM THAILAND

WING BEAN SALAD

THIS IS A FRESH, CRUNCHY SALAD THAT LOOKS GOOD ON THE TABLE. WING BEANS HAVE FOUR FRILLY EDGES TO THEM AND AN INTERESTING CROSS SECTION WHEN CUT.

oil, for frying
75 g (3 oz) Asian shallots,
    finely sliced
175 g (6 oz) wing beans
55 g (2 oz) cooked chicken,
    shredded
1 lemongrass stalk, white part only,
    finely sliced
2 tablespoons dried shrimp, ground
1½ tablespoons fish sauce
3–4 tablespoons lime juice
½ long red chilli or 1 small red chilli,
    finely chopped
55 g (2 oz) whole salted roasted
    peanuts
125 ml (½ cup) coconut milk
    (see recipe on page 468),

SERVES 4

HEAT 2.5 cm (1 inch) oil in a wok or deep frying pan over a medium heat. Deep-fry the shallots for 3–4 minutes until they are light brown (without burning them). Lift out with a slotted spoon and drain on paper towels.

SLICE the wing beans diagonally into thin pieces. Blanch the wing beans in boiling water for 30 seconds, then drain and put them in cold water for 1–2 minutes. Drain. Transfer to a bowl.

ADD the cooked chicken, lemongrass, dried shrimp, fish sauce, lime juice, chilli and half the peanuts. Mix with a spoon. Taste, then adjust the seasoning if necessary.

PUT the wing bean salad in a serving bowl, drizzle with coconut milk and sprinkle with the crispy shallots and the rest of the peanuts.

STIR-FRIED WATER SPINACH

THE VEGETABLE THAT THE CHINESE CALL 'ONG CHOY' IS POPULAR IN THAILAND WHERE IT'S CALLED 'PHAK BUNG'. IT HAS LONG THIN STALKS AND LEAFY TOPS, ALL OF WHICH ARE GOOD TO EAT. BUY IT FROM ASIAN SUPERMARKETS WHERE IT IS SOMETIMES CALLED MORNING GLORY.

1½ tablespoons oyster sauce
1 teaspoon fish sauce
1 tablespoon yellow bean sauce
¼ teaspoon sugar
1½ tablespoons vegetable oil
2–3 garlic cloves, finely chopped
350 g (12 oz) water spinach,
    cut into 5 cm (2 inch) lengths
1 red bird's eye chilli, slightly
    crushed (optional)

SERVES 4

MIX the oyster sauce, fish sauce, yellow bean sauce and sugar in a small bowl.

HEAT the oil in a wok or a frying pan and stir-fry the garlic over a medium heat until light brown.

INCREASE the heat to very high, add the stalks of the water spinach and stir-fry for 1–2 minutes.

ADD water spinach leaves, the sauce mixture and the crushed chilli and stir-fry for another minute.

STIR-FRIED WATER SPINACH

FROM JAPAN

EGGPLANT WITH DASHI

THE EGGPLANT (AUBERGINE), *NASU*, IS ONE OF THE FAVOURITE SUMMER VEGETABLES IN JAPANESE CUISINE, AND ALSO, INCIDENTALLY, A POPULAR DECORATIVE MOTIF ON TABLEWARE. ITS TENDER TEXTURE AND MILDNESS ARE WELL SUITED TO THE FLAVOURED DASHI SEASONING IN THIS DISH.

6 baby or slender eggplants
   (aubergines)
oil, for brushing
60 ml (2 fl oz/¼ cup) dashi II
   (see recipe on page 483)
1½ tablespoons shoyu (Japanese
   soy sauce)
1 teaspoon mirin
½ teaspoon fresh ginger , grated,
   and its juice
pinch caster (superfine) sugar
fine katsuobushi (bonito flakes),
   to garnish

SERVES 6

PREHEAT a grill (broiler) to high. Brush the eggplants with oil, then prick a few times with a skewer. Put the eggplants under the grill and cook for 12–15 minutes, turning regularly, until the skin is slightly blackened and wrinkled and the flesh feels soft to the touch. Immediately plunge into iced water until cool enough to handle, then peel, discarding the skin. Cut the flesh into 5 cm (2 inch) lengths. Arrange in a bundle in a serving dish.

COMBINE the dashi, shoyu, mirin, ginger and juice, and sugar and pour over the eggplant. Sprinkle the katsuobushi over the top of the eggplants just before serving.

Katsuobushi, or bonito flakes, is a unique flavouring ingredient essential to everyday cooking. Fillets of bonito fish, called *katsuo*, are steamed, smoked, mould-cured and dried hard as wood.

STIR-FRIED LETTUCE

LETTUCE IS GENERALLY EATEN COOKED IN CHINA AND MANY DIFFERENT VARIETIES ARE AVAILABLE. LETTUCE IS ADDED TO SOUPS, STIR-FRIES AND CASSEROLES, AS WELL AS COOKED ON ITS OWN AS A VEGETABLE. YOU CAN USE ANY CRISP LETTUCE FOR THIS RECIPE.

750 g (1 lb 10 oz) crisp lettuce
1 tablespoon oil
4 tablespoons oyster sauce
1 teaspoon roasted sesame oil

SERVES 4

CUT the lettuce in half and then into wide strips, trimming off any roots that may hold the pieces together. Wash well and dry thoroughly (if too much water clings to the lettuce it will cause it to steam rather than fry).

HEAT a wok over high heat, add the oil and heat until very hot. Toss the lettuce pieces around the wok until they start to wilt, then add the oyster sauce and toss everything together.

SPRINKLE with the sesame oil, season and serve.

BEAN SPROUTS STIR-FRY

BEAN SPROUTS CAN MEAN EITHER SOYA BEAN SPROUTS OR MUNG BEAN SPROUTS AND BOTH ARE USED IN THIS RECIPE. SOYA BEAN SPROUTS ARE SLIGHTLY BIGGER AND MORE ROBUST FOR COOKING, AS WELL AS BEING MORE COMMONLY FOUND IN CHINA.

200 g (7 oz) mung bean sprouts
200 g (7 oz) soya bean sprouts
1 tablespoon oil
1 red chilli, finely chopped
1 spring onion (scallions), finely chopped
2 tablespoons light soy sauce

SERVES 4

WASH the bean sprouts, discarding any husks and straggly end pieces, and drain thoroughly.

HEAT a wok over high heat, add the oil and heat until very hot. Stir-fry the chilli and spring onion for 30 seconds, add the bean sprouts and toss until they start to wilt. Add the soy sauce and toss for 1 minute, then season and serve.

BEAN SPROUTS STIR-FRY

FROM INDIA
POTATO MASALA

THIS FILLING IS TRADITIONALLY ROLLED IN DOSAS TO MAKE MASALA DOSA, WHICH IS SERVED FOR BREAKFAST OR AS A SNACK IN SOUTHERN INDIA. HOWEVER, IT ALSO MAKES AN EXCELLENT SPICY POTATO SIDE DISH.

2 tablespoons oil
1 teaspoon black mustard seeds
10 curry leaves
¼ teaspoon ground turmeric
1 cm (½ inch) piece of ginger,
  grated
2 green chillies, finely chopped
2 onions, chopped
500 g (1 lb 2 oz) waxy potatoes,
  cut into 2 cm (¾ inch) cubes
1 tablespoon tamarind purée
  (see recipe on page 467)

SERVES 4

HEAT the oil in a heavy-based frying pan, add the mustard seeds, cover and when they start to pop add the curry leaves, turmeric, ginger, chilli and onion and cook, uncovered, until the onion is soft.

ADD the potato cubes and 250 ml (8 fl oz/1 cup) water to the pan, bring to the boil, cover and cook until the potato is tender and almost breaking up. If there is any liquid left in the pan, simmer, uncovered, until it evaporates. If the potato isn't cooked and there is no liquid left, add a little more and continue to cook.

ADD the tamarind and season with salt, to taste.

PAPAYA MUSTARD PICKLE

THIS IS A WONDERFUL PICKLE SUITABLE FOR SERVING WITH ROAST LAMB RAAN OR WITH PIECES OF ROTI AND A QUICK DAL CURRY OR SAMBAR. MAKE SURE YOU USE A GREEN PAPAYA AND NOT A RIPE ONE, OTHERWISE THE FLESH WILL DISINTEGRATE WHEN YOU COOK IT.

5 red chillies, seeded and chopped
1 large red onion, chopped
5 cm (2 inch) knob of ginger, grated
3 garlic cloves, chopped
60 g (2¼ oz) black mustard seeds
500 ml (17 fl oz/2 cups) clear
  vinegar
1 tablespoon oil
3 green chillies, seeded and
  chopped
200 g (7 oz) sugar
¼ teaspoon salt
¼ teaspoon ground turmeric
500 g (1 lb 2 oz) green papaya, cut
  into 1 cm (½ inch) cubes

MAKES 1 LITRE (35 FL OZ/4 CUPS)

CHOP the red chilli, onion, ginger, garlic, mustard seeds and 125 ml (4 fl oz/½ cup) vinegar in a food processor or pestle and mortar to form a paste. The mustard seeds will not break up completely.

HEAT the oil in a large heavy-based saucepan and cook the paste and remaining vinegar until aromatic and reduced.

ADD the green chilli and sugar and stir until the sugar is dissolved. Add salt, turmeric and papaya and simmer for 2 minutes, making sure papaya stays firm.

POUR the pickle into sterilised jars (wash the jars in boiling water and dry in a warm oven) and leave to cool completely. Store in a cool place, or in the fridge after opening.

PAPAYA MUSTARD PICKLE

POTATO MASALA

SHIITAKE SIMMERED IN SOY

DRIED SHIITAKE ARE PRIZED IN CERTAIN RECIPES FOR THEIR MORE PRONOUNCED TASTE AND DENSER TEXTURE THAN THEIR FRESH COUNTERPART. IT IS THESE QUALITIES THAT MAKE IT THE MUSHROOM OF CHOICE FOR THIS SLOW-SIMMERED AND INTENSELY FLAVOURFUL SIDE DISH.

8 large dried shiitake mushrooms
375 ml (13 fl oz/1½ cups) dashi II
   or konbu dashi II (see recipes on
   page 483)
2 tablespoons mirin
2 tablespoons sake
2 tablespoons shoyu (Japanese soy
   sauce)
1 tablespoon dark brown sugar

SERVES 4–6

SOAK the shiitake in hot water for 30 minutes, then drain well. Discard the stems.

COMBINE the dashi, mirin, sake, shoyu and sugar in a small saucepan. Put the pan over high heat and stir until the sugar has dissolved. Bring to the boil. Add the shiitake, return to the boil, then reduce to a simmer and cook for 1 hour, or until the liquid has almost evaporated.

SERVE the shiitake in a small bowl either warm or at room temperature as a condiment, part of a multicourse meal or served over rice as a snack.

SIMMERED shiitake can also be thinly sliced to use in sushi or savoury Japanese custard.

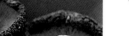

Since ancient times, wild shiitake have been gathered in Japanese forests where they thrive on fallen and decaying trees, often a variety of oak called shii, for which they were named. Shiitake exude a woodsy aroma and have a deep flavour. Fresh and dried shiitake each have their own role in recipes and are not considered interchangeable. Shiitake are thought to have impressive nutritional and medicinal benefits.

SWEET TOMATO CHUTNEY

THIS IS AN EASY STORE-CUPBOARD CHUTNEY. IT IS AN ESPECIALLY HANDY RECIPE IF YOU HAVE AN ABUNDANCE OF VERY RIPE TOMATOES (YOU WILL NEED ABOUT 800 G/1 LB 12 OZ PEELED FRESH TOMATOES). IF YOU CAN'T FIND CLEAR VINEGAR AT INDIAN FOOD SHOPS, USE WHITE VINEGAR.

8 garlic cloves, roughly chopped
5 cm (2 inch) piece of ginger, roughly chopped
2 x 400 g (14 oz) tins chopped tomatoes
310 ml (10 fl oz/1¼ cups) clear vinegar
350 g (12 oz) palm sugar (jaggery) or soft brown sugar
2 tablespoons sultanas
2 teaspoons salt
¾ teaspoon cayenne pepper
chilli powder (optional)

MAKES 500 ML (17 FL OZ/2 CUPS)

COMBINE the garlic, ginger and half the tomatoes in a blender or food processor and blend until smooth. If you don't have a blender, crush the garlic, grate the ginger and push the tomatoes through a sieve before mixing them all together.

PUT the remaining tomatoes, the vinegar, sugar, sultanas and salt in a large, heavy-based saucepan. Bring to the boil and add the garlic and ginger mixture. Reduce the heat and simmer gently for 1½–1¾ hours, stirring occasionally, until the mixture is thick enough to fall off a spoon in sheets. Make sure the mixture doesn't catch on the base.

ADD the cayenne pepper. For a hotter chutney, add a little chilli powder. Leave to cool, then pour into sterilised jars (wash the jars in boiling water and dry them in a warm oven). Store in a cool place, or in the fridge after opening.

Shelled tamarind husk and pulp.

TAMARIND AND RAISIN CHUTNEY

2 teaspoons fennel seeds
250 ml (1 cup) tamarind purée (see recipe on page 467)
50 g (¼ cup) pitted dates, chopped
30 g (¼ cup) raisins
1 teaspoon chilli powder
180 g (6 oz) jaggery or soft brown sugar
1 tablespoon oil
½ teaspoon black mustard seeds
6 green chillies, slit in half and seeded but left whole

MAKES 250 ML (8 FL OZ/1 CUP)

PLACE a small frying pan over low heat and dry-roast the fennel seeds, stirring constantly until aromatic. Grind the seeds to a fine powder using a spice grinder or pestle and mortar. Mix the ground fennel with the tamarind, dates, raisins, chilli powder, jaggery and a pinch of salt.

HEAT the oil in a large, heavy-based saucepan over medium heat, add the mustard seeds, then cover and shake the pan until they start to pop. Add date mixture and chillies, bring to the boil and cook 3 minutes, or until mixture starts to thicken. Reduce the heat and simmer for 40 minutes until the chutney is thick enough to fall off a spoon in sheets. Cool, then put in a sterilised jar (wash the jar in boiling water and dry in a warm oven). Store in a cool place. Refrigerate after opening.

TAMARIND AND RAISIN CHUTNEY

FROM INDIA

KOSAMBRI

KOSAMBRI ARE SALAD-LIKE DISHES FROM MYSORE. THIS ONE USES A COMBINATION OF CARROTS OR RADISHES AND DAL BUT THERE ARE MANY VARIATIONS. THIS IS AN EXCELLENT COMBINATION OF INGREDIENTS AND CAN BE SERVED ALONGSIDE MOST INDIAN DISHES.

EGGPLANT SAMBAL

60 g (2 oz/½ cup) moong dal
200 g (7 oz) carrots or white radish
25 g (1 oz) grated coconut
   (see recipe on page 468)
25 g (1 oz/¾ cup) coriander
   (cilantro) leaves
½ tablespoon oil
½ teaspoon yellow mustard seeds
2 dried chillies
2 tablespoons lemon juice

SERVES 4

SOAK the dal in plenty of boiling water for 3 hours, then drain.

FINELY grate the carrot or radish and combine with the dal, coconut and coriander leaves in a salad bowl. Heat the oil in a small saucepan over medium heat, add the mustard seeds, then cover and shake the pan until the seeds start to pop. Add the chillies, remove from the heat and add the lemon juice. When cold, pour over the remaining ingredients and toss well. Season with salt, to taste.

EGGPLANT SAMBAL

EGGPLANT, OR AUBERGINE, IS ALSO KNOWN BY ITS INDIAN NAME BRINJAL. FOR THIS RECIPE, IT IS PREFERABLE TO USE THE LONG, THIN, ASIAN EGGPLANTS. USE THE SAMBAL AS AN ACCOMPANIMENT OR EAT IT AS A DIP WITH PIECES OF INDIAN BREAD.

2 medium (about 500 g/1 lb 2 oz)
   eggplants (aubergines)
½ tablespoon oil
½ teaspoon ground turmeric
3 tablespoons lime juice
2 red chillies, seeded and finely
   diced
1 small red onion, finely diced
4 tablespoons thick plain yoghurt
   (see recipe on page 467)
coriander (cilantro) leaves

SERVES 4

PREHEAT the oven to 200°C (400°F/Gas 6). Slice each eggplant in half and brush the cut halves with the oil and ground turmeric. Place the eggplants in a roasting tin and roast them for 30 minutes, or until they are browned all over and very soft.

SCOOP eggplant pulp into a bowl. Mash pulp with the lime juice, chilli and onion, reserving some chilli and onion for garnish. Season with salt, to taste, then fold in the yoghurt.

GARNISH with coriander leaves and the remaining onion and chilli.

DESSERTS

Anko is a sweet bean paste made by slow-cooking adzuki beans in a sugar syrup.

CHOCOLATE PUDDING WITH ADZUKI HEART

A TRULY PERFECT CONCOCTION COMBINING THE FLAVOURS OF BOTH EAST AND WEST, THIS PLEASING CHOCOLATE BAKED PUDDING FEATURES A HEART OF CHOCOLATE-INFUSED SWEET ADZUKI BEAN PASTE. A SPRINKLE OF COCOA POWDER GIVES THIS DESSERT A CONTRASTING FINISH.

1 tablespoon anko (sweet adzuki bean paste)
150 g (5 oz) dark cooking chocolate, chopped
125 g (4½ oz) unsalted butter, chopped
90 g (3¼ oz/¾ cup) plain (all-purpose) flour
90 g (3 oz/⅓ cup) caster (superfine) sugar
½ teaspoon baking powder
4 eggs, lightly beaten
1 teaspoon unsweetened cocoa powder

MAKES 6

PUT the anko and 25 g (1 oz) of the chocolate in a small heatproof bowl over simmering water and stir until melted and combined. Cover and refrigerate for 3 hours.

PUT the remaining chocolate and butter in a heatproof bowl and place over a saucepan of simmering water for 10–15 minutes, stirring often, until completely melted and combined. Remove from the heat.

COMBINE the flour, sugar and baking powder in a large bowl and beat in the eggs until the mixture is smooth. Beat in the chocolate mixture until smooth. Cover and refrigerate.

PREHEAT the oven to 220°C (425°F/Gas 7).

GREASE six 125 ml (4 fl oz/½ cup) ramekins. Spoon enough of the pudding mixture into the ramekin to come two-thirds of the way up the side. Spoon 1 teaspoon of the anko mixture into the middle of each pudding, then spoon over the remaining pudding mixture. Bake for about 15 minutes, or until the mixture has risen to the top of the ramekins. Remove from the oven and cool for a few minutes. Invert onto a plate, sieve cocoa powder over the top and serve.

STICKY RICE WITH MANGO

4 large ripe mangoes
1 quantity of steamed sticky rice
  with coconut milk (see recipe on
  page 459)
180 ml (6 fl oz/⅔ cup) coconut
  cream (see recipe on page 468)
  mixed with ¼ teaspoon salt, for
  garnish
2 tablespoons dry-fried mung beans
  (optional)

SERVES 4

PEEL the mangoes and slice off the two outside cheeks of each, removing as much flesh as you can in large pieces. Avoid cutting very close to the stone where the flesh is fibrous. Discard the stone. Slice each cheek lengthways into four or five pieces.

ARRANGE the mango pieces on a serving plate. Spoon a portion of steamed sticky rice with coconut milk near the mango slices. Spoon the coconut cream garnish on top and sprinkle with mung beans.

SERVE at room temperature.

BANANA IN COCONUT CREAM

400 ml (13 fl oz/1⅔ cups) coconut
  milk (see recipe on page 468)
4 tablespoons sugar
5 just-ripe bananas
½ teaspoon salt

Serves 4

PUT the coconut milk, sugar and 125 ml (4 fl oz/ ½ cup) water in a saucepan and bring to a boil. Reduce heat and simmer until sugar dissolves.

PEEL the bananas and cut them into 5 cm (2 inch) lengths. If you are using very small bananas, leave them whole.

WHEN the sugar in the coconut milk dissolves, add the bananas and salt. Cook gently over a low to medium heat for 5 minutes or until the bananas are soft.

DIVIDE the bananas and coconut cream among four bowls.

SERVE warm or at room temperature.

BANANA IN COCONUT CREAM

Black sticky rice is commonly used for desserts and, when cooked, is actually a dark purplish-red.

FROM THAILAND

BLACK STICKY RICE WITH TARO

VEGETABLES LIKE TARO ARE OFTEN USED IN THAI DESSERTS. BLACK STICKY RICE IS SIMPLY WHITE RICE WITH THE BRAN LEFT ON AND IS ACTUALLY MORE PURPLE THAN BLACK. YOU MUST COOK THE RICE BEFORE ADDING ANY SUGAR OR IT WILL TOUGHEN AND NEVER BECOME TENDER.

175 g (6 oz) black sticky rice
  (black glutinous)
280 g (10 oz) taro, cut into 1 cm
  (½ inch) squares and soaked in
  cold water
150 g (5 oz) palm sugar (jaggery)
1 teaspoon salt
185 ml (6 fl oz/¾ cup) coconut milk
  (see recipe on page 468)

SERVES 6

PUT the rice in a bowl and pour in cold water to come 5 cm (2 inches) above the rice. Soak for at least 3 hours, or overnight if possible.

DRAIN the rice and add clean water. Scoop the rice through your fingers four or five times to clean it, then drain. Repeat two or three times with clean water to remove the unwanted starch. (The water will never be completely clear when using black rice, even when all the unwanted starch has gone.) Put rice in a pan. Add 625 ml (21 fl oz/2½ cups) cold water. Bring to the boil, stirring rice frequently as it reaches boiling point. Reduce the heat to medium. Stir and simmer for 30–35 minutes or until nearly all the liquid has been absorbed. Rice should be very moist, but with hardly any water remaining in the bottom of the saucepan. (Taste a few grains to check whether the rice is cooked.)

MEANWHILE, drain the taro, spread it on a plate and transfer it to a bamboo steamer or other steamer. Taking care not to burn your hands, set the basket over a pan of boiling water over a high heat. Cover and steam for 8–10 minutes or until the taro is cooked and tender.

WHEN the rice is cooked, add the sugar and gently stir until the sugar has dissolved. Add the taro and gently mix.

MIX the salt into the coconut milk.

DIVIDE the pudding among individual bowls and drizzle the coconut milk on top. Serve warm.

FROM JAPAN

PLUM WINE GRANITA

FOR A REFRESHING CLOSE TO A SOPHISTICATED DINNER ON A HOT SUMMER EVENING, THIS GRANITA IS AN IDEAL CHOICE. FRUITY, WITH A TART SWEETNESS AND A HINT OF GINGER, AS WELL AS LIGHTLY ALCOHOLIC, THIS BRIGHT DESSERT MAKES A BEAUTIFUL PRESENTATION.

115 g (4 oz/½ cup) caster (superfine) sugar
a few strips lemon zest
2 cm (¾ inch) piece young fresh ginger, thinly sliced
500 g (1 lb 2 oz) ripe plums, seeded
500 ml (17 fl oz/2 cups) Japanese plum wine

SERVES 6

COMBINE the sugar with the lemon zest, ginger and 375 ml (13 fl oz/1½ cups) water. Stir over high heat until the sugar has dissolved, then bring to the boil. Reduce the heat to low and simmer for 10 minutes. Cool completely, then strain.

PURÉE the plum flesh in a food processor, then strain through a fine sieve to extract the juice – you will need about 250 ml (9 fl oz/1 cup).

ADD to the cooled syrup with the plum wine, then pour into a shallow 30 x 20 cm (12 x 8 inch) metal container. Place in the freezer until the mixture begins to freeze around the edges.

REMOVE from the freezer and scrape the frozen sections back into the mixture with a fork. Repeat every 30 minutes, until the mixture has even-sized ice crystals.

JUST before serving, beat the mixture with a fork, then spoon into six bowls or glasses.

Just before serving, beat the mixture with a fork.

Umeshu is commonly called 'plum wine'. It is a sweet liqueur with an almond flavour. Made from *ume*, a Japanese apricot, which, curiously, is more often referred to as a plum.

Roll the gulab jamun into smooth balls. When they have fried to a deep golden brown, add them to the flavoured sugar syrup.

GULAB JAMUN

SYRUP
440 g (15 oz/2 cups) sugar
4–5 drops rosewater

GULAB JAMUN
100 g (3 oz/1 cup) low-fat
    powdered milk
2 tablespoons self-raising flour
2 teaspoons fine semolina
2 tablespoons ghee
4 tablespoons milk, to mix
24 pistachio nuts (optional)
oil for deep-frying

MAKES 24

TO MAKE syrup, put the sugar in a large heavy-based saucepan with 850 ml (28 fl oz/3⅓ cups) water. Stir over low heat to dissolve the sugar. Increase the heat and boil for 3 minutes. Stir in the rosewater and remove from the heat.

TO MAKE gulab jamun, combine powdered milk, flour, semolina and ghee in a bowl. Add enough milk to make a soft dough, mix until smooth, then divide into 24 portions. If using the pistachio nuts, press each piece of dough in the centre to make a hole, fill with a pistachio, then roll into a ball. If not using pistachios, just roll each piece into a ball.

FILL a karhai or deep saucepan one-third full with oil. Heat the oil to 150°C (300°F). A cube of bread should brown in it in 30 seconds. Fry balls over low heat until golden brown all over. Remove with a slotted spoon and transfer to the syrup. When all the balls are in the syrup, bring the syrup to boiling point, then remove from the heat. Cool and serve the gulab jamun at room temperature.

SHRIKHAND

½ teaspoon saffron strands
3 cardamom pods
250 ml (8 fl oz/1 cup) thick plain
    yoghurt (see recipe on page 467)
3 tablespoons caster (superfine)
    sugar
a few toasted flaked almonds

SERVES 4

SOAK the saffron in 1 teaspoon boiling water. Remove the cardamom seeds from the pods and coarsely crush them in a spice grinder or pestle and mortar.

PUT the yoghurt, sugar, cardamom and saffron in a bowl and beat until well mixed. Divide among four bowls and refrigerate before serving. Serve with toasted almonds sprinkled on top.

SHRIKHAND

FROM JAPAN

NASHI AND GINGER STRUDEL

THE CRISPY APPLE-SHAPED JAPANESE PEAR MAKES AN EXCELLENT STRUDEL FILLING, ITS FLAVOUR ACCENTED BY AROMATIC GINGER. THE CHOPPED WALNUTS AND SESAME SEEDS SCATTERED BETWEEN BUTTERY LAYERS OF PASTRY, AND THE TOUCH OF KINAKO ON TOP, ADD MORE APPEAL.

4 small nashi pears, peeled, cored and sliced

1 tablespoon lemon juice

2 teaspoons fresh ginger, finely grated

30 g (1 oz/½ cup) panko (Japanese breadcrumbs)

230 g (8 oz/1 cup) caster (superfine) sugar

40 g (1½ oz/¼ cup) sesame seeds, lightly toasted, plus extra to garnish

60 g (2 oz/½ cup) walnuts, very finely chopped

1½ teaspoons ground cinnamon

1 teaspoon ground ginger

8 sheets filo pastry

150 g (5 oz) unsalted butter, melted

2 tablespoons icing (confectioners') sugar

2 tablespoons kinako (roasted soya bean flour)

SERVES 6–8

PREHEAT the oven to 180°C (350°F/Gas 4). Lightly grease a baking tray.

PUT the nashi slices in a bowl with the lemon juice, fresh ginger, panko and half the sugar and stir well.

COMBINE the sesame seeds, walnuts, cinnamon, ground ginger and remaining sugar in a separate bowl.

LAY one sheet of filo on a work surface with the long edge towards you, brush lightly with a little melted butter, then lay another sheet on top so it overlaps the edge furthest away from you by about 5 cm (2 inches). Brush with a little more butter. Sprinkle about one-quarter of the sesame mixture over the top of the two pastry sheets, then keep layering in the same position with the rest of the filo and sesame mix, brushing each sheet of pastry with melted butter. Leave a 4 cm (1½ inch) border along the edge of the pastry closest to you and on both sides, and place the nashi mixture in a neat log along the edge closest to you. Carefully roll up, folding in the sides about halfway along, then continue rolling to the end.

CAREFULLY transfer the strudel to the prepared tray, seam side down, and brush all over with melted butter. Bake for 50 minutes, or until golden.

ALLOW to cool slightly before sprinkling with sifted combined icing sugar and kinako. Slice on the diagonal and serve with lightly whipped cream, if desired.

Nashi pears are firm with a sweet flesh. The colour can vary from pale yellow–green to brown. The darker the colour, the richer the flavour.

Dip your thumb in some flour and make an indent in each biscuit to hold the almonds.

ALMOND BISCUITS

125 g (4½ oz) unsalted butter, softened
185 g (6 oz) sugar
1 egg, lightly beaten
200 g (7 oz) plain (all-purpose) flour
½ teaspoon baking powder
½ teaspoon salt
150 g (5 oz) finely chopped almonds
1 teaspoon almond extract
1 egg, lightly beaten, extra
25 whole blanched almonds

MAKES 25

PREHEAT the oven to 180°C (350°F/Gas 4). Lightly grease a baking tray.

CREAM the butter and sugar for 5 minutes. Add the egg and beat until smooth. Sift together the flour, baking powder and salt and slowly add to the butter, stirring until smooth. Add the almonds and extract and stir until smooth.

DROP tablespoons of the mixture onto the baking tray, 3 cm (1¼ inches) apart. Dip your thumb into some flour and make an indentation in the centre of each biscuit. Brush each biscuit with the beaten egg and place an almond in the centre of each indentation.

BAKE for 10–12 minutes, or until the biscuits are golden and puffed. Cool slightly, then transfer to a rack to cool completely.

STEAMED PEARS IN HONEY

STEAMED PEARS IN HONEY

100 g (3½ oz) jujubes (dried Chinese dates)
6 nearly ripe pears
6 tablespoons honey

SERVES 6

SOAK the jujubes in hot water for 1 hour, changing the water twice. Drain, stone and cut crosswise into strips. Cut a slice off the bottom of each pear so that it will sit flat. Cut a 2.5 cm (1 inch) piece off the top and set it aside. Using a fruit corer or knife, remove cores without cutting through to the base.

ARRANGE the pears upright on a heatproof plate. Place 1 tablespoon of honey and some jujubes into the cavity of each pear. Replace the tops and, if necessary, fasten with toothpicks.

PUT the plate in a steamer. Cover and steam over simmering water in a wok for about 30 minutes, or until tender when pierced with a knife. Serve pears hot or cold.

Ready-made eight-treasure rice.

Fresh longans.

FROM CHINA
EIGHT-TREASURE RICE

THIS CHINESE RICE PUDDING IS A FAVOURITE AT BANQUETS AND CHINESE NEW YEAR. THE EIGHT

TREASURES VARY, BUT CAN ALSO INCLUDE OTHER PRESERVED FRUITS.

12 whole blanched lotus seeds

12 jujubes (dried Chinese dates)

20 fresh or tinned gingko nuts, shelled

225 g (8 oz/1 cup) glutinous rice

2 tablespoons sugar

2 teaspoons oil

30 g (1 oz) slab sugar

8 glacé cherries

6 dried longans, pitted

4 almonds or walnuts

225 g (8 oz) red bean paste

SERVES 8

SOAK the lotus seeds and jujubes in bowls of cold water for 30 minutes, then drain. Remove the seeds from the jujubes. If using fresh gingko nuts, blanch in a pan of boiling water for 5 minutes, then refresh in cold water and dry thoroughly.

PUT glutinous rice and 310 ml (10 fl oz/1¼ cups) water in a heavy-based saucepan and bring to the boil. Reduce the heat to low and simmer for 10–15 minutes. Stir in the sugar and oil.

DISSOLVE the slab sugar in 185 ml (6 fl oz/¾ cup) water and bring to the boil. Add the lotus seeds, jujubes and gingko nuts and simmer for 1 hour, or until lotus seeds are soft. Drain, reserving liquid.

GREASE a 1 litre (35 fl oz/4 cup) heatproof bowl. Decorate the base with the lotus seeds, jujubes, gingko nuts, cherries, longans and almonds. Smooth two-thirds of the rice over this to form a shell on the surface of the bowl. Fill with the bean paste, cover with the remaining rice and smooth the surface.

COVER the rice with a piece of greased foil and put the bowl in a steamer. Cover and steam over simmering water in a wok for 1–1½ hours, replenishing with boiling water during cooking.

TURN the pudding out onto a plate and pour the reserved sugar liquid over the top and serve hot.

Eight-treasure rice can be made in any round dish. If you want it to sit higher on the plate, choose a deep bowl. Remember that the pattern you make on the bottom will come out on top.

FROM INDIA

APRICOTS IN CARDAMOM SYRUP

300 g (10 oz/1⅔ cups) dried
    apricots
3 tablespoons caster (superfine)
    sugar
3 tablespoons slivered, blanched
    almonds
1 cm (½ inch) piece of ginger,
    sliced
4 cardamom pods
1 cinnamon stick
4 pieces edible silver leaf (varak),
    (optional)

SERVES 4

SOAK the apricots in 750 ml (26 fl oz/3 cups) water in a large saucepan for 4 hours, or until plumped up.

ADD the sugar, almonds, ginger, cardamom and cinnamon to the apricots and bring slowly to the boil, stirring until the sugar has dissolved. Reduce the heat to a simmer and cook until the liquid has reduced by half and formed a thick syrup. Pour into a bowl, then refrigerate.

SERVE in small bowls with a piece of silver leaf for decoration. To do this, invert the piece of backing paper over each bowl. As soon as the silver leaf touches the apricots it will come away from the backing and stick to them.

KHEER

KHEER

150 g (5 oz/¾ cup) basmati rice
20 cardamom pods
2.5 litres (67 fl oz/10 cups) milk
30 g (1 oz/⅓ cup) flaked almonds
165 g (5½ oz/¾ cup) sugar
30 g (¼ cup) sultanas

SERVES 6

WASH the rice, then soak for 30 minutes in cold water. Drain well. Remove the seeds from the cardamom pods and lightly crush them in a spice grinder or pestle and mortar.

BRING the milk to the boil in a large heavy-based saucepan and add the rice and cardamom. Reduce the heat and simmer for 1½–2 hours, or until the rice has a creamy consistency. Stir occasionally to stop the rice sticking to the pan.

DRY-FRY the almonds in a frying pan for a few minutes over medium heat. Add the sugar, almonds and sultanas to the rice, reserving some almonds and sultanas. Mix, divide among bowls.

SERVE warm, garnished with the almonds and sultanas.

FROM THAILAND

PUMPKIN WITH CUSTARD

THIS TRADITIONAL THAI DESSERT, MADE WITH COCONUT MILK AND PALM OR COCONUT SUGAR, IS
SWEET AND RICH IN TASTE. CHOOSE HONEY-COLOURED PUMPKINS, EITHER ONE SMALL TO MEDIUM,
OR FOUR VERY SMALL ONES. WHEN COOKED AND COOLED, CUT THEM INTO WEDGES FOR SERVING.

2 tablespoons coconut milk
(see recipe on page 468)
2 eggs
150 g (5 oz) palm sugar (jaggery),
cut or shaved into very small
pieces
2–3 pandanus leaves, dried
and cut into small pieces,
and bruised, or 1 teaspoon
vanilla essence
1 small to medium or 4 very small
pumpkins

SERVES 4

TO MAKE a custard, stir the coconut milk, eggs,
palm sugar, pandanus leaves and a pinch of salt in
a bowl, using a spoon, for 10 minutes or until the
sugar has dissolved. Pour the custard through a
sieve into a jug to discard the pandanus leaves.

CAREFULLY cut off the top of the pumpkin/s.
Try not to pierce the pumpkin at any other point
with the knife as it is more likely to crack or leak
around such punctures. Using a spoon, scrape
out and discard all the seeds and fibres.

POUR the custard into the pumpkin/s, filling to
within 2.5 cm (1 inch) from the top.

FILL a wok or a steamer pan with water, cover and
bring to a rolling boil over a high heat. Place the
pumpkin/s on a plate. Use a plate that will fit on
the rack of a traditional bamboo steamer basket or
on a steamer rack inside the wok. Taking care not
to burn your hands, place the plate on the rack or
steamer inside the wok. Cover, reduce the heat to
low and cook for 30–45 minutes or until the
pumpkin is cooked and the custard puffed up.
Check and replenish water every 10 minutes or so.

TURN off the heat and remove the cover. Carefully
remove the pumpkin and set aside to cool. If you
prefer, you can leave the pumpkin in the steamer
to cool to room temperature.

CUT the pumpkin into thick wedges for serving.
Serve at room temperature or chilled.

AS an alternative, you can steam the mixture in a
shallow tin, such as a pie tin or cake pan, and
serve it in small spoonfuls on top of mounds of
steamed sticky rice with coconut milk.

Cut off the tops of the pumpkins
and scrape out the seeds. Sieve
the custard, discard the leaves,
then pour into the pumpkins.

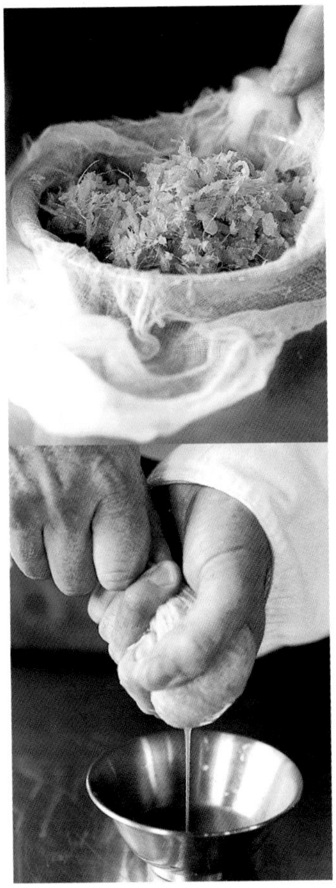

FROM CHINA

GINGER PUDDING

200 g (7 oz) young ginger
1 tablespoon sugar
500 ml (17 fl oz/2 cups) milk

SERVES 4

GRATE the ginger as finely as you can, collecting any juice. Place it in a piece of muslin, twist the top hard and squeeze out as much juice as possible. You will need 4 tablespoons. Alternatively, push the ginger through a juicer.

PUT 1 tablespoon of ginger juice and 1 teaspoon of sugar each into four bowls. Put the milk in a saucepan and bring to the boil, then divide among the bowls. Leave to set for 1 minute (the ginger juice will cause the milk to solidify). Serve warm.

Squeeze the juice out of the ginger by twisting it up in a piece of muslin.

ALMOND TOFU WITH FRUIT

2½ tablespoons powdered gelatine
  or 6 gelatine sheets
90 g (3 oz/⅓ cup) caster
  (superfine) sugar
2 teaspoons almond extract
125 ml (4 fl oz/½ cup) condensed
  milk
400 g (14 oz) tin lychees in syrup
400 g (14 oz) tin loquats in syrup
½ papaya, cut into cubes
½ melon, cut into cubes

SERVES 6

PUT 125 ml (4 fl oz/½ cup) water in a saucepan. If you are using powdered gelatine, sprinkle it on the water and leave to sponge for 1 minute. If you are using sheets, soak in the water until floppy. Heat mixture slightly, stirring to dissolve gelatine.

PLACE the sugar, almond extract and condensed milk in a bowl and stir to combine. Slowly add 625 ml (21 fl oz/2½ cups) water, stirring to dissolve the sugar. Stir in the dissolved gelatine. Pour into a chilled 23 cm (9 inch) square tin. Chill for at least 4 hours, or until set.

DRAIN half the syrup from the lychees and the loquats. Place the lychees, loquats and remaining syrup in a bowl. Add the papaya and melon. Cut the almond tofu into diamond-shaped pieces and arrange on plates. Spoon the fruit around the tofu.

ALMOND TOFU WITH FRUIT

FROM JAPAN

BANANA TEMPURA

BATTER-FRIED BANANAS ARE A FURTHER TAKE ON THE TEMPURA TECHNIQUE, WHICH LENDS ITSELF NICELY TO A BROAD VARIETY OF INGREDIENTS. SERVED WARM WITH HONEY AND ICE CREAM, OR JUST WITH A CUP OF GREEN TEA, THEY MAKE A DELIGHTFUL DESSERT.

TEMPURA BATTER
(MAKES 1 BATCH)
310 ml (10¾ fl oz/1¼ cups) iced
   water
45 g (1½ oz/¼ cup) potato starch,
   sifted
140 g (5 oz/1 heaped cup) plain
   (all-purpose) flour, sifted
¼ teaspoon baking powder

oil, for deep-frying
4 small bananas
caster (superfine) sugar, to serve
warmed honey, to serve

SERVES 4

TO MAKE one batch of the tempura batter, pour the iced water into a bowl. Add the sifted potato starch, flour, baking powder and ¼ teaspoon salt all at once and give just a few strokes with a pair of chopsticks to loosely combine. There should be flour all around the edges of the bowl and the batter should be lumpy. (If the kitchen is hot, place the bowl over a bowl of iced water.)

FILL a deep-fat fryer or large saucepan one-third full of oil. Heat to 170°C (325°F), or until a cube of bread dropped into the oil browns in 20 seconds.

SPLIT the bananas in half lengthways, then in half crossways. Dip the banana quarters into the batter and deep-fry a few at a time for about 2 minutes, or until crisp and golden. Drain on paper towels and sprinkle with sugar.

SERVE drizzled with warmed honey and a scoop of sesame seed ice cream or green tea ice cream.

Gently stir the tempura mixture – do not whisk the batter – it should be lumpy.

Deep-fry the bananas, a few at a time until crisp and golden.

COCONUT ICE CREAM

400 ml (13 fl oz/1²⁄₃ cups) coconut
    milk (see recipe on page 468)
250 ml (8 fl oz/1 cup) thick
    (double/heavy) cream
2 eggs
4 egg yolks
160 g (5½ oz/²⁄₃ cup) caster
    (superfine) sugar
¼ teaspoon salt

SERVES 10

POUR the coconut milk and cream into a medium saucepan. Stir over a gentle heat without boiling for 2–3 minutes. Remove from the heat, cover and keep warm over a bowl of boiling water.

PUT the eggs, egg yolks, sugar and salt in a large heatproof bowl. Beat the mixture with electric beaters for 3 minutes or until frothy and thickened.

PLACE the bowl over a pan of simmering water. Continue to beat the egg mixture, slowly adding all the coconut mixture until the custard thickens lightly. This process will take 8–10 minutes. The mixture should be a thin cream and easily coat the back of a spoon. Do not boil it or it will curdle. Set aside until cool. Stir the mixture occasionally while it is cooling. Pour into a freezer box or churn in an ice cream machine. If you are using a freezer box, take the mixture out of the freezer and beat it with electric beaters at least twice during the freezing. You want it to get plenty of air whipped into it. Cover and freeze completely.

TO SERVE, remove ice cream from the freezer for 10–15 minutes until slightly softened. Serve in scoops with slices of coconut.

MANGO SORBET

3 ripe mangoes
150 g (5½ oz) palm sugar (jaggery)
zest and juice from 1 lime

SERVES 4

MANGO SORBET

PEEL the mangoes and cut flesh off the stones. Chop into small pieces.

PUT the sugar and 185 ml (6 fl oz/¾ cup) water in a saucepan and bring to the boil. Reduce the heat and simmer until the liquid reduces by half.

PUT sugar syrup, mango and lime zest and juice in a food processor or blender. Whiz until smooth.

POUR into a freezer box or churn in an ice cream machine. If you are using a freezer box, take the mixture out of the freezer and beat it with electric beaters at least twice during the freezing time. You want it to have plenty of air whipped into it or it will be too icy and hard. Cover and freeze completely.

BREADS, RICE & BASICS

Make sure that the naan dough is very soft but not sticky. Shape it by pulling it into the right shape with your hands.

FROM INDIA

NAAN

PERHAPS THE MOST FAMOUS LEAVENED BREAD FROM NORTH INDIA, TRADITIONALLY THIS BREAD IS COOKED ON THE WALLS OF A TANDOOR (CLAY OVEN). IT IS NOT EASY TO RECREATE THE INTENSE HEAT IN A DOMESTIC OVEN SO THE TEXTURE IS SLIGHTLY DIFFERENT BUT THE TASTE IS DELICIOUS.

500 g (1 lb 2 oz/4 cups) maida or plain (all-purpose) flour
310 ml (10 fl oz/1¼ cups) milk
2 teaspoons (7 g/¼ oz) easy-blend dried yeast or 15 g (½ oz) fresh yeast
2 teaspoons kalonji (nigella seeds), (optional)
½ teaspoon baking powder
½ teaspoon salt
1 egg, beaten
2 tablespoons oil or ghee
185 ml (6 fl oz/¾ cup) thick plain yoghurt (see recipe on page 467)

MAKES 10

SIFT the maida into a large bowl and make a well in the centre. Warm the milk over low heat in a saucepan until it is hand hot (the milk will feel the same temperature as your finger when you dip your finger into it). If you are using fresh yeast, mix it with a little milk and a pinch of maida and set it aside to activate and go frothy.

ADD yeast, kalonji, baking powder and salt to the maida. In another bowl, mix egg, oil and yoghurt. Pour into maida with 250 ml (8 fl oz/1 cup) of the milk and mix to form a soft dough. If the dough seems dry, add the remaining milk. Turn out onto a floured work surface and knead for 5 minutes, or until smooth and elastic. Put in an oiled bowl, cover and leave in a warm place to double in size. This will take several hours.

PREHEAT the oven to 200°C (400°F/Gas 6). Place a roasting tin half-filled with water at the bottom of the oven. This provides moisture in the oven which prevents the naan from drying out too quickly.

PUNCH down the dough, knead it briefly and divide it into 10 portions. Using the tips of your fingers, spread out one portion of dough to the shape of a naan bread. They are traditionally tear-drop in shape, so pull dough on one end. Put the naan on a greased baking tray. Bake on the top shelf for 7 minutes, then turn the naan over and cook for another 5 minutes. While the first naan is cooking, shape the next one. If your tray is big enough, you may be able to fit two naan at a time. Remove cooked naan from the oven and cover with a cloth to keep it warm and soft.

REPEAT the cooking process until all the dough is used. You can only use the top shelf of the oven because naan won't cook properly on the middle shelf. Refill baking tray with boiling water as needed.

FROM INDIA

CHAPATIS

CHAPATIS ARE THE MOST BASIC FORM OF UNLEAVENED BREAD. THEY SHOULD BE COOKED ON A HIGH HEAT TO PREVENT THEM BECOMING TOUGH. YOU CAN USE EQUAL AMOUNTS OF WHOLEMEAL (WHOLE WHEAT) AND MAIDA IF YOU CAN'T BUY CHAPATI FLOUR.

200 g (7 oz/1⅓ cups) atta (chapati flour)
½ teaspoon salt
100 g (3½ oz) ghee or clarified butter

MAKES 8

SIFT the atta and salt into a bowl and make a well in the centre. Add about 170 ml (6 fl oz/⅔ cup) tepid water, enough to mix to form a soft, pliable dough. Turn the dough out onto a floured work surface and knead for 5 minutes. Place in an oiled bowl, cover and allow to rest for 30 minutes.

PUT a tava or griddle, or a heavy-based frying pan over medium heat and leave it to heat up. Divide dough into eight equal portions. Working with one portion at a time and keeping the rest covered, on a lightly floured surface roll out each portion to form a 15 cm (6 inch) diameter circle. Keep the rolled chapatis covered with a damp cloth while you roll them and cook them. Remove the excess surface flour on the chapati prior to cooking by holding the chapati in the palms of your hands and gently slapping it from one hand to the other. If you leave the flour on it may burn.

PLACE each chapati on the tava and leave it for 7–10 seconds to brown, then turn it over to brown on the other side. Depending on the hotness of the griddle, the second side should take about 15 seconds. Turn over the chapati again and, using a folded tea towel (dish towel), apply gentle pressure to the chapati in several places to heat it and encourage it to puff up like a balloon. It is this puffing up process that gives the chapati its light texture. Smear the hot chapati with a little of the ghee or butter, and leave stacked and covered with a tea towel (dish towel) until all the chapatis are cooked.

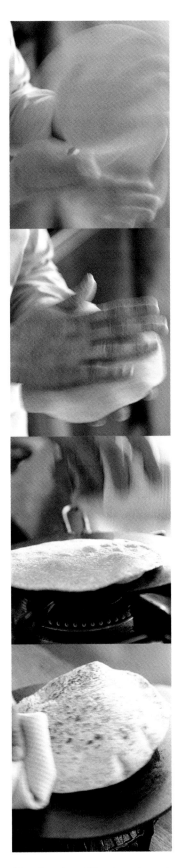

Slap the chapati backwards and forwards to remove excess flour. Press with a tea towel (dish towel) to make it puff up as it cooks.

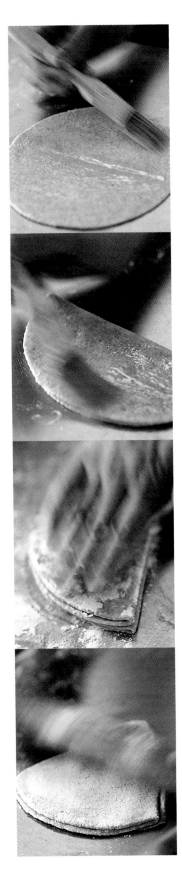

The ghee folded and rolled into the parathas will separate out the layers as they cook. Try to keep the shape neat as you roll.

FROM INDIA

PARATHAS

THIS FRIED UNLEAVENED BREAD IS OFTEN EATEN ON SPECIAL OCCASIONS. IT IS BEST COOKED ON A TAVA OR IRON GRIDDLE. YOU CAN USE EQUAL AMOUNTS OF WHOLEMEAL (WHOLE WHEAT) AND MAIDA IF YOU CAN'T BUY CHAPATI FLOUR.

200 g (7 fl oz/1⅓ cups) atta
  (chapati flour)
½ teaspoon salt
1 tablespoon oil or ghee
oil or ghee for cooking
  and brushing

MAKES 6

SIFT atta and the salt into a bowl and make a well in the centre. Add about 170 ml (6 fl oz/⅔ cup) tepid water and the oil or ghee and mix to form a soft pliable dough. Turn dough out onto a floured work surface and knead for 5 minutes. Place in an oiled bowl, cover and allow to rest for 30 minutes. Divide dough into six equal portions.

ROLL each portion into a 15 cm (6 inch) diameter circle. Using a pastry brush, cover the surface of each paratha with a very thin coating of oil or ghee. Fold each into a semicircle and brush thinly with oil. Fold into quarters. Roll out each quarter to roughly three times its original size. Cover the rolled-out parathas with a cloth and cook them one at a time.

PLACE a tava, griddle or a heavy-based frying pan over medium heat and leave it to heat up. Lightly brush the surface of the tava or griddle with oil. Remove the excess surface flour on each paratha prior to cooking by holding it in the palms of your hands and gently slapping it from one hand to the other. If you leave the flour on, it may burn.

PUT a paratha on the tava and cook for 1 minute. Turn it over and cook for another minute, or until surface has brown flecks. This cooking process should be quick to ensure the parathas remain soft. Repeat until all the parathas are cooked. Cover the cooked ones with a cloth.

PARATHAS must be served warm and can be reheated in a microwave oven, or wrapped in oil and heated in a conventional oven at 180°C (350°F/Gas 4) for 10 minutes.

BASIC YEAST DOUGH

CHINESE CHEFS USE TWO TYPES OF BREAD DOUGH FOR MAKING STEAMED BREADS, ONE MADE WITH
YEAST AS HERE, THE OTHER MADE WITH A YEAST STARTER DOUGH.

3 tablespoons sugar
250 ml (8 fl oz/1 cup) warm water
1½ teaspoons dried yeast
    or 10 g (¼ oz) fresh yeast
400 g (13 oz/3¼ cups) plain
    (all-purpose) flour
2 tablespoons oil
1½ teaspoons baking powder

MAKES 1 QUANTITY

DISSOLVE the sugar in the water, then add the yeast. Stir lightly, then set aside for 10 minutes, or until foamy.

SIFT the flour into a bowl and add the yeast mixture and the oil. Using a wooden spoon, mix the ingredients to a rough dough. Turn mixture out onto a lightly floured surface and knead for about 10 minutes, or until dough is smooth and elastic. If it is very sticky, knead in a little more flour. The dough should be soft. Lightly grease a bowl with the oil. Place the dough in the bowl and turn it so that all sides of the dough are coated. Cover the bowl with a damp cloth and set aside to rise in a draught-free place for 3 hours.

UNCOVER the dough, punch it down, and turn it out onto a lightly floured surface. If you are not using the dough straight away, cover it with plastic wrap and refrigerate.

WHEN you are ready to use the dough, flatten it and make a well in the centre. Place the baking powder in the well and gather up the edges to enclose the baking powder. Pinch the edges to seal. Lightly knead the dough for several minutes to evenly incorporate the baking powder, which will activate immediately.

USE the prepared dough as directed.

This bread dough is double risen, first with yeast and then with baking powder, which is kneaded into the dough, making it very light and fluffy.

Folding sesame oil into the dough means that when the breads are steamed, the layers will spring open.

STEAMED BREADS

THE BASIC YEAST DOUGH CAN BE USED TO MAKE LOTS OF DIFFERENT STEAMED BUNS, CALLED MANTOU IN CHINA. FLOWER ROLLS ARE ONE OF THE SIMPLEST SHAPES, WHILE SILVER THREAD ROLLS REQUIRE MORE DEXTERITY. THESE BREADS ARE DELICIOUS WITH RED-COOKED MEATS INSTEAD OF RICE.

1 quantity basic yeast dough
   (see recipe on page 451)
3 tablespoons roasted sesame oil

MAKES 12 FLOWER ROLLS
OR 6 SILVER THREAD LOAVES

CUT the dough in half and, on a lightly floured surface, roll out each half to form a 30 x 10 cm (12 x 4 inch) rectangle. Brush the surface of the rectangles liberally with the sesame oil. Place one rectangle directly on top of the other, with both oiled surfaces facing up. Starting with one of the long edges, roll up the dough swiss-roll style. Pinch the two ends to seal in the sesame oil.

LIGHTLY flatten the roll with the heel of your hand and cut the roll into 5 cm (2 inch) pieces. Using a chopstick, press down on the centre of each roll, holding the chopstick parallel to the cut edges. (This will cause the ends to 'flower' when they are steamed.) Arrange shaped rolls well apart in four steamers lined with greaseproof paper punched with holes. Cover and let rise for 15 minutes.

COVER and steam each steamer separately over simmering water in a wok for 15 minutes, or until the rolls are light and springy. Keep rolls covered until you are about to eat to ensure they stay soft.

THE dough can also be shaped in other ways, one of the most popular being silver thread bread. Divide the dough in half and roll each half into a sausage about 3 cm (1¼ inches) in diameter, then cut each sausage into six pieces. Roll six of the pieces into rectangles 20 x 10 cm (8 x 4 inches) and set aside. Roll the remaining pieces into rectangles 20 x 10 cm (8 x 4 inches), brush each with a little sesame oil and fold in half to a 10 cm (4 inch) square. Brush with more sesame oil and fold in half again. Cut into thin strips crossways. Place one of the rectangles on the work surface and stretch the strips so they fit down the centre. Fold the ends and sides in to completely enclose the strips. Repeat with the remaining dough until you have six loaves. Steam as for the flower rolls for 20–25 minutes.

Steaming mantou being sold in the streets in Beijing.

MANDARIN PANCAKES

THESE THIN PANCAKES ARE ALSO CALLED DUCK PANCAKES AND ARE USED FOR WRAPPING PEKING DUCK AND SEVERAL OTHER NORTHERN DISHES, SUCH AS CRISPY SKIN DUCK, MU SHU PORK AND MONGOLIAN LAMB.

450 g (1 lb) plain (all-purpose) flour
310 ml (10 fl oz/1¼ cups) boiling water
1 teaspoon oil
roasted sesame oil

MAKES 24–30

SIFT the flour into a bowl, slowly pour in the boiling water, stirring as you pour, then add the oil and knead into a firm dough. Cover with a damp tea towel (dish towel) and set aside for 30 minutes.

TURN the dough out onto a lightly floured surface and knead for 8–10 minutes, or until smooth. Divide the dough into three equal portions, roll each portion into a long cylinder, then cut each cylinder into 8 to 10 pieces.

ROLL each piece of dough into a ball and press into a flat disc with the palm of your hand. Brush one disc with a little sesame oil and put another disc on top. Using a rolling pin, flatten each pair of discs into a 15 cm (6 inch) pancake.

HEAT an ungreased wok or frying pan over high heat. Reduce heat to low and place the pairs of pancakes, one at a time, in pan. Turn over when brown spots appear on the underside. When the second side is cooked, lift the pancakes out and carefully peel them apart. Fold each pancake in half with the cooked side facing inwards, and set aside under a damp cloth.

JUST before serving, put the pancakes on a plate in a steamer. Cover and steam over simmering water in a wok for 10 minutes.

TO STORE the pancakes, put them in the fridge for 2 days or in the freezer for several months. Reheat either in a steamer for 4–5 minutes or a microwave for 30–40 seconds.

Mandarin pancakes are always rolled and cooked as a pair; the two pancakes are separated by a layer of sesame oil.

RICE

BASMATI IS A FRAGRANT, LONG-GRAIN RICE THAT GETS ITS UNIQUE FLAVOUR FROM THE SOIL IN WHICH IT IS GROWN. WE HAVE COOKED IT BY THE ABSORPTION METHOD BUT, IF YOU PREFER, YOU CAN ADD THE RICE TO A SAUCEPAN OF BOILING WATER AND BOIL THE RICE UNTIL READY.

400 g (13 oz/2 cups) basmati rice

SERVES 6

RINSE the rice under cold running water until the water running away is clear, then drain well.

PUT the rice in a heavy-based saucepan and add enough water to come about 5 cm (2 inches) above the surface of the pan. (If you stick your index finger into the rice so it rests on the bottom of the pan, the water will come up to the second joint.) Add 1 teaspoon of salt and bring the water quickly to the boil. When it boils, cover and reduce the heat to a simmer.

COOK for 15 minutes or until the rice is just tender, then remove the saucepan from the heat and rest the rice for 10 minutes without removing the lid. Fluff the rice with a fork before serving.

Rinse the rice very thoroughly under cold running water until the water running through it is completely clear.

BOILED ROSEMATTER OR PATNI RICE

ROSEMATTER IS EATEN IN SOUTHERN INDIA AND PATNI IN CENTRAL AND WESTERN INDIA. BOTH LOOK RED AND SPECKLED BECAUSE THE RICE HAS BEEN PRECOOKED IN ITS HUSK, LEAVING SOME BRAN AND HUSK STUCK TO THE GRAIN. COOK THEM AS WE HAVE, RATHER THAN BY THE ABSORPTION METHOD.

400 g (13 oz/2 cups) rosematter or patni rice

SERVES 6

RINSE the rice under cold running water until the water running away is clear, then drain well.

BRING a large, heavy-based saucepan of water to the boil and add 1 teaspoon of salt. When the water is at a rolling boil, add rice and bring back to the boil. Keep at a steady boil for 20 minutes, then test a grain to see if it is cooked. Drain and serve.

ROSEMATTER RICE

STICKY RICE

400 g (13 fl oz/2 cups) sticky rice

SERVES 4

PUT the rice in a bowl and pour in cold water to come 5 cm (2 inches) above the rice. Soak for at least 3 hours, or overnight. Drain and transfer to a bamboo basket specially made for steaming sticky rice, or to a steamer lined with a double thickness of muslin. Spread the rice in the steamer. Bring the water in the bottom of the steamer to a rolling boil. Taking care, set rice over the water. Lower heat, cover and steam for 20–25 minutes or until rice swells and is glistening and tender. Cooking time will vary depending on the soaking time. Check and replenish the water every 10 minutes or so.

WHEN the rice is cooked, tip it onto a large tray and spread it out to help it cool quickly. If it cools slowly it will be soggy rather than sticky.

SERVE warm or cold.

STICKY RICE

STEAMED RICE

400 g (13 fl oz/2 cups) jasmine rice

SERVES 4

RINSE the rice until the water runs clear. Put rice in a saucepan. Add enough water to come an index-finger joint above the rice. Bring to the boil, cover and cook at a slow simmer for 10–15 minutes. Remove from the heat and leave to rest for about 10 minutes.

STEAMED STICKY RICE WITH COCONUT MILK

200 g (7 oz/1 cup) sticky rice

170 ml (6 fl oz/⅔ cup) coconut milk (see recipe on page 468), well stirred
1 tablespoon palm sugar (jaggery) (not too brown)
½ teaspoon salt

SERVES 4

COOK the sticky rice according to the instructions in the recipe above.

WHILE the rice cooks, stir coconut milk, sugar and salt in a small saucepan over low heat until sugar has dissolved.

AS soon as rice is cooked, use a wooden spoon to gently mix it with the coconut milk. Set aside for 15 minutes.

STEAMED STICKY RICE WITH COCONUT MILK

STEAMED RICE

Combine the rice and liquid gently with a wooden rice paddle or thin wooden spoon.

PERFECT SUSHI RICE

SUSHI IS MADE USING A TYPE OF SHORT-GRAIN RICE, SOMETIMES CALLED STICKY RICE, AND IS PREPARED WITH SWEETENED VINEGAR. ONCE COOKED, THE RICE GRAINS STICK TOGETHER, MAKING IT IDEAL FOR SUSHI OR FOR EATING WITH CHOPSTICKS.

550 g (1 lb 3 oz/2½ cups)
   Japanese short-grain white rice
4 cm (1½ inch) piece of konbu,
   wiped with a damp cloth, optional
2 tablespoons sake, optional
80 ml (3 fl oz/⅓ cup) Japanese rice
   vinegar
1½ tablespoons caster (superfine)
   sugar
½ teaspoon salt

MAKES 6 CUPS

RINSE the rice several times in cold water or until the water runs clear, then drain in a colander for 1 hour.

PLACE rice in a saucepan with 750 ml (26 fl oz/ 3 cups) cold water and, if you wish, add konbu and sake. Bring to the boil, then remove konbu. Cover with a tight-fitting lid, reduce heat to low and simmer for 15 minutes. Turn off the heat but leave the pan on the hotplate. Working quickly, remove the lid and place a clean tea towel (dish towel) across the top (to absorb excess moisture), then replace lid for a further 15 minutes. Or, cook the rice in a rice cooker, following manufacturer's instructions.

TIP the rice into a wide, shallow non-metallic container and spread it out. Combine the vinegar, sugar and salt until the sugar is dissolved, then sprinkle over the warm rice. With quick, short strokes, combine the rice and liquid using a damp wooden rice paddle or a thin wooden spoon or spatula, being careful not to mash up the rice. Traditionally, the rice is cooled with a hand-held fan while mixing the liquid into the rice.

WHEN cooled, cover with a clean, damp tea towel (dish towel). To get the best results, use the rice immediately and do not refrigerate it.

Note: If you are not making your sushi within 1–2 hours, the rice must be refrigerated or bacteria may develop.

BOILED OR STEAMED RICE

200 g (7 oz/1 cup) white long-grain rice

SERVES 4

PUT the rice in a bowl and, using your fingers as a rake, rinse under cold running water to remove any dust. Drain the rice in a colander.

TO BOIL the rice, put the rice in a heavy-based saucepan with 420 ml (14 fl oz/1⅔ cups) water and bring to the boil. Reduce heat to low. Simmer, covered, for 15–18 minutes, or until the water has evaporated and craters appear on the surface.

TO STEAM the rice, spread the rice in a steamer lined with greaseproof paper punched with holes, damp cheesecloth or muslin. Cover and steam over simmering water in a wok for 35–40 minutes, or until tender.

FLUFF the rice with a fork to separate the grains. Serve or use as directed.

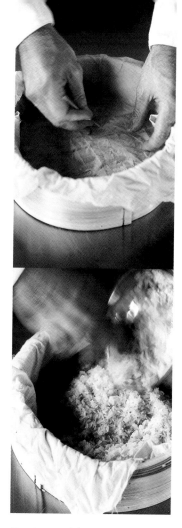

For steamed rice, line a steamer with greaseproof paper punched with holes, or use cheesecloth or muslin, to let in the steam. Spread the rice in an even layer.

CRISPY RICE

135 g (4½ oz/⅔ cup) white long-grain rice

SERVES 4

PUT the rice in a bowl and, using your fingers as a rake, rinse under cold running water to remove any dust. Drain the rice in a colander.

PUT the rice and 200 ml (7 fl oz) water in a heavy-based saucepan and bring to the boil. Reduce the heat to low. Simmer, covered, for 15–18 minutes.

CONTINUE to cook uncovered until the rice has formed a cake that comes loose from the pan. Leave to cool. Tip cake out and dry completely.

FILL a wok one-quarter full of oil. Heat the oil to 180°C (350°F), or until a piece of bread fries golden brown in 15 seconds when dropped in the oil. Cook the rice cake until it is brown and crisp.

CRISPY RICE

FROM INDIA

PANCH PHORON

PANCH PHORON IS A FIVE-SPICE MIX USED TO FLAVOUR VEGETABLES AND PULSES. THE MIX IS FRIED

AT THE BEGINNING OF A DISH, OR FRIED AND ADDED AS A FINAL SEASONING (TARKA).

1 teaspoon cumin seeds
1 teaspoon fennel seeds
1 teaspoon fenugreek seeds
1 teaspoon brown mustard seeds
1 teaspoon kalonji (nigella seeds)

GRIND all the spices to a fine powder in a spice grinder, a pestle and mortar, or with a grinding stone. Store in a small airtight container until you need it.

MAKES 1 TABLESPOON

PANCH PHORON

CHAAT MASALA

CHAAT MASALA IS A SALTY, TANGY SEASONING USED IN POPULAR SNACKS SUCH AS BHEL PURI. IT CAN

BE TOSSED THROUGH DRY SNACK MIXES OR SPRINKLED ONTO FRUIT AND VEGETABLES AS A SEASONING.

4 tablespoons coriander seeds
2 tablespoons cumin seeds
1 teaspoon ajowan
3 tablespoons black salt
1 tablespoon amchoor powder
2 dried chillies
1 teaspoon black peppercorns
1 teaspoon pomegranate seeds

PLACE a small frying pan over low heat and dry-roast the coriander seeds until aromatic. Remove from the pan and dry-roast the cumin seeds, then separately, the ajowan. Grind the roasted mixture to a fine powder with the other ingredients, using a spice grinder or pestle and mortar. Store in an airtight container.

MAKES 10 TABLESPOONS

GARAM MASALA

GARAM MASALA MEANS 'WARMING SPICE MIX'. IT CAN BE A MIXTURE OF WHOLE OR GROUND SPICES.

RECIPES ARE NUMEROUS BUT THEY ARE ALL AROMATIC, RATHER THAN 'HOT' MIXES.

GARAM MASALA

8 cardamom pods
2 Indian bay leaves (cassia leaves)
1 teaspoon black peppercorns
2 teaspoons cumin seeds
2 teaspoons coriander seeds
5 cm (2 inch) cinnamon stick
1 teaspoon cloves

REMOVE the seeds from the cardamom pods. Break the bay leaves into small pieces. Put them in a spice grinder or pestle and mortar with the remaining spices and grind to a fine powder. Store in a small airtight container until needed.

MAKES 3 TABLESPOONS

FROM INDIA

TAMARIND PUREE

150 g (5½ oz) tamarind block,
broken into small pieces

MAKES ABOUT 310 ML
(10 FL OZ/1¼ CUPS)

PUT tamarind in a bowl, pour in 250 ml (8 fl oz/ 1 cup) very hot water and soak for 3 hours or until the tamarind is soft. (If you are in a hurry, simmer the tamarind in the water for 15 minutes. Although this is efficient, it doesn't give as good a result.) Mash the tamarind thoroughly with a fork.

PUT the mixture through a sieve and extract as much of the pulp as possible by pushing it against the sieve with the back of a spoon. Put tamarind in the sieve back in the bowl with another 125 ml (4 fl oz/½ cup) hot water and mash again. Strain again. Discard fibres left in the sieve. Purée can be frozen in 1 tablespoon portions and defrosted as needed.

TAMARIND PUREE

YOGHURT

625 ml (21 fl oz/2½ cups) milk
2 tablespoons thick plain yoghurt
(see recipe on page 467)

MAKES 625 ML
(21 FL OZ/2½ CUPS)

BRING the milk to the boil in a heavy-based saucepan. Allow to cool to lukewarm. Stir in the yoghurt, cover and leave in a warm place for about 8 hours, or overnight. The yoghurt should be thick. If it is too runny, the milk was probably too hot for the starter yoghurt; if it is too milky, the yoghurt was probably not left in a warm enough place to ferment. From each batch, use 2 tablespoons to make the next batch.

WHEN the yoghurt is set, put it in a sieve lined with a piece of muslin and leave to drain overnight. This will give a thick yoghurt which does not contain too much moisture.

GINGER JUICE

GINGER JUICE

5 cm (2 inch) piece of ginger

MAKES 2 TABLESPOONS

POUND the ginger in a pestle and mortar, or grate with a fine grater into a bowl. Put the ginger in a piece of muslin, twist it up tightly and squeeze out all the juice.

GRATED COCONUT

GRATED COCONUT IS BEST WHEN IT IS FRESH. DRIED OR DESICCATED COCONUT CAN ALSO BE USED BUT IT NEEDS TO BE SOAKED, THEN CHOPPED MORE FINELY OR GROUND TO A PASTE, OTHERWISE IT WILL BE FIBROUS. IF YOU CAN BUY A PROPER COCONUT GRATER, YOUR LIFE WILL BE MUCH EASIER.

1 coconut

MAKES 300 g (10½ OZ)

DRAIN the coconut by punching a hole in two of the dark, coloured eyes. Drain out the liquid and use it as a refreshing drink. Holding the coconut in one hand, tap around the circumference firmly with a hammer or pestle. This should cause the coconut to split open evenly. If it doesn't crack easily, put it in a 150°C (300°F/Gas 2) oven for 15 minutes. This may cause it to crack as it cools. If not, it will crack easily when hit with a hammer.

IF YOU would like to use a coconut grater (hiramne), the easiest ones to use are those that you sit on at one end, then scrape out the coconut from each half on the serrated edge, catching it in a large bowl. If you don't have a coconut grater, prise the flesh out of the shell, trim off the hard, brown, outer skin and grate either by hand on a box grater or chop in a food processor. Grated coconut can be frozen in small portions.

Crack the coconut by tapping it around the circumference with a heavy object. It will open neatly.

COCONUT MILK AND COCONUT CREAM

COCONUT MILK IS NOT THE LIQUID WHICH IS FOUND INSIDE THE COCONUT (WHICH IS THE JUICE OR WATER), BUT IS MADE BY SOAKING THE GRATED COCONUT FLESH IN WATER AND THEN SQUEEZING IT. THE FIRST SOAKING AND SQUEEZING GIVES A THICKER MILK, SOMETIMES CALLED CREAM.

1 quantity grated coconut

MAKES 125 ML (4 FL OZ/½ CUP) COCONUT CREAM AND 250 ML (8 FL OZ/1 CUP) COCONUT MILK

MIX grated coconut with 125 ml (4 fl oz/½ cup) hot water and leave to steep for 5 minutes. Pour the mixture through a sieve lined with muslin, then gather the muslin into a ball to squeeze out any extra liquid. This will make a thick coconut milk. Repeat the process with another 250 ml (8 fl oz/ 1 cup) water to make thinner coconut milk.

COCONUT MILK AND
COCONUT CREAM

FROM THAILAND
GREEN CURRY PASTE

1 teaspoon ground coriander

1 teaspoon ground cumin

8–10 small green chillies, seeded

2 lemongrass stalks, white part only, finely sliced

2.5 cm (1 inch) piece of galangal, finely chopped

1 teaspoon very finely chopped makrut (kaffir lime) skin or leaves (about half the skin from a makrut or 4–5 leaves)

4–5 garlic cloves, finely chopped

3–4 Asian shallots, chopped

5–6 coriander (cilantro) roots, finely chopped

a handful of holy basil leaves, finely chopped

2 teaspoons shrimp paste

MAKES 125 G (4 OZ/½ CUP)

DRY-ROAST the coriander in a small frying pan for 1 minute until fragrant, then remove from the pan. Repeat with the cumin.

USING a pestle and mortar, pound the chillies, lemongrass, galangal and makrut skin or leaves into a paste. Add the garlic, shallots and coriander roots and pound together. Add the remaining ingredients and dry-roasted spices one at a time and pound until the mixture forms a smooth paste.

ALTERNATIVELY, you can use a food processor or blender to blend all the ingredients into as smooth a paste as possible. Add cooking oil as needed to assist the blending.

USE as required or keep in an airtight jar. Paste will keep for at least two weeks in the refrigerator and for two months in a freezer.

Whether using makrut skin or leaves, chop them very finely. Dry-roasting the ground spices helps to bring out the flavour.

YELLOW CURRY PASTE

3 teaspoons coriander seeds, dry-roasted

1 teaspoon cumin seeds, dry-roasted

2–3 dried long red chillies

2 lemongrass stalks, white part only, finely sliced

3 Asian shallots, finely chopped

2 garlic cloves, finely chopped

2 tablespoons grated turmeric or 1 teaspoon ground turmeric

1 teaspoon shrimp paste

MAKES 250 G (8 OZ/1 CUP)

GRIND the coriander seeds to a powder with a pestle and mortar. Repeat with the cumin seeds.

REMOVE the stems from the chillies and slit the chillies lengthways with a sharp knife. Discard the seeds and soak the chillies in hot water for 1–2 minutes or until soft. Drain and roughly chop.

USING a pestle and mortar, pound the chillies, lemongrass, shallots, garlic and turmeric to as smooth a paste as possible. Add the shrimp paste, ground coriander and ground cumin and pound until the mixture forms a smooth paste.

ALTERNATIVELY, use a small processor or blender, blend all the ingredients into a very smooth paste. Add cooking oil as needed to ease the grinding.

USE as required or keep in an airtight jar. Paste will keep for at least two weeks in the refrigerator and for two months in a freezer.

YELLOW CURRY PASTE

Before soaking the dried chillies in hot water, slit lengthways and remove all the seeds.

RED CURRY PASTE

3–4 dried long red chillies, about 13 cm (5 inches) long
8–10 dried small red chillies, about 5 cm (2 inches) long, or 10 fresh small red chillies, seeded
2 lemongrass stalks, white part only, finely sliced
2.5 cm (1 inch) piece of galangal, finely sliced
1 teaspoon very finely chopped makrut (kaffir) lime skin or makrut lime leaves (about half the skin from a makrut lime or 4–5 leaves)
4–5 garlic cloves, finely chopped
3–4 Asian shallots, finely chopped
5–6 coriander (cilantro) roots, finely chopped
2 teaspoons shrimp paste
1 teaspoon ground coriander, dry-roasted

MAKES 125 G (½ CUP)

REMOVE the stems from the dried chillies and slit the chillies lengthways with a sharp knife. Discard the seeds and soak the chillies in hot water for 1–2 minutes or until soft. Drain and roughly chop.

USING a pestle and mortar, pound the chillies, lemongrass, galangal and makrut skin or leaves into a paste. Add the remaining ingredients and pound together until the mixture forms a smooth paste.

ALTERNATIVELY, you can use a food processor or blender to blend all the ingredients into as smooth a paste as possible. Add cooking oil, as needed, to assist the blending.

USE as required or keep in an airtight jar. The paste will keep for at least two weeks in the refrigerator and for two months in a freezer.

MASSAMAN CURRY PASTE

MASSAMAN CURRY PASTE

2 dried long red chillies, about 13 cm (5 inches) long
1 lemongrass stalk, white part only, finely sliced
2.5 cm (1 inch) piece of galangal, finely chopped
5 cloves
10 cm (4 inch) piece of cinnamon stick, crushed
10 cardamom seeds
½ teaspoon freshly grated nutmeg
6 garlic cloves, finely chopped
4 Asian shallots, finely chopped
4–5 coriander (cilantro) roots, finely chopped
1 teaspoon shrimp paste

MAKES 250 G (4 OZ/1 CUP)

REMOVE the stems from the chillies and slit the chillies lengthways with a sharp knife. Discard the seeds and soak the chillies in hot water for 1–2 minutes or until soft. Drain and roughly chop.

USING a pestle and mortar, pound the chillies, lemongrass, galangal, cloves, cinnamon, cardamom seeds and nutmeg to a paste. Add garlic, shallots and coriander roots. Pound and mix together. Add the shrimp paste and pound until the mixture is a smooth paste.

ALTERNATIVELY, use a food processor or blender to grind or blend all the ingredients into as smooth a paste as possible. Add cooking oil, as needed, to assist the blending.

USE as required or keep in an airtight jar. The paste will keep for two weeks in the refrigerator and for two months in a freezer.

DRY CURRY PASTE

2 dried long red chillies, about
   13 cm (5 inches) long
2 lemongrass stalks, white part only,
   finely sliced
2.5 cm (1 inch) piece of galangal,
   finely chopped
4–5 garlic cloves, finely chopped
3–4 Asian shallots, finely chopped
5–6 coriander (cilantro) roots,
   finely chopped
1 teaspoon shrimp paste
1 teaspoon ground cumin,
   dry-roasted
3 tablespoons unsalted peanuts,
   chopped

MAKES 90 G (3 OZ/2⅓ CUP)

REMOVE the stems from the chillies and slit the chillies lengthways with a sharp knife. Discard the seeds and soak the chillies in hot water for 1–2 minutes or until soft. Drain and roughly chop.

USING a pestle and mortar, pound the chillies, lemongrass and galangal into a paste.

ADD the remaining ingredients one at a time and pound until the mixture forms a very smooth paste.

ALTERNATIVELY, you can use a food processor or blender to blend all the ingredients together into as smooth a paste as possible. Add cooking oil, as needed, to assist the blending.

USE as required or keep in an airtight jar. Paste will keep for at least two weeks in the refrigerator and for two months in a freezer.

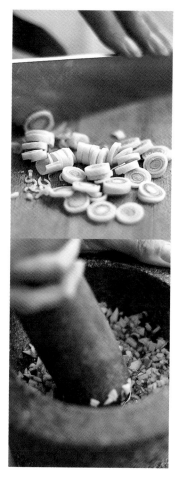

Pound the chopped ingredients until a smooth paste is formed.

CHIANG MAI CURRY PASTE

1 tablespoon coriander seeds
2 teaspoons cumin seeds
2 dried long red chillies, about
   13 cm (5 inches) long
½ teaspoon salt
5 cm (2 inch) piece of galangal,
   grated
1 lemongrass stalk, white part only,
   finely chopped
2 Asian shallots, chopped
2 garlic cloves, chopped
1 teaspoon grated turmeric or
   a pinch of ground turmeric
1 teaspoon shrimp paste
½ teaspoon ground cassia
or cinnamon

MAKES 185 G (6 OZ/¾ CUP)

DRY-ROAST the coriander seeds in a small frying pan for 1 minute until fragrant, then remove from the pan. Repeat with the cumin seeds. Grind them both to a powder with a pestle and mortar.

REMOVE the stems from the chillies and slit the chillies lengthways with a sharp knife. Discard the seeds. Soak the chillies in hot water for 1–2 minutes or until soft. Drain and roughly chop.

USING a pestle and mortar, pound the chillies, salt, galangal, lemongrass, shallots, garlic and turmeric to as smooth a paste as possible.

ADD shrimp paste, ground coriander, cumin and cassia and mix until a smooth paste forms.

ALTERNATIVELY, use a small processor or blender to blend all the ingredients into a very smooth paste. Add a little cooking oil, as needed, to ease the grinding.

CHIANG MAI CURRY PASTE

PLUM SAUCE

PEANUT SAUCE

PLUM SAUCE

185 ml (6 fl oz/¾ cup) white vinegar
8 tablespoons sugar

1 preserved plum (available in jars)
  without liquid

MAKES 60 ML (2 FL OZ/¼ CUP)

IN a small saucepan, heat the vinegar and sugar quickly, stirring constantly, until it reaches boiling point. Lower the heat to medium and simmer for 15–20 minutes until it forms a thick syrup.

ADD the preserved plum and mash it with a spoon or fork. Cook for 1–2 minutes to form a smooth paste, then pour into a bowl ready to serve.

SWEET CHILLI SAUCE

7 long red chillies, seeded and
  roughly chopped

185 ml (6 fl oz/¾ cup) white vinegar
8 tablespoons sugar
½ teaspoon salt

MAKES 60 ML (2 FL OZ/¼ CUP)

USING a pestle and mortar or a small blender, pound or blend the chillies into a rough paste.

IN a small saucepan, boil vinegar, sugar and salt over a high heat to boiling point, stirring constantly. Reduce heat to medium. Simmer for about 20 minutes, or until the mixture forms a thick syrup. Spoon the paste into the syrup, cook for 1–2 minutes. Pour into a bowl ready to serve.

PEANUT SAUCE

2 garlic cloves, crushed
4 Asian shallots, finely chopped
1 lemongrass stalk, white part only,
2 teaspoons Thai curry powder

1 tablespoon tamarind purée
1 tablespoon chilli paste
160 g (5 oz/1 cup) unsalted roasted
  peanuts, roughly chopped
375 ml (12½ fl oz/1½ cups)
  coconut milk (see recipe on
  page 468)
2 teaspoons palm sugar (jaggery)

MAKES 375 G
  (12½ FL OZ/1½ CUPS)

HEAT 1 tablespoon vegetable oil in a saucepan and fry garlic, Asian shallots and finely chopped lemongrass for a minute. Add Thai curry powder and stir until fragrant.

ADD the remaining ingredients and bring slowly to the boil. Add enough boiling water to make a spoonable sauce and simmer for 2 minutes. Season with salt to taste.

FROM THAILAND

CURRY POWDER

1 tablespoon black peppercorns
2 teaspoons white peppercorns
1 tablespoon cloves
3 tablespoons coriander seeds
3 tablespoons cumin seeds
1 tablespoon fennel seeds
seeds from 8 cardamom pods
3 tablespoons dried chilli flakes
2 tablespoons ground ginger
3 tablespoons ground turmeric

MAKES 125 G (4 OZ/½ CUP)

DRY-ROAST the peppercorns, cloves, coriander, cumin and fennel seeds, doing one ingredient at a time, in a frying pan over a low heat until fragrant.

TRANSFER to a spice grinder or pestle and mortar and grind to a powder. Add the remaining ingredients and grind together. Store in an airtight container.

CURRY POWDER

SALTED EGGS

10 fresh duck eggs (if available), or large chicken eggs, cleaned
175 g (6 oz) salt
a preserving jar, big enough to hold all the eggs

MAKES 10

IN a saucepan, heat 625 ml (21 fl oz/2½ cups) water and the salt until the salt has dissolved. Allow to cool.

BEING very careful not to crack the shells, place the eggs into a large jar. Pour in the cool salt water. Seal the jar and leave for only three weeks. If you leave them any longer they will get too salty. Salted eggs will last for up to two months in their jar. Drain and use as required: boil the eggs, then scoop out the yolks and discard the whites.

CUCUMBER RELISH

CUCUMBER RELISH

4 tablespoons rice vinegar
125 g (½ cup) sugar
1 small red chilli, seeded and chopped
1 teaspoon fish sauce
80 g (½ cup) peanuts, lightly roasted and roughly chopped
1 Lebanese cucumber, unpeeled, seeded, finely diced

MAKES 185 G (6 OZ/¾ CUP)

PUT the vinegar and sugar in a small saucepan with 125 ml (4 fl oz/½ cup) of water. Bring to the boil, then reduce heat and simmer for 5 minutes.

ALLOW to cool before stirring in the chilli, fish sauce, peanuts and cucumber.

SALTED EGGS

CHILLI JAM

FROM THAILAND

CHILLI JAM

oil, for frying
20 Asian shallots, sliced
10 garlic cloves, sliced

3 tablespoons dried shrimp
7 dried long red chillies, chopped
3 tablespoons tamarind purée or
  3 tablespoons lime juice
6 tablespoons palm sugar (jaggery)
1 teaspoon shrimp paste

MAKES 250 G (8 OZ/1 CUP)

HEAT the oil in a wok or saucepan. Fry the shallots and garlic together until golden, then transfer from the wok to a blender or food processor.

FRY the dried shrimp and chillies for 1–2 minutes, then add these to the blender along with the remaining ingredients and blend. Add as much of the frying oil as necessary to make a paste that you can pour.

PUT the paste back in a clean saucepan and bring to a boil. Reduce the heat and simmer until thick. Be careful because if you overcook this you will end up with a caramelised lump. Season sauce with salt or fish sauce.

CHILLI jam is used as base for recipes, especially stir-fries, as well as a seasoning or accompaniment. It will keep for several months in an airtight jar in the refrigerator.

GARLIC AND CHILLI SAUCE

ROAST CHILLI SAUCE

90 ml (3 fl oz/⅓ cup) oil
2 Asian shallots, finely chopped
2 garlic cloves, finely chopped
40 g (1½ oz) dried chilli flakes
¼ teaspoon palm sugar (jaggery)

MAKES 185 G (6 OZ/¾ CUP)

HEAT the oil in a small saucepan and fry the shallots and garlic until brown. Add the chilli flakes and palm sugar and stir well. Season with a pinch of salt.

USE as a dipping sauce or accompaniment. The sauce can be stored in a jar in the refrigerator for several weeks.

GARLIC AND CHILLI SAUCE

4 garlic cloves, finely chopped
3 bird's eye chillies, mixed red and
  green, stems removed, lightly
  crushed
2 tablespoons lime juice
1 tablespoon fish sauce
1 teaspoon sugar

MAKES 125 ML (4 FL OZ/½ CUP)

COMBINE all the ingredients in a small bowl.

THE sauce can be stored in a jar in the refrigerator for several weeks.

ROAST CHILLI SAUCE

FROM JAPAN

THREE WAYS WITH DASHI

SO ESSENTIAL IS DASHI BROTH TO JAPANESE COOKERY THAT IT IS OFTEN RIGHTFULLY CALLED THE SOUL OF JAPANESE CUISINE. DASHI FORMS THE BASE OF MANY JAPANESE SOUPS, IS USED TO SIMMER VEGETABLES AND DILUTES AND FLAVOURS DRESSINGS. INSTANT DASHI GRANULES CAN BE A TIME-SAVING SUBSTITUTE.

DASHI I

10 cm (4 inch) square piece of konbu

20 g (½ oz/1 cup) katsuobushi (bonito flakes)

MAKES ABOUT 1 LITRE (35 FL OZ/4 CUPS)

WIPE the konbu with a damp cloth but do not rub off the white powdery substance that will become obvious as it dries. Cut the konbu into strips. Place the konbu and 1.5 litres (52 fl oz/6 cups) cold water into a saucepan and slowly bring to the boil, then remove the konbu. Quickly add 60 ml (2 fl oz/¼ cup) cold water to stop the boiling process. Add bonito flakes, then allow it to return to the boil. Remove from the heat. Allow bonito flakes to sink to the bottom of the pan, then strain the liquid through a fine sieve. This stock is now ready for making clear soups.

DASHI I

DASHI II

10 cm (4 inch) square piece of konbu

20 g (½ oz/1 cup) katsuobushi (bonito flakes)

MAKES ABOUT 1 LITRE (35 FL OZ/4 CUPS)

WIPE the konbu with a damp cloth but do not rub off the white powdery substance that will become obvious as it dries. Cut the konbu into strips. Place the konbu and 1.5 litres (52 fl oz/6 cups) cold water into a saucepan and slowly bring to the boil. Quickly add 60 ml (2 fl oz/¼ cup) cold water to stop the boiling process. Add the bonito flakes, then allow it to return to the boil and simmer for 15 minutes. Remove from the heat. Allow the bonito flakes to sink to the bottom of the pan then strain the liquid through a fine sieve. This stock is now ready for stews and thick soups.

DASHI II

KONBU DASHI

15 cm (6 inch) square piece of konbu

MAKES 1.25 LITRES (43 FL OZ/5 CUPS)

FOR konbu dashi I, cut the konbu into strips and place in a saucepan with 1.5 litres (52 fl oz/6 cups) cold water. Bring to the boil, then remove konbu.

FOR konbu dashi II, leave the konbu in the pot, reduce to a simmer and cook 10 minutes longer.

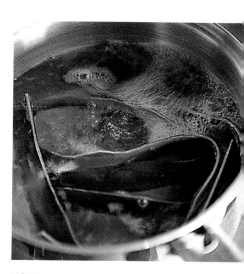

KONBU DASHI

PONZU

SESAME SEED SAUCE

TEMPURA DIPPING SAUCE

THREE WAYS WITH SAUCES

JAPANESE SAUCES ARE TYPICALLY LIGHT, AND ARE APPLIED WITH A LIGHT HAND TOO. SAUCES NEVER OVERWHELM THE NATURAL FLAVOURS AND TEXTURES OF THE FOODS THEMSELVES, BUT SERVE AS AN ACCENT TO THEM.

PONZU

1 tablespoon lemon juice
1 tablespoon lime juice
1 tablespoon rice vinegar
60 ml (2 fl oz/¼ cup) Japanese soy sauce
1 tablespoon mirin
60 ml (2 fl oz/¼ cup) sake
1 teaspoon sugar
4 cm (1½ inch) square piece of konbu
1 tablespoon katsuobushi (bonito flakes)

MAKES ABOUT 250 ML
(9 FL OZ/1 CUP)

WIPE the konbu with a damp cloth but do not rub off the white powdery substance that will become obvious as it dries. Cut the konbu into strips. Place all ingredients in a non-metallic bowl and stir until the sugar is dissolved. Cover with plastic wrap and refridgerate for 24 hours. Strain through muslin or a fine sieve before using.

SESAME SEED SAUCE

100 g (3½ oz/⅔ cup) sesame seeds
2 teaspoons oil
125 ml (4 fl oz/½ cup) shoyu (Japanese soy sauce)
2 tablespoons mirin
3 teaspoons caster (superfine) sugar
½ teaspoon dashi granules
125 ml (4 fl oz/½ cup) warm water

MAKES ABOUT 435 ML
(15¼ FL OZ/1¾ CUPS)

Toast the sesame seeds in a dry frying pan over medium heat for 3–4 minutes, shaking the pan gently, until the seeds are golden brown. Remove from the pan at once to prevent burning. Grind the seeds using a mortar and pestle or a suribachi (Japanese ribbed mortar) until a paste is formed. Add oil, if necessary, to assist in forming a paste. Mix the paste with shoyu (Japanese soy sauce), mirin, caster (superfine) sugar, dashi granules and 125 ml (4 fl oz/½ cup) warm water. Store, covered, in the refrigerator and use within 2 days of preparation.

TEMPURA DIPPING SAUCE

310 ml (10 fl oz/1¼ cups) dashi II
60 ml (2 fl oz/¼ cup) mirin
80 ml (⅓ cup) Japanese soy sauce

MAKES 685 ML
(23 FL OZ/2¾ CUPS)

COMBINE all the ingredients in a small saucepan and bring to the boil over high heat. Reduce the heat to low and keep warm until ready to serve.

FROM CHINA

SOY AND VINEGAR DIPPING SAUCE

125 ml (4 fl oz/½ cup) light soy
    sauce
3 tablespoons Chinese black
    rice vinegar

MAKES 225 ML
    (ABOUT 8 FL OZ/1 CUP)

COMBINE the soy sauce and vinegar with
2 tablespoons water in a small bowl, then
divide among individual dipping bowls.

SOY AND VINEGAR DIPPING
SAUCE

SOY, VINEGAR AND CHILLI DIPPING SAUCE

125 ml (4 fl oz/½ cup) light soy
    sauce
2 tablespoons Chinese black
    rice vinegar
2 red chillies, thinly sliced

MAKES 200 ML
    (ABOUT 7 FL OZ/¾ CUP)

COMBINE the soy sauce, vinegar and chilli in a
small bowl, then divide among individual dipping
bowls.

SOY, VINEGAR AND CHILLI
DIPPING SAUCE

RED VINEGAR DIPPING SAUCE

125 ml (4 fl oz/½ cup) red rice
    vinegar
3 tablespoons shredded ginger

MAKES 225 ML
    (ABOUT 8 FL OZ/1 CUP)

COMBINE the rice vinegar, 2½ tablespoons water
and the ginger in a small bowl, then divide among
individual dipping bowls.

SOY, CHILLI AND SESAME DIPPING SAUCE

125 ml (4 fl oz/½ cup) light soy
    sauce
2½ tablespoons chilli oil
1 tablespoon roasted sesame oil
1 spring onion (scallion), finely
    chopped

MAKES 200 ML
    (ABOUT 7 FL OZ/ ¾ CUP)

COMBINE the soy sauce, chilli oil, sesame oil
and spring onion in a small bowl, then divide
among individual dipping bowls.

SOY, CHILLI AND SESAME
DIPPING SAUCE

RED VINEGAR DIPPING SAUCE

FROM CHINA

SPICY SALT AND PEPPER

1 tablespoon salt
2 teaspoons ground Sichuan
  peppercorns
1 teaspoon five-spice powder

MAKES 2 TABLESPOONS

COMBINE the salt, Sichuan peppercorns and five-spice powder. Dry-fry over low heat, stirring constantly, for 2–3 minutes, or until aromatic. This mix can be used as an ingredient or as a dipping condiment for roast duck or chicken.

SPICY SALT AND PEPPER

CHILLI SAUCE

1 kg (2 lb 4 oz) red chillies,
  stalks removed
3 teaspoons salt
4 tablespoons sugar
170 ml (6 fl oz/²⁄₃ cup) clear rice
  vinegar

MAKES 400 ML (ABOUT 1 ½ CUPS)

PUT the chillies in a saucepan with 5 tablespoons water, cover and bring to the boil. Cook until the chillies are tender, then add the salt, sugar and vinegar. Blend the mixture to a paste in a blender or food processor, or push through a sieve. Store in the fridge for up to 1 month or freeze in small portions. Use as an ingredient or dipping sauce.

CHILLI OIL

CHILLI OIL

50 g (1¾ oz) dried chilli flakes
125 ml (4 fl oz/½ cup) oil
60 ml (2 fl oz/ ¼ cup) roasted
  sesame oil

MAKES 200 ML
  (ABOUT 6 FL OZ/¾ CUP)

PUT the chilli in a heatproof bowl. Put the oils in a saucepan and heat until they are very hot but not smoking. Pour onto chilli and leave to cool. Try not to breathe in the fumes. When cool, transfer to a jar. Store in fridge for up to 6 months. The oil can be used as a flavouring, and chilli at the bottom of the jar can be used instead of fresh chilli.

GINGER JUICE

GINGER JUICE

200 g (7 oz) young ginger

MAKES ABOUT 60 ML
  (2 FL OZ/¼ CUP)

GRATE the ginger as finely as you can, collecting any juice. Combine the ginger with an equal volume of cold water and place it in a piece of muslin, twist the top hard and squeeze out as much juice as possible. Alternatively, push the ginger through a juicer, then combine with an equal quantity of cold water. Use as an ingredient.

CHICKEN AND MEAT STOCK

650 g (1 lb 7 oz) chicken
  carcasses, necks, pinions and
  feet
650 g (1 lb 7 oz) pork spare ribs
4 spring onions (scallions), each tied
  into a knot
12 slices ginger, smashed with the
  flat side of a cleaver
4 litres (16 cups) water
80 ml (⅓ cup) Shaoxing rice wine
2 teaspoons salt

MAKES 3 LITRES (12 CUPS)

REMOVE any excess fat from the chicken and
meat, then chop into large pieces and place in a
stockpot with the spring onions, ginger and water
and bring to the boil. Reduce the heat and simmer
gently for 3½–4 hours, skimming the surface to
remove any impurities.

STRAIN through a fine strainer, removing the
solids, and skim the surface to remove any fat.
Return to the pot with the rice wine and salt. Bring
to the boil and simmer for 3–4 minutes. Store in
the fridge for up to 3 days or freeze in small
portions.

CHICKEN AND MEAT STOCK

CHICKEN STOCK

1.5 kg (3 lb 5 oz) chicken
  carcasses, necks, pinions and
  feet
250 ml (8 fl oz/1 cup) Shaoxing rice
  wine
6 slices ginger, smashed with the
  flat side of a cleaver
6 spring onions (scallions), ends
  trimmed, smashed with the flat
  side of a cleaver
4 litres (140 fl oz/16 cups) water

MAKES 3 LITRES
  (105 FL OZ/12 CUPS)

REMOVE any excess fat from the chicken, then
chop into large pieces and place in a stockpot
with the rice wine, ginger, spring onions and water
and bring to the boil. Reduce the heat and simmer
gently for 3 hours, skimming the surface to remove
any impurities.

STRAIN through a fine strainer, removing the
solids, and skim the surface to remove any fat.
If the stock is too weak, reduce it further.
Store in the fridge for up to 3 days or freeze in
small portions.

VEGETABLE STOCK

500 g (1 lb 2 oz) fresh soya
  bean sprouts
10 dried Chinese mushrooms
6 spring onions (scallions), each tied
  into a knot (optional)
4 litres (140 fl oz/16 cups) water
3 tablespoons Shaoxing rice wine
2 teaspoons salt

MAKES 3 LITRES
  (105 FL OZ/12 CUPS)

DRY-FRY the sprouts in a wok for 3–4 minutes.
Place the sprouts, mushrooms, spring onions and
water in a stockpot and bring to the boil. Reduce
the heat and simmer for 1 hour.

STRAIN through a fine strainer, removing the solids
(keep the mushrooms for another use). Return to
the pot with the rice wine and salt. Bring to the boil
and simmer for 3–4 minutes. Store in the fridge for
up to 3 days or freeze in small portions.

VEGETABLE STOCK

GLOSSARY OF ASIAN FOOD AND COOKING

Abura-age Deep-fried sheets of tofu. *See page 22.*

agar-agar Is a setting agent made from certain types of seaweed. It is sold as strips, sheets, flakes or powder, dissolves in boiling water, and unlike gelatin will set at room temperature.

ajowan A spice that looks like miniature cumin seeds and has a similar aroma but stronger flavour. Use sparingly.

amaranth A leafy green vegetable. *See page 280.*

amchoor/amchur powder A fine beige powder made by drying green mangoes.

anko A sweet bean paste made by slow-cooking adzuki beans in a sugar syrup.

asafoetida This yellowish powder or lump of resin is made from the dried latex of a type of fennel. Asafoetida has an extremely pungent smell which has earned it the name 'devil's dung'. It is used to make pulses and legumes more digestible and Hindu Brahmins and Jains use it instead of garlic and onions which are forbidden to them. Asafoetida is always fried to calm its aroma. *See page 306.*

asian shallots Small reddish-purple shallots used in South-East Asia. French shallots can be used instead.

atta Sometimes called *chapati flour*, this is made from finely ground whole durum wheat. Atta is much finer and softer than wholemeal flour so if you can't find it, use half wholemeal and half maida or plain (all-purpose) flour.

bamboo shoots The young, pale shoots of certain types of bamboo, which have a mellow flavour. The fresh ones require some preparation before use, but the precooked, tinned ones are easier because they can be used as they are. *See page 146.*

banana flower or blossom The purple, teardrop-shaped flower of the banana plant. The purple leaves and pale yellow buds that grow between them are discarded. Only the inner pale core is eaten and this needs to be blanched in boiling water to remove any bitterness. It is advisable to wear rubber gloves to prepare banana flower as it has a gummy substance that can stain.

banana leaves Large green leaves, which can be used as a wrapping (dip briefly in boiling water or put in a hot oven for 10 seconds to soften them before use) for foods, or to line plates. Young leaves are preferable.

bean sprouts These can be sprouted mung or soya beans. Soya bean sprouts are bigger and more robust, but the two are usually interchangeable.

bean thread noodles Are not true noodles, these are made from mung bean starch and are also labelled as cellophane or glass noodles. They come as vermicelli or as slightly thicker strands and need to be soaked. They have no flavour of their own but soak up flavourings when they are cooked with ingredients.

besan Also known as *gram flour*, is a yellow flour made from ground Bengal gram or chickpeas. It has a nutty flavour and is used as a thickener in curries, as well as in batters, dumplings, sweets and breads.

betel leaves Known also as *piper leaves* or *wild tea leaves*, these are not true betel but are a close relative. They are used to wrap some snacks. Use baby spinach leaves if you can't get betel leaves.

bitter melon Looks like a pale cucumber with a warty skin. The flesh is bitter and needs to be blanched or degorged, then married with strong flavours.

black fungus Also known as *wood* or *cloud ears*, this is a cultivated wood fungus, which is dried. When reconstituted, it expands to up to five times its original size. It is used in recipes for both its colour and slightly crunchy, rubbery texture.

black salt A rock salt mined in central India. Available as black or dark brown lumps, or ground to a pinkish grey powder. Unlike white salt, it has a tangy, smoky flavour.

black sugar A dark brown sugar with a rich molasses flavour, usually sold in small rough lumps or rocks. It is commonly used to make a syrup, which is sometimes available pre-prepared. Crush the lumps before use.

black-eyed beans Also called *black-eyed peas*, these are actually dried cow peas and are also known as *chowli dal* when split. Buff-coloured beans with a small dark eye on one side, they need to be soaked overnight or pre-cooked before use. Avoid dark or wrinkled beans as they are old.

bok choy Also called a *little Chinese white cabbage*, this is a mild, open-leaved cabbage with a fat white or pale-green stem and dark-green leaves.

cardamom Dry green pods full of sticky, tiny brown or black seeds which have a sweet flavour and pungent aroma. If you need ground cardamom, open the pods and grind the seeds. Ready-ground cardamom quickly loses flavour. Use pods whole or crushed.

cassia The bark of the cassia tree is similar to cinnamon (which can be used instead), though cassia has a more woody flavour. It is used as a flavouring, especially in braises, and is a component of five-spice powder.

cayenne pepper A very hot red chilli powder made from sun-dried red chillies.

chaat masala Seasoning used for various snacks known as *chaat* (which means 'to lick' in Hindi). The spice blend uses a variety of flavourings including asafoetida, amchoor, black salt, cumin, cayenne, ajowan and pepper.

chana dal Also known as *gram lentils*. These are husked, split, polished, yellow Bengal gram, the most common type of gram lentil in India. They are often cooked with a pinch of asafoetida to make them more easy to digest.

chickpeas Chickpeas *(chana)* come white or black. White chickpeas are actually a tan colour and the black ones are dark brown. Usually sold whole, but also sold split, dried chickpeas need to be soaked for 8 hours in cold water before use. They will double in size. Tinned ones can be used but need to be added at the end of the cooking time as they are already very soft.

chilli bean paste Made from broad beans fermented with chillies and salt to give a browny-red sauce, this is an important ingredient in Sichuan cooking. Other pastes, called hot or Sichuan bean pastes, can be substituted. It is hard to judge their heat, so take care when adding a new one to a recipe.

chilli flakes Dried, coarsely ground chillies with the seeds included – usually hot.

chilli jam A thick, sweet chilli relish that can also be used as a sauce.

chilli oil A condiment made by pouring smoking hot oil over chilli flakes and seeds.

chilli powder A wide variety of chillies are dried and crushed to make chilli powders. Some, such as Kashmiri chilli powder and paprika, are used for colour, whereas others like cayenne are used for heat. Don't use chilli powder indiscriminately. The amount used can be varied, to taste, so start with a small amount and determine how hot it is.

chilli sauce Made from fresh chillies and a variety of other ingredients, such as garlic and vinegar, the thicker version is good for cooking and the thinner for a dipping sauce.

chillies Red and green chillies are widely used in Asian cuisine. Recipes generally give a colour, rather than a variety. Many varieties are grown throughout Asia.

chillies, dried Dried whole chillies of various shapes, sizes and heat levels. Sometimes soaked to soften them. Remove the seeds if they are very hot.

Chinese broccoli This has dark-green stalks and leaves and tiny florets.

Chinese cabbage A white cabbage also known as *Chinese leaf, Tianjin, Beijing, napa cabbage,* or *wong bok.* There are two main types: one is long with pale-green leaves and a thick white stem, while the other is pale yellow with curlier leaves and a rounder shape.

Chinese curry powder A strong and spicy version of five-spice powder, with additional spices including turmeric and coriander, which lend the curry flavour.

Chinese shrimp paste Very pungent pulverised shrimp. Refrigerate after opening.

Chinese turnip Looking like a huge white carrot, this is actually a type of radish. It has a crisp, juicy flesh and mild radish flavour. The Japanese name is *daikon.*

choy sum A green vegetable with tender pale-green stalks, small yellow flowers and dark-green leaves. It has a mild flavour and is often just blanched and eaten with a simple flavouring like garlic or oyster sauce.

cloves The dried, unopened flower buds of the clove tree. Brown and nail-shaped, they have a pungent flavour and should be used in moderation. Use cloves whole or ground.

coconut milk powder A powdered form of coconut which when mixed with water makes coconut milk or cream.

coconut sugar Is made from the sap from coconut trees. Dark brown in colour, it is mainly used in sweet dishes. Palm sugar or unrefined soft brown sugar can be used instead.

coriander *(dhaniya)* seeds The round seeds of the coriander plant. The seeds have a spicy aroma. To intensify the flavour, dry-roast the seeds until aromatic, before crushing them. Best freshly ground for each dish. Available whole or ground.

coriander Fresh coriander *(cilantro)* leaves are used in recipes and as a colourful garnish. The roots are chopped or ground and used in curry pastes and sauces. Buy bunches that have healthy green leaves and avoid any that are yellowing.

creamed coconut A solid block of coconut cream which needs to be reconstituted with water, or can be added straight to a dish to give a strong coconut flavour. Slice pieces off the block as required.

cumin The elongated ridged seeds of a plant of the parsley family, these have a peppery, slightly bitter flavour and are used in some curry pastes. To intensify the flavour, dry-roast the seeds before crushing them. Best freshly ground for each dish. Available whole or ground. *See page 68.*

curry leaves Smallish green aromatic leaves of a tree native to India and Sri Lanka. They are usually fried and added to the dish or used as a garnish at the end.

curry pastes All curry pastes are ground and pounded together in a pestle and mortar until they are very smooth. *See page 216.*

curry powder Usually bought ready-made as it is not widely used except in a few stir-fries, marinades, sauces and in curry puffs.

daikon A mildly flavoured giant white radish. It is an important staple of the Japanese diet. Raw daikon is finely grated for dipping sauces or dressings and shredded for salads. Daikon is believed to aid the digestion of oily foods. Daikon can have a pungent aroma, not dissimilar to cabbage, when cooked and it can become bitter with age. The leaves can be used in stir-fries or soups. Daikon has a high water content and is very porous. To store daikon, wrap it with plastic wrap and refrigerate to prevent from drying out.

dal *(dhal)* Is used to describe not only an ingredient but a dish made from it. In India, dal relates to any type of dried split pea, bean or lentil. The cooking times vary as do the texture and flavour. A dal dish can be a thin soup or more like a stew. All dal should be rinsed before use.

dashi granules Made from konbu and katsuobushi and available also in powder form, this is an instant version of the essential Japanese stock, dashi.

dried shrimp These are tiny, orange, saltwater shrimps that have been dried in the sun. They come in different sizes and the really small ones have their heads and shells still attached. Dried shrimp need to be soaked in water or rice wine to soften them before use and are used as a seasoning, not as a main ingredient.

dumpling wrappers Also called *Shanghai wrappers, wheat dumpling skins, gow gee wrapper* or *egg dumpling skins,* they are white and can be round or square.

edamame Young soya beans in the pod, available fresh when in season, otherwise frozen.

egg noodles come fresh and dried in varying thicknesses. In recipes they are interchangeable, so choose a brand that you like and buy the thickness appropriate to the dish you are making.

eggplant There are lots of varieties of eggplant *(aubergine)* used in Asian cuisine and, unlike in the West, bitterness is a prized quality. Common eggplants include *Thai eggplant* which are pale green, orange, purple, yellow or white and golf-ball sized. *Long eggplant* are long, skinny and green. *Pea eggplant* are tiny, bitter and look like large peas. Cut eggplant using a stainless steel knife and store in salted water to prevent them from turning black.

enoki mushroom A Japanese mushroom with a long, thin white stem and tiny white cap. Enoki mushrooms grow in clumps and can be pulled apart quite easily. They require very little cooking and can be eaten raw in salads.

fennel seeds The dried seeds of a Mediterranean plant, fennel seeds are oval, greenish yellow, with ridges running along them, and look like large cumin. Used as an aromatic and a digestive. To intensify the flavour, dry-roast the seeds before crushing them. Available whole or ground. Best freshly ground.

fenugreek seeds Not a true seed, but a dried legume. Ochre in colour and almost square, with a groove down one side, fenugreek has a curry aroma (it is a major ingredient in commercial curry powders) and is best dry-roasted for a few seconds before use. Don't brown them too much or they will be bitter.

fermented tofu A marinated tofu that is either red, coloured with red rice, or white, and may also be flavoured with chilli. It is sometimes called preserved tofu or tofu cheese and is used as a condiment or flavouring.

fish sauce Made from salted anchovy-like fish that are left to break down naturally in the heat, fish sauce is literally the liquid that is drained off. It varies in quality.

five-spice powder A Chinese mixed spice generally made with star anise, cassia, Sichuan pepper, fennel seeds and cloves, which gives a balance of sweet, hot and aromatic flavours

flat cabbage Is a type of bok choy. It looks like a giant flower with shiny, dark-green leaves that grow out flat.

galangal or galingale A rhizome, similar to ginger, used extensively in Thai cooking, usually in place of ginger.

garam masala A northern Indian spice mix which means 'warming spice mix', it mostly contains coriander, cumin, cardamom, black pepper, cloves, cinnamon and nutmeg. There are many versions and you can buy ready-ground mixes or make your own. Garam masala is usually added to meat dishes as a final seasoning.

garlic Usually smashed with the side of a cleaver rather than being crushed before use. Deep-fried garlic is used as a garnish as is garlic oil. Deep-fried garlic can be bought in jars.

garlic chives *(Chinese chives)* Have a long, flat leaf and are green and very garlicky, or yellow with a milder taste. Flowering chives are round-stemmed with a flower at the top, which can be eaten. Both are used as a vegetable rather than a herb.

ghee A highly clarified butter made from cow or water buffalo milk. Ghee can be heated to a high temperature without burning and has an aromatic flavour. Vegetable ghees are also available but don't have the same aromatic qualities. You can substitute clarified butter, or make your own ghee by melting unsalted butter in a saucepan, bringing it to a simmer and cooking it for about 30 minutes to evaporate out any water. Skim any scum off the surface, then drain the ghee off, leaving the white sediment behind. Leave to cool.

ginger Fresh young ginger should have a smooth, pinkish beige skin and be firm and juicy. As it ages, the skin toughens and the flesh becomes more fibrous. Avoid old ginger which is wrinkled as it will be tough. Ginger is often measured in centimetre (inch) pieces.

gingko nuts Not strictly a nut, this is the very small and pale yellow fruit of the Ginkgo biloba tree. Fresh ginkgo nuts have a crisp shell that must be removed. The pre-prepared tinned, frozen or vacuum-packed nuts are easier to use than the fresh. Cooked ginkgo nuts have a creamy, nutty flavour and slightly chewy texture.

gobo The long root of edible burdock. Found fresh in season with a very thin brown skin that needs to be lightly scraped off to reveal the cream-coloured flesh. It is also available pre-scraped, cut and frozen ready for use. It has a wonderful earthy flavour and is great in soups and simmered dishes. Gobo is high in dietary fibre and is believed to aid digestion.

guilin chilli sauce From the southwest of China, this sauce is made from salted, fermented yellow soya beans and chillies. If it is unavailable, use a thick chilli sauce instead.

harusame Also called *spring rain noodles*. These are very thin, clear noodles of Chinese origin, usually made from mung bean starch, but sometimes made from potato starch or sweet potato starch. They are popular in stews, hotpots and soups and are sometimes finely chopped as a coating for fried foods because they puff up and turn white when they hit the hot oil.

hoisin sauce This sauce is made from salted, yellow soya beans, sugar, vinegar, sesame oil, red rice for colouring and spices such as five-spice or star anise. It is generally used as a dipping sauce, for meat glazes or in barbecue marinades.

Holy basil Is either red or green with slightly pointed, variegated leaves. *See page 228.*

ichimi togarashi This is a chilli powder made from the dried togarashi chilli, a hot red Japanese pepper. It is used predominantly for sprinkling over soups, noodles and simmered dishes.

inari abura-age Are sheets of tofu that have been simmered in a sweet soy broth. These prepared sheets are used to make inarizushi.

Indian bay leaves These are the dried leaves of the cassia tree. They look somewhat like dried European bay leaves but they have a cinnamon flavour.

jackfruit A large spiky fruit with segmented flesh enclosing large stones. It tastes like fruit salad and is used unripe in curries.

jaggery Made from sugar cane, this is a raw sugar with a caramel flavour and alcoholic aroma. Jaggery, which is sold in lumps, is slightly sticky and varies in colour depending on the juice from which it is made. Jaggery can also refer to palm sugar. Soft brown sugar can be used as a substitute.

Japanese curry powder A flavoursome, aromatic curry powder available in varying degrees of heat. It can be substituted with Indian curry powder.

Japanese mayonnaise It has a slightly salty–sweet egg flavour and contains soya bean oil. The most superior brand is called variously QP, kyuupii or kewpie mayonnaise. *See page 357.*

Japanese mustard Looks and tastes a little like English mustard but is hotter and spicier. It should be used sparingly. Serve as a condiment or add to dressings.

Japanese rice vinegar *(komesu)* Made from vinegar and a natural rice extract, this slightly sweet and refreshing vinegar is less sharp than other types. Used in dressings and marinades. Choose a Japanese brand when cooking Japanese food.

Japanese short-grain rice A short-grained rice with a high starch content. When cooked, the rice is a little sticky, but still firm to the bite.

Japanese soy sauce *(shoyu)* Available in heavy and light varieties, the heavy is less salty and slightly sweeter than light. Light soy sauce is more often used in cooking and the heavy is more often used as an accompaniment. They are suitable substitutes for each other.

jujubes Also known as *Chinese dates*. They are an olive-sized dried fruit with a red, wrinkled skin. They need to be soaked and are used in eight-treasure or tonic-type dishes. They are thought to be lucky because of their red colour.

kalonji *(nigella seeds)* Small teardrop-shaped black seeds with an onion flavour, used both as a spice in northern India and as a decoration for breads such as naan.

kamaboko A small white loaf of steamed fish paste, made from the flesh of a variety of fish, processed with starch to help hold its shape. It comes attached to a small wooden board and is sometimes tinted bright pink. It should be sliced before eating and requires little cooking to warm through. Usually added at the end of cooking to simmered dishes. It can also be grilled (broiled).

kanpyo The pale flesh of a bottle-shaped gourd, cut into long thin strips, then dried. It must be fully rehydrated before use and, as it has little flavour of its own, should be cooked with other flavours, which it readily absorbs. Prepared kanpyo has been simmered in a sweet soy-based sauce ready for use in various sushi or as an appetiser with drinks or even as an edible tie for bundles of vegetables in vegetarian cuisine.

Kashmiri chilli powder Made from ground red Kashmiri chillies which have a deep red colour but little heat. A mild, dark red chilli powder can be substituted.

katakuriko A starch made from a plant called *Japanese dog tooth violet*. It is valued for the way it thickens sauces, resulting in a smooth, clear sauce. It also makes for a crispy coating on deep-fried foods. It can be quite expensive so is often substituted with potato starch.

katsuobushi *(bonito flakes)* The dried, smoked and cured flesh of the bonito, a member of the tuna family. It has a strong aroma but a smoky mellow flavour. It is usually shaved into large flakes before using as a base for home-made dashi or shaved into smaller flakes for garnishing. *See page 403.*

ketchap manis A thick, sweet soy sauce used as a flavouring.

kokum The dried purple fruit of the gamboge tree which is used in southern Indian, Gujarati and Maharashtran cuisine to impart an acid fruity flavour. Kokum looks like dried pieces of purple/black rind and is quite sticky. It can be bought from Indian food shops and is sometimes called cocumful. A smoked version which is called *kodampodli* is also available. Kokum needs to be briefly soaked before use.

konbu *(kombu)* A dried kelp essential for making dashi. It can turn bitter if cooked for very long so it is often simply soaked overnight to add flavour to cooking liquid. Tasting of the sea and packed full of vitamins and minerals, dried konbu strips can be grilled, deep-fried or simmered in sweet soy sauce as a healthy snack food. Konbu comes covered with a white powdery substance. Wipe with a damp cloth to remove any grit, but do not wash.

konnyaku A gelatinous paste made from the starchy root of the konjac plant, it is formed either into blocks or 'noodles' called *shirataki*. It comes in white or speckled grey. It has little flavour or nutritional value but no fat and, as it readily absorbs surrounding flavours, it is often used as a bulking ingredient or for texture. Commonly used in simmered dishes and sometimes salads, it should always be boiled before eating.

kuzu A high-quality thickening starch made from the *kudzu* or *kuzu vine*. It is added to sauces to help them glaze well, used to set foods and even to make certain noodles. It comes as a powder or as small rocks, which should be crushed before use. It is often labelled, or substituted with, arrowroot. *See page 191.*

lemongrass The fibrous stalk of a citrus perfumed grass, it is finely chopped or sliced or cut into chunks. Discard the outer layers until you reach a softer purple layer.

lemon basil Is also called *mint basil*. It is less common and is used in curries and stir-fries and as a condiment with rice noodles.

longans From the same family as lychees, these are round with smooth, buff-coloured skins, translucent sweet flesh and large brown pips. Available fresh, tinned or dried.

lotus leaves The dried leaves of the lotus, they need to be soaked before use and are used for wrapping up food like sticky rice to hold it together while it is cooking.

lotus root A rhizome with a crisp texture and a delicate, fresh flavour. It has small holes through the centre and, when sliced, looks like a flower. Once sliced, submerge it in vinegared water so it does not discolour. Fresh lotus root needs to be cooked before eating. It is also available peeled, thickly sliced and frozen, and in vacuum packs.

lotus seeds These seeds from the lotus are considered medicinal and are used in eight-treasure dishes as well as being roasted, salted or candied and eaten as a snack. Lotus seeds are also made into a sweet paste to fill buns and pancakes. Fresh and dried lotus seeds are both available and dried seeds need to be soaked before use.

lychees Small round fruit with a red leathery skin and translucent white flesh surrounding a brown stone.

maida Plain white flour used for making naan and other Indian recipes. Plain (all-purpose) flour is a suitable substitute.

makrut (kaffir) limes These knobbly skinned fruit are used for their zest rather than their bitter juice. Leaves are double leaves with a fragrant citrus oil. They are used very finely shredded or torn into large pieces. Frozen leaves are available but less fragrant than fresh ones. *See page 116.*

maltose A sweet liquid of malted grains used to coat Peking duck and barbecued meats. Honey can be used instead.

masoor dal (red lentils) When whole (known as *matki* or *bagali*) these are dark brown or green. When split, they are salmon in colour. The split ones are the most common as they cook more easily and do not usually need soaking as the whole ones do.

methi (fenugreek leaves) The leaves of young fenugreek plants, these are used as a vegetable and treated much like spinach. They have a mildly bitter flavour. Strip the leaves off the stalks as the stalks are often tough. English spinach leaves can be used but will not give the same flavour. Available fresh or dried.

mirin A sweet spirit-based rice liquid sometimes referred to as sweet rice wine. It is manufactured for use in cooling rather than drinking. It is commonly used in sauces, dressing and marinades. Look for bottles labelled *hon mirin* 'true mirin'. *See page 64.*

miso A rich, earthy paste made from fermented soya beans. There are different grades and colours of miso. Generally, the lighter the colour, the sweeter and less salty the taste. The base flavour in miso soup, it is also added to other dishes. The names are a little misleading as white miso (*shiromiso*) is pale gold, while red miso (*akamiso*) is a mid caramel colour with a reddish tinge. Brands can vary in colour and quality and be confusingly labelled. Since white and red miso can look quite similar, compare the colours when you are buying them. *Shinshu* is an all-purpose yellowish miso that makes a good substitute in most circumstances. *Hatcho miso* is dark reddish brown with a very strong, salty flavour and should be used sparingly. Don't confuse it with red miso. *See page 95.*

mitsuba (trefoil/Japanese parsley) Is a long thin-stemmed herb with three leaves,

resembling coriander (*cilantro*) or flat-leaf (*Italian*) parsley. It has a fresh, lightly peppery flavour similar to chervil and cucumber and is used predominantly in soups and salads. If not in season, it can be substituted with flat-leaf parsley.

mizuna A large-leafed peppery herb with slight mustardy flavour, used in salads and sometimes added to simmered dishes. If not in season it can sometimes be substituted with rocket (*arugula*).

moong dal Split and skinned mung beans, which are pale yellow. The dal does not always need to be soaked. Whole mung beans must be soaked before use.

mung bean starch noodles Are very thin white translucent noodles that go clear when soaked. They are much tougher than rice noodles.

mushrooms Straw mushrooms are usually found tinned except in Asia. Replace them with oyster mushrooms if you need to. Shiitake are used both fresh and dried. Dried ones need to be soaked in boiling water before they are used. The soaking liquid can be used to add flavour to dishes.

mustard oil Made from pressed brown mustard seeds, this is a strongly flavoured oil. Usually preheated to smoking point and then cooled to temper its strong aroma.

mustard seeds Yellow, brown and black mustard seeds are used in Indian cooking. Brown and black are interchangeable. The seeds are either added to hot oil to pop, to make them taste nutty rather than hot, or are ground to a paste before use in which case they are still hot. Split mustard seeds are called *mustard dal*.

nashi A type of round Japanese pear with firm, sweet flesh. The slightly rough texture of the skin can vary in colour from pale yellow–green to brown. The darker the colour, the richer the flavour of the flesh. *See page 427.*

nori Green paper-like sheets, the result of compressing and drying a particular marine algae found on the surface of the sea off Japan, China and Korea. A popular wrap for sushi and is sold in pre-cut and toasted squares specifically for this purpose. Also available in strips or flakes for garnishing other savoury foods. *See page 141.*

okra Are green, fuzzy, tapered pods with ridges running down them. When cut they give off a mucilaginous substance which disappears during cooking.

oyster sauce A fairly recent invention, this is a Cantonese speciality made with oyster extract. Add to dishes at the end of cooking or use as a dipping sauce or marinade.

palm sugar Is made by boiling sugar palm sap until it turns into a granular paste. Sold in hard cakes of varying sizes or as a slightly softer version in tubs. Unrefined, soft light brown sugar can be used instead.

panch phoron (panch phora) Meaning five spices, it contains fennel, brown mustard, kalonji, fenugreek, and cumin seeds in equal amounts. It can be used whole or ground.

pandanus leaves Long green leaves are shaped like blades and are used as a flavouring in desserts and sweets, as well as a wrapping for small parcels of food. Pandanus leaves are often sold frozen.

paneer A fresh cheese made by coagulating milk with lemon juice and leaving it to drain. It is usually pressed into a block.

panko Crisp white breadcrumbs available in fine and coarse grades. Usually larger than traditional breadcrumbs, they make a very crisp coating for deep-fried foods.

pepper Used as an ingredient rather than as a condiment, most hot dishes were originally flavoured with copious quantities of pepper rather than the chillies used now. White pepper is used rather than black.

peppercorns Green peppercorns are used fresh in curries. Dried white peppercorns are used as a seasoning in dishes and as a garnish but black pepper is seldom used.

pickled ginger Thinly sliced ginger that has turned pink in the pickling process. It has a sharp but sweet and refreshing flavour. It is used as a palate refresher and can be chopped and added to cooked dishes for flavour or as a garnish.

plum sauce This comes in several varieties, with some brands sweeter than others and some adding chilli, ginger or garlic. It is often served with Peking duck rather than the true sauce and is a good dipping sauce.

plum wine A sweet liqueur with an almond flavour. Made from ume, a Japanese apricot, which, curiously, is more often referred to as a plum. It is usually drunk neat or on the rocks but is also used as a flavouring for desserts.

pomegranate seeds Sun-dried whole or ground sour pomegranate seeds, used to add a sour, tangy flavour to north Indian dishes. They are also used as a garnish.

pomfret A silvery seawater fish with tiny black spots. Pomfret is expensive and hard to find outside India, although it is sometimes available frozen. Sole, flounder, leatherjacket or John Dory fillets can be substituted.

ponzu The name of a dressing or dipping sauce combining lemon juice with soy sauce, katsuobushi and other flavourings.

poppadom *(papadam, papad, appalam)* These are quite thin wafers made from a paste of lentil (gram) flours, rice flour or even tapioca or sago flour, which is rolled out very thin and then sun-dried. Poppadoms come in different sizes and flavours.

poppy seeds In India, white poppy seeds are used rather than European black or grey ones. They are used either whole or ground. Don't use black poppy seeds as a thickener or the colour of your dish will be greyish.

potato starch A thickening starch with similar qualities to katakuriko. It is great for thickening sauces and coating deep-fried foods to give extra crunch.

preserved ginger Ginger pickled in rice vinegar and sugar, typically used for sweet-and-sour dishes. Japanese pickled ginger could be used as a substitute.

ramen noodles Thin yellow noodles made from wheat flour and eggs. Available fresh, dried and instant.

red bean paste Made from crushed adzuki beans and sugar, this sweet paste is used in soups and to fill dumplings and pancakes.

rice flour Is finely ground rice, often used to make rice noodles. Glutinous rice flour, used for making sweet things, makes a chewier dough.

rice noodles Are made from a paste of ground rice and water and can be bought fresh or as dried rice sticks or vermicelli. Fresh noodles are white and can be bought in a roll.

rice vinegar Made from fermented rice, Chinese vinegars are milder than Western ones. Clear rice vinegar is mainly used for pickles and sweet-and-sour dishes. Red rice vinegar is a mild liquid used as a dipping sauce. Black rice vinegar is used in braises. Rice vinegars can last indefinitely but may lose their aroma, so buy small bottles. If you can't find them, use cider vinegar instead of clear and balsamic instead of black.

rosewater Made from rose essence and water, this is used to perfume sweets, desserts and drinks. It has an aroma but no flavour. Use sparingly.

saag A generic term for leafy greens.

saffron strands The dried stigmas of a crocus flower. The strands give an intense yellow colour and musky aroma. Only a few are needed for each dish.

sago Small dried balls of sago palm sap which are used for milky desserts and savoury dishes. Cooked sago is transparent and soft with a silky texture.

sake An alcoholic liquid made by fermenting cooked, ground rice mash. It has a dry flavour, somewhere between vodka and dry sherry. In its less refined form it is light amber in colour and is used in cooking. *See page 227.*

salted, fermented black beans Very salty black soya beans that are fermented using the same moulds as are used for making soy sauce. Added to dishes as a flavouring, they must be rinsed before use and are often mashed or crushed. You can also use a black bean sauce.

semolina A fine, coarse or medium grain made from processed wheat with the wheat germ removed. It swells when cooked to give a creamy, textured effect. Used for sweets and upama.

sesame oil A strongly flavoured oil extracted from roasted sesame seeds, it should be used sparingly. A spicy version infused with chilli is drizzled over noodle soups.

sesame paste Made from ground, roasted white sesame seeds, this is a fairly dry paste. It is more aromatic than tahini, which can be used instead by mixing it with a little Chinese sesame oil.

Sesame seeds Small, nutty-flavoured seeds. They are most often available in a cream colour but there is also a black variety, which is popular in Japan because of its value as a garnish. The oil-rich seeds are usually toasted to enhance the flavour before grinding to a paste for dressings or simply used as a garnish. *See page 392.*

sevian Very fine noodles made from wheat flour. They have a biscuity flavour.

Shaoxing rice wine Made from rice, millet, yeast and Shaoxing's local water, this is aged for at least 3 years, then bottled either in glass or decorative earthenware bottles. Several varieties are available. Dry sherry is the best substitute.

shichimi togarashi A spice mix containing seven different flavours. It always includes togarashi, a hot red Japanese chilli. The remaining ingredients are flexible but often include mustard, sesame seeds, poppy seeds, sansho, shiso or nori flakes.

shiitake mushroom Has a unique and relatively strong flavour. It has a flattish cap with edges that curl under. The woody stem should be discarded. Available fresh or dried. *See page 408.*

shimeji mushroom A mushroom that grows in a cluster. The cluster can be easily pulled apart to reveal individual long-stemmed, pale-coloured mushrooms with small grey–brown caps.

Sichuan peppercorns Not a true pepper, but the berries of a shrub called the prickly ash. Sichuan pepper, unlike ordinary pepper, has a pungent flavour and the aftertaste, rather than being simply hot, is numbing. The peppercorns should be crushed and dry-roasted to bring out their full flavour.

slab sugar Dark brown sugar with a caramel flavour sold in a slab. Soft brown sugar can be used instead.

snake (yard long) beans Are sold in coils or tied together in bunches. Eaten fresh and cooked. Green beans can be used instead.

soba noodles Made from buckwheat flour, they have a slightly nutty flavour. Available dried and fresh, they are sometimes flavoured with green tea and are then known as cha soba. *See page 377.*

somen noodles Fine white noodles made from wheat flour. They are usually eaten cold, often on a bed of rice, or in a light broth. Also popular in salads.

soya beans Are oval, pale-green beans. The fresh beans are cooked in their fuzzy pods and served as a snack. Dried beans can be yellow or black and need to be soaked in water overnight. *See page 236.*

split peas (matar dal) Split dried peas which need to be soaked before they are cooked and have a slightly chewy texture. Green and yellow ones are available.

spring-roll sheets Wheat and egg dough wrappers. Squares of filo can also be used.

tamarind A fruit whose flesh is used as a souring agent. Usually bought as a dried cake or prepared as a purée, tamarind is actually a pod filled with seeds and a fibrous flesh. If you buy tamarind cake, then it must be soaked in hot water and then rubbed and squeezed to dissolve the pulp around the fibres. The fibres are then sieved out. Pulp is sold as purée or concentrate but is sometimes referred to as tamarind water in recipes. Freshly made tamarind water has a fresher, stronger flavour.

tandoori food colouring A bright red powder which is added to tandoori pastes to give it colour.

Thai sweet basil Has purplish stems, green leaves and an aniseed aroma and flavour. It is aromatic and is used in curries, soups and stir-fries, as well as sometimes being served as an accompaniment. *See page 279.*

tiger lily buds Are not from tiger lilies but are the unopened flowers from another type of lily. The buds are bought dried and then soaked. *See page 322.*

tofu Also known as bean curd and is made by coagulating soya bean milk. The curds are sold in blocks, either soft, firm or pressed. Keep the blocks in water in the fridge, changing the water frequently, for up to 2 to 3 days. *See page 79.*

toor dal Also called yellow lentils, these come oiled and plain. Oiled ones look slightly greasy and need to be soaked in hot water to remove the oil. Soak the dal for a few hours before cooking.

turmeric Dried turmeric, sold whole or ground, is a deep yellow colour. It has a slightly bitter flavour and a pungent aroma. Turmeric is used for both colour and flavour.

udon noodles Thick white Japanese noodles made from wheat flour, available in various widths. The noodles are available both fresh and dried. Udon noodles are most often eaten in soups but they may also be served in braised dishes. *See page 119.*

umeshu (plum wine) Is a sweet liqueur with an almond flavour. *See page 423.*

urad dal The split variety is a cream colour with black skin. The skinned variety is cream. Urad dal does not usually need to be soaked. The dal is used when making dosa and idli batters and it becomes glutinous and creamy when cooked.

vinegar White coconut vinegar is the most common. Any mild white vinegar or better still, rice vinegar, can be used as a substitute.

wakame A curly leafed seaweed, usually dehydrated and broken into very small pieces. It swells considerably and quickly when added to water and has a soft texture, which can become slimy if left to soak for too long. It has a mild, pleasant green leafy vegetable taste.

wasabi Wasabi paste is a hot, pungent mixture made from the knobby green root of the Japanese wasabi plant. It is also available in powdered form to be mixed to a paste when needed, and as a pre-prepared paste. It is sometimes referred to as Japanese horseradish because of its flavour but in fact it is not related to horseradish. The fresh root can be finely grated when in season and has a better flavour and less heat than wasabi paste. Use it sparingly as a condiment for sushi and sashimi and to add to dipping sauces to serve with noodles. *See page 165.*

water chestnuts These are the rhizomes of a plant that grows in paddy fields in China. The nut has a dark-brown shell and a crisp white interior. The raw nuts need to be peeled with a knife and blanched, then stored in water. Tinned ones need to be drained and rinsed. Freshly peeled nuts are sometimes available from Chinese shops.

water spinach (phak bung) Is a leafy green vegetable that has hollow stems. Used as an ingredient as well as an accompaniment.

wheat starch A powder-like flour made by removing the protein from wheat flour. It is used to make dumpling wrappers.

whole black gram This whole urad dal has a black skin. Usually it has to be soaked or precooked before use.

wing beans Also called *angle beans*, these have four frilly edges. Used cut into cross sections in salads and stir-fries. Buy as fresh as you can.

winter melon A very large gourd or squash that looks like a watermelon. The skin is dark green, often with a white waxy bloom, and the flesh is pale green.

won ton sheets These sheets or wrappers are available from the refrigerator or freezer cabinets of Asian food shops. Some are yellow and include egg in the pastry and others are white. Gow gee and gyoza wrappers can also be used.

yakisoba noodles Chinese-style yellow egg noodles that are partly cooked and oiled ready for use. They are usually sold in plastic bags. If not available, you can substitute with thin Hokkien noodles.

yard long beans Also called *snake* or *long beans*, these are about 40 cm (16 inches) long. The darker green variety has a firmer texture.

yellow bean sauce This is actually brown in colour and made from fermented yellow soya beans, which are sweeter and less salty than black beans, mixed with rice wine and dark brown sugar. It varies in flavour and texture (some have whole beans in them) and is sold under different names – *crushed yellow beans, brown bean sauce, ground bean sauce* and *bean sauce*.

INDEX

Published in 2009 by Murdoch Books Pty Limited

Murdoch Books Australia
Pier 8/9
23 Hickson Road
Millers Point NSW 2000
Phone: +61 (0) 2 8220 2000
Fax: +61 (0) 2 8220 2558
www.murdochbooks.com.au

Murdoch Books UK Limited
Erico House, 6th Floor
93–99 Upper Richmond Road
Putney, London SW15 2TG
Phone: +44 (0) 20 8785 5995
Fax: +44 (0) 20 8785 5985
www.murdochbooks.co.uk

Chief Executive: Juliet Rogers
Publishing Director: Kay Scarlett
Commissioning Editor: Lynn Lewis
Design Concept: Vivien Valk
Senior Designer: Heather Menzies
Designer/cover design: Wendy Inkster
Photographers: Jason Lowe, Alan Benson, Gorazd Vilhar, Ian Hofstetter
Production: Alexandra Gonzalez
Index: Jo Rudd

National Library of Australia Cataloguing-in-Publication Data

Title: The Food of Asia: a journey for food lovers / editor, Lynn Lewis
ISBN: 9781741964196 (pbk.)
Notes: Includes index.
Subjects: Cookery, Asian.
Dewey Number: 641.595

A catalogue record for this book is available from the British Library.

Printed by C & C Offset Printing Co. Ltd in 2009. PRINTED IN CHINA.

IMPORTANT: Those who might be at risk from the effects of salmonella poisoning (the
elderly, pregnant women, young children and those suffering from immune deficiency
diseases) should consult their doctor with any concerns about eating raw eggs.

OVEN GUIDE: You may find cooking times vary depending on the oven you are using. For
fan-forced ovens, as a general rule, set the oven temperature to 20°C (32°F) lower than
indicated in the recipe.